Twenty-First Century Fictions of Terrorism

Twenty-First Century Fictions of Terrorism

Arin Keeble

EDINBURGH
University Press

Edinburgh University Press is one of the leading university presses in the UK. We publish academic books and journals in our selected subject areas across the humanities and social sciences, combining cutting-edge scholarship with high editorial and production values to produce academic works of lasting importance. For more information visit our website: edinburghuniversitypress.com

© Arin Keeble 2024, 2025

Edinburgh University Press Ltd
13 Infirmary Street
Edinburgh EH1 1LT

First published in hardback by Edinburgh University Press 2024

Typeset in 11/13pt Adobe Sabon by
Cheshire Typesetting Ltd, Cuddington, Cheshire

A CIP record for this book is available from the British Library

ISBN 978 1 4744 7867 0 (hardback)
ISBN 978 1 4744 7868 7 (paperback)
ISBN 978 1 4744 7869 4 (webready PDF)
ISBN 978 1 4744 7870 0 (epub)

The right of Arin Keeble to be identified as the author of this work has been asserted in accordance with the Copyright, Designs and Patents Act 1988, and the Copyright and Related Rights Regulations 2003 (SI No. 2498).

Contents

List of Figures	vi
Acknowledgements	vii
Introduction: From Traumatic Rupture to Systemic Crisis in the Twenty-First Century Novel of Terrorism	1
1. Revisiting the Anglophone 9/11 Novel: Domesticity, Metafiction and Exceptionalism	40
2. Writing the 'Clash of Civilizations': Racism, Difference and Terrorism	111
3. The Novel of Terrorism and the War on Terror	168
4. Contemporary Historical Novels of Terrorism	210
5. Genre, Policing and Terrorism	253
Conclusion: New Event-Based Narratives of Terrorism	291
Index	299

Figures

1.1 The cover images for *The Good Life* and *A Disorder Peculiar to the Country* both featured illustrations of the twin towers of the World Trade Center casting a shadow of a man and a woman. Cover image for *The Good Life* (2006) by Jay McInerney. With thanks to Bloomsbury Publishing Plc. — 55

4.1 The American cover for Rachel Kushner's *The Flamethrowers* (2013). Cover design © Scribner. — 221

Acknowledgements

I am grateful and indebted to too many people to name individually. The unwavering love, support and solidarity of my family and friends has kept me going during some difficult moments. My colleagues at Edinburgh Napier University have been understanding and generous. The people I have co-edited, co-authored and variously collaborated with in recent years have been inspiring and caring, and have helped me shift my professional priorities to collaboration and exchange. My students have sustained my belief in the importance and value of what I do. I am truly grateful to you all.

Introduction: From Traumatic Rupture to Systemic Crisis in the Twenty-First Century Novel of Terrorism

Event to System

This book discusses the novel of terrorism in the early twenty-first century, focusing on twenty-two works published between 2003 and 2021. Since the '9/11' attacks in 2001, the term 'terrorism' has been misused in troubling ways, its value stretched to the limit. It has been reduced and narrowed to serve Islamophobic agendas, and expanded into a nearly meaningless label, liberally deployed by various parties to demonise political adversaries. Yet, it remains important given the continued prevalence of political violence usefully understood as terrorism. Often such instances have taken forms that do not resemble the types of threat that America-driven 'post-9/11' security paradigms have emphasised. Indeed, from police shootings and other forms of state terrorism to white supremacist attacks, terrorism in the twenty-first century frequently relates to structural or institutional failures rather than fringe radicals. My argument in this book is that the novel of terrorism has moved away from the event-based narratives that emerged with such prominence in the years after September 11. Instead, a diverse range of fiction about terrorism has focused on systemic and slow violence. These novels explore the social and cultural conditions that foster extremism and depict the wider permutations of terrorism: the impact it has on human relationships in families and in communities, on victims, suspects and the wrongly accused, and between cultures and nations. Some of these works have begun to depict the intersections of systemic violence and traumatic rupture, too, responding to what many feel is a new twenty-first century sensibility of 'crisis ordinariness'. Indeed, as Melanie Wattenberger notes, the 'invasion of terrorist violence into the mundane is the marker of a recent trend in literature, and arguably as well as more significantly, a feature of lived reality' (685). Such texts depict terrorism or the threat of terrorism as part of a situation where the 'long-term problems of embodiment within capitalism' are 'less successfully addressed in the temporalities of crisis and require other frames for understanding the contexts of doing, being, and thriving' (Berlant 105). In tracking the changing ways in which novelists are depicting terrorism, I also track the steady, global advances of neoliberalism. But by emphasising systemic and slow violence, I do not mean to deny the popular notion that the world order shifted in the wake of the September 11 attacks. However, what is critically important to recognise, and what underpins many new novels of terrorism, is the fact that it was not 9/11 itself that changed the world; rather, it was America and its allies' response to the attacks, over the past twenty years, that has caused seismic, material changes. Moreover, this response has in many ways followed deeper historical patterns of American imperialism and drawn on systems and institutional phenomena long in development; not least of all the rise of neoliberalism, a definitive feature of the 'war on terror'. Yet we continue to identify this period – even now – as the 'post-9/11 era', rather than, say, the 'war on terror era', which would be more accurate.

I begin with a set of short examples from contemporary texts that are not centrally about terrorism but are useful here in locating and understanding this movement away from event-based paradigms. In Teju Cole's *Open City* (2011), the elusive narrator, Julius, a recently qualified psychiatrist, begins wandering New York City in the autumn of 2006. As he walks, ostensibly a 'postcolonial migrant-flaneur of the global city', Julius recalls his childhood in the Nigerian capital, Lagos, along with other more recent experiences as an immigrant, and has a series of banal but charged interactions with strangers and friends (Krishnan 682). Central to his encounters and the reflections he shares are his experiences of multiculturalism – in New York and Brussels, where Julius visits in the second half of the novel – fraught in both cases amidst the expanding war on terror and its climate of fear. The spectre of September 11 pervades certain sections of the novel, and is finally addressed directly, late on. The passage begins with Julius's thoughts on Freud's writing about mourning, and what happens when mourning is curtailed or 'does not proceed normally' (208). He notes:

The neatness of the line we had drawn around the catastrophic events of 2001 seemed to me to correspond to this kind of sectioning off. There had been great heroism, of course, though, as the years passed, it had become clear that aspects of this heroism were overstated. There was firmness of purpose, too, in the language of the president, there was certainly political squabbling, and there was a determination to rebuild right away. But the mourning had not been completed, and the result had been the anxiety that cloaked the city. (209)

This passage functions as a meditation on the way the attacks have been historicised. Julius's account of misguided priorities and unresolved trauma might even be more explicitly connected as, actually, the 'official narratives' of September 11 short-circuited mourning by precipitously advancing their architects' drive for geopolitical conflict and a set of new domestic agendas. Furthermore, the American government's response to the attack eroded wider historical contexts by characterising the event as unprecedented and unforeseeable. Moreover, the emphasis on mourning, trauma and victimhood – at the heart of so many early narratives of the attacks – was actually one of the reasons September 11 was not contextualised in ways that might have been very useful: as part of a complex, ongoing ideological conflict, and within the global machinations and unevenness of the capitalist world-system. As Ronak Kapadia has noted, we might understand this moment 'not as a radical historical or political rupture, but rather as a continuation of a longer history of US imperialism that has been erased or evaded' (36). In a sense, then, while the mourning or trauma of 9/11 might have been (and might still be) unresolved, the ongoing fixation on the events as traumatic fostered a certain insularity and exceptionalisation. *Open City* both participates in this fixation and challenges it.

This contradiction is made more vivid by considering an earlier scene in which Julius attends an exhibition at the International Center of Photography, showcasing the work of Hungarian photographer Martin Munkácsi. He ruminates on the famous photo of three Liberian boys on a beach running into the surf, from which, he notes, Henri Cartier-Bresson 'developed the ideal of the decisive moment' (150). Julius's thoughts on this clearly resonate in the context of the still-traumatised city: '[one] moment, in all of history, was captured but the moments before and after it disappeared into the onrush of time; only that selected moment itself was privileged' (150). This comment foreshadows a shocking moment of personal violence which is revealed shortly after but is also pointedly connected to the novel's interest in the aftermath of the September 11 attacks, and calls to mind Marianne Hirsch's memorable account of the photographic response to the attacks. In a personal essay, Hirsch argued that still photography was the medium that best captured 'the trauma and loss associated with September 2001' because its ability to freeze time addressed 'the feeling that time stopped around 9:00 am on September 11', a feeling that, for Hirsch, 'created an immeasurable gulf between the before and after' (71–2). Such notions now seem imbued with the rhetoric of exceptionalism, and certainly this kind of framing has been routinely challenged, at least since Zadie Smith's well-known *New York Review of Books* essay 'Two Paths for the Novel', which interrogated the inflated importance attached to 9/11 in literary spheres.[1] This said, it is a useful way of locating the contradiction at the centre of Cole's novel's musings on September 11, a contradiction that, I argue, cuts to the heart of the legacy of that historical moment and the ways we understand 'events' and crises more broadly, in a contemporary period where emphasis has shifted away from 'decisive moments', towards the less visible or less spectacular phenomena of slow violence and systemic crisis. In *Open City* there is, on the one hand, a suggestion that the process of mourning September 11 was curtailed by the need to move on too quickly, which meant that trauma was unresolved and real understanding impossible. On the other hand, though, the novel reminds us that fixation on a singular traumatic event 'privileges' it, severs it from its contexts and potentially – as was the case with 9/11 – exceptionalises it.

Ultimately, *Open City*'s depictions of multiculturalism and its sustained interest in global systems, flows of migration and, as Daniel O'Gorman has noted, 'the structures of global power that acts of terror are located within' cut against exceptionalist rhetoric and emphasise systemic phenomena (458). Moreover, the shocking late revelation that – despite his ostensible social liberalism and anti-violent ethos – Julius has potentially suppressed a horrific personal history of perpetrating rape is, if not allegorical, then deeply suggestive of his adopted country's unwillingness to examine or even acknowledge its own violent history.[2] Yet, despite these compelling challenges to conventional histories and narratives of September 11, the novel also insists that the mourning process is incomplete and it remains haunted or 'cloaked in anxiety' (209). In a broad sense, Cole's novel, published ten years after the attacks, exemplifies a tension between two impulses: to examine the effects of a singular traumatic rupture, on one hand, and entrenched systemic violence, on the other. The 'evasiveness' or 'fugitivity' of the flaneur narrator might also be understood in these terms, as signalling a movement away from the shadow of event-based logics (von Gleich). Consequently, though September 11 or terrorism more generally are not the central concern or subject of *Open City*, Cole's novel is a useful point of reference in considering the way emphasis has shifted in twenty-first century fiction about terrorism, from the discourse of 'the event' towards depictions of terrorism as a violent symptom of neoliberalism and systemic and institutional failures.

Another useful way of considering this shift, which is at the heart of my project in this book, is via Porochista Khakpour's comments on the impact of the September 11 attacks in her memoir, *Sick* (2017). Analysis of Khakpour's work will feature later in this book, and her two novels, *Sons and Other Flammable Objects* (2007) and *The Last Illusion* (2014), and many of her personal essays, recently collected in *Brown Album* (2020), have sought to decentre September 11, either by situating the attacks in the context of other historical ruptures, such as the Islamic Revolution in Iran, which Khakpour's family fled when she was a small child, or by examining the experience of xenophobia in America before and after the attacks. Nevertheless, in *Sick*, a book that trenchantly critiques the systemic failures of the American healthcare system, Khakpour is quick to cite September 11 as a defining moment – a personal and collective trauma that 'changed everything' and one that was decisive for her generation. Khakpour notes in *Sick*:

> What 9/11 did was give us the gift of time running out; it put limits on things, stamped expiration dates on us. Suddenly I watched the news, the clock, the calendar. Age meant something. And I looked at my life just months before with a sort of mix of horror and envy. (66)

Khakpour's comments, which convey the shock of the attacks and align closely to Hirsch's feeling that the event created 'an immeasurable gulf between the before and after', seem to sit uneasily alongside her sustained interest in de-exceptionalising the attacks. In actuality, though, in the context of her wider oeuvre, Khakpour's comments speak to what we must see as a fundamental aporia in the study of September 11, its impacts and legacies. This is, that, in one sense, the notion that the attacks have been exceptionalised and ascribed far more importance than any number of world historical crises that have included mass death is undeniable, and we should continue to interrogate the ways this has happened. In another sense, though, there is no doubt that the world did change in material ways in the immediate aftermath of the attacks, which saw the global war on terror, increasingly flagrant forms of racism and xenophobia, new mandates for surveillance and securitisation, and the global tightening of borders; and certainly the current prevalence of the discourses of migration in electoral politics and the post-2016 turn towards right-wing populism can be traced back to this period. But again, these global shifts were not caused by the September 11 attacks; rather, it was America and its allies' response to the attacks, over the past twenty years – including instances of what we must consider state terrorism – that have reshaped the world order. As Richard Jackson points out, 'the response to the threat of terrorism since 9/11 has been one of unnecessary and counterproductive overreaction' and September 11 'has been leveraged for much more profound and invasive processes of surveillance, securitisation, border management, social control, democratic constriction, neoliberalisation, legal transformation, and exceptional politics' (4). This is undeniably the case, but the exceptional historical status of the attacks shows no sign of diminishing. Moreover, separating the event itself and its aftermath remains difficult because of the emotive power it retains. For instance, in May of 2019, then President Donald J. Trump waged a sustained and hateful critique of Democratic Congresswoman Ilhan Omar on Twitter, based on an objectively true comment the latter had made about the September 11 attacks engendering a rise in Islamophobia, which was taken out of context and deemed to trivialise the event.[3] That President Trump was able to repeatedly use still and video images of the attacks to condemn his political opponent, and elicit an extraordinarily emotional and violent demonisation of Congresswoman Omar with these tactics, is testament to the continued rhetorical power of 9/11 in America.[4]

I make these preliminary observations to begin to establish the primary concerns of this book. First, I seek to show how contemporary fiction has begun to move away from 'event-based' narratives of terrorism – and the '9/11 novel' is paradigmatic here – towards representations of the wider social and political contexts that engender radicalisation or extremism, positioning terrorism as a consequence of both world-systemic phenomena and more localised systemic crises and failures. In doing this, I examine the changing ways literature has sought to make sense of both the reasons why terrorism occurs and the effects it has on victims, survivors and international and intercultural relations. Not only can we discern a significant shift in the way novels have depicted terrorism over the past twenty years, but also the fiction of terrorism gives us real insight into the nature and intricacies of global patterns of terrorism and how the threat and fear of terrorism has shaped global relations between nations and cultures. These shifts are still unfolding and remain dynamic, attached as they are to world historical events. With this in mind, I wish to be cautious in the gestures I make towards periodisation, and I am eager to note that many of the novels I discuss, particularly in the second half of the book, feature a sense of reflexivity about periodisation. Ben Lerner's novel *Leaving the Atocha Station* (2011), which is also a kind of flaneur narrative, comes immediately to mind here, though like *Open City* and *Sick* it does not feature in the chapters to come. It is notable, though, for the way its narrator, a young American poet on a visiting fellowship in Madrid, witnesses the Atocha Station attacks of March 2004, where 191 people died and thousands more were injured. The narrator, who is selfish and oblivious to his own privilege, and the subject of much of the novel's satire, makes an astute observation: 'I overheard conversations about the role of photography *now*, where "now" meant post-March 11. A "post" was being formed, and the air was alive less with the excitement of a period than the excitement of periodization' (140). Though the narrator is discussing the Madrid attacks, these observations clearly evoke the previously cited comments of Hirsch, or many like hers, in the aftermath of September 11. Crucially, this scene in Lerner's novel registers a suspicion about the clamour to declare a new epoch, which is precisely what occurred in the autumn of 2001. In the context of the novel's many other critiques of the Bush administration's foreign policy, this comment immediately evokes the way such precipitous acts of periodisation were and are mobilised ideologically. Many commentators, such as David Holloway, have noted that the idea of the 'post-9/11' quickly became a rhetorical tool for the Bush administration. Holloway notes that the idea 'of 9/11 as the moment when everything changed became the ideological lynch-pin of the "war on terror"' and critique of this idea is also at the heart of Giorgio Agamben's influential formulation of a 'state of exception' (4). For Agamben, the Bush administration's rhetoric of a new world order enabled undemocratic policies and laws that collapse 'the very distinction between peace and war' and erase 'the legal status of the individual' (22, 3).

This book, then, is partly driven by a scepticism of the politics of periodisation and forming 'posts', even if it is in some ways complicit in the project of constructing a broad, early twenty-first century period. As such, it will remain attuned to the processes and impulses of periodisation. My core aim is to examine the novel of terrorism's transition and to trace the permutations of this transition towards a theorisation of the contemporary novel of terrorism. In doing this, I will also discuss the ways these novels have both exemplified and resisted some of the broader frames of literary periodisation that have emerged in the twenty-first century, alongside the 9/11 novel. These period frames have often been imbricated in the discourses of 9/11 and its aftermath, and though it is not uncommon for 'watershed historical moments' to function in this way, this imbrication has particular inflections (Eaglestone 1094). In a *Guardian* article from October 2001, James Wood anticipated the end of the 'false zaniness' of what he termed 'hysterical realism', while also calling for an abandonment of the big novel of society, exemplified by Don DeLillo's *Underworld* (1997). Both modes, Wood argued, devalue the interior worlds of characters, and he framed his critique in relation to the newly sombre post-9/11 mood, calling for novels of 'human consciousness' that reflect 'the newly dark lights of the age' (n.p.). For Wood, the 'tentacular ambition' of big social novels, 'the effort to pin down an entire writing culture, to be a great analyst of systems, crowds, paranoia, politics', had effaced emotion, and he cited Zadie Smith's comment that the writer's job is 'not to tell us how somebody felt about something' but to 'tell us how the world works', as emblematic of this trend (n.p.). Smith's own critique of the early twenty-first century literary landscape cited a 9/11 novel – Joseph O'Neill's *Netherland* (2008) – as a case study example of 'lyrical realism', a mode she sees as unambitious and lacking invention. For Smith 'lyrical realism' registers anxiety about the potential of its own formal dimensions, without the will to innovate. Smith is frustrated with this unadventurous mode which 'has the freedom of the highway for some time', and with the fixation in anglophone literary culture on 9/11 (71).

This divergence of priorities in the criticism by Wood and Smith exemplifies the difficulty in trying to periodise after 9/11, though many such attempts have been made via scholarly paradigms including post-postmodernism, meta-modernism, the 'genre turn' and, most persuasively, 'New Sincerity'. Drawing these together, Daniel O'Gorman and Robert Eaglestone have argued that some 'consensus has emerged around the idea that postmodernism, the critical paradigm of late twentieth century arts and culture, has begun to fizzle out gradually, replaced by works that maintain postmodernism's self-reflexive playfulness while also adhering to an underlying sense of emotional truthfulness' (2). However, this combination of self-reflexivity and emotional truth sounds quite a lot like what

Rachel Greenwald Smith has identified as 'compromise aesthetics' (2021, 11). For Greenwald Smith, such fiction takes the 'provocative experiments' of the avant-garde and embeds them in an 'easily consumable shape' (2021, 11). Here, too, the debate over period is linked to the discourse of 9/11 and the 9/11 novel, as Greenwald Smith notes that early 9/11 novels like Jonathan Safran Foer's *Extremely Loud and Incredibly Close* (2005) 'articulate the events as world-changing while remaining formally familiar' (2015, 62). This is paradoxical, as while these works obviously seek to evoke a newly changed world, they use a narrative mode that emerged in the 1990s alongside and in tune with the consolidation of social and cultural neoliberalism.[5]

This study begins with a set of American and America-centric novels published in the decade after 9/11. Beginning in the second but mostly in the third, fourth and fifth chapters, in addition to exploring different vectors of departure from this paradigm, it identifies some formal links across a diverse selection of more recent novels of terrorism. In some cases, these are usefully understood in relation to the broader debates about periodisation sketched above, and I will note instances where these debates come into focus. Ultimately, I arrive at a cautious and loosely defined theorisation of the contemporary novel of terrorism that is distinct from the event-based fiction exemplified by the 9/11 novel; and the postmodern and Modernist novel of terrorism before it, even while traces of each remain visible. The contemporary novel of terrorism frequently draws on established genre frames – both popular and 'literary'. In some cases, this provides narrative familiarity that aids the project of depicting the unknowable 'mind of the terrorist'. More often, genre reinforces the historical gestures of these works through its inherent intertextuality. As Theodore Martin notes, genres 'lead distinctly double lives, with one foot in the past and the other in the present; they contain the entire abridged history of an aesthetic form while also staking a claim to the form's contemporary relevance' (6). This is very much the case, for instance, in Percival Everett's *The Trees* (2021) (discussed in Chapter 5), where the detective genre framework and modulation to Southern gothic places the novel's representation of lynching – America's most pervasive form of domestic terrorism – within a genre tradition with significant historical resonances. Similarly, Kamila Shamsie's *Home Fire* (2017) (discussed in my third chapter) uses the narrative frame of *Antigone* to 'draw not only on Sophocles' tragedy, but also on the postcolonial legacy it has built' (Pishotti 350).

Just as prevalent in the contemporary novel of terrorism is a metafictional fixation on acts of reading and writing. In some cases, this too functions historically, as the kind of historiographic metafiction typical of the postmodern novel of terrorism, in which 'the writing of history is deconstructed and its authority challenged' (del Pont 84). More often, however, acts of reading and writing are strategies for survival. In Anna Burns's *Milkman* (2018) (discussed in Chapter 4), for instance, protagonist middle sister has an idiosyncratic habit of reading while walking for which she is repeatedly reproached, even by friends. Yet, in a climate of suspicion and violence, she remains defiant, describing the practice as her 'one bit of power in a disempowering world' (205). Equally, in Ayad Akhtar's autofictional novel *Homeland Elegies* (2020) (discussed in Chapter 3), writing is a kind of ongoing process of building self-knowledge and withstanding the systemic violence of the neoliberal present. This is not the kind of 'curious knot', doubling or zero-sum competition between writer and terrorist staged in Don DeLillo's *Mao II* (1991), but a repeated pattern of mitigation and survival amid systemic violence. In addition to the uses of genre and metafictional strategies discussed above, the most prominent form of connective tissue across these works is their interest in systemic malaise. In some instances, this works formally, recalling what Tom LeClair theorised in 1987 as 'the systems novel', but mostly it is simply a shared engagement with structural violence via an array of different formal strategies. In the chapters to come I trace the connections between these various fictional engagements with systemic phenomena in detail and show how they can be located within broader literary and cultural currents.

This movement from event to system is not straightforwardly linear, and it is certainly the case that many contemporary texts remain fundamentally interested in traumatic rupture or 'events' alongside and as part of their depictions of systemic phenomena. Equally, comparative reading reveals surprising points of connection between seemingly disparate novels of terror, across the five chapters to come. For instance, I will consider the ways that Don DeLillo's *Falling Man* (2007), Yasmina Khadra's *The Attack* (2005) and Anna Burns's *Milkman* (discussed in my first, second and fourth chapters, respectively) all feature a kind of structural circularity, ostensibly beginning where they end. In DeLillo's novel this evokes the circularity of trauma; in Khadra's novel it suggests the cycles of violence and counter-violence in Palestine and Israel; and in *Milkman* it invites the reader to focus on the affective richness of middle sister's retrospective narration and her experiences of various forms of terror, rather than a single moment. Many other connections come into view. For example, while *Milkman* depicts a specific historical conflict in a unique way, its vision of predation amidst a climate in which sectarian violence, state violence and imperial violence intersect resonates with other contemporary novels of terrorism. Like Ahmed Saadawi's *Frankenstein in Baghdad* (2013), discussed in my third chapter, it depicts the intersections of sectarian conflict, occupation and state violence, each figured as forms of terrorism. Both novels raise questions about the nature and language of terrorism in such circumstances, and this is one of many examples of fruitful if unexpected lines of connection between the novels discussed here. While I seek to examine a certain trajectory in the fiction of terrorism, I am careful to keep sight of such continuities.

Despite these continuities, and my interest in systemic phenomena, the nature of terrorism as a tactic requires some attention to the discourse of 'events', rupture, spectacle and trauma. This remains the case in the novels I analyse in later chapters, which focus on the processes of radicalisation, ever-increasing wealth disparities, climates of intolerance, racism, state violence, surveillance and counter-terrorist tactics – rather than singular violent events and their aftermaths. Indeed, many of these texts dramatise the intersections of these different kinds of violence. In my Conclusion, I even consider new forms of event-based narratives of terrorism, focusing on Megha Majumdar's *A Burning* (2020) and Preti Taneja's *Aftermath* (2021), and address the ways their central events actually open up sustained depictions of systemic phenomena. Unlike DeLillo's *Falling Man*, for example (which begins with September 11 and focuses mostly on the trauma of one family), these works probe the wider political and social systems in which the events occur, consider them within wider historical contexts, and centre the perspectives of victims, perpetrators, colluders and conspirators, and the wrongly accused, while keeping the impact of psychological trauma in sight. In doing this they align with Michael Rothberg's resonant call for scholars of trauma and memory (and I suggest here that we add terrorism) to take on the task of considering 'two forms of violence': sudden traumatic events, as well as the less visible and more entrenched phenomenon of 'exploitation in an age of globalized, neo-liberal capitalism' (xiv).

While I adopt Rothberg's call to understand how these very different forms of violence interact, the movement away from event-based narratives of terrorism that I track in the chapters that follow broadly aligns with a wider turn towards the systemic.[6] One influential example of this is Lauren Berlant's *Cruel Optimism* (2011), which examines the way people in Western capitalist democracies remain so fixated on fantasies of the 'good life' and upwards mobility, when there is so much evidence of decline, structural inequality and the impossibility of such fantasies being realised. Central to Berlant's argument is the notion that we should be 'moving away from the discourse of trauma – from Caruth to Agamben – when describing what happens to persons and populations as an effect of catastrophic impacts' (9). For Berlant, the emphasis on trauma has meant that the present is continually viewed as a state of exception where people are waiting to resume 'some ongoing, uneventful ordinary life' in which they are able to feel 'solid and confident' but which actually does not exist (10).

Berlant's notion of a contemporary 'crisis ordinariness' and call to refocus on 'systemic crisis' (10) aligns with another key intervention that emerged from the humanities that was published in the same year, Rob Nixon's *Slow Violence and the Environmentalism of the Poor*. Nixon's theory of 'slow violence' emphasises the need to attend to phenomena that are 'neither spectacular nor instantaneous but rather incremental and accretive', and he notes that the effort to 'make forms of slow violence more urgently visible suffered a setback in the United States in the aftermath of 9/11, which reinforced a spectacular, immediately sensational, and instantly hyper-visible image of what constitutes a violent threat' (1, 13). Though Nixon's analysis is focused on anthropogenic climate change, the logic of slow violence, and the way it has been perpetuated by capitalism, has meant that many recent analyses of systemic crisis and neoliberalism have adopted the term, too, focusing on the slow violence of incarceration, institutional racism or colonial legacies. Anna Hartnell, writing about Hurricane Katrina and Naomi Klein's argument in *The Shock Doctrine* (2007) that rupture or 'shock' has driven neoliberalisation historically and in the specific case of Katrina, notes that this emphasis on shock 'fails to track the progression of neoliberal policies as forms of "slow violence" that had been in train for decades' (173). Like Berlant, Nixon and Hartnell are focused on a kind of violence that is 'nonspectacular and human-engineered' (Berlant 9).

While terrorism is by nature spectacular, there are many reasons why the fiction of terrorism has followed this turn and moved away from a focus on singular events. Many of the texts discussed in the chapters that follow address systemic phenomena that perpetuate violent extremism and contextualise terrorism in depictions of slow forms of violence. Event-based narratives have been unable to interrogate such phenomena. In the growing discipline of Critical Terrorism Studies (CTS) – which formed in response to the war on terror – a similar project is under way. As Bart Schuurman notes in a recent state-of-the-discipline essay in *Critical Studies on Terrorism*, 'event-driven critiques' have 'served to prioritize particular subjects . . . while others, such as state-terrorism or right-wing extremist violence, are by this same logic left un- or under-examined' (464). Additionally, contemporary novels of terror have responded to the landscape of 'crisis ordinariness' and to the different ways catastrophe has come to be expected. For instance, in *Training for Catastrophe: Fictions of National Security After 9/11* (2021), Lindsay Thomas analyses various 'preparedness materials', including 'policy documents, workplace disaster training manuals, emergency management textbooks, training exercises, preparedness plans' and other objects, as 'state-sponsored fictions' of security that depoliticise and normalise disaster (4–5). Thomas notes that such 'state-sponsored fictions' elide emerging and urgent threats, and points specifically to systemic phenomena, noting how this discourse teaches people to 'ignore or deny the existence of the many disasters of white supremacy' (5). However, for Thomas, rather than 'emphasizing the shock of the unexpected disaster or the terror of violent acts, preparedness materials advance an understanding of catastrophe as expected and as recurring' (13). In this light we might wonder if some novels fall in line with these state-sponsored 'fictions of preparedness' that both normalise crisis and elide certain forms of institutional violence. I argue here that this is increasingly infrequent and show how a diverse range of novels work to reveal the perniciousness of systemic malaise.

This book traces the shift I have described in the twenty-first century novel of terrorism, in relation to and as part of this wider turn to the systemic exemplified by Berlant and Nixon. However, I now focus attention on a set of preliminary matters. First, it is necessary to revisit the perennially troubled task of defining terrorism and, in doing so, address the question of how our understanding of terrorism has evolved in the twenty-first century. This includes analysis of scholarly approaches and interventions in terrorism studies, and I will introduce two theoretical frameworks that I draw from: the transnational and feminist dimensions of CTS, and the binary formations of Alex Houen and Peter C. Herman, who have understood terrorism in terms of the 'symbolic and real' and the 'speakable and unspeakable'. I will then define other key interpretive terms that I use, all of which have dynamic vectors of meaning: trauma and 'cultural trauma' and 'the systemic' and 'world-systemic'.[7]

Terrorism: Definitions and Approaches

That terrorism is difficult to define is a point laboured by every study even tangentially about the topic. This section will clarify the applications of the term adopted by this book and introduce some interpretative tools that help locate a productive way of using it, while acknowledging that the contemporary discourse of terrorism has frequently been toxic and racist. It is necessary, though, to outline the ways it has been defined, and the challenges and ideological imperatives that have shaped debate over its meanings.

One of the reasons that 'terrorism' and 'terrorist' are such elusive terms is because they are simultaneously elastic and singular. The old notion that 'one person's terrorist is another person's freedom fighter' remains broadly true insofar as such maxims can be, but despite this ambiguity, it is also the case that the emotive power of these terms means they are a first recourse for commentators who wish to label an individual or group as irredeemably evil. This can be, and has been, acutely reductive; as Herman notes, the only real consensus is that 'terrorism is always the work of another' and that it generally approximates 'violence you don't like by people you don't like' (2020, 5). This is acute in the early twenty-first century where we routinely see calls for activist and interest groups – including nonviolent ones – from Extinction Rebellion and Antifa to the National Rifle Association (NRA) to be classified as 'terrorist organisations'.[8] Much of the impetus behind such calls comes from the rhetorical power of the term, and associated terms like 'extremist' or 'fundamentalist'. It is also the case that the power of official and legislative definitions, and the penalties they stipulate for committing or attempting terrorist acts, drive the imperative for categorisation. So while such calls are often hyperbolic, in the current post-2016 climate of right-wing populism and white nationalism, there is a legitimate urgency and need to legally define the violent activities of organisations like the Aryan Brotherhood (AB), the Russian Imperial Movement, the Atomwaffen Division and even the growing 'incel' phenomenon, which is often linked to white nationalism. One reason this is important in the West is because counter-terror resources remain disproportionately focused towards Islamist terrorism despite an overwhelming consensus that white nationalist terrorism is a far greater threat.[9] Yet, the variation in the groups that have been referred to as domestic terrorist organisations – including the Earth Liberation Front alongside the KKK – stretch the viability of the term. I am not arguing for an expansion of the term, which might be counterproductive in numerous ways. As Taneja notes in *Aftermath*, this might equate to a 'call to feed the prison's cells' (135). Instead, I want to question its uneven applications and underrepresented histories, such as America's history of lynching, and make comparative gestures only when useful lines of connection are visible.

Definitional debates have played out in various political contexts and in the disciplines of Terrorism Studies and Critical Terrorism Studies. Definitions vary from nation to nation, but in some countries, and particularly America, they vary within government bodies, too.[10] As Herman has noted, different US agencies 'employ their own definitions of the term', and there are notable divergences regarding the question of whether terrorism is a crime or act of war (2018, 2). However, while there are distinctions between the ways these institutions define and legislate against terrorism, they remain broad, enabling a flexibility of legal application. And, because of this broadness, there are some consistencies. They all identify terrorism as a category of political violence perpetrated by insurgents seeking to disrupt civilian life and/or challenge state authority to advance political agendas. The prevalence of the state as victim and never perpetrator of terrorism is a troubling feature here, especially when, as Deepa Kumar shows, the condemnation of terrorism is often articulated by state representatives who wilfully ignore the 'political violence of allies', and 'state-sponsored violence against civilians is rarely, if ever, categorized as terrorism' (108).

Definitions in other Western capitalist democracies are similar. The Terrorism Act 2000 in the UK cites the 'use or threat of action' to 'influence the government' or 'intimidate the public' to advance a 'political, religious, racial or ideological cause' (s. 1). A wave of updated definitions appeared in the early war on terror era, largely retaining this tendency towards the opaque. In 2004, the United Nations Security Council Resolution 1566 named a set of designed to 'provoke a state of terror in the general public or in a group of persons or particular persons, intimidate a population or compel a government or an international organization to do or to abstain from doing any act' (2).

Contemporary Western definitions mostly approximate the description issued by the United Nations General Assembly after the Munich Airport attack of 1972, and many current legal definitions remain, in their openness and avoidance of state violence, close to the one posed by the League of Nations in 1937: 'All criminal acts directed against a State and intended or calculated to create a state of terror in the minds of particular persons or a group of persons or the general public.'[11] As Ben Saul notes, this definition 'has proved remarkably durable, influencing approaches to definition in a variety of legal contexts in subsequent years' (79). This durability is visible in the *European Union Terrorism Situation and Trend Report 2020* (TE-SAT), which covers 'specific violent extremist acts and activities as reported by EU Member States, when these aim to intimidate a population or compel a government or have the potential to seriously destabilise or destroy the fundamental political, constitutional, economic or social structures of a country' (Europol 8). The definition used by the Center for Strategic and International Studies (CSIS) is similar. Its report 'The Escalating Terrorist Problem in the United States' (2020) breaks activity into four categories but the broad definition is familiar: 'the deliberate use – or threat – of violence by non-state actors in order to achieve political goals and create a broad psychological impact' (n.p.). It identifies 'right-wing, left-wing, religious, and ethnonationalist' terrorism, with the caveats that such activities are perpetrated by fringe extremists not related to mainstream political parties or religions; though it is notable that this influential report identified an alarming rise in 'right wing' terrorism.[12] But while there is some coherence around terrorism as designed to create a 'broad psychological impact', as politically, ideologically or religiously motivated, and as designed to destabilise governments, these definitions remain unsatisfactory in their disavowal of state terrorism and strict emphasis on rogue actors. Additionally, the almost antithetical notions that terrorism involves either the indiscriminate killing of innocents or specific symbolic targets remains unsettled, and the distinction between terrorism as a criminal act or an act of war remains unresolved.

Consideration and analysis of state terrorism has been at the heart of the recent work done in Critical Terrorism Studies, a discipline that emerged in the twenty-first century and has made a substantial impact in shaping how we understand terrorism now. The recent *Routledge Handbook of Critical Terrorism Studies* (2016), edited by Richard Jackson, makes a sustained case for the inclusion of state terrorism, and even the 795-page *Oxford Handbook of Terrorism* (2019), edited by Erica Chenoweth et al,. has a substantial section on state terrorism and a chapter by Jackson. Some recent scholarship still seeks to keep terrorism and state terrorism separate, though. In *Terror in Our Time* (2012), a study of the first decade of the war on terror, Ken Booth and Tim Dunne acknowledge the existence of state terror but argue that while Islamist terrorism has increased after September 11, 'there is little that is new about state terrorism', and that 'governments have wielded terror and committed egregious human wrongs against their citizens ... for centuries' (21). The notion that there is little new about state terrorism is hard to accept given the proliferation of drone attacks during a period that Kapadia refers to as 'the drone age': where this form of violence 'manipulates, conflates, and destroys communal bonds, stripping away our sense of responsibility to the racialized targets of US war-making in the frontiers of the forever war' (74). Moreover, while torture and rendition are not new phenomena, many high-profile instances, and new practices, have characterised the war on terror. It is also important to note that many non-Western nations specifically designate state violence as terrorism. While Iraq's Counter Terrorism Service, established by the US in 2005, initially followed the broad definitions outlined above, Iran has designated all American forces as terrorist organisations, in legislation passed after the drone assassination of Qassem Soleimani in 2020. Similarly, the Palestine Authority has frequently named US and Israeli instances of state violence as terrorism. In the early stages of the war on terror, Yasser Arafat famously asserted that the Palestinian people 'stand firmly against all kinds of terrorism, whether it is by states, groups or individuals' (Schanzer 55). This entirely sensible logic underpins several recent literary representations. A scene in Shamsie's *Home Fire*, discussed in my third chapter, comes to mind here. One protagonist, Isma, is being profiled at Heathrow airport. She is asked questions about her Britishness and asserts to her interrogator, 'Killing civilians is sinful – that is equally true if the manner of killing is a suicide bombing or aerial bombardments or drone strikes' (5).

In this book, I follow a set of scholarly interventions in tracing contemporary fiction's growing interest in state or 'proto-state' terrorism. I note Marita Sturken's thoughtful and robust call for a redefinition of terror that is inclusive of America's history of lynching. Sturken addresses an absurd American reality where 'practices of racial terrorism, such as lynching, have evaded being labeled as such' (17). As Sturken points out, to understand terrorism 'not as a foreign project only but as a US-based and generated force would require grappling with the history of racial terrorism as state-sanctioned terrorism' (17). In the era of Ron DeSantis and the curtailment of Critical Race Theory, even such unambiguous truths are rejected, as they challenge received notions of what America is. To define lynching and other acts of state terror this way is, as Sturken notes, 'to understand terrorism as an integral active force in the origins of the United States and its very social fabric' (18). In broad alignment but with an international focus is Arun Kundnani's argument that to 'designate an act of violence as terrorism is to arbitrarily isolate it from other acts of violence considered normal, rational or necessary' (21). Specifically, Kundnani points to the fact that neither 'the military violence of Western states' or the 'daily reality of gender-based violence . . . both of which ought also to be labelled terrorism according to the term's usual definition: violence against innocent civilians designed to advance a political cause (the patriarchy is eminently political)' (21). I agree with Sturken and Kundnani, and the novels discussed in the chapters to come repeatedly reinforce these ideas, too. Moreover, in some compelling instances the novels under discussion depict situations in which state terrorism operates in similar terms and with similar tactics to non-state terrorism.

The emergence of CTS broadly follows the same post-September 11 timeline this book does. Central to the discipline is the idea that terrorism 'is a socially constructed category or signifier without any essential ontological content' (Jackson 3). This means that much CTS work focuses on scrutinising categorisation and labelling, and much of this work is focused on practices associated with the war on terror. As Jackson notes, the ever-expanding CTS project constitutes a probing 'scepticism towards official counterterrorism culture and practice', and a 'sustained normative critique of the war on terror and Western counterterrorism practices' (2).[13] The argument that terrorism is a social construct and that the war on terror has been premised on a conservative ideological agenda means that its other core concern, defining state terrorism, is complex and at times contradictory. For instance, we might ask how we can understand state terrorism as a social construct. Jackson points to specific practices such as the use of 'terror-directed violence for political purposes', and the 'long history of Western state terrorism and practices of torture, rendition and targeted killing' (6). The specific kinds of violence named here overlap significantly with the kinds routinely listed in the legal definitions I have cited and broadly share the same aims: they are violent actions designed to shock, intimidate, engender fear and panic, and challenge ideological formations (whether framed by nationhood or not).

In the face of the definitional challenges outlined here, I draw from two theoretical formations that provide definitional clarity and coherence in discussing the literary departure from event-based narratives of terrorism. First is the CTS approach outlined above with a particular emphasis on its comparative, transnational and feminist dimensions. My arguments align with approaches that are prevalent in CTS and particularly its critique of the 'exceptionalisation of 9/11' in Chapters 1 and 2. I draw inspiration from the key ideas in two innovative, CTS-inflected works that address the relationship between terrorism and literature: Preti Taneja's *Aftermath* (2021) and Basuli Deb's *Transnational Feminist Perspectives on Terror in Literature and Culture* (2015). Part memoir, part essay, part polemic, part theory, part trauma narrative, *Aftermath* (discussed in depth in my Conclusion) resists easy categorisation. Taneja tells the story of the Fishmongers' Hall attack of 29 November 2019 from her unique vantage point, as someone for whom one of the victims, Jack Merritt, was a colleague and friend, and as someone who had taught creative writing to the 'terrorist' Usman Khan as part of the prison education imitative, Learning Together. *Aftermath* interrogates racist definitions of terrorism, and addresses contemporary legacies of colonialism and forms of state violence. Its achievement lies in its generosity and intimacy, and in how it shows how traumatic rupture can occur amid the less visible but equally pernicious forces of systemic violence. Taneja immerses the reader in what she calls the 'atro-city', probing its painful edges. In *Aftermath*, the 'atro-city' is at once a single event that is all-encompassing and, conversely, a world of structural violence crystallised in a single event. It is 'the outside world turned inwards', a place where endemic poverty, lack of opportunity, entrenched prejudice and punitive justice violently collide (12). For my purposes it is critically important in the way it exemplifies and theorises the ways terror can be understood within the context of slow violence. Deb's transnational feminist scholarship addresses the 'problem of a pervasive public misunderstanding of terrorism conditioned by a foreign and domestic policy perspective' (2). Deb's approach is particularly useful in challenging promiscuous applications of the terms 'terrorist' and 'terrorism', which in some instances have extended to the 'demonization of entire populations as terrorists' (5). Not only does Deb's framework resist conventional readings of the war on terror, challenging 'associations that have emerged under the ideological/material conditions of Euro-American imperialism and postcolonial nationalism', it also establishes an itinerary for attending to a shift, in contemporary fictions of terrorism that has been concurrent with the movement away from event-based narratives: the movement away from hetero-normative formations (23). This logic will underpin my analysis of novels that reflexively address the ways 'terror is created, perpetuated, and sustained by dominant gender ideologies within a global order of unequal geopolitical power relationships' (4). The de-exceptionalising trajectory of CTS, and the emphasis on deep-rooted structures of systemic violence in the works by Taneja and Deb provide critically important analytical frameworks for my study.

The second critical formation I draw on here is an approach that has sought to understand terrorism in binary terms, and I draw heavily on two studies: Alex Houen's *Terrorism and Modern Literature* (2002), which explores interactions between 'the symbolic and the real' in the literature of terrorism, and Peter C. Herman's *Unspeakable: Literature and Terrorism from the Gunpowder Plot to 9/11* (2020), which focuses on literature's depictions of an impasses between 'speakable' and 'unspeakable' dimensions of terrorism. I draw cautiously on these works, noting that they focus on twentieth-century writing. For Houen, the 'terrifying effects of terrorism are produced and exacerbated' by interactions between the real and symbolic, and the figurative 'can affect the nature of material events, just as material events can modulate discursive practices' (6). Herman reframes this, using the language of trauma, arguing that 'terrorism's perpetrators always mean to convey some sort of message', but that 'the message terrorism means to send often goes unheard because, to those on the receiving end, terrorism is unspeakable' (2020, 6). For Herman, this means that cycles of terrorism continue because the messages or grievances of the terrorists go unheard – the symbolic short-circuited by the material horrors. Despite the apparent contradictions here, these formations represent useful tools and help us understand why this violent phenomenon has been so contested, and why the terms 'terrorism' and 'terrorist' have been so misused.

Houen's *Terrorism and Modern Literature* covers twentieth-century representations, from Conrad's *The Secret Agent* (1907) to Ciaran Carson's and Seamus Heaney's poetry of the Troubles, in the newly periodised post-September 11 climate. At the heart of the book is research carried out in the late 1990s that was given an abrupt new context, and Houen has noted recently that he had finished the book and was halfway through the introduction when the September 11 attacks occurred (2018, 505). Yet Houen's introduction handles this with a clarity that is rare, even in scholarly work from this period. One reason this work is so important is precisely because it emerged in a context where, in mass media and conservative political narratives, terrorism was increasingly taking on monolithic meanings: Islamophobic abstractions of evil. This meant that *Terrorism and*

Modern Literature was, without fully intending to be, a stern rebuke to those who were dutifully ignoring complex histories of terrorism, many involving white Christians. In the context of my argument here, it is also significant in that its analysis of the evolution of the literature of terrorism in the long twentieth century can be contrasted with the shift I identify in the early twenty-first century. Houen notes that the texts he analyses are 'experiments in the force of literature' and 'refigurings of modernist and postmodernist literary practices' (20). But while Houen tracks two divergent literary movements, noting seismic shifts, the focus on spectacle, event and mediation remains stable. Houen's attention to the consistency of this emphasis over a century of literary output underlines the significance of the shift away from a central focus on events during the last twenty years that this book examines.

The aspect of *Terrorism and Modern Literature* that I draw on, though, is its theorisation of the interplay between the symbolic and real that continues to characterise acts of terrorism and preoccupy authors. This book will take up questions that Houen addresses via the set of twentieth-century texts he analyses: 'is the figurative as volatile in what it can signify and do as the violence itself ... does the history of terrorism show that violence and the figurative, have interacted differently according to historical context?' (7). These questions are critical to my analysis of the shift in fictions of terrorism in the early twenty-first century and can be usefully extended. Many of these narratives of systemic violence are highly reflexive in their uses and depictions of the symbolic, and they often recalibrate DeLillo's famous notion of a 'curious knot that binds novelists and terrorists' in evocative ways (1991, 41). Long before the September 11 attacks, and the 9/11 novels that followed, DeLillo's *Mao II* (1991) explored the similarities between novelists and terrorists in their use of symbols, plots and rhetoric, while also suggesting that novelists have lost ground to terrorists. Protagonist Bill Gray, a reclusive novelist, laments this lost ground:

> Years ago I used to think it was possible for a novelist to alter the inner life of the culture. Now bomb-makers and gunmen have taken that territory. They make raids on human consciousness. What writers used to do before we were all incorporated. (41)

This 'zero-sum' struggle that Gray and other characters debate does not prevent the emergence of clear lines of connection between the novel's depiction of the writer and the terrorist. Margaret Scanlan's *Plotting Terror: Novelists and Terrorists in Contemporary Fiction*

(2001) – published just two months prior to September 11 – focused precisely on these connections. Scanlan argued that in a set of novels published in the 1980s and 1990s, novelists and terrorists are consistently 'doubled', and that these novels are metafictionally obsessed with 'exploring the influence of fiction on history and politics, the relation between language and violence, the nature of power, and the impetus to resist' (14).

Tracing these connections remains vitally important, even if they are premised on some outdated assumptions. It seems unlikely, now, that even the most popular novelists could compete for attention with the media spectacles that have occurred in the early twenty-first century, much less the flows of commentary that circulate via social media. Certainly the recent novels of terrorism that I will discuss in later chapters, such as Shamsie's *Home Fire* and Majumdar's *A Burning*, are acutely attuned to the power of social media and biased mainstream media, in driving systemic prejudice, corruption and repressive government agendas. This book takes up Houen's insistence that 'the figurative has been imbricated in terrorism's events and history in complex, material ways' (2002, 6) as one part of a more substantial and meaningful way of defining terrorism, and as a phenomenon to track alongside the movement away from event-based narratives.

Where Houen sees terrorism's force deriving from the interaction of the figurative and real, Herman emphasises their mitigating functions. Herman argues that a consistency of terrorism is its sense of design or purpose: it is employed to deliver a message or tell a story. So, while specific tactics may vary from suicide-martyrdom to hostage-taking or drone strikes, there is always a message. This may be 'a protest against political oppression, an act of vengeance, a blow supporting a national independence movement' or any 'ideological statement' (2020, 5). But while terrorism is always 'speakable', it is also inevitably 'unspeakable' because of the traumatic or unprecedented impact of the attacks, which break 'previous limits and conventions, thus rendering the audience speechless' (2020, 6). This ostensible paradox remains useful in defining terrorism and helps us understand the persistence of the phenomenon through the decades and centuries.

This said, part of my purpose in working with these theoretical formations will be to show how contemporary novels of terrorism resist their frameworks – particularly as they begin to eschew depictions of spectacle or the gravitational focus on 'events'. For instance, these formations are less persuasive in relation to novels such as *Milkman*. As Patricia Malone has shown, *Milkman* is a novel of voice that mounts a 'radical challenge to the received wisdom of trauma as "unspeakable"', and instead of an event-based model, of rupture, aftermath and working through, it renders inherited and entrenched colonial trauma (1145). These formations are also less persuasive when considered in relation to the literature of racist terrorism – like lynching or police shootings – where the symbolic dimensions are very different. Where some instances of terrorism are atrocities committed in the name of understandable grievances, racist terrorism is obviously not. Yet, the ideas of Houen and Herman provide a useful analytical lens for Everett's *The Trees*, in which these forms of terrorism happen with such frequency that, despite the spectacle of lynching – America's most egregious form of domestic terrorism – the victims are not remembered as individuals. The ideas of Houen and Herman also remain potent in relation to novels such as *Home Fire*, which is deeply preoccupied with sound and listening, literally addressing the speakable/unspeakable paradox. Claire Chambers meticulously examines this leitmotif, noting how the novel's 'tropes of noise and violence' invite us to listen 'to others, to individuals who are usually unattended to: most notably, radicalized subjects' (202).

In consideration of the ongoing definitional debates and theorisations of terrorism I have outlined, I define terrorism in the following terms and with the caveats below:

- Terrorism is politically driven violence by state or non-state actors.
- Terrorism is designed to shock and cause fear.
- Terrorism is designed to deliver a message.
- Terrorism should be understood in the context of structural violence.
- The ideological framing of the term 'terrorism' should always be questioned.

Traumatic and Systemic Violence

Two other terms (and variants) are critical to this book: 'trauma' (almost as contested as 'terrorism') and 'systemic'. As noted with reference to Berlant, Nixon and Hartnell, there has been a growing interest in systemic crises and slow violence in the humanities in the last decade. In some ways this has manifest as a turning away from 'the discourse of trauma', but it might more accurately be described as a growing interest in phenomena that are adjacent to but outside the remit of trauma studies (Berlant 9). This is registered in the *Routledge Companion to Literature and Trauma* (2020), which features new work by influential scholars of trauma studies of the past three decades such as Cathy Caruth and Michael Rothberg. The parameters of trauma studies have long been scrutinised, first with a set of challenges to the eurocentrism of the discipline, but also, and of particular importance here, with Rothberg's assertion that it is vital to attend to 'two forms' of violence – traumatic and systemic (xiv). Though it is disingenuous to suggest that increasing attention to systemic violence has resulted in a turning away from trauma, there are useful ways in which we can understand these phenomena in dialectical tension. One route is to consider how trauma and slow violence pose antithetical representational challenges. As Anne Whitehead has noted, the term 'trauma fiction' represents a paradox: 'if trauma comprises an event or experience which overwhelms the individual and resists language or representation, how then can it be narrativised in fiction?' (4). However, while traumatic ruptures are impossible to fully apprehend and therefore a challenge to represent, they often at least have dramatic potential. The lack of such potential has, as Nixon has noted, proven to be the critical representational challenge for slow violence because it is 'neither spectacular nor instantaneous, but rather incremental and accretive, its calamitous repercussions playing out across a range of temporal scales' (2). The difficulty of representing both phenomena gives us further pause to reflect on their natures, and this book will attend to the strategies contemporary novels employ to meet these challenges; and to note instances of intersection where traumatic ruptures punctuate ongoing systemic crises.

Despite these representational challenges and the growing interest in systemic phenomena, a basic understanding of individual psychological trauma, defined in the humanities by Cathy Caruth in the 1990s, has remained relatively stable.[14] There is consensus that a traumatic event is that which exceeds comprehension and the ability to process or understand in real time: it is belated or, as Caruth memorably describes it, an 'unclaimed experience' (1996). Caruth defines trauma in temporal relation to PTSD as 'a response, sometimes delayed, to an overwhelming event or events, which take the form of repeated, intrusive hallucinations, dreams, thoughts or behaviours stemming from the event, along with numbing that may have begun during or at the experience' (1995, 4). Richard Crownshaw, writing fifteen years later, echoes this, asserting that 'trauma is that which defies witnessing, cognition, conscious recall and representation' (4).

Crownshaw echoes Whitehead in noting that trauma 'defies representation' but also argues that literature can be vital in working through trauma via its capacity to 'narrativise' traumatic events. As Kristiaan Versluys notes, writing about September 11, narrativising traumatic events can begin 'uncoiling the trauma' which can 'only be dealt with when a traumatic memory gets situated within a series of events' (28).

While these tenets of individual psychological trauma are broadly agreed upon, notions of 'collective trauma' are more contested. As Lucy Bond and Stef Craps note, some commentators 'understand trauma to occur in collectives in much the same ways as it does in individuals' whereas others see collective trauma as a 'social construct' (9). At the very least, collective traumas experienced by large groups must be seen as multifaceted, and one useful way of understanding this is via Ron Eyerman's theory of 'cultural trauma' (2015). Eyerman defines 'cultural trauma' as dynamic:

> Cultural traumas are not things, but processes of meaning-making and attribution, contentious contests in which various individuals and groups struggle not only to define a situation but also to manage and control it. That is, they struggle to push collective understanding in particular directions. (9)

Eyerman's insistence on process and debate is useful in probing the ways terrorism is socially and culturally constructed, and immediately evokes the licentious use of the terms 'terrorist' and 'terrorism'. This is a useful way of understanding both the collective experience of trauma and post-September 11 culture wars, and is also a meaningful entry point into examining twenty-first century systemic crises.

In my analyses of the ways contemporary fiction represents systemic violence, I use the term 'systemic' in two intersecting ways. First, I refer to phenomena that are structural or entrenched in social and cultural institutions of government, media or industry. Second, I refer to 'world-systems' as theorised by Immanuel Wallerstein, which are not always global or planetary, but which refer to a 'large unit in terms of population or area' and are characterised by the axial divisions of core–periphery–semiperiphery (518). In Wallerstein's formation and in world-systems analysis in general, there are multiple 'world-systems'. This includes the 'modern capitalist world-system' as theorised by the Warwick Research Collective (WReC). For the WReC, this is a *world-system* that is also, uniquely and for the first time, a *world* system, whose defining characteristic is a 'combined and uneven' modernity (49). Despite obvious intersections, these formations are useful in distinct ways.

Though LeClair's influential study of the 'systems novel' is in some ways outdated, certain aspects of his 'systems theory' are remarkably prescient. Discussing the appeal of systems theory, he noted in 1987, with reference to the 'late 1960s and 1970s':

> Systems theory respond to, connects and makes sense of ... the accelerating specialization (and alienation) of knowledge and work; the tremendous growth of information and communications media into mass markets and the attendant reductiveness of messages into commodities; large-scale geopolitical crises over energy ... growing awareness of planetary ecological threats by man yet now seemingly beyond his control. (10)

The WReC offers an elegant update, noting that systemic phenomena are 'characterised by vertical and horizontal integration, connection and interconnection, structurality and organisation, internal differentiation, a hierarchy of constitutive elements governed by specific "logics" of determination and relationality' (8). Specific examples of such systemic phenomena that I will discuss include Islamophobia, which is driven by complex interactions between government, media and cultural representations. I draw heavily on the work of Deepa Kumar, Arun Kundnani, and Peter Morey and Amina Yaqin. The latter identify repeated occurrences where events are 'initiated by a tiny fringe group, picked up in the new media, broadcast by mainstream agencies, and given a boost by high-level political interventions', ultimately triggering 'a raw emotional response' in the public and creating various vectors of prejudice and bigotry (213). This is what Nathan Lean refers to as the 'Islamophobia Industry'.

Another systemic phenomenon I refer to is systemic racism, particularly in Chapter 5. In the United States, institutional power and cultures can be traced back over centuries, and some of America's most violent systems can be traced back to slavery. The justice and penal systems, as shown in Michelle Alexander's *The New Jim Crow* (2011), and other invaluable work in Critical Race Studies, often functions as an instrument of oppression and segregation. Alexander demonstrates in painful detail how a vast swathe of American society still suffers radically curtailed and limited rights, and is 'subject to legalized discrimination in employment, housing, education, public benefits and jury service, just as their parents, grandparents, and great-grandparents once were' (2). Alexander's analysis shows that this contemporary systemic oppression functions 'automatically', and that the deeper histories of racism and oppression have meant that 'the prevailing systems of racial meanings, identities, and ideologies already seemed natural' (58).

A third example of analysis of systemic phenomena that I will draw on is Taneja's *Aftermath*. Like Morey and Yaqin's work on Islamophobia, and Alexander's work on systemic racism and the slow violence of incarceration, Taneja traces current logics of incarceration and racism in the UK back to colonialism.

Though contemporary US racism, endemic police brutality, and discriminatory justice and penal policies might exemplify 'systemic' phenomena, the roots of such systems in slavery and colonialism mean their roots are world-systemic. Wallerstein characterises world-systems analysis as a 'knowledge movement', and emphasises the distinction of the world-system as a 'unit of analysis' that might stand in for a 'state/society/social formation' (518). Sharae Deckard and Stephen Shapiro's recent configuration is useful in approaching literary texts that often dramatise human stories of family and relationships in the context of wider geopolitical events. They note that contemporary world-systems of core–semiperiphery–periphery 'operate on multiple scales, rather than strictly national spheres', including 'household, city, region, nation or macro-area' (9). Such notions are useful in elucidating the broad trajectory of twenty-first century literatures of terrorism, which first approach September 11 and the shock of terror and then, as Peter Boxall notes, 'stage a kind of encounter between Islam and the West' – both reinforcing and critiquing Samuel P. Huntington's famous clash of civilisations theory – before moving towards the broader issues of inequality, radicalisation, neoliberalism and neoliberalisation, and systemic violence (128). World-systems analysis is also useful here in the sense that the movement to narratives of systemic crisis is characterised by a movement away from insularity and 'the domestic' towards the global and towards a sustained interest in dramas of world-systems or of the modern capitalist world-system.[15]

This is not to say that the novels under discussion here are 'systems novels' in the formal sense. They mostly do not resemble the works discussed by LeClair, in his 1987 study of DeLillo, Pynchon, Coover and Gaddis, as authors formally and thematically engaged with 'global ecology' and the 'inherent circularity and strange loops of living systems'; though sections on novels by both DeLillo and Pynchon follow (10). Nor am I focused on contemporary forms of maximalism, encyclopaedism or the 'big social novels' that Wood critiques for their exhaustive efforts to 'pin down an entire writhing culture, to be a great analyst of systems, crowds, paranoia, politics' (n.p.).

Chapter Outlines

My first chapter, 'Revisiting the Anglophone 9/11 Novel: Domesticity, Metafiction and Exceptionalism', returns to paradigmatic event-based novels of terrorism. This is the longest chapter, and I recognise that because of this, in some senses I too am exceptionalising 9/11. This length is necessary, though, in order to properly contextualise the chapters to come and to understand the paradigm shift at the heart of this book. In this chapter I analyse six novels published between 2005 and 2013 with additional commentary on others.[16] Discussions of these works have focused on the perceived domestication of the attacks in early novels and the eventual appearance of political 9/11 novels. I focus on a set of striking continuities in the genre, despite this turn: the prevalence of particular metafictional strategies, a central interest in American domesticity, and the depiction of psychological trauma – arguing that these works mostly reinforce the exceptionalisation of 9/11. I begin by discussing the metafictional conceits of Jonathan Safran Foer's *Extremely Loud and Incredibly Close* (2005) with some comment on Frédéric Beigbeder's *Windows on the World* (2003). Both novels deploy narrative devices that were innovations of late-twentieth century postmodernism but seem less experimental in the early twenty-first century, and represent an inwards reflex more than traumatic disorientation. I then discuss Lynne Sharon Schwartz's *The Writing on the Wall* (2005) and Don DeLillo's *Falling Man* (2007) with some comment on Jay McInerney's *The Good Life* (2005), Claire Messud's *The Emperor's Children* (2006) and Ken Kalfus's *A Disorder Peculiar to the Country* (2006). While these novels have legible critical dimensions, they too ultimately reinforce an insular and limited understanding of 9/11. I then analyse two novels – Joseph O'Neill's *Netherland* (2008) and Amy Waldman's *The Submission* (2011) – which have been praised for their outward-facing narratives of 9/11. Though they are undoubtedly more political than the earlier texts, and critique post-9/11 racism, they too envision 9/11 as a totalising, exceptional event. I conclude this chapter with analysis of Thomas Pynchon's *Bleeding Edge*, arguing that it is the first anglophone 9/11 novel to properly reject the exceptionalisation of the attacks. It does this, I posit, by locating 9/11 within a set of historical ruptures including a deeper history of neoliberalism.

In the second chapter, 'Writing the "Clash of Civilizations": Racism, Difference and Terrorism', I discuss works that were published during the same period as the 9/11 novels discussed in Chapter 1, noting the way they begin to challenge a notion that underpinned the exceptionalisation of 9/11: the alleged 'clash of civilisations'. I begin with two further 9/11 novels, Mohsin Hamid's *The Reluctant Fundamentalist* (2007), described neatly by Ambreen Hai as a 'Pakistani postcolonial novel that explicitly makes 9/11 its center-point' (435), and Khakpour's *Sons and Other Flammable Objects* (2007), a 'clash of generations' story of an Iranian family that flee Tehran to a Los Angeles suburb in the late 1970s. Both novels fit into the 9/11 novel genre in that relationship or family narratives are central and domestic formations are used to register the shock of the attacks. Like Waldman's *The Submission*, these novels also address post-9/11 racism and xenophobia, though they do so with more historical depth and international context, and in ways that destabilise the normative whiteness of the 9/11 novel genre. Following this, I consider two novels that seek to understand the inner world of the Islamic terrorist 'other'. I discuss Yasmina Khadra's novels *The Attack* (2005) and *The Sirens of Baghdad* (2006), which offer inverted perspectives of suicide terrorism: the former depicts the traumatic aftermath of a suicide attack in Tel Aviv and the latter depicts the 'radicalisation' of a young man in Iraq, plotting an attack 'a thousand times more awesome than the attacks of September 11' (11). Though very different, both novels seek to understand the rationale of a terrorist. I conclude this chapter with a lengthy analysis of Nadeem Aslam's multigenerational novel *The Blind Man's Garden* (2013), which powerfully critiques clash of civilisations logic by staging and restaging various forms of impasse, while simultaneously exploring a set of doubles. *The Blind Man's Garden*, I argue, is a complex depiction of war on terror-era violence and counter-violence that should be read as a forceful critique of the normative discourse of the war on terror.

My third chapter, 'The Novel of Terrorism and the War on Terror', considers the way four novels reject the narrow understandings of terrorism that became hegemonic during the war on terror. I begin with Ahmed Saadawi's *Frankenstein in Baghdad*, first published in Arabic in 2013 and translated to English by Jonathan Wright in 2018. Saadawi's novel is a genre hybrid that offers a nuanced portrait of conflict in Baghdad in 2005, following the US invasion and occupation, as the country leans towards civil war. It uses the Frankenstein story to interrogate the nature of terrorism, terror and the 'terrorist other', against the backdrop of a conflict where imperial and state violence overlaps with sectarian conflict. I then discuss

Karan Mahajan's *The Association of Small Bombs* (2016) a novel that follows the aftershocks of a deadly 'small bomb' that devastates two families in 1996 over a period of upheaval in India from that moment until 2003, including the 2002 anti-Muslim riots in Gujarat, described by many as a state-sponsored pogrom.[17] Mahajan's novel builds in layers of context and a panorama of perspectives including that of the terrorists, and its depictions of radicalisation and terrorism are in sharp contrast to typical war on terror-era representations. I then turn to Kamila Shamsie's *Home Fire* (2017), which uses the narrative frame of *Antigone* to tell the story of a London-based family torn apart by state violence and inequality under neoliberalism. I focus on its devastating critique of what Jodi Melamed calls 'neoliberal multiculturalism', in which citizens are inundated with dishonest visions of freedom and meritocracy that elide structural inequality. This aspect of Shamsie's novel has sometimes been overlooked because of its well-known foresight in 'predicting' the rise of Sajid Javid, its resonance with the Shamima Begum case, and its prescient depiction of the British government's 'hostile environment' policies. I conclude this chapter with discussion of another transatlantic post-2016 narrative – Ayad Akhtar's autofictional 'novel', *Homeland Elegies* (2020), which critiques the way the discourse of terrorism has evolved from 9/11 to the Trump era.

In my penultimate chapter, 'Contemporary Historical Novels of Terrorism', I examine two works that have looked back on episodes of terrorism and conflict in the late twentieth century. I begin by considering Rachel Kushner's *The Flamethrowers* (2013), a story of escalating leftist violence in the 1970s that is couched in a much deeper, global, historical narrative. Kushner's novel challenges stereotypes about the motivations and aesthetics of terrorists, while insisting on the underlying context of the capitalist world-system. Kushner also contextualises her depiction of the Red Brigades with depictions of various and sometimes contradictory forms of revolutionary energy. I compare Kushner's novel with another recent novel of terrorism and violence in the 1970s, Anna Burns's *Milkman* (2018). Unlike Kushner's widescreen approach, Burns is more interested in the intense and violent divisions of Northern Ireland in the early stages of the Troubles, though the world the novel creates is every bit as capacious, and it also insists on context in its depiction of terrorism, showing how it interacts with various other forms of state and paramilitary violence.

In my final chapter, 'Genre, Policing and Terrorism', I analyse depictions of the kinds of terrorism that have emerged or re-emerged with frightening force in recent years; and with particular ferocity since 2016. I focus here on three novels that all operate within the crime fiction genre and consider them within their respective series and alongside related novels. I begin with Ausma Zehanat Khan's *A Deadly Divide* (2020), the fifth book in her Rachel Getty and Esa Khattak series, and with Attica Locke's celebrated *Heaven, My Home* (2019) the second of her Darren Mathews mysteries, following *Bluebird, Bluebird* (2017). Finally, I discuss Percival Everett's *The Trees* (2021), a novel that considers the history and legacies of America's most egregious form of domestic terrorism: lynching. In Everett's novel, police shootings are a form of lynching and so a form of terrorism. Indeed, each of these crime novels of terrorism considers state terrorism alongside white nationalist terrorism and offers self-reflexive comment on a genre that has come under new scrutiny in the aftermath of the killing of George Floyd in 2020.

In my Conclusion, I discuss Megha Majumdar's *A Burning* (2020) alongside Preti Taneja's *Aftermath* (2021) in the context of the early, event-based narratives of September 11 as they each examine the fallout of 'events'. *A Burning* does this in the broad context of Hindu nationalism and the oppression of the Muslim minority population in Narendra Modi's India. It foregrounds the experience of the wrongly accused and the complicit, and focuses squarely on state violence and neoliberalism. I end the book with some further comparative reflections on *Aftermath*, which, I argue, points to new directions in understanding violent 'events' in its conception of the 'atro-city', a place where systemic and historical violence converge with traumatic rupture.

Notes

1. Zadie Smith's essay 'Two Paths for the Novel', which focuses on Tom McCarthy's *Remainder* (2005) and Joseph O'Neill's *Netherland* (2007) as examples of progressive and conservative modes, framed the expectation and anticipation for 9/11 novels in a suggestive way. Smith wrote of *Netherland*, 'it's the post-September 11 novel we hoped for. (Were there calls, in 1915, for the *Lusitania* novel? In 1985, was the Bhopal novel keenly anticipated?) It's as if, by an act of collective prayer we have willed it into existence' (72).
2. As I have noted elsewhere, *25th Hour*'s allegorical narrative suggests that America might usefully 'look to its own actions for answers' in the disorienting aftermath of the September 11 attacks (Keeble 2017 n.p.).

3. Donald Trump's Twitter campaign against Congresswoman Ilhan Omar repeatedly used images and videos of the September 11 attacks to stir the emotions of his supporters following reporting on a comment Omar made about the violent rise of Islamophobia after 'some people did something'. Omar's slightly clumsy expression was clearly, in context, pointing out that a whole population had been vilified because of the actions of a small minority. Removed from context, it seemed to trivialise the attacks. Trump's demonisation of the Congresswoman on Twitter culminated with the retweet of a false claim that a video of Omar dancing to Lizzo at the Congressional Black Caucus event portrayed her 'dancing on 9/11'. Trump has subsequently made several racist attacks to demonise Omar, a Muslim, along other members of 'The Squad' – Alexandria Ocasio-Cortez, Ayanna Pressley and Rashida Tlaib, all women of colour.
4. I follow Rachel Sykes's argument that '9/11' is an exceptionalising coinage. Sykes argues that the 'terminology is ideologically problematic, perpetuating an idea of the events' exceptionalism by referring to the attacks as a symbol' (n.p.). This is also implied by the narrator of Thomas Pynchon's 2013 novel *Bleeding Edge*, who uses '11 September' throughout and critiques the adoption of 'Ground Zero': 'those who repeat "Ground Zero" over and over do so without shame or concern for etymology. The purpose is to get people cranked up in a certain way. Cranked up and scared' (328).
5. In *Affect and American Literature in the Age of Neoliberalism*, Rachel Greenwald Smith notes that neoliberalism hegemony was secured in the 1990s, and in the introduction to *Neoliberalism and Contemporary Literary Culture*, Greenwald Smith and Mitchum Huehls posit their influential four phases theory, in which the third phase occurs in the 1990s when neoliberalism becomes socially and culturally entrenched.
6. In *Narratives of Hurricane Katrina in Context: Literature, Film and Television* (2019), I discuss the ways in which Jesmyn Ward's novel *Salvage the Bones* (2011) and Dave Eggers's work of narrative nonfiction *Zeitoun* (2009) dramatise 'intersections and overlaps between traumatic rupture and slow or systemic violence' (32).
7. In *Combined and Uneven Development: Towards a New Theory of World-Literature* (2015), the WReC makes an important distinction between 'world-systems' analysis, which can refer to multiple separate 'world-systems', and 'the combined and uneven, modern capitalist world-system' (8).
8. On 31 May 2020, in the midst of global protesting against police brutality in the wake of the murder of George Floyd, President Trump tweeted his intention to designate Antifa, a loosely connected international anti-fascist organisation that is mostly nonviolent and responsible for no deaths, a terrorist organisation. This tweet was widely condemned and Trump has been unable to make such a designation

official; however, the former president's influence means that many Americans now feel strongly that members of this anti-fascist collective are 'terrorists'. Moreover, as Sahar Aziz has noted, 'Designating Antifa as a terrorist organisation would not only change the public view of Antifa as a radical political group that, while fringe and occasionally violent, falls under Americans' expansive notions of free speech. It would unleash the full force of the government's counterterrorism regime against political dissidents on the left' (n.p.).

9. Detailed, refereed reports by the Soufan Center, Europol and the Center for Strategic and International Studies, all show that white nationalist or right-wing terrorism is by far the most significant threat in the USA and the world.

10. Alex Schmid also identifies differences between definitions of terrorism in four influential US government bodies. In 2002, the United States House of Representatives gave this definition: 'Terrorism is the illegitimate, premeditated violence or threat of violence by subnational groups against persons of property with the intent to coerce a government by installing fear amongst the populace.' In 1984, the State Department asserted that 'Terrorism means premeditated, politically motivated violence perpetrated against noncombatant targets by subnational groups or clandestine agents, usually intended to influence an audience.' In 1999, the FBI (Federal Bureau of Investigation) stated that 'Terrorism is defined as the unlawful use, or threatened use, of force or violence by a group or individual committed against persons or property by subnational groups or clandestine agents, usually intended to influence an audience' (Schmid 377).

11. In 'The Legal Response of the League of Nations to Terrorism' (2006), Ben Saul examines the history and impact of the League of Nations' definition of terrorism from 1937, showing how many of the points of contention and debate that are so prevalent today can be traced back to the drafting of this statement over eighty years ago.

12. Notably, the CSIS report of June 2020, cited in prominent articles in *The Guardian* and elsewhere, which analysed a 'data set of 893 incidents that occurred in the United States between January 1994 and May 2020', showed that a substantial majority were perpetrated by right-wing groups, and particularly white nationalists, and that this majority has steadily increased in the twenty-first century (n.p.).

13. There has been criticism of some of the central arguments of Critical Terrorism Studies, including its insistence on state terrorism as a central subject of analysis. For example, in a scholarly article entitled 'Terrorism', published in 2019 in *Israel Studies*, Jonathan Schanzer points out that the many unambiguous ways in which the Israeli and American governments have terrorised Palestinian citizens have usually not been understood as acts of terrorism. Schanzer dismisses the 'attempt to frame as terrorism Israel's military control of the West

Bank and the Gaza Strip', stating that this eventuality is 'born of a conflict instigated by the Palestinians and the Arab states in 1948' (55). Schanzer goes on to argue that while 'this interpretation has gained resonance among Arab states and a number of like-minded terrorist groups', the 'notion of Israeli enforcement terrorism has generally failed to gain traction' (55).
14. Cathy Caruth's monograph and edited collection of essays from the mid-1990s have been particularly influential: Cathy Caruth, *Unclaimed Experience: Trauma, Narrative and History* (Baltimore: Johns Hopkins University Press, 1996) and Cathy Caruth (ed.), *Trauma: Explorations in Memory* (Baltimore: Johns Hopkins University Press, 1995).
15. For Richard Gray, these novels are 'domestic' in two senses, both representing conservative impulses: they are novels of the home and family and they are novels of America and American life.
16. My first book, *The 9/11 Novel: Trauma, Politics and Identity* (2014), examined a fundamental tension between continuity and discontinuity in the fiction of September 11. I have updated and applied these ideas in numerous journal articles and a recent essay in *The Routledge Companion to Twenty-First Century Literary Fiction* (2019).
17. The description of the 2002 Gujarat massacre as a 'pogrom' is common. Parvis Ghassem-Fachandi makes a particularly compelling case for this in *Pogrom in Gujarat: Hindu Nationalism and Anti-Muslim Violence in India*.

Works Cited

Agamben, Giorgio, *State of Exception*, trans. by Kevin Attell (Chicago: Chicago University Press, 2005).

Akhtar, Ayad, *Homeland Elegies: A Novel* (New York: Little, Brown, 2020).

Alexander, Michelle, *The New Jim Crow: Mass Incarceration in the Age of Colorblindness* (New York: New Press, 2011).

Aslam, Nadeem, *The Blind Man's Garden* (London: Faber, 2013).

Aziz, Sahar, 'A Domestic Terror Law Could Quash Political Dissent in the US', *Aljazeera*, 13 June 2020 <https://www.aljazeera.com/indepth/opinion/trump-call-label-antifa-domestic-terrorists-dangerous-200611134333479.html> [accessed 21 July 2020].

Beigbeder, Frédéric, *Windows on the World*, trans. by Frank Wynne (London: Harper Perennial, 2005).

Berlant, Lauren, *Cruel Optimism* (Durham, NC: Duke University Press, 2011).

Bond, Lucy, and Stef Craps, *Trauma* (Abingdon: Routledge, 2020).

Booth, Ken, and Tim Dunne, *Terror in Our Time* (Abingdon: Routledge, 2012).

Boxall, Peter, *Twenty-First-Century Fiction: A Critical Introduction* (Cambridge: Cambridge University Press, 2013).
Burns, Anna, *Milkman* (London: Faber, 2018).
Caruth, Cathy, 'Trauma and Experience: Introduction', in *Trauma: Explorations in Memory*, ed. by Cathy Caruth (Baltimore: Johns Hopkins University Press, 1995), pp. 3–12.
Caruth, Cathy, *Unclaimed Experience: Trauma, Narrative and History* (Baltimore: Johns Hopkins University Press, 1996).
Chambers, Claire, 'Sound and Fury: Kamila Shamsie's *Home Fire*', *The Massachusetts Review*, 59.2 (2018), 202–19.
Chenoweth, Erica, Richard English, Andreas Gofas and Stathis N. Kalyvas (eds), *The Oxford Handbook of Terrorism* (Oxford: Oxford University Press, 2019).
Cole, Teju, *Open City* (London: Faber, 2011).
Crownshaw, Richard, *The Afterlife of Holocaust Memory in Contemporary Literature and Culture* (Basingstoke: Palgrave Macmillan, 2010).
CSIS (Center for Strategic and International Studies), 'The Escalating Terrorist Problem in the United States', 17 June 2020 <https://www.csis.org/analysis/escalating-terrorism-problem-united-states> [accessed 21 July 2020].
Davis, Colin, and Hanna Meretoja (eds), *The Routledge Companion to Literature and Trauma* (New York: Routledge, 2020).
Deb, Basuli, *Transnational Feminist Perspectives on Terror in Literature and Culture* (Abingdon: Routledge, 2015).
Deckard, Sharae, and Stephen Shapiro, *World Literature, Neoliberalism, and the Culture of Discontent* (Basingstoke: Palgrave Macmillan, 2019).
DeLillo, Don, *Falling Man* (New York: Scribner, 2007).
DeLillo, Don, *Mao II* (London: Vintage, 1991).
del Pont, Xavier Marcó, 'Metafiction', in *The Routledge Companion to Twenty-First Century Literary Fiction*, ed. by Daniel O'Gorman and Robert Eaglestone (Abingdon: Routledge, 2019), pp. 80–8.
Eaglestone, Robert, 'Contemporary Fiction in the Academy: Towards a Manifesto', *Textual Practice*, 27.7 (2013), 1089–101.
Europol, *European Union Terrorism Situation and Trend Report 2020 (TE-SAT)* (The Hague: Europol, 2020) <https://www.europol.europa.eu/cms/sites/default/files/documents/european_union_terrorism_situation_and_trend_report_te-sat_2020_0.pdf> [accessed 5 October 2023].
Everett, Percival, *The Trees* (Minneapolis: Graywolf, 2021).
Eyerman, Ron, *Is This America? Katrina as Cultural Trauma* (Austin: University of Texas Press, 2015).
Ghassem-Fachandi, Parvis, *Pogrom in Gujarat: Hindu Nationalism and Anti-Muslim Violence in India* (Princeton, NJ: Princeton University Press, 2012).
Gray, Richard, 'Open Doors, Close Minds: American Prose Writing at a Time of Crisis', *American Literary History*, 21.1 (2009), 128–51.

Greenwald Smith, Rachel, *Affect and American Literature in the Age of Neoliberalism* (Cambridge: Cambridge University Press, 2015).

Greenwald Smith, Rachel, *On Compromise: Art, Politics, and the Fate of an American Ideal* (Minneapolis: Graywolf, 2021).

Hai, Ambreen, 'Pitfalls of Ambiguity in Contexts of Islamophobia: Mohsin Hamid's *The Reluctant Fundamentalist*', *Studies in the Novel*, 52.4 (2020), 434–58.

Hartnell, Anna, *After Katrina: Race, Neoliberalism and the End of the American Century* (New York: State University of New York Press, 2017).

Herman, Peter C. (ed.), *Terrorism and Literature* (Cambridge: Cambridge University Press, 2018).

Herman, Peter C., *Unspeakable: Literature and Terrorism from the Gunpowder Plot to 9/11* (Abingdon: Routledge, 2020).

Hirsch, Marianne, 'I Took Pictures: September 2001 and Beyond', in *Trauma at Home: After 9/11*, ed. by Judith Greenberg (Lincoln: University of Nebraska Press, 2003), pp. 69–86.

Holloway, David, *9/11 and the War on Terror* (Edinburgh: Edinburgh University Press, 2008).

Houen, Alex, 'Afterword', in *Terrorism and Literature*, ed. by Peter C. Herman (Cambridge: Cambridge University Press, 2018), pp. 505–14.

Houen, Alex, *Terrorism and Modern Literature* (Oxford: Oxford University Press, 2002).

Huehls, Mitchum, and Rachel Greenwald Smith, 'Four Phases of Neoliberalism and Literature: An Introduction', in *Neoliberalism and Contemporary Literary Culture*, ed. by Mitchum Huehls and Rachel Greenwald Smith (Baltimore: Johns Hopkins University Press, 2017), pp. 1–18.

Jackson, Richard, 'Introduction: A Decade of Critical Terrorism Studies', in *Routledge Handbook of Critical Terrorism Studies*, ed. by Richard Jackson (New York: Routledge, 2016), pp. 1–13.

Kapadia, Ronak, *Insurgent Aesthetics: Security and the Queer Life of the Forever War* (Durham, NC: Duke University Press, 2019).

Keeble, Arin, *Narratives of Hurricane Katrina in Context: Literature, Film and Television* (Cham: Palgrave Macmillan, 2019).

Keeble, Arin, 'The 9/11 Novel', in *The Routledge Companion to Twenty-First Century Literary Fiction*, ed. by Daniel O'Gorman and Robert Eaglestone (Abingdon: Routledge, 2019), pp. 273–85.

Keeble, Arin, *The 9/11 Novel: Trauma, Politics and Identity* (Jefferson, NC: McFarland, 2014).

Keeble, Arin, 'Why Spike Lee's 25th Hour Is the Most Enduring Film about 9/11', *The Conversation*, 8 September 2017 <https://theconversation.com/why-spike-lees-25th-hour-is-the-most-enduring-film-about-9-11-82020> [accessed 21 July 2020].

Khakpour, Porochista, *Brown Album* (London: Penguin, 2020).

Khakpour, Porochista, *Sick* (Edinburgh: Canongate, 2017).

Khadra, Yasmina, *The Attack*, trans. by John Cullen (London: Vintage, 2007).
Khadra, Yasmina, *The Sirens of Baghdad*, trans. by John Cullen (London: Vintage, 2008).
Klein, Naomi, *The Shock Doctrine* (London: Penguin, 2007).
Krishnan, Madhu, 'Postcoloniality, Spatiality and Cosmopolitanism in *Open City*', *Textual Practice*, 29.4 (2015), 675–96.
Kumar, Deepa, *Islamophobia and the Politics of Empire: 20 Years After 9/11* (London: Verso, 2021).
Kundnani, Arun, *The Muslims Are Coming: Islamophobia, Extremism, and the Domestic War on Terror* (London: Verso, 2015).
Kushner, Rachel, *The Flamethrowers* (London: Vintage, 2013).
Lean, Nathan, *The Islamophobia Industry* (London: Pluto, 2012).
LeClair, Tom, *In the Loop: Don DeLillo and the Systems Novel* (Chicago: Chicago University Press, 1987).
Lerner, Ben, *Leaving the Atocha Station* (Minneapolis: Coffee House Press, 2011).
Mahajan, Karan, *The Association of Small Bombs* (London: Viking, 2016).
Majumdar, Megha, *A Burning* (New York: Knopf, 2020).
Malone, Patricia, 'Measures of Obliviousness and Disarming Obliqueness in Anna Burns' *Milkman*', *Textual Practice*, 36.7 (2022), 1143–74.
Martin, Theodore, *Contemporary Drift: Genre, Historicism, and the Problem of the Present* (New York: Columbia University Press, 2017).
Melamed, Jodi, *Represent and Destroy: Rationalizing Violence in the New Racial Capitalism* (London: University of Minnesota Press, 2011).
Morey, Peter, and Amina Yaqin, *Framing Muslims: Stereotyping and Representation After 9/11* (Cambridge, MA: Harvard University Press, 2011).
Nixon, Rob, *Slow Violence and the Environmentalism of the Poor* (Cambridge, MA: Harvard University Press, 2011).
O'Gorman, Daniel, 'Global Terror | Global Literature', in *Terrorism and Literature*, ed. by Peter C. Herman (Cambridge: Cambridge University Press, 2018), pp. 446–68.
O'Gorman, Daniel, and Robert Eaglestone, 'Introduction', in *The Routledge Companion to Twenty-First Century Literary Fiction*, ed. by Daniel O'Gorman and Robert Eaglestone (Abingdon: Routledge, 2019), pp. 1–10.
O'Neill, Joseph, *Netherland* (London: Fourth Estate, 2008).
Pishotti, Gabriella, 'Materializing Grief: The Reclamation of Loss in Kamila Shamsie's *Home Fire*', *Journal of Postcolonial Writing*, 58.3 (2022), 349–60.
Pynchon, Thomas, *Bleeding Edge* (London: Penguin, 2013).
Rothberg, Michael, 'Preface', in *After Trauma Theory*, ed. by Robert Eaglestone, Gert Buelens and Sam Durrant (Abingdon: Routledge, 2014), pp. xi–xviii.

Saadawi, Ahmed, *Frankenstein in Baghdad*, trans. by Jonathan Wright (London: Oneworld, 2018).
Safran Foer, Jonathan, *Extremely Loud and Incredibly Close* (London: Penguin, 2005).
Saul, Ben, 'The Legal Response of the League of Nations to Terrorism', *Journal of International Criminal Justice*, 4.1 (2006), 79–102.
Scanlan, Margaret, *Plotting Terror: Novelists and Terrorists in Contemporary Fiction* (Charlottesville: University of Virginia Press, 2001).
Schanzer, Jonathan, 'Terrorism', *Israel Studies*, 24.2 (2019), 52–61.
Schmid, Alex, 'Terrorism – the Definitional Problem', *Case Western Reserve Journal of International Law*, 36.2/3 (2004), 375–420.
Schuurman, Bart, 'Topics in Terrorism Research: Reviewing Trends and Gaps 2006–2017', *Critical Studies on Terrorism*, 12.3 (2019), 463–80.
Shamsie, Kamila, *Home Fire* (London: Bloomsbury, 2017).
Smith, Zadie, 'Two Paths for the Novel', *New York Review of Books*, 55.18 (20 November 2008), 34–9; repr. as 'Two Directions for the Novel', in *Changing My Mind: Occasional Essays* (London: Penguin, 2009), pp. 71–96.
Soufan Center, 'White Supremacy Extremism: The Transnational Rise of the Violent White Supremacist Movement', 27 September 2019 <https://thesoufancenter.org/research/white-supremacy-extremism-the-transnational-rise-of-the-violent-white-supremacist-movement/> [accessed 5 October 2023].
Sturken, Marita, *Terrorism in American History: Memorials, Museums, and Architecture in the Post-9/11 Era* (New York: New York University Press, 2022).
Sykes, Rachel, '"All that howling space": "9/11" and the Aesthetic of Noise in Contemporary American Fiction', *C21 Literature*, 4.1 (2016) <http://doi.org/10.16995/c21.2>.
Taneja, Preti, *Aftermath* (Oakland, CA: Transit Books, 2021).
Terrorism Act 2000, UK Government <https://www.legislation.gov.uk/ukpga/2000/11/section/1> [accessed 22 July 2020].
Thomas, Lindsay, *Training for Catastrophe: Fictions of National Security After 9/11* (Minneapolis: University of Minnesota Press, 2021).
United Nations Security Council, Resolution 1566 (2004) <https://digitallibrary.un.org/record/532676?ln=en> [accessed 1 September 2023].
Versluys, Kristiaan, *Out of the Blue: September 11th and the Novel* (New York: Columbia University Press, 2009).
von Gleich, Paula, 'The "fugitive notes" of Teju Cole's Open City', *Atlantic Studies*, 19.2 (2022), 334–51.
Waldman, Amy, *The Submission* (London: Windmill, 2011).
Wallerstein, Immanuel, 'World-Systems Analysis as a Knowledge Movement', in *The Routledge Handbook of World-Systems Analysis*, 2nd edition, ed. by Salvatore J. Banones and Christopher Chase-Dunn (Abingdon: Routledge, 2016), pp. 515–22.

Wattenberger, Melanie R., 'When Person Becomes Problem', *Interventions: International Journal of Postcolonial Studies*, 20.5 (2018), 682–96.

Whitehead, Anne, *Trauma Fiction* (Edinburgh: Edinburgh University Press, 2004).

Wood, James, 'Tell Me How Does It Feel?', *The Guardian*, 6 October 2001, <https://www.theguardian.com/books/2001/oct/06/fiction> [accessed 31 August 2023].

WReC (Warwick Research Collective), *Combined and Uneven Development: Towards a New Theory of World-Literature* (Liverpool: Liverpool University Press, 2015).

Chapter 1

Revisiting the Anglophone 9/11 Novel: Domesticity, Metafiction and Exceptionalism

Conjuring the 9/11 Novel

The mid to late-2000s saw the publication of a sequence of English language novels centrally depicting the September 11, 2001 terror attacks. These quickly became known – in Western literary journalism, literary scholarship and university syllabi, and to general readers – as '9/11 novels'. Nobody was surprised by the rapid proliferation of these works. It seemed inevitable from the early days and weeks after the attacks, when newspapers and magazines clamoured to publish the thoughts of the period's pre-eminent writers, that a wave of '9/11 fiction' would follow. These novels – narratives of rupture, trauma and aftermath – are paradigmatic event-centred narratives of terrorism and, as such, they are the obvious starting point for this book.

Though there are recent 9/11 novels like Anissa M. Bouziane's excellent *Dune Song* (2019), and while there will undoubtedly be more, a substantial cluster were published over a decade bookended by Frédéric Beigbeder's *Windows on the World* (2003) and Thomas Pynchon's *Bleeding Edge* (2013). While this might suggest it is best considered a cycle of context-specific fictions, there are enough shared narrative conceits, recurring tropes and themes – beyond just the centrality of the September 11 attacks – for us to also consider the anglophone 9/11 novel as a genre in its own right; and this is reinforced by the numerous scholarly articles, monographs and collections of essays addressing these works. These novels diverge in important ways, especially in their engagement (or lack of engagement) with post-9/11 racism, Islamophobia and the alleged 'clash of civilisations', and the genre certainly evolves over this decade. However, there are some remarkably consistent features: heteronormative depictions of marital discord, parents struggling to protect children, a re-evaluation of what is important in life, and narrative arcs of catastrophe, traumatic disorientation and eventual recovery. There are variations in how the novels depict trauma, but as Lucy Bond has shown, there is a distinction between '9/11 trauma fiction' and the more experimental models of trauma fiction theorised by Anne Whitehead, in which conventional narrative frameworks are questioned, rejected or repurposed; or 'traumatic realism' as theorised by Michael Rothberg (409). Bond is mostly discussing the early iterations of the genre, but there have been no genuinely experimental formal anglophone 9/11 novels, and of these works only *Bleeding Edge* offers a sophisticated reflection on the traumas of 9/11 within a wider historical context.

Indeed, the trauma narratives of so many 9/11 novels have, as Rachel Greenwald Smith shows, actually attested to the 'disturbing resiliency of narrative form in the face of the event that was supposed to change everything' (2015, 62). In one sense we might interpret this as a rarely registered critical dimension of these works where the 'everything's changed' rhetoric of the Bush administration is questioned by the 'resiliency' of their formal features (which suggest continuity rather than discontinuity). However, their event-centred narratives have mostly reinforced the exceptionalisation of 9/11, a phenomenon that has meant an exaggerated importance has been attached to this event as a defining moment. Moreover, while Greenwald Smith makes an astute point about the contradictory situation that saw a lack of any bold narrative or aesthetic responses to this allegedly world-changing event, the event-centred shapes of these novels warrant further scrutiny. Indeed, these novels reveal much about the social and cultural conditions that have driven this exceptionalisation.

It is useful to make a distinction between the 9/11 novel as a genre and the broader categories of 'post-9/11 novel' or 'post-9/11 fiction'; a distinction that, somewhat curiously, has not often been made. While the term '9/11 novel' quickly became common, the term 'post-9/11 novel' has often been used synonymously. Hamilton Carroll refers to '9/11-centred novels', but this distinction is unusual and the common interchangeability of '9/11 novel' and 'post-9/11 novel' should be questioned (281). The latter term might refer to '9/11-centred' novels or to works that deal with certain post-9/11 realties of securitisation, fear and intolerance; and sometimes it simply denotes fiction published after 9/11. Making a distinction is important because of the way 9/11 novels, which I define here as works that deal centrally with the attacks, are uniquely framed in ways that reinforce (and very occasionally challenge) the exceptionalisation of 9/11. These novels have frequently, as Sarah O'Brien notes, proffered 'narrow conceptualisations of 9/11 that situate it singularly, or even primarily, as an American or Western trauma that represents a unique instance of rupture in human history' (4). Indeed, the singularity and prominence of 9/11 in these works means that they are aligned – mostly inadvertently – with the Bush administration's notion of a new world order which, as David Holloway has noted, was ultimately the 'ideological lynchpin' of the 'war on terror' (4). The world has changed in profound ways since 9/11, of course, but this was not because of the attacks themselves as a singular event, rather it was because of America and its allies' disproportionate response to the attacks. Yet we continue to identify this period – even now – as the 'post-9/11' era. Moreover, the anglophone 9/11 novels published during the ongoing war on terror rarely even reference it. I welcome the calls for a move towards proper consideration of 'how different peoples and cultures may represent and understand their post-9/11 worlds in non-US centered ways', and the chapters following this one do precisely this (Cilano 16–17). Here, though, I argue for the value in understanding how these novels have reinforced the exceptionalisation of 9/11 – a phenomenon of great consequence – and how they consolidated an 'event-centred paradigm' of writing about terrorism.

Periodisation is another reason that the 9/11 novel has been one of the most read, studied and critiqued genres of early twenty-first century fiction: there was a sense that these novels might somehow register not just the attacks, but this new era more broadly. This is a lot of responsibility and, as I have noted, pressure steadily grew from the very early aftermath of the attacks, when this body of work was already being conjured. Literary magazines like the *New Yorker* and *Harper's* and broadsheet newspapers like *The Guardian* and *New York Times* sought out novelists to help make sense of the attacks in the days and weeks after, publishing work by Ian McEwan, Jay McInerney, Martin Amis, Umberto Eco, Arundhati Roy, Don DeLillo, John Updike, Jonathan Franzen and Amitav Ghosh, among others. As Alex Houen has pointed out, this recourse to 'call in the novelists', the 'experts at imagining the unimaginable', seemed logical in the face of the incomprehensible (419). And, while it was not fiction that the novelists produced, this wave of writing stoked anticipation for the novels that would eventually come; particularly from DeLillo, who had been depicting political violence for decades. Charlie Lee Potter has argued that these novelists 'rehearsed their later fictional responses by acting as journalists, writing commentaries, essays and fragments of prose for the newspapers and magazines that queued up to commission salving words' (3). But as Potter concedes, the novels that eventually appeared bore little resemblance to the short, elegiac articles published in the initial weeks after. In fact, those works are usefully understood in relation to another journalistic response to the attacks, the *New York Times*' 'Portraits of Grief', which ran between 15 September and 31 December 2001, offering short, poetic glimpses into the lives lost in the attacks. Editor Janny Scott described them as 'informal and impressionistic' and 'utterly democratic' (ix). They were undoubtedly popular, and were soon published in anthology form in 2002; an odd proposition that David Simpson felt was 'formulaic ... regimented, even militarized, made to march to the beat of a single drum' (2006, 23). This aside, they were influential as an early approach to writing about the tragedy. Some of the novelists' articles offered broader context than what was common in the portraits, but they were similar in the emphasis placed on shared grief over ordinary lives, love and consolation. John Updike et al.'s *New Yorker* piece is a good example. Updike described watching from the roof of his building as 'the south tower dropped from the screen of our viewing': 'we knew we had witnessed thousands of deaths; we clung to each other as if we ourselves were falling' (n.p.). This personal and consoling tone also characterised many contributions to Ulrich Baer's collection of short 'stories', *110 Stories* (2002), a volume of very short works by New York writers, designed to capture the 'boundless complexity, polyglot energy' (1) as well as the 'regenerative imagination' of New York (New York University Press n.p.). The 'Portraits', Baer's collection and this profusion of non-fiction by prominent novelists all emphasised the idea that words could repair; but the particular visibility of these celebrated novelists created palpable anticipation for the 9/11 novel which might also help people process or 'understand' what had happened. As Zadie Smith has noted, the 9/11 novel was practically 'willed into existence' (71), and these early works foreshadowed the exceptionalist vision of the novels that would follow in their emphasis on the unique greatness of New York, the white heteronormative American family – what Kenneth Millard has described as the 'sacred cornerstone of the American social project' (2) – and portrayals of Americans as, strictly, victims or heroes.

As noted, the first 9/11 novels were subject to polarised critical debates about the perceived 'domestication' of the attacks. In particular, Pankaj Mishra, Richard Gray and Michael Rothberg focused their critical attention on Claire Messud's *The Emperor's Children* (2006), Jay McInerney's *The Good Life* (2005), Ken Kalfus's *A Disorder Peculiar to the Country* (2006) and Don DeLillo's *Falling Man* (2007). These critiques elicited strong rejoinders from John Duvall and Robert P. Marzec, and though I will not restage these much-discussed debates here, I would like to note that they focused attention on this particular set of domestic novels and a sequence of subsequent, conspicuously political (but also very much domestic) 9/11 novels, positioned as a response to the earlier texts: Joseph O'Neill's *Netherland* (2008), Mohsin Hamid's *The Reluctant Fundamentalist* (2007) and Amy Waldman's *The Submission* (2011).[1] Partly because of the profile of this initial critical debate, these clusters of 9/11 novels have had more attention than others that warrant consideration. For example, Lynne Sharon Schwartz's *The Writing on the Wall* (2005), very much a novel of trauma and family relationships, has received little critical attention. Schwartz's novel is another instance of trauma being measured through family upheaval, but it also has some distinct features worthy of further attention; for instance, out of all these domestic fictions, its criticisms of the Bush administration's post-9/11 family values rhetoric are the most potent. Similarly, Jess Walter's detective novel *The Zero* (2006) offers under-appreciated variations on the '9/11 trauma narrative' and is perhaps as close as the genre gets to formal experimentation in its potent satire and traumatic realism. As Timothy Melley notes, *The Zero* depicts 'collective American befuddlement and naïveté through a protagonist whose traumatic amnesia after 9/11 prevents him from understanding . . . how his work for a top-secret security agency produces the very threats he is investigating' (276). Porochista Khakpour's evocative family novel, *Sons and Other Flammable Objects* (2007), discussed at length in my next chapter, has also been neglected, possibly (as with *The Zero*) because of its irreverent humour and refusal to grant any concessions to the many advocates for sombre and unironic narratives of 9/11. Khakpour's novel is a vital contribution to the literature of 9/11 in its depiction of the pre- and post-9/11 experiences of an Iranian family that fled the Islamic revolution of 1979, positioning the attacks on a useful historical continuum shaped by two moments of rupture.

This chapter contains analysis of some of the most discussed 9/11 novels and some that have been neglected, and focuses on how they work as event-based narratives. Though most analyses of these novels have participated in the debates about the perceived 'failure of imagination', I focus here on what I have called the 'exceptionalisation of 9/11' (Gray 130). I examine the ways these novels have mostly affirmed President Bush's sombre proclamation on 20 September 2001, to a joint session of Congress, that '[a]ll of this was brought upon us in a single day – and night fell on a different world'. The 9/11 novel genre is, in some ways, defined by the alleged singularity of this event, and its most prominent feature is a combination of domestic realism and a set of curiously limited metafictional conceits, which, rather than posing 'questions about the relationship between fiction and reality', mostly perpetuate the centring of 9/11, consolidating its exceptionalisation (Waugh 2).

Though 9/11 remains a totalising event in each novel discussed here (apart from *Bleeding Edge*), these texts begin to build in layers of context, considering extraterritoriality, American empire and state violence, and it would be unfair to ignore such gestures. Moreover, while formal experimentation in 9/11 fiction never really arises, a perceptible discomfort with exceptionalisation occasionally comes into view – at formal, thematic and diegetic levels. This is inevitably paradoxical, because even the 9/11 novels most suspicious of the exceptionalisation of this historical moment are in some ways participant in it simply by centring this event (as, of course, am I, writing again about it). But as the genre has evolved, the critical reflexes, and contextualising or historicising gestures of these works, have become more visible.

In previous analyses, I have focused on tensions that run throughout this body of work, arguing that it is 'characterized by anxiety and internal conflict relating to a set of competing impulses' (Keeble 10). I build on this notion here, while shifting focus to the ways the novels are imbricated in wider exceptionalist agendas, and though this chapter maps the evolution of the genre over a decade, I will also focus on narrative strategies and conceits that have remained consistent. I attend to two interrelated formal features: the unsubtly metafictional devices of the novels and their central interest in (mostly white, heteronormative) American domesticity. These features, clearly conceived of as ways to depict or respond to psychological trauma, mean their political visions remain limited, even as gestures towards wider contexts emerge.

What follows in this chapter is detailed analysis of six anglophone 9/11 novels in four sections with some contextualising comment on others. I begin by considering the conflicting impulses of Jonathan

Safran Foer's *Extremely Loud and Incredibly Close* (2005) with some discussion of Frédéric Beigbeder's *Windows on the World* (2003), too. These novels are simultaneously transatlantic and parochial, in their focus on the private traumas of individual families. They are both earnest and conspicuously playful, and exemplify a confluence of impulses towards literary prestige and mass appeal, embodying what Greenwald Smith calls 'compromise aesthetics', where formal experiments are embedded in an 'easily consumable shape' (2021, 11). The metafictional reflexivity of *Extremely Loud and Incredibly Close* is limited to the specific challenges of narrating and describing 9/11. This is not the kind of trauma narrative that addresses the question of how to represent what cannot be fully understood, as theorised by Whitehead in *Trauma Fiction* (2004), but rather, is nicely described as '9/11 trauma fiction': a mode that 'frames disaster within sentimental domestic settings, assimilating trauma into conventional narrative structures, and generating a standardized almost homogenized portrait of post-9/11 America' (Bond 409).

In the subsequent section, I consider a set of novels published between 2005 and 2007 that are built around stories of heteronormative marital and relationship discord. These are the novels that consolidate what Georgiana Banita describes as 'the formula of the 9/11 novel': 'urban and emotional architectures organize an endless loop of marriage, divorce, and other prefabricated plots' (154). Couples separate and reform as characters take stock and re-evaluate what is important in life. Additionally, though, they operate via a similar kind of metafiction-lite, which draws attention to practices of writing and reading as characters diegetically puzzle over the ways they might write about the 9/11 crisis. I focus on DeLillo's *Falling Man* (2007) and Schwartz's *The Writing on the Wall* (2005) with some discussion of Messud's *The Emperor's Children* (2006) and McInerney's *The Good Life* (2005). I note that while these insular narratives of privileged couples reinforce the singularity of the 9/11 attacks, some of their important features have been neglected. First, their visions of marriage and relationships rarely suggest the marital home as a place of stability, refuge or strength in the aftermath of 9/11. *The Writing on the Wall* skewers the post-9/11 fantasies of 1950s-style domesticity peddled by the Bush administration and conservative American media; fantasies which were later meticulously laid bare in Susan Faludi's *The Terror Dream* (2007, 9).[2] Additionally, little attention has been given to the fact that while these novels are, at least in Bond's definition, '9/11 trauma' narratives, they also, to varying degrees, depict the resolution of trauma and return to normalcy. Even in *Falling Man*, with its circular narrative that ends just before the novel begins, in the towers, there is a sense of recovery for one central protagonist. *Falling Man* also makes some provisional but provocative references to late-twentieth-century terrorism, in that a peripheral character is an ex-member of Kommune 1 and potential affiliate of the Red Army Faction, and certainly a critic of American imperialism and power. However, such contextual gestures are ultimately minimal, and while these novels signal some discomfort with the insularity of their own narrative modes, they remain decidedly aligned with the notion of 9/11 as a singular, world-changing event.

In the penultimate section I discuss two novels that are, again, metafictional narratives of trauma and recovery where privileged, heteronormative domesticity is central. However, these novels – O'Neill's *Netherland* (2008) and Waldman's *The Submission* (2011) – offer fuller forms of political critique. *Netherland* is the first 9/11 novel that reflexively responds to the early critical accusations of domestication that the early 9/11 novels accrued, and *The Submission* is uniquely self-conscious as a novel that is both about and an example of the memorialisation of 9/11. Both texts engage meaningfully with intolerance, Islamophobia and racism and are more attuned to perspectives other than those of privileged white Manhattanites. This said, *Netherland*'s central sporting metaphor (the civility and level playing field of cricket) elides structural inequalities in favour of an ideological vision of meritocratic, aspirational multiculturalism. In Donald E. Pease's reading, this informs a kind of 'neo-liberal fantasy work' that many critical and scholarly readings have actually reinforced (140). Waldman's novel is certainly metafictional as a work that is both about and an example of representation and memorialisation, but this reflexivity is also short-circuited by the all-encompassing trauma of 9/11. Moreover, despite the important critical dimensions these novels include, they continue to imagine 9/11 as a totalising event, the shadow of which is, in some ways, inescapable.

Finally, I consider Pynchon's *Bleeding Edge* (2013), with some commentary on Walter's earlier novel *The Zero* (2006), both noirish, detective novels. In surprising ways, *Bleeding Edge* is conspicuously aligned with the early 9/11 novels; certainly in its domestic architecture. Nevertheless, I argue that it includes the most important departures and developments of the genre, consistently challenging the singularity of 9/11 by contextualising it within a historical narrative of other key moments from the turn-of-the-millennium years in which it is set and a deeper history of neoliberalism beginning with the 'other 9/11', the bombing of the presidential palace in Chile on 11 September 1973, and CIA-sponsored coup that installed Augusto Pinochet. In addition to locating 9/11 on a meaningful historical continuum – and de-exceptionalising it as a historical event – *Bleeding Edge* depicts a world where the experience of neoliberalism is one of process and immaterial exchange in America but an experience of violence for those in peripheral zones. In *Bleeding Edge*, the 9/11 attacks are positioned as a *choc en retour* where the violence of neoliberalism rebounds against its source.

Extremely Loud and Incredibly Close

Extremely Loud and Incredibly Close (2005) and *Windows on the World* (2003) have striking similarities. They are both transatlantic novels featuring dual narratives unfolding in Europe and in New York which alternate with every chapter. Additionally, they are conspicuously metafictional, without being particularly challenging or experimental. Their metafiction is derived from conceits that were once innovations of postmodernist fiction but are now familiar and even banal. The author is a character/protagonist in *Windows on the World*, and *Extremely Loud and Incredibly Close* features a range of still images, typographical play and literary allusions. In both cases the supposed limits of language and fiction are clearly signposted, and attention is drawn to the novel's own artifice. Both texts are also concerned with children, exemplifying what Holloway has identified as a dominant trope in 9/11 novels: 'children and youths, or adult sons and daughters involved in distressing relationships with parents or "guardian" figures' (108). Holloway persuasively reads this as an allegory for the American state's failure to protect its citizens – 'children/citizens divested of parental/state protection' (110–11) – and this is perhaps the most evocative feature of both novels, despite their conspicuous aesthetic conceits. *Extremely Loud* centres on nine-year-old Oskar Schell, whose father died in the attacks, and who embarks on an eccentric quest to find the keyhole for a mysterious key he has discovered, belonging to his father. The novel also gives substantial space to the story of his grandparents, traumatised survivors of the Dresden fire-bombings during World War II. *Windows on the World* tells the story of an American man, Carthew Yorston, who is having breakfast in the Windows on the World restaurant (which occupied the 106th and 107th floors of the North

Tower) with his two young children on the morning of the attacks, and it alternates between his perspective and that of the author, who is his European double, and who meditates on the tragedy and on transnational relations before and after 9/11.

The aesthetic strategies of the novels are linked to their openly signalled struggles to represent 9/11. In *Windows*, the narrator remarks that 'writing this hyperrealist novel is made more difficult by reality itself ... it's impossible to write about this subject, and yet impossible to write about anything else' (3). An even more acute sense of anxiety pervades Safran Foer's novel. The tensions between its will to build in meaningful historical analogy and its rhetoric of traumatic rupture are compounded by its preoccupation with the inescapable nature of trauma. The narrative centres around the precocious Oskar, who has lost his father in the 9/11 attacks a year earlier. He listens to his father's final answering machine messages, and begins to search for a lock for the key he has found in his father's closet, sensing meaning or healing in this quest: 'Every time I left our apartment to go searching for the lock, I became lighter, because I was getting closer to Dad' (52). Oskar's quest mirrors the wider project of the book, and he has even created his own book, *Stuff That Happened to Me*, his 'scrapbook of everything that happened' which helps him manage his trauma (42). When Oskar describes opening the book to try to help him get to sleep, *Stuff that Happened to Me* and *Extremely Loud* converge, as the next eight pages the reader encounters show the fourteen different images that Oskar sees in his book, including two of the famous falling man photos taken by Richard Drew. Running parallel are the stories of Oskar's grandparents, whose lives were violently upended by the Dresden fire-bombings during World War II, and who came together in the US after those events. The traumas of Oskar's grandparents are, like his, understood in relation to acts of writing, as their stories, in the form of letters (from Oskar's grandfather to his father, and his grandmother to him), are the stories of how they worked through (and failed to work through) these traumas.

Ostensibly, this narrative of generational trauma forces the reader to locate 9/11 in the context of previous instances of political violence and to think internationally; and in addition to the Dresden fire-bombings, there is a powerful scene where the Hiroshima atomic bomb is discussed. Kristiaan Versluys suggests that these episodes resonate throughout the novel, arguing that 'this seemingly apolitical family novel has history inscribed in every sentence' (81). But what connects 9/11 and the traumas of World War II are private stories of loss. The sequence of family tragedies is certainly caused by moments of historic political violence, but they are not discussed or understood as such and instead are expressed almost entirely via commonplace notions of trauma. Describing the first post-Dresden meeting between Oskar's grandparents, Oskar's grandmother states, 'The seven years were not seven years. They were not seven hundred years. Their length could not be measured in years, just as an ocean could not explain the distance we had travelled, just as the dead can never be counted' (81). This image of unquantifiable, frozen traumatic time is typical of the novel's approach to historical violence and is echoed by Oskar's experiences and his collection of images: 'It was like time stopped. I thought about the falling body' (97).

Later in the novel Oskar plays a recording of an oral testimony of Hiroshima during a school presentation, but despite the graphically violent descriptions the episode is similar in what it offers as historical analogy. The interviewee on the recording recalls the gruesome effects of the attack, which upsets and sickens Oskar's classmates: 'there were maggots in her wounds and a sticky yellow liquid. I tried to clean her up. But her skin was peeling off' (188). But there is no real discussion of the politics of the event, and the interview ends with a sentiment that might accurately describe the novel's – death and suffering is universally horrible: 'That is what death is like. It doesn't matter what uniforms the soldiers are wearing . . . I thought if everyone could see what I saw, we would never have any more war' (189). It is certainly notable that Hiroshima and Dresden both represent American violence perpetrated against other states, and in a broad sense this represents a challenge to narratives (prevalent at the time the novel was published) that, as Versluys notes, perennially reduced geopolitics of the war on terror 'to a pitched battle of "us" versus "them" or good versus evil' (83). Nevertheless, the novel mostly positions the attacks as an apolitical event experienced as a family tragedy. The impact of 9/11 is confined to the Schell family narrative, meaning that, as Deborah Shostak notes, it turns 'inward rather than toward the historical world', reducing 'historical rupture to a personal rupture, the transnational to the domestic, and most notably, to the familial' (23). Ultimately, the novel's conspicuous historical and transnational components signal a will to situate 9/11 internationally but its rhetoric of rupture and domestic crisis pulls the novel in the opposite direction, inwards. Indeed, Oskar's refrain that September 11 – the day he lost his father – was 'the worst day', falls into explicit alignment with the Bush administration's notion that '[a]ll of this was brought upon us in a single day – and night fell on a different world', a singular and absolute rhetoric that elides context and other forms of suffering. Crucially, the limited historical outlook of the novel includes no commentary on the conflicts in which 9/11 occurred and remains 'isolated from any larger geopolitical frame', leaving 9/11 as a totalising event (Greenwald Smith 2015, 65).

The stylistic conceits of the novel add complexity to some of its opposing impulses. Its visual flourishes – which are substantial, and include sixty-four still images, sections annotated with red pen, pages of numeric code, and type which overlaps until blacked out – seem initially to signal a desire to find new tools of expression. But they also strengthen the novel's traumatic impulse, suggesting an attempt to articulate what is 'beyond words'. The novel's use of images evokes trauma by harnessing the formal quality of the still photograph, often seen as the archetypal traumatic form. Marianne Hirsch has noted that '[p]hotography interrupts, actually stops time, freezes a moment: it is inherently elegiac', and as we have seen, the notion that 'time stopped' on 9/11 is a major preoccupation of the novel (71). In addition to this conflict between the ostensible innovation and traumatic freeze of the photograph, there is yet another layer of tension. Just as Safran Foer's metafictional project lacks the experimental sophistication of some of the late-twentieth-century writing that preceded it, it also should be understood as part of what we can now, in the twenty-first century, see as an established literary tradition. This was pointed out as early as Walter Kirn's review, in which he noted that it 'can't really be called experimental', because its 'signature high jinks, distortions and addenda first came to market many decades back' (n.p.). Indeed, by 2005, the metafictional tools Safran Foer employs are hardly unprecedented, even if they are conspicuous. Consequently, Safran Foer's aesthetics carry a tension between the continuity of tradition and the discontinuity of traumatic rupture which mirrors the tension between its transnational historical gestures and its drive inwards towards private, family traumas. More importantly, just as its historical analogies fail to meaningfully contextualise 9/11, its metafictional apparatus directs its turn inwards, furthering its understanding of 9/11 as a totalising and inescapable trauma.

In my first book, I scrutinised in depth the 'conflictedness' described above. Since its publication, two more sophisticated readings have made better sense of the novel's internal contradictions. Bond identifies 'oppositional narrative tendencies: first, a retreat from the disorder of public life into the familiar environs of the home; second, the hyperbolic encoding of personal issues as national problems' (408). Bond describes this as a kind of 'scalar telescoping' which sought to 'simultaneously shrink the narrative of 9/11 to the confines of the home and symbolically expand the boundaries of the domicile to the borders of the Homeland' (409). This reading astutely captures the exceptionalist logic of the novel in which 'the worst day' for Oskar and the Schell family is also a national tragedy. Greenwald Smith also identifies a contradiction here, and shows how the novel exemplifies a paradox in the advance of neoliberalism. Puzzling over the novel's formal conceits, which, as I have noted, seem to signal rupture while also belonging to decades-old conventions, she points out that our present moment is 'characterized by a surprising intimacy between seemingly world-changing catastrophes and the expansion of existing political policies' (2015, 67). For Greenwald Smith, the Bush administration's 'changed world' rhetoric coincided with a policy agenda built around the continued advance of neoliberalism that had been in train for decades. In this sense, the conflictedness of the novel's formal gestures tracks the Bush administration's simultaneous imperatives of announcing a new world order while continuing to operate from an entrenched, long-standing ideological position. Nevertheless, the tension between notions of continuity and discontinuity in no way mitigates the exceptionalising work of *Extremely Loud*. Greenwald Smith's point that despite the singularity of the Bush administration's rhetoric, the neoliberal agenda which underpinned its policymaking had been long in the making, is persuasive; and I agree that this is mirrored by the ostensible 'experimentation' of Safran Foer's novel, which actually signals aesthetic continuity. This said, the Bush administration's narrative of 9/11 as a totalising traumatic event distracted from the ongoing systemic violence of neoliberalism – the erosion of the welfare state, the continued privatisation of public services, and increasingly transactional, competition-based social and cultural formations – which, as Mitchum Huehls and Greenwald Smith have shown, became hegemonic in these realms in the 1990s.[3] This is another reason why it is important to track the movement away from event-based narratives of terrorism to storytelling that engages critically with neoliberalisation. For now, though, I turn to the wave of domestic novels that followed *Extremely Loud*. These, I argue, shift in some ways, while retaining combinations of domestic realism and metafiction as their strategy for dealing with trauma.

Falling Man and The Writing on the Wall

If Safran Foer's novel is an example of a conservative form of 9/11 trauma fiction as defined by Bond, then so is DeLillo's *Falling Man*. Where the former's signature formal features – the typographical gimmickry and use of still photos discussed above – telegraph to the reader that words are not enough, *Falling Man*'s circular narrative, which ends just before the novel begins, is another conspicuous evocation of trauma in its modelling of traumatic repetition. These novels are, undoubtedly, exemplars of 9/11 trauma fiction; and just as Safran Foer's narrative is defined by 'the worst day', *Falling Man* emphasises the notion that 'everything now is measured by after' (138). In other words, they also align in the ways their trauma narratives function to exceptionalise. But *Falling Man* adjusts focus to marital discord rather than parental relations and loss, and its metafictional moves are slightly different. Though it is certainly preoccupied with the limits of language, and fundamentally interested in acts of writing and artistic representation in response to 9/11, it begins to move towards a meaningful consideration of how narrative hegemony is formed and how personal stories relate to such narratives. Protagonist Lianne Glenn, an editor of academic books, runs a writing group for Alzheimer's sufferers which has clear figurative resonances. Linda Kaufman suggests that in *Falling Man*, Alzheimer's becomes a 'metaphor for the post-September 11 condition: all the characters are living in a state of abeyance, with a sense of impending doom that they are powerless to prevent' (145). This is an astute reading, though it is also the case that through the writing group and other diegetic acts of representation, the novel registers some discomfort with the way trauma or 'abeyance' can unwittingly accord with exceptionalist logic, and the impulses of the group do not always align with the 'official narrative' of 9/11.

Nevertheless, *Falling Man* has frequently been assessed alongside other 9/11 novels published between 2005 and 2007 that function mainly as relationship melodramas: Ken Kalfus's *A Disorder Peculiar to the Country* (2006), Jay McInerney's *The Good Life* (2005), and Claire Messud's *The Emperor's Children* (2006). These are the works – with *Falling Man* – that are clustered together in the forceful critiques of 'domestication' by Richard Gray, Michael Rothberg, Pankaj Mishra and, to a lesser extent, Bimbisar Irom. In David Cowart's more charitable assessment, they are novels that 'foreground a dysfunctional or faltering marriage' because 'husband

and wife are themselves twin towers that marital discord threatens to bring down' (n.p.). It is worth noting that later 9/11 novels from Hamid's *The Reluctant Fundamentalist* and Khakpour's *Sons and Other Flammable Objects* (both discussed in the next chapter) to O'Neill's *Netherland* and Waldman's *The Submission* as well as Pynchon's *Bleeding Edge* are also relationship or marital dramas. But unlike these later novels, the works by DeLillo, McInerney, Kalfus and Messud are domestic-focused both in the sense of the domicile and in terms of national insularity. Indeed, Cowart's reading, which connects the attack on the twin towers of the World Trade Center with a crisis in heteronormative relationships and marriage, evokes the kind of 'scalar' telescopic connection between 'home and homeland' described by Bond.

While the problems inherent in this kind of 'telescoping' are clear, there can also be value in the project of depicting intersections between private and public events. As Banita notes, 'at their best, these texts reflect on how personal and historical tragedy collide to create art that gives both deeper meaning' (154). *Falling Man* certainly does this more persuasively than the novels by McInerney, Messud and Kalfus, as does a less-recognised 9/11 novel, Lynne Sharon Schwartz's *The Writing on the Wall* (2005). Schwartz's novel is another narrative of before and after measured via the domestic turmoil of a privileged, white American couple, but the intricate backstory of protagonist Renata, who lost her twin sister as a teenager, mobilises an affecting evocation of how reverberations between private family traumas and public catastrophe can manifest. Moreover, its own metafictional conceit – the protagonist's obsession with the nature and power of language – enables the narrative to explore the 'interconnection of public language and personal grief' and it is fruitfully compared to *Falling Man* in this way (Uytterschout and Versluys 131).

In examining the domestic narratives of *Falling Man* alongside *The Writing on the Wall*, this section makes a series of observations relating to the ways these novels reinforce – and in places question – the exceptionalisation of 9/11. I begin by discussing the depictions of domesticity in these novels, noting that they are not images of stability and security. Critiques of these works as novels that retreat into the domestic have mostly failed to reckon with this point while echoing Mishra's critique of the idea of 'marital discord as a metaphor for 9/11' (4). In *Falling Man*, Keith Neudecker, bloodied and disoriented, walks out of the burning North Tower and back to his previously abandoned marital home, seeking to restore relationships

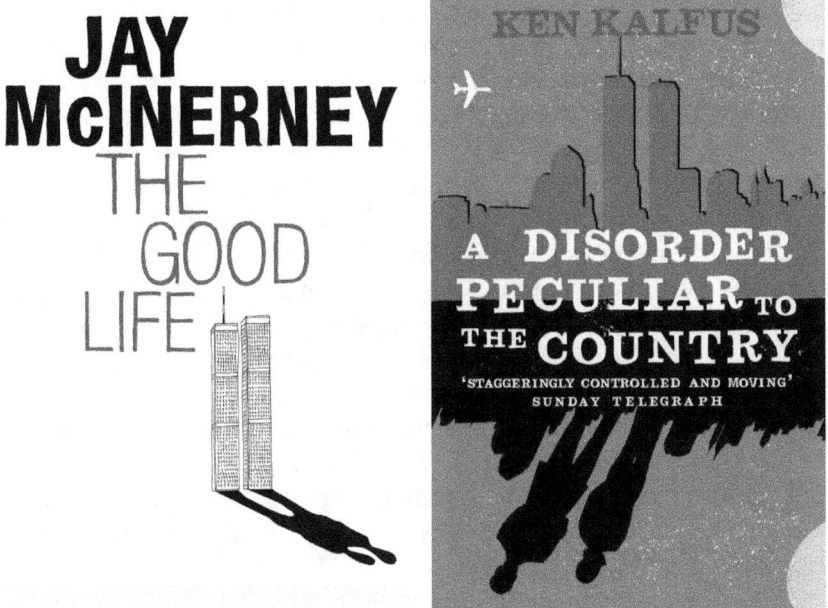

Figure 1.1 The cover images for *The Good Life* and *A Disorder Peculiar to the Country* both featured illustrations of the twin towers of the World Trade Center casting a shadow of a man and a woman. Cover image for *The Good Life* (2006) by Jay McInerney. With thanks to Bloomsbury Publishing Plc.

with his estranged wife, Lianne, and their son, Justin. But his new sense that life is 'meant to be lived seriously and responsibly' (137) is short-circuited by trauma, and he has an affair with another survivor and withdraws into the hypnotic repetitions of gambling. Not only is this not an image of security and stability, but it also skewers the cartoonish, family values rhetoric that was stridently proffered by the Bush administration and mainstream media in America after 9/11, which is trenchantly analysed in Faludi's *The Terror Dream*. In *The Writing on the Wall*, Renata looks after a baby belonging to her partner's work associate, who dies at the World Trade Center. In the weeks after, she temporarily gives up her work, looks after the baby and her partner, while making explicit jibes at such formations: 'For now, she's glad enough to wait for Jack and greet him with a kiss and a drink like a 1950s suburban wife' (87). But while such gestures have a critical component, the dramatic thrust of these novels remains rooted in the private domestic turmoil of privileged white New Yorkers and these critiques remain muted. Additionally, and despite the underpinning exceptionalist logic that 'everything now is measured by after', there are some subtle but not insignificant contextual gestures that merit further consideration. Lianne's mother's German partner, Martin Ridnour, is a former associate of Kommune 1 and possibly the Red Army Faction in the 1970s – an important detail given he is the only character interested in the terrorists' motivations. Speaking to Lianne just days after 9/11, he describes the event as an attack on a 'great power that interferes, that occupies' (46). Such comments draw attention to myopic American responses that were uninterested in understanding 'why', and while Ridnour is a peripheral character, contextual details such as this were too hastily dismissed in some critiques of *Falling Man* and this wave of domestic fiction more generally. As noted, these novels also feature conspicuous metafictional conceits, but here, instead of posing searching questions about the relationship between fiction and reality, these conceits read as acts of self-obsession and reinforce the insularity of the narratives.

A final element of these novels, exemplified by *Falling Man* and *The Writing on the Wall*, has been under-analysed: the recoveries they dramatise. In *Falling Man*, the circular narrative which ends where it began is only the story of one of the two central protagonists – Keith – and Lianne notes, near the end, that she is 'ready to be alone, in reliable calm . . . the way they were before the planes appeared that day, silver crossing blue' (236). As Simpson has noted, it is unclear whether the restorations of equilibrium articulated in these novels (Kalfus, McInerney, Messud, DeLillo and Schwartz) indicates 'the resilience of ordinary life' or whether it is actually a 'damning indictment of the sheer indifference and self-centeredness of the homeland mainstream' (2007, 216). Simpson's question takes on further weight when considering the exceptionalisation of September 11, and we might reframe it: does this return to normalcy question exceptionalist notions of the attacks as unprecedented and world-changing or does it reinforce exceptionalist notions of America's singular greatness? Ultimately, I argue that it is the latter, though I want to qualify this by first attending to some ways that these novels express discomfort with exceptionalist logic.

Falling Man's narrative begins where DeLillo originally suggested 'the writer' should start, in his *Harper's* essay from December 2001, 'In the Ruins of the Future': 'The writer begins in the towers, trying to imagine the moment, desperately. Before politics, before history and religion, there is the primal terror' (2001, 33). The novel opens with an image of falling, its central leitmotif, which is also an image of the event as totalising and all encompassing: 'It was not a street anymore but a world, a time and space of falling ash and near night' (3). Here, Keith is exiting the burning towers, injured and disoriented. These opening paragraphs, which contain some vivid descriptive writing, convey the traumatic disorientation of the attacks, while repeatedly evoking 9/11 as totalising. Keith attempts to find his way from the site but is surrounded and enveloped by 'noise' and 'stratified sound' and is unable to get beyond it: 'he walked away from it and into it at the same time' (4). In *The Writing on the Wall*, Renata witnesses the attacks from the Brooklyn Bridge, and the explosions are curiously described like flowers: 'a huge marigold bursting open in the sky, across the river, flinging petals into the blue' (45). However, there is a striking similarity between DeLillo's and Schwartz's apocalyptic descriptions: 'the pillar of smoke began surging across the river, walling the skyline, making it seem there was nothing behind the wall' (46). In these scenes, there is literally no way to see beyond the attack. These are, of course, depictions of the immediate emergency, which would have felt overwhelming and encompassing for anyone. But they were published in 2005 and 2007, during the second term of the Bush administration, when the ideological underpinnings of the war on terror were finally being properly interrogated and the entire basis for the conflict questioned; a point when proper contextualisation of September 11 would be expected. With this in mind, Rachel Sykes's observation that such crisis scenes set up narratives where characters are consumed by 'the event's singularity', where 'the cacophonous noise echoing through the city, the impact of the event spreads at an alarming rate', is important (n.p.).

In both works – as well as the other domestic novels – the domestic space is the magnetic centre around which all other activity orbits. Heteronormative relationships are central, and they are introduced through an initial fixation on sex. There is a temptation in some instances to interpret this as what certain media outlets described, in the immediate aftermath, as 'terror sex', a phenomenon whereby New Yorkers, gripped by collective trauma, were allegedly experiencing heightened sexual activity (Kazdin n.p.). In retrospect, perhaps the most interesting thing about the terror sex myth is that it contradicts the conservative family values and gendered moral obligations that were espoused with renewed force by the conservative media and US government in the aftermath of 9/11. In *Falling Man*, sex is actually another way of articulating the totalising nature of the event, and a way of folding all aspects of life into the domicile. The second chapter of the novel establishes this: 'sex was everywhere at first, in words, phrases, half gestures' (2). This sense that in the days after, 'the simplest intimation of altered space' 'was sex' quickly moves into a scene where Lianne is considering this in relation to the larger narrative of her life with Keith, reflecting on 'the early times, eight years ago, of the eventual extended grimness called their marriage' (7). Then, as days pass and Keith continues to recover in the marital home, Lianne begins anticipating the consummation of their recoupling: 'she knew the time was coming when he'd press her to the wall before she finished dressing' (18). The novel continues to fixate on the possibility of the couple re-establishing sexual intimacy, and the narrative shifts briefly – but suggestively – to second person, opening this fixation out and inviting readers to empathise and relate: 'its interesting isn't it, the way you move about the bedroom, routinely near-naked and the respect you show the past, the deference to its fervors of the wrong kind, its passions of cut and burn'(35). The section concludes with the explicit statement that she 'wanted contact and so did he', and later, when they do have sex, it 'was the tenderest sex she'd known with him' (35, 60).

In *Falling Man*, sex establishes Keith and Lianne's history, it invites investment, establishing their relationship as the novel's gravitational centre, and it draws the reader in with formal gestures like this use of the second person. The story of Keith and Lianne's marriage then becomes a story of re-evaluation, as both characters reappraise what is important in their lives, in the wake of catastrophe. Together, they discuss the possibility that they are 'done with conflict' and 'everyday friction' (75). Lianne listens to Keith purposefully, 'mind and body', because 'listening is what would save them this time, keep them from falling into distortion and rancor' (104). Keith feels a new sense that life is 'meant to be lived seriously and responsibly, not snatched in clumsy fistfuls' (137). This period of re-evaluation and recoupling coincides with Keith's physical recovery, which is also reliant on a notion of 'home': 'home' becomes a site of marital recovery (initially) and the site of Keith's physical recovery, too. For Keith, recovery is contingent on 'home': it 'was not the MRI and not the surgery that brought him closer to well-being' but 'this modest home program, the counting seconds, the counting of repetitions, the times of day he reserved for the exercises' (40).

The Writing also establishes the central relationship via sex, but in different terms. As in *Falling Man*, the centrality of a relationship between woman and man is introduced in this way, and again the domesticity of a heteronormative relationship and home is conflated with the domestic as national. Renata, the central protagonist, is awakened early on the morning of September 11, 2001, by her partner Jack's convulsive movements. She at first interprets this as an erotic dream and then realises it is a nightmare (which might be premonitory). Here, Schwartz's novel establishes the central relationship drama and connects this to the attacks. It is also, simply, a way of introducing a strong but untested relationship between two people that have not fully revealed themselves to each other. The opening chapter shows Renata and Jack, who 'radiated sex', to have a powerful physical connection, mutual admiration, but also secrets, and it foreshadows the ways their relationship will be put under pressure (8). For instance, the opening scenes reveal some of Renata's eccentricities and unusual habits, including her many 'files' of clippings on topics like 'Transformed Lives' or 'Everyone Wants to Be Changed', and walls covered with panels of Chinese calligraphy; eccentricities that Jack does not understand. Her passion for language and idiosyncratic habits of collection and cataloguing relate to her professional role as a linguist and librarian, but also, we will learn, to a set of formative traumas: becoming estranged from her twin, Claudia (with whom she shared a made-up language) as an adolescent, who later died in tragic circumstances as a seventeen-year-old; and then attempting to raise Claudia's baby as her own, only to have the child abducted a few short years later.

As in *Falling Man*, *The Writing* emphasises the ways the crisis intensifies feelings between its central couple, and Renata 'finds herself loving Jack as never before with a piercing, apocalyptic urgency' (103). However, in this passage she also wonders if this is 'love or fear', and, as noted, the novel offers a series of knowing reflections on the stereotypes of post-September 11 relationships. A key plot development occurs when a colleague of Jack's, Carmen, dies in the attack after he had requested she drop off some documents at their World Trade Center office. Jack and Renata begin taking care of her baby, who was left at daycare, as Carmen's family are in Puerto Rico. Jack's job running a non-profit 'social service agency' that works with homeless and vulnerable people becomes demanding and urgent in the immediate aftermath, and so Renata begins looking after the baby, occupying a traditional domestic role (54). Renata basks in this oddly contrived domesticity and is warmed by the thought of them as a 'makeshift family, strangers thrown together by disaster or war' (90). Renata becomes attached to the baby – Julio – and immerses herself in the roles of wife and mother, busying herself with 'groceries and errands' and feeling 'exactly like a young mother pushing her stroller through the day' (94). Eventually, they 'squabble like a married couple' and when Jack finally contacts Julio's grandparents, Renata is devastated to learn that they are coming to collect the baby, and 'wildly' beseeches Jack, insisting they should adopt him (168).

Renata's backstory is critical here, particularly her perceived failure to raise her twin sister's baby, Gianna. Indeed, the multiple traumas of this story – as well as the novel's eventual discussion of child abuse and child sexual abuse – mean that despite its 'comforting ending', which Peter C. Herman describes as a 'retreat into domesticity' (182), there is a pervasive sense of malaise. Renata's backstory is one that is elaborately – but powerfully – linked to the 9/11 attacks. We learn that her original estrangement from her sister, Claudia, occurred over a $20 bill that Renata believed her sister had stolen. This seemingly petty accusation caused a devastating conflict between the inseparable twins and Renata identifies it as the beginning of a rift that would precipitously deepen. Oddly, just after the attack, as the air fills with smoke and ash, she finds a $20 bill: 'She had the absurd notion that it might be the same twenty dollars that went missing when she was eleven years old, causing the estrangement from her now-dead twin sister and lasting grief. Changing the course of her life' (47). This slightly overdetermined connection between the trauma of the 9/11 terror attack and Renata's personal trauma plays out over the course of the whole novel. She becomes attached to the orphaned child, first, and then to a lost and clearly traumatised teenager she keeps encountering, and who, she mistakenly believes, could be Gianna, the niece who was abducted from her care years before. Her obsessive behaviour, evidently a response to the intersection of personal and public traumas, begins affecting her relationship with Jack; and subsequently, and as in the other 'domestic' 9/11 novels, melodrama ensues in the disorienting aftermath.

As noted, both *Falling Man* and *The Writing* have features that unsettle their somewhat parochial relationship narratives, and I agree with Bimbisar Irom's argument that they 'are engaged with imagining possibilities beyond the process of grieving' (532). These gestures are worth tracking even if they do not amount to any substantial questioning of the insular narrative architectures in which they appear (532). *Falling Man* is a carefully structured novel of three parts which, as noted, ends just before it begins (in the North Tower). This circular structure, which has frequently been read as a replication of traumatic repetition, mostly applies to Keith, and *Falling Man* gives equal emphasis to Lianne's story of recovery. This divergence is also a key structural element of the novel and is at least as important as its circularity. The central narrative of Keith and Lianne rebuilding their marriage and then eventually disconnecting to the point that Lianne is 'ready to be alone, in reliable calm, she and the kid', is augmented by story strands that widen context (236). First, is the story of Hammad, one of the terrorists, who is the subject of three short interludes. A generous reading of these sections is that while the 'origin, motivation, and goal' of Hammad and his organisation are 'not part of the novel's scope', they show a man who, as Michael C. Frank notes, needs 'structure' and 'purpose' in relatable ways (350). Hamza Karam Ally describes the Hammad story as 'the novel's most calculated depoliticisation', in that it portrays the terrorist as a reluctant participant more than a 'fanatical extremist', who articulates no real ideological position (359). Indeed, DeLillo's attempt to give the 'terrorist's view' is the least persuasive part of the novel, relying on stereotypes and offering no real insight into the group's grievances or motivations. But while Hammad's motivations are not clear, some insight is suggested by the previously mentioned Martin Ridnour, also known as 'Ernst Hechinger', whose characterisation is subtly evocative.

Martin/Ernst is a German art dealer who, it is eventually revealed, was a former associate of Kommune 1 – and possibly the Red Army Faction – and he implies some broad continuities between the grievances of the 9/11 terrorists and these late-twentieth-century leftist organisations. He is the only character interested in the terrorists' motivations, and the grievances he cites might easily be attributed to the Red Army Faction: 'lost lands, failed states, foreign intervention, money, empire, oil, the narcissistic heart of the West' (113). Indeed, just days after the attacks, Martin argues that they struck a 'blow to this country's dominance ... to show how a great power can be vulnerable. A great power that interferes, that occupies' (46). Martin even ventriloquises well-known interpretations of the events proffered by European philosophers like Jean Baudrillard and Slavoj Žižek. During one exchange with Lianne he argues that the World Trade Center towers were built as 'fantasies of wealth and power that would one day become fantasies of destruction' (116). He goes on, asking what 'other reason would there be to go so high and then to double it, do it twice ... You are saying, Here it is, bring it down' (116). The novel features three scenes where Martin and Lianne discuss the events in an adversarial dynamic, and one of the novel's three sections' titles is his given name, 'Ernst Hechinger', clearly signposting his importance. Ultimately, though, the exchanges between him and Lianne reinforce her determination to rebuild with Keith.

During one of these moments, frustrated with Martin's rhetoric, she even reflects that Keith is 'an American, not a New Yorker, not one of the Manhattan elect' (44). Moreover, while Martin's rhetoric is evocative, he fades out of the narrative and is ultimately not as consequential as his name's use for a section title suggests.

There are other story strands that challenge the gravitational pull of the novel's domestic narrative. One is Lianne's volunteer work, leading 'storylines' sessions with sufferers of Alzheimer's, which, for Kaufman, becomes a 'metaphor for the post-September 11 condition' (145). But this metaphor and Lianne's experiences in the group also drive the novel's metafictional impulses, as the group begins trying to write about the attacks. Usually the sessions with 'five or six or seven men and women in the early stages of Alzheimer's', would consist of discussion of world events followed by writing on topics set by Lianne (29). Participants, under Lianne's guidance, 'worked into themselves, finding narratives that rolled and tumbled, and how natural it seemed to do this, tell stories about themselves' (30). But in the first of four scenes with the 'storylines' group, we learn there 'was one subject the members wanted to write about insistently ... the planes' (31). In the second scene, we learn that they have been writing about 'where they were when it happened', about people they knew who had been in the towers, and about God and spirituality. However, to Lianne's frustration, nobody 'wrote a word about the terrorists' and 'no one spoke about the terrorists' (63–4), which is difficult not to read as self-reflexive or possibly as a comment, as Frank has suggested, 'on writerly engagement with 9/11 more generally' (340). Lianne manages to draw out some responses that she interprets as angry or 'defined in terms of revenge', and these speak to her own unarticulated anger and grief (64). Eventually, though, Lianne begins to move beyond the anger that had seen her lash out at a neighbour for playing vaguely Eastern music, and she does this via participation in the storytelling. Indeed, Lianne's eventual recovery is tracked through these episodes with the Alzheimer's group and through repeated references to it in other scenes. In the fourth of these sections, she tells the group about Justin, her son, and about her own fears, which leads to meditative thoughts on the loss of her father, years before, to suicide. When she addresses the group, she attempts to construct a narrative that works methodically, 'one thing following sensibly upon another', even as it follows digressions and diversions (as the novel does) with 'moments where she wasn't talking so much as fading into time, dropping back into some funnelled stretch of recent past' (127). Eventually these sessions help her address her grief and they lead directly to her feeling ready 'to be alone, in reliable calm' (236). It is a powerful sequence of events and undoubtedly propelled by the metafictional connection between Lianne's acts of writing, reading and recovering and the novel's own work towards that end. But again, this is not the kind of metafictive device that invites the 'reader to question the construction of meaning, narrative and truth' (del Pont 86). Instead, the diegetic pursuit of stability and recovery after 9/11 via domesticity is simply connected and aggregated to the novel's own pursuits.

The other strand of *Falling Man* which ostensibly offers a metafictional unsettling of the novel's domestic architecture is the figure of the 'Falling Man' performance artist, aka David Janiak, who suspends himself in mid-air in crowded areas in New York City. Like 'Ernst Hechinger' (Martin Ridnour) and 'Bill Lawton' (Justin and his friends' name for Osama bin Laden), 'David Janiak' is also the title of one of the novel's three sections, signalling his importance. Like the novel, the Falling Man is trying to 'represent crisis', and there is an air of knowing in the newspaper articles Lianne reads about Janiak near the end of the novel: one is titled, 'Falling Man as Heartless Exhibitionist or Brave New Chronicler of the Age of Terror'. Given that DeLillo has been seen as an important chronicler of terror for some decades, it is difficult not to read some alignment here. But like Lianne's writing group and the acts of reading and writing the crisis that occur there, the Falling Man/Janiak episodes simply fall in line with the novel's depiction of trauma, aggregating diegetic and self-conscious attempts to address trauma. This is not an examination of the nature of representation versus reality, but actually a doubling down and even a kind of self-absorption redolent of American exceptionalism.

The Writing on the Wall also contains a conspicuous metafictional conceit that is connected to Renata's role as a linguist. Ostensibly, this is a device that allows the novel to introduce nuanced critiques of the way the Bush administration shaped the language of 9/11 and the war on terror. Renata continually scrutinises the public discourse of 9/11, and particularly the hyperbole and dishonesty of the government and media. At first, watching the President on TV, 'declaring for the tenth time that he would find the folks who did this and smoke them out of their caves', she tries to 'make allowances', acknowledging that 'there were no proper words' (74). However, she soon becomes outraged by what she perceives as 'false language' and 'wrong words' or '*Prashmensti*' (87, 104). Renata is disgusted by how the Bush administration's use of language has shaped public discourse and turns to her collections, files and work for 'truth in language that refreshes, now that the ambient language is so stale and sour that it reeks' (102). David Cockley notes how the novel's 'preoccupation with language confronts the media's ability to force meaning on a particular situation. The media constantly names and defines the event, and with its perceived authority and repetitive force it fills in meaning where otherwise confusions exists' (15). This is an accurate account, but the protagonist's obsession with language, which began with her and Claudia's creation of their own language, is also folded into her struggle to resolve the private traumas of her past and to find meaning in the aftermath of the attacks. Partially driven by readings from her 'Transformed Lives' clippings, and with the pain of her private losses stoked by the public catastrophe, Renata begins to contrive and inhabit new narratives of family. Moreover, as Irom notes, 'Renata's search for her lost family' is 'inseparably entwined with her search for an authentic language to represent her experiences'; consequently, her quest is entangled in the novel's metafictional reflections on the language of crisis, and the question of what the 'right words' for crisis are (533).

Sien Uytterschout and Kristiaan Versluys read this as a successful depiction of interactions between 'little' private narratives and the 'grand narrative of 9/11', echoing Banita's point about the potential for the domestic fiction of 9/11 to 'reflect on how personal and historical tragedy collide' and to give 'both a deeper meaning' (128). For Uytterschout and Versluys, 'the intricate interplay' between the little and grand narratives – or private and public – as well as the 'incisive interrogations of the role of language in the post-9/11 context', mean that *The Writing on the Wall* withstands the many critiques of domestication these texts have received (129). But while Schwartz's novel is very different to *Falling Man*, ending on a hopeful note, it is similar in the way its metafictional impulses reinforce the diegetic stories of grief and trauma in the domestic realms of privileged New Yorkers. Patricia Waugh's theorisation of metafiction focused on 'writing which consistently displays its conventionality, which explicitly and overtly lays bare its condition of artifice, and which thereby explores the problematic relationship between life and fiction' (4). This might have been a provocative and productive mode for representing 9/11, given its popular framing as an 'unreal' or traumatic event which, as Carroll notes, 'was commonly understood to have produced' a 'break with the past' (271). But neither *Falling Man* nor *The Writing on the Wall* could persuasively be called experimental and neither addresses the questions Waugh poses. Rather, like *Extremely Loud*, these novels sit more comfortably alongside the kind of fiction that emerged in the 1990s which balances an earnest kind of realism with some formal play: 'often aiming to reconcile the challenging experimental writing associated with the avant-garde with the accessibility of more traditional forms of literature' (Greenwald Smith 2021, 11). Rather than offering an oppositional narrative that works to both 'create a fiction and to make a statement about the creation of that fiction', the reflexive components of Safran Foer's, DeLillo's and Schwartz's novels align in their inwards turn (Waugh 6). In the case of *Falling Man*, this is brought into focus by considering DeLillo's previous novels of terrorism, like *Mao II* (1991), which posits a 'curious knot between terrorists and novelists' (41). In this novel, the novelist protagonist Bill Gray thinks that writers and terrorists are playing a 'zero-sum game' where the former are losing the ability to shape the 'inner life of the culture' (41). Though this kind of binary might also slip easily into 'us against them' formations, *Mao II* is very different in shape and texture. It does not have a central event and aftermath, and ultimately Bill's formation collapses as his own self-mythologising replicates stereotypes of terrorists and when an explosion occurs it is described in literary terms – as 'well authored' (156). It may be less possible, in the twenty-first century, for metafiction to be considered 'experimental', but it can still play with contradiction in fruitful ways and, as Xavier Marcó del Pont argues, while metafiction was innovative and 'experimental' in the 1960s and 1970s, in the digital age of textual production 'it is finely timely' now (86). However, in what I am calling '9/11 metafiction', a self-consciousness about the specific difficulty of writing about 9/11 replaces more evocative reflections on the blurred boundaries between the real and fictional, the waning power of literature and/or 'reality hunger'.

I would like to make a final observation about the novels by DeLillo and Schwartz, which extends to the early domestic fictions of 9/11 by McInerney, Messud and Kalfus as well. Each of these texts depicts a restoration of equilibrium, and as event-based narratives, understanding this is crucial. Some commentators – including Versluys – have argued that 'the endless re-enactment of trauma' presented in *Falling Man* 'allows for no accommodation or resolution' (30). I agree that the novel is fundamentally about trauma, but it ascribes equal importance to Keith and Lianne; and Lianne's already-quoted declaration that she is ready to return to her pre-9/11 life with Justin is a potent gesture of recovery and rebalancing. While *Falling Man* depicts an estranged couple recoupling to find new purpose and direction and then reverting to estrangement, McInerney's *The Good Life* reverses this: a couple separates seeking something more meaningful, and then gets back together. In both cases, reflection and re-evaluation occurs, but does not stick. McInerney sees this as a commonly experienced phenomenon, and in discussing his novel insists 'the collective trauma of 9/11 prompted many of us, especially those of us in New York, to re-evaluate our lives, to re-examine our values, our careers, our marriages' (n.d.). For McInerney, this re-evaluation period was temporary, and at the end of *The Good Life*, Luke McGavock notes that 'the satori flash of acute wakefulness and connectedness that had followed the initial confrontation with mortality in September was already fading behind them' (353). In a review, Benjamin Strong argued that '*The Good Life* may be the most provocative novel yet about September 22, precisely because it dares to suggest that most of us weren't changed at all' (n.p.). One might apply the same logic to another, much-critiqued domestic novel of 9/11, Messud's *The Emperor's Children*. In this novel, the return to normalcy is even more striking as the novel spends so much time on its characters' pre-9/11 tribulations and a set of personal traumas. Not only do we see a restoration of equilibrium in the characters and their relationships after the rupture of 9/11, but we see this in spite of the attacks. Things do not fundamentally change for them, despite the major disruptions in their lives, and furthermore, the ostensible new seriousness of life after the attacks does not shed light on these disruptions either. In reading this novel, Simpson notes that ultimately 'nothing has changed' for these privileged characters, and 'life is not very interesting or stratifying' despite the rupture of 9/11 (2007, 216). Simpson reads this as a kind of suspicion of 'the rhetoric of 9/11 as a world changing event' and, as noted, asks a question we might extend to all these novels, of whether they depict a 'tribute to the resilience of ordinary life or a more damning indictment of the sheer indifference and self-centeredness of the homeland mainstream' (2007, 216). I reframed this question as: does this return to normalcy question exceptionalist notions of the attacks as unprecedented and world-changing or does it reinforce exceptionalist notions of America's singular greatness? I have argued that it is the latter. In *Falling Man* and *The Writing*, 9/11 remains a seismic and defining rupture, whose impact is the central narrative focus. While this drama unfolds, there is a conspicuous disavowal of the geopolitics of 9/11. *Falling Man* and *The Writing on the Wall* feature some limited engagement with the wider contexts of the attacks, but their obsessive struggles to represent or respond to 9/11 – diegetically and metafictionally – reinforce the hegemonic, exceptionalist framing of the attack.

Netherland and The Submission

Just as Bond has made a critical distinction between trauma fiction and 9/11 trauma fiction, we might make a similar distinction between more critical and evocative forms of metafiction, as theorised by Waugh, and 9/11 metafiction. In both the cases, theoretical formations which have opened a range of interpretive possibilities – trauma fiction and metafiction – become one-dimensional and closed. While I have attended closely to the kinds of metafictional reflexivity that are fundamental to *Extremely Loud*, *Falling Man* and *The Writing on the Wall*, I argue in this section that 9/11 metafiction is exemplified by Joseph O'Neill's *Netherland* (2008) and Amy Waldman's *The Submission* (2011). Their reflexive gestures about the difficulty of representing crisis are similar but they are also shaped by a keen awareness of the limitations of previous 9/11 novels and carry a certain 'anxiety' about their own status within this genre. Like the novels by Safran Foer, DeLillo and Schwartz, they are usefully understood within a larger set of trends that followed the peak period of postmodernism, trends that have been interpreted and theorised in sometimes conflicting ways. Daniel O'Gorman and Robert Eaglestone offer a useful starting point, noting that

> [a] consensus has emerged around the idea that postmodernism, the critical paradigm of late twentieth century arts and culture, has begun to fizzle out gradually, replaced by works that maintain postmodernism's self-reflexive playfulness while also adhering to an underlying sense of emotional truthfulness. (3)

This is at least partially explained by the notion that

> [t]he irony and occasional cynicism that is often seen to characterize postmodern writing has, for some, come to feel self-indulgent in an era in which, for instance, it has become indisputable that humanity will face mass displacement and famine in the absence of urgent and committed collective action against climate change. (4)

As noted, other critics have seen this combination of sincerity, earnestness and/or realism with 'postmodernism's self-reflexive playfulness' as an act of compromise. For instance, Greenwald Smith, while noting that hybrid forms can be potent 'vessels for tension', argues that hybrid forms might also take 'provocative experiments' and embed them in 'easily consumable shape[s]', ultimately using 'compromise as a solution rather than as a form of trouble' (2021, 11). This logic underpins Zadie Smith's oft-quoted essay-review 'Two Paths for the Novel', which examines Tom McCarthy's *Remainder* (2005) and O'Neill's *Netherland* as 'antipodal' novels, the former a provocative and vital experiment and the latter a 'function of our alling literary culture' (71). Smith's critique of *Netherland*'s 'lyrical realism' focuses on a certain kind of metafictional gesture or reflexivity that, rather than opening critical trajectories, represents a form of insularity. For Smith, *Netherland* is a novel that 'wants you to know that it knows you know it knows' (74). I agree here that the novel's metafictional conceits turn inwards rather than opening questions and allegorical possibilities, but my reading in this chapter diverges from Smith's as I argue that the novel's anxiety is best understood in specific relation to the September 11 attacks, rather than its own formal dimensions. Both *Netherland* and Waldman's novel *The Submission* are realist novels that simultaneously value 'emotional truthfulness' while offering vectors of self-consciousness. What makes these novels exemplars of 9/11 metafiction is the way they both replicate and conspicuously depart from the 'domesticity' that was so heavily critiqued in the earlier 9/11 novels. In doing this they consolidated their place in the canon of 9/11 fiction while registering their awareness not just of the challenges of representing 9/11, but of the specific preoccupations and 'failures' of previous iterations of the genre.

In previous analyses, I have championed these novels for their corrective gestures – their diverse milieus and the political critiques they mobilise – and I retain this position here. However, despite these laudable qualities, the metafictional features of these novels ultimately serve, in both cases, to reinforce a totalising view of the attacks. This is paradoxical: their awareness of the emerging discourse around the 'domestication' of 9/11 seems to drive their gestures outwards and towards more diverse and international narratives, but ultimately, by remaining fixated on the impact of this single event, they – inadvertently – reinforce exceptionalist logics. One dramatic highpoint from *Netherland* exemplifies and models this and makes for a useful starting point for discussion of both novels.

Some context is necessary. *Netherland* is narrated by Hans van den Broek, a talented and privileged Dutch financial analyst, who is married to a British woman, Rachel, a lawyer, with whom he has a young son, Jake. Hans tells the story from the present day of 2006, looking back to the years immediately following 9/11. From the family home in London, he recalls the experience of living in New York when 9/11 happened and the subsequent post-9/11 period during which he and Rachel separated. His flashback narrative is triggered by news of the death of Chuck Ramkissoon, who he had befriend when Rachel and Jake returned to London, leaving him unmoored in New York. He came to know Chuck, a Trinidadian man, when he began playing cricket for the first time since his youth, with a group of mostly South Asian players. Chuck is an aspiring entrepreneur, and he gravitates to Hans because of his professional position amongst the financial sector elite, while Hans is beguiled by Chuck's charisma and optimism. Through Chuck, Hans begins to see a part of New York that had been invisible to him, and he is encouraged to reflect on his own immigrant status and colonial heritage. He is also invited to invest in Chuck's dream of bringing cricket to America on a large scale via his 'Bald Eagle Field' project.

The scene I want to consider, to introduce my discussion of *Netherland* and *The Submission*, and my argument about the ways they reinforce exceptionalist logics despite their more political narratives, happens near the end of the novel. Hans describes a dinner party in London, after he and Rachel have reconciled. At the party, the host, Matt, remarks on Tony Blair's 'catastrophic association with George W. Bush, whom Matt describes as the embodiment of a distinctly American strain of stupidity and fear'; a 'commonplace judgement' that Hans essentially agrees with (175). But then conversation turns to 9/11, and Matt argues that it was not really 'a big deal' considering 'what has happened since'. Hans has not 'the slightest urge to contradict' Matt's argument, based on the 'arithmetic' or 'numbers of Iraqi dead', and concedes that 'most of the rest of the world' has observed the war on terror with a 'dark amazement' (175). Despite this, he speaks up, interrupting the conversation to say that he does think it was a big deal. When Rachel reminds the group that they were there, he interrupts again to say, 'That's not my point, I'm just saying, it was a big deal' (176). Discussion moves on, but when he catches Matt exchanging bemused whispers with another guest he is 'filled with rage', looks at Rachel and says, 'let's go' (177). Rachel, a fierce critic of the Bush administration, who had left Hans partially for his lack of political conviction in the early aftermath, tells Matt to 'piss off' and they exit 'holding hands' with a 'tang of glory in the air' (177). In this scene, despite the insight his association with Chuck has provided, and the polarised political debates he has had with Rachel, and without really knowing why, Hans cannot accept Matt's comments. It is tempting to read this response as redolent of the way his personal crisis has interacted with the public trauma of 9/11. But Hans explicitly states that his insistence that 9/11 was a 'big deal' was not about his experience of being in New York during the attacks but relates to something else, that he has not fully understood. This curious scene thus models the larger narrative logic of both *Netherland* and *The Submission*. They move beyond the early domestic fictions, offering political critique and more diverse milieus, and repeatedly question political positions that have shaped the exceptionalist framing of September 11 and the war on terror. Yet, they also circle back to the singularity of this moment, depicting it as an event which has defined the lives of their characters.

Like the early 9/11 novels, both texts depict the heteronormative familial relationships of privileged white New Yorkers. This said, they depart from the other sense of 'domesticity' attached to these novels: the narrowly national. Suggestively, these departures start from the family homes of each novel's focalising protagonists. In *Netherland* Hans, Rachel and Jake were living in a Tribeca loft when the attacks occurred and were forced to relocate to the Chelsea Hotel, where they occupied an apartment that had 'extraordinary acoustics': 'a goods truck smashing into a pothole sounded like an explosion, and the fantastic howl of a passing motorbike once caused Rachel to vomit with terror' (17). Rachel soon decides to move back to London with Jake, fleeing terror but also because of a growing sense of disconnection from Hans. Rachel is alarmed by the Bush administration's response to the attacks and is critical of its 'right-wing plan to destroy international law and order as we know it' (93). She is also frustrated with Hans's lack of outrage and political vision. Returning to London, she participates in anti-war protests and begins a new job with a humanitarian NGO. Hans, on the other hand, is a self-described 'political-ethical idiot' who is unsure what his position is and stays in New York, alone and directionless: 'lost in invertebrate time' (28). Indeed, the disorientation he feels having lost his family intensifies his lack of political vision: 'I could not tell where I stood. If pressed to state my position, I would confess the truth: That I had not succeeded in arriving at a position' (96).

Ostensibly, the novel's frame narrative, through which Hans narrates by flashback, suggests that he has found his way back to Rachel at least partly by gaining some political and ethical knowledge; and the natural assumption is that this has come via his association with Chuck and the immigrant cricketers who have afforded him new lines of sight into a hitherto invisible New York. However, by the novel's conclusion it seems doubtful that Hans has reflected meaningfully on the 'real' New York. The story of his friendship with Chuck certainly opens new and fruitful terrain for the anglophone 9/11 novel, and it is worth noting that this emerges from the novel's central marital crisis. Just as Rachel and Hans's impasse is often framed in the terms of a political-ethical debate about the war on terror, Rachel's return to London 'opens up space for the world of Chuck' and, as I have previously suggested, for 'areas that 9/11 fiction has avoided or excluded' (Keeble 144). This point has been reaffirmed and better contextualised in Daniel Dufournaud's article about domesticity in *Netherland*, which notes that 'family dysfunction' in the novel 'is ultimately what imbues it with a worldly quality, opening it up to ethico-political issues that outweigh the private drama unfolding within the dwelling' (6).

In a sense, the political dimensions of Waldman's *The Submission* also emerge via a privileged domestic sphere, as the novel's central protagonist, Claire Burwell, whose husband Cal died in the attacks, is forced to reconcile her grief, anger and the ostensibly liberal political position she shared with her husband. But while *Netherland* mobilises the unlikely central metaphor of cricket and explores forms of 'seeing', Waldman employs a more explicit and provocative conceit. Published in 2011, on the tenth anniversary of the attacks, *The Submission* also looks back to the early aftermath. Its central premiss is that an anonymous competition to design the 9/11 memorial is won by a secular Muslim man, Mohammad 'Mo' Khan, which causes a divisive furore, and amplifies post-9/11 racism and Islamophobia. Burwell is on the 'jury' of individuals who chose the anonymous 'submission' and, on the disclosure of the identity of the architect, is thrown into an epistemological crisis. Moreover, this conceit enables the novel to engage with the racism and identity politics of post-9/11 America. The political acumen of the novel resonated with public debates about the Park51 Islamic Community Center project, a controversy that gained international media attention in 2010 when high-profile Islamophobes labelled it the 'Ground Zero Mosque'. But despite its journalistic, panoramic framework and its meta-reflections on representation and memorialisation, *The Submission* also presents an image of September 11 as world-changing and at least tacitly reinforces exceptionalist logics. Both novels make conspicuous moves away from privileged domestic spheres and notably build in the views and positions of non-white and non-American subjects. This departure from the kinds of domesticity that dominated anglophone 9/11 fiction is, itself, a metafictional gesture that was registered in reviews of both novels. Here, however, I examine the ways their metafictional impulses circle back to the inescapable impacts of 'the event'.

Netherland's 'anxiousness' is focused on how to represent and understand 9/11 and how it might reject the homogenous visions of domesticity in earlier 9/11 novels. Discussion of how to interpret the attacks appears diegetically, early on. Hans recalls that 'little about anything seemed intelligible or certain' (21) and recounts his and Rachel's attempts to understand the event historically:

> We were trying to avoid what might be termed a historic mistake. We were trying to understand, that is, whether we were in a pre-apocalyptic situation like the European Jews in the thirties or the last citizens of Pompeii, or whether our situation was merely near-apocalyptic, like that of the Cold War inhabitants of New York, London, Washington and, for that matter, Moscow. (21)

Hans even phones Rachel's father, to ask how his generation dealt with the Cold War threat. He recalls wanting 'to believe that this episode of history, like those old cataclysms that deposit a geologically telling layer of dust on the floors of seas, had sooted its survivors with special information' (22). These moments where Hans is trying to understand the impact of 9/11 and trying to seek a way of interpreting the attacks speak to the novel's broader project and are legible in two key structuring conceits. First, cricket, which Hans begins playing after Rachel's departure for London, becomes a metaphor for civilised multiculturalism, and second, the theme of 'seeing' (as understanding), which is most potent in Hans's use of Google Earth and his car rides around New York with Chuck. The early cricket scenes are the first of a set of passages where Hans catalogues the multiculturalism that becomes visible to him via Chuck and his cricket team, and the reader is invited to consider Hans's immigrant status in relation to Chuck's and his teammates'. Early in the narrative Hans notes that in the summers of 2002 and 2003, when he played cricket in New York he was 'the only white man' on the fields, and that his 'teammates variously originated from Trinidad, Guyana, Jamaica, India, Pakistan and Sri Lanka' (8). Noting how this group is united by a love of cricket, he names their religious differences, too, in a description of a pre-match prayer: 'We huddled with arms round one another's shoulders – nominally, three Hindus, three Christians, a Sikh and four Muslims' (9). As Hans gets to know Chuck, the diversity he experiences on the cricket field is extended to new parts of the city, hitherto unexplored by the privileged, white protagonist. In one memorable episode, after a fraught exchange at the DMV (Department of Motor Vehicles), where Hans's Green Card is questioned, he walks home through neighbourhoods that are outside his zone of familiarity, and New York's distinct multiculture is vividly evoked:

> The route, unfamiliar to me, passed through the old Tin Pan Alley quarter, blocks now given over to wholesalers and street vendors and freight forwarders and import-exporters ... Arabs, West Africans, African Americans hung out on the sidewalks among goods trucks, dollies, pushcarts, food carts, heaped trash, boxes and boxes of merchandise. I might have been in a cold Senegal. (66)

Unsurprisingly, this route leads him to Chuck's office and eventually, via Chuck, he sees other parts of the city that had been invisible to him. *Netherland* revels in these descriptive passages, locating and emphasising a quotidian beauty. As David James has noted, the novel 'not only introduces us to the process of noticing how unexpectedly ordinary the sublime can be, but also simulates and thereby involves us in the experience of deliberating over commonplace moments of wonder that we may register yet disregard' (870). For example, in one scene, Hans describes a typical instance of him and Chuck driving around the city:

> I became familiar with the topical sights: the chiming, ceaselessly peregrinating ice-cream truck, driven by a Turk; the Muslim funeral home on Albemarle Road out of which watchful African American men spilled in sunglasses and black suits; the Hispanic gardeners working on the malls; the firehouse on Cortelyou that slowly gorged on reversing fire trucks; the devout Jewish boulevardiers on Ocean Parkway; the sticks of light that collected in the trees as though part of the general increase. (147)

A final example of the novel's meticulous cataloguing of a diverse and vibrant city, newly visible to Hans, occurs when they drive 'the length of Coney Island Avenue' through 'the real Brooklyn' (141) to Bald Eagle Field:

> gas stations, synagogues, mosques, beauty salons, bank branches, restaurants, funeral homes, auto body shops, supermarkets, assorted small businesses proclaiming provenances from Pakistan, Tajikistan,

> Ethiopia, Turkey, Saudi Arabia, Russia, Armenia, Ghana, the Jewry, Christendom, Islam: it was on a subsequent occasion, that Chuck and I came upon a bunch of South African jews, in full sectarian regalia, watching televised cricket with a couple of Rastafarians in the front office of a Pakistani-run lumber yard. (141)

These passages, which map out a multicultural New York, offer a conspicuous corrective to the white, privileged class milieu of the early 9/11 novels. This said, the listing and repetition here is overdetermined and while these scenes are vivid, it is difficult not to read them as redolent of the anxieties identified by Smith and as a kind of recognition of the whiteness and middle-classness of early 9/11 fiction. Moreover, Hans's friendship with Chuck and immersion in 'the real' New York seems to open an integral period of reflection and growth that enables him to reconcile with Rachel. This is suggested from the beginning of the novel when Chuck memorably addresses a group of cricketers (of which Hans is the only white member) after an on-field altercation: 'I sometimes tell people, you want a taste of how it feels to be a black man in this country? Put on the white clothes of the cricketer. Put on white to feel black' (13). This, it is implied, is the beginning of Hans's political awakening.

The idea that Hans begins to see the previously unseen via Chuck is developed through other evocative references to 'seeing'. The most prominent of these is Hans's use of Google Earth, after Rachel and Jake return to London, on which he 'surreptitiously' travels, 'night after night', to England (119). It is an evocative passage that sweeps from the global to the local. Hans opens the application to a 'hybrid map of the United States', then travels across the North Atlantic, slowly homing in on a 'brown and beige and greenish Europe', and then to England and the house on Landford Road in London, where his wife and son are and where it is 'always a clear and beautiful day' (119). Here, though, the ability to see is limited as everything is static – a potent metaphor – and Hans admits, 'there was no way to see more, or deeper. I was stuck' (119). Something of a contradiction emerges as these two conceits are established: Hans is introduced to new routes, new people, new ways of living, but is also stuck and unable to see deeper. It is in this context that Chuck and Hans become friends and Chuck attempts to secure Hans's investment and support for his dream of Bald Eagle Field. But this meditation on seeing is also resonant in relation to the project of representing 9/11. Sarah Wasserman notes that *Netherland* 'lays out a new mode of seeing, one that prizes distance over intimacy, mutability over memory, and the transnational over the national' (251). Wasserman argues that, in doing this, the novel shows how

> fiction about 9/11 may take up the paradoxical task of turning away from the United States, from New York, from Ground Zero, and from the spectacular images that became a grim token of home. Only by looking away, O'Neill indicates, can one elude the captivating powers of spectacle. (268)

I agree that questions of seeing are fundamental to the novel's laudable impulse to offer a corrective to previous 9/11 novels, and that in certain ways it attempts to 'to go deeper'. Nevertheless, *Netherland* is ultimately about a man's struggle to better understand a personal and public crisis and Hans's development as a character, and the extent to which he gains new social vision has been overplayed. Moreover, the potential to open meaningful vectors of global and political context via the connections between Hans's profession as an oil futures analyst and the ongoing war on terror – a conspicuously unexplored global dimension of the text – are not pursued.

Readers of *Netherland* should be cautious about locating the novel's ethics in strict relation to Hans's world view, despite this being a common – and understandable – impulse. Donald E. Pease notes, citing essays by Elizabeth Anker, Michael Rothberg, Christian Moraru and John Duvall, that the 'hypercanonization' of the novel has 'drawn on a pre-existing fund of democratizing values they have projected onto the cricket dream at the center of the novel' (139). For Pease, what is missed in these readings is the fact that the relationship between Chuck and Hans is based on business, not on a 'post-racial, post-national vision for which the cricket field creates a cosmopolitan fold' (139). Pease notes that

> the cultural and political values that critics have attributed to *Netherland* are saturated with the liberal multi-culturalist tropes – the social justice of cricket, its transnational and post-national participation, the multicultural legacy – that Chuck himself deploys to persuade Hans to proffer the mezzanine financing his scheme requires. (141)

Hans describes Chuck as a friend, and clearly has an emotional attachment to him, but he is also simply drawn to his unflappable optimism at a time when he is struggling to orient himself, and, ultimately, Chuck disappears from his life when he recouples with Rachel. Moreover, while Hans certainly enters previously invisible (to him) sections of society, he does not meaningfully reflect on his own role in the 'financialized-military complex' he 'depends on for his livelihood' (Pease 140). Hans is an equities analyst specialising in oil and gas stocks, and it is notable that he never connects his work to the conflict in Iraq playing out during his time on the cricket fields of New York. In fact, he only mentions this conflict in relation to Rachel's opposition to it or 'on television' where 'dark Baghdad glittered with American bombs' (118). Additionally, though there are numerous opportunities for Hans to reflect on the discrepancies between his and Chuck's immigrant experiences, and about his own colonial heritage, no particularly meaningful conclusions are drawn. Moreover, an infrequently discussed episode of the novel, where Hans reflects on a one-night stand with a Danielle, a Black woman, that occurred during his post-9/11, post-break-up years of friendship with Chuck, suggests that Hans's social vision remains limited.

The scene begins with a chance encounter with Danielle, whom he had known briefly in London, eight years earlier, during the period when he first got together with Rachel. In describing this encounter, where they recall sharing a cab together on Edgeware Road, O'Neill's leitmotif of seeing is again prominent. They meet at a diner with a mirrored back wall which creates a 'temporary illusion that the back room did not actually exist and was no more than a trick of reflection' (102). Moreover, we learn that this diner, a favourite of Hans's, is frequented by 'blind people who lived in a special residence of the street' (103). He even recalls thinking of this, his own neighbourhood, as the 'quarter of the blind', evoking his own lack of vision. Hans and Danielle become reacquainted, agree to meet, and eventually spend a subdued evening eating and drinking before arriving back at Hans's building where a party is occurring. Buoyed by the celebratory mood, they end up in Hans's apartment, and after some initial intimacy, Hans begins to ponder the 'ins and outs of her Anglo-Jamaican parentage' (110). Shortly after this, Danielle initiates a BDSM session, handing Hans a belt. He willingly participates and watches in the window reflection as he beats Danielle (with her consent), 'a pale white hitting a pale black', and wonders 'how it could be that I should find myself living in a hotel in a country where there was no one to remember me, attacking a woman who'd boomeranged in from a time I could not claim as my own' (111).

As Lenore Bell shows, this encounter begins in ways that recall Keith's fling with Florence in *Falling Man*, as both white men experience a kind of 'delayed attraction' to Black women and are surprised at this feeling; though as Bell notes, this encounter is differentiated by a taboo, BDSM 'race-play', and Danielle never returns Hans's call after the first date (83). Susana Araújo identifies a complex evocation of colonial violence which works in two directions. It functions as a 'transgenerational phantom', a 'symptom of devastating trauma which unlocks an unspeakable but consummated desire', by resurrecting a 'historical marker of his "superior" cast and her "inferior" race' (95). It also, however, evokes the novel's geopolitical present, which, as noted, is rarely discussed in the diegetic world of the novel. For Araújo, 'Danielle's fetishistic reenactment of racial violence' is reminiscent of the famous Abu Ghraib images, 'where torture and abuse (physical and sexual) were theatrically reproduced' through references to 'iconic images of racial oppression' (95). Crucially, Danielle's Jamaican heritage is connected to Chuck's Trinidadian roots, and the shocking nature of this encounter should evoke a more thoroughgoing consideration of the colonial history Hans has begun considering via his relationship with Chuck. Moreover, if Chuck's archetypally American entrepreneurialism elides the violence of colonial history, then Hans's experience with Danielle should counteract Chuck's Gatsbyesque optimism. However, despite this scene beginning with multiple iterations of the 'seeing' leitmotif, Hans fails to make any fruitful reflections on this episode.

As noted, Chuck is explicitly connected to the eventual recovery of Hans and Rachel's marriage as, ostensibly, a figure who helps Hans change into the person Rachel wants him to be. However, the recoupling is staged in a way that reveals precisely how Hans has failed to 'see' Chuck. It begins with a trip to Goa, originally planned for Rachel, her boyfriend Martin and Jake. Rachel is 'jilted' by Martin, though, and she invites Hans, and they begin to reconnect. Hans looks back on this trip as the beginning of his reconciliation with Rachel, but a particular memory from the trip – once again, framed around acts of seeing – recurs, inevitably leading him to thoughts of Chuck. Hans recalls seeing a group of poor local workmen, who were 'almost unnoticeable, and when they were noticeable it was only for an instant' (222). What Hans remembers is that they 'were small and thin and poor and dark-skinned' and this memory haunts him in the way it leads his thoughts to Chuck (222):

> For some reason, I keep on seeing these men. I do not think of Chuck as one of them, even though, with his very dark skin, he could have been one of them. I think of Chuck as the Chuck I saw. But whenever I see these men I always end up seeing Chuck. (222)

Shortly after this Hans meditates on his belief that the recovery of his marriage has been made possible by the inexorable changes in himself and, in fact, sees himself as a new person. He notes that while Rachel saw their reunion as a 'continuation', he understands it as a coming together of two people who have fallen in love with 'third parties to whom, fortuitously, we were already married' (222).

It is clear, then, that Hans sees himself as changed, and that he sees Chuck as instrumental to that change. However, Hans never interrogates the links between his profession as an oil futures analyst and the ongoing war on terror and he never meditates on the gulf between his immigrant experience and Chuck's. This said, the novel does, in its closing passage, suggest that we adopt a critical stance in relation to Hans's vision. In the final scenes the novel depicts a happy, reunited family in London, in front of – inevitably – the 'London Eye' Ferris wheel. Here, Hans's thoughts drift to a memory of travelling on the Staten Island Ferry, staring with other passengers at a dusky vision of the World Trade Center towers and experiencing 'extraordinary promise' and imagining a 'people risen in light' (247). His memory is broken by his son's voice, demanding his attention, and he turns to 'look for what it is we're supposed to be seeing' (247). This is a pointed evocation of Hans's continued struggle to 'see' and reinforces a critical reading of the failures of vision I have outlined above. It even suggests that his vision of a 'people risen in light' belongs in the realms of the 'neo-liberal fantasy work' described by Pease. However, despite the critical avenues this final statement on Hans's lack of vision unlocks, and even if the reader is distanced from Hans's world view here, it remains the case that the wider historical contexts of colonialism and American empire, and of the racialised war on terror, are treated with only cursory comment in the novel, despite the entry points it presents. Moreover, 9/11 remains the novel's central point of rupture and a life-altering occurrence for its central protagonist. In fact, the novel's closing scene of marital happiness combined with a flashback memory of the twin towers, bathed in sunlight, is an explicit evocation of this, 'fantasy work'.

The Submission is a counterfactual novel about a controversy over the memorialisation of 9/11, and its premiss evokes two recent controversies over the public memory of violence and loss in America. Mo Khan wins an anonymous competition to design the September 11 memorial and quickly becomes subjected to an Islamophobic campaign against him and his design, 'The Garden', when it is revealed that he is a Muslim. This echoes the controversy surrounding Maya Lin, who won a public competition to design the Vietnam Veterans Memorial, which was eventually built in 1982, and Waldman has acknowledged that this story was an inspiration for the novel. Like the fictional Mo, Lin was subject to racist abuse and questions about hidden 'unAmerican' meanings in the design. Though the writing of *The Submission* began before 2010, the novel was also uncannily resonant when published just after the high-profile Islamophobic protests over a planned community centre, proposed by the experienced and revered Manhattan cleric Imam Feisal Abdul Rauf. Originally proposed as Cordoba House – a reference to Cordoba, Spain, once an intellectual centre where Christians, Muslims and Jews flourished together – the project was eventually renamed Park51. It was conceptualised as a multipurpose facility that, had it been built, would have been a thirteen-storey building featuring a culinary school, art studio, basketball court and swimming pool; and a prayer space for local Muslims. The Park51 project never came to fruition because of vicious protests led by a coalition of Islamophobes including extremists like Robert Spencer (founder of 'Jihad Watch') and Pamela Geller, who first labelled it the 'Ground Zero Mosque'. In their terms, it was an affront to the memory of victims of September 11 and would become a centre for the 'Islamification' of America. The irrational fears protesters expressed are very similar to those faced by Khan in *The Submission* when his design, 'The Garden', is hysterically decried as a 'Victory Garden' or 'Martyrs Garden'. In this sense, *The Submission* is more aligned to the history of Park51 than the Vietnam Veterans Memorial controversy. The novel is attuned to the way fringe fundamentalists on the far right find mainstream traction, which is exactly what happened with Park51. As Deepa Kumar notes, citing Newt Gingrich's infamous but widely circulated comparison between Park51 and Nazis putting up a 'sign next to the Holocaust Museum', 'Muslims were so vilified after 9/11' that this argument 'seemed acceptable' (184). Nathan Lean locates the 'interconnected confederation of fear merchants' that drove the protests as part of the mechanisms of an 'Islamophobia Industry' (41). Unlike Lin's Vietnam Veterans Memorial, Park51 did not go ahead – and neither does Khan's garden, in the novel, as he ultimately withdraws his submission under extreme stress from the force of this 'industry' (41). Ultimately, Khan immigrates to India and is forever changed – as are other key characters, who struggle to emerge from the shadow of the event.

Though these real histories are important contexts for *The Submission*, Waldman's novel is usefully read as part of the 9/11 novel genre, and it formally acknowledges its place in the genre through its metafictional conceits. This was noted by the novel's reviewers – including Claire Messud and Kamila Shamsie. Shamsie places *The Submission* in the context of previous anglophone writing about 9/11:

> Perhaps the representatives of fiction writing and non-fiction writing in America didn't gather in a smoke-filled room at the end of 2001 and divide territory. Perhaps the fiction writers didn't claim for themselves the individual tales of trauma around the day itself (signatories include Jonathan Safron [sic] Foer, Don DeLillo, Claire Messud) while the non-fiction writers held on to History and Politics leading up to and on from 9/11. (n.p.)

Shamsie rightly sees *The Submission* as a new kind of anglophone 9/11 novel but also understands it within the canon. Alluding to the maligned domestic novels, she asks, rhetorically:

> How do you take the trauma and grief of 9/11 as the starting point of a novel and move on to a tale of suspended civil liberties and prejudices without the former entirely overshadowing the latter? Waldman takes hold of this potential stumbling block and turns it into the bedrock of her novel. (n.p.)

This is an insightful observation and useful way of reading *The Submission* – as a response to the 'problem' of the 9/11 novel. Waldman does this in two interconnected ways. First, the overarching preoccupation of the novel is the politics and processes of representation – whether this is artistic representation, media representation, legal representation, or the representation of a community or culture by an individual spokesperson. This is a pointed reaction to a genre that has been repeatedly criticised for its narrowness of representation. Second, it is a novel that is structured as a kind of panorama offering perspectives of people from contrasting subject positions. Central protagonist Claire Burwell, a '9/11 widow' and privileged, archetypal centrist Democrat, is mirrored in two ways: by another 9/11 widow, Asma Anwar, whose husband was an undocumented Bangladeshi janitor, and Sean Gallagher, a surly, blue-collar Republican whose brother, a fireman, also died in the tragedy. We also get the perspectives of activists, politicians, handlers and, of course, Mo – an aspirational, talented architect who becomes the victim of some of the most vicious and violent tenets of American intolerance.

These two features, the theme of 'representation' and the panoramic structure of the novel, are often linked to Waldman's background as a *New York Times* journalist – a career which included three years as co-chief of the South Asian bureau. Christian Lorentzen's review argued that *The Submission* reads like a novel 'written by the *New York Times* itself', and that 'Waldman has so thoroughly internalized the paper's worldview that she can't see things any other way' (n.p.). There may be a certain alignment between Waldman's world view, the *New York Times* and central protagonist Claire Burwell, but one of the strengths of the novel is the way it depicts the nefarious practices of the media across ostensible party lines – from the unscrupulous *New York Post* reporter Alyssa Spier to the ostensibly progressive *New Yorker*'s failure to support Khan. Waldman has insisted that the novel is not an indictment of 'all of journalism' but rather a depiction of 'how the media itself is an actor in history' (Potter 198). It certainly depicts practices – appeals to populism and emotion, and the erosion of even the pretence of objectivity – that feel prescient more than a decade after publication. As Kristine Miller notes, these features have ensured its 'continued relevance today, as American citizens struggle to make sense, rather than confusion, of what many have called our "post-fact" or "post-truth" world' (216). My interest is in showing how the journalistic structure and style of the novel – and its diegetic preoccupation with the media – should be read as an expression of anxiety about its own place in the 9/11 novel canon and an attempt to transcend the narrow world views of early 9/11 novels. If *Netherland*'s engagement with multicultural New York is a welcome, if at times overdetermined, corrective to the dominant milieus of the early 9/11, then the subversive potential of *The Submission*'s depiction of representation and its panoramic structure should be qualified in similar terms. These features of the novel offer forceful critiques of the media and Islamophobia, but *The Submission* ultimately privileges one subject position, Claire Burwell's, and maintains the genre's exceptionalising function.

The public 'debate' at the centre of the narrative expands into a complex portrayal of the internal divisions within each 'side' of crude polarisations like the 'clash of civilisations' or 'Islam versus the West'. It also focuses on the internal conflicts of key characters, too. As the controversy escalates, both 'sides' begin 'wearing American flag pins to prove their patriotism' – another resonant detail in the context of post-2016 culture wars – yet it cuts through the simplistic binaries and one-dimensional subject positions (161). Its cast of Muslim characters have divergent beliefs and visions; though Waldman's journalist logic is legible here as these characters occupy certain established 'types'. The two most prominent Muslim women are set up as antithetical. Asma is an undocumented Bangladeshi immigrant whose husband, a janitorial worker, died in the World Trade Center on 9/11. She resides in an insular community in Brooklyn known as 'Little Dhaka', wears traditional attire, and before her husband's death was a housewife, who spent her days looking after their son, Abdul. But in contrast to stereotypes of the 'submissive' Muslim woman, Asma is a courageous, capable and impassioned woman who will not accept her husband being erased from history (he is not recognised as a victim) and is willing to engage in a toxic public debate to stand up for his memory. In a dramatic scene, she tells her story at a public hearing in front of a rabid and hostile media. The depiction of her inner world – to which we get some insight (though nothing compared with that of the other 9/11 widow, Claire Burwell) also resists stereotypes. Asma's internal musings on her community and the world present her as a critical thinker, and she is sexually liberal, too, recounting sexual pleasure 'so deep that she couldn't find words' – traits that resist the stock caricatures of deferential Muslim women that are a staple of American representations of Islam. Laila is an equally complex character, even if she too, is presented on the surface via cliché. She is politically savvy, sensitive and, like Mo, an aspirational young professional in neoliberal New York. She wears expensive suits and works for an elite Manhattan law firm, but we also learn about 'her passions' which include 'food of all kinds; Persian poetry and Iranian films' and 'her large and extended family' (144).

The characterisation of Mo is another challenge to stereotypes, primarily in that he is secular – a fact that makes the demonisation he experiences particularly perverse. These characters are all designed to counter stereotypes, and Mo becomes an example of how such stereotypes originate and how they are perpetuated. His defining characteristic is ambition, and we learn that his motivation for entering the memorial competition was about career aspiration. He is a stylish, successful bachelor whose many ex-girlfriends of multiple ethnicities are frequently mentioned. Crucially, his embodiment of the social and ideological facets of capitalism is clearly a strategy of characterisation designed to emphasise his Americanness – precisely the part of his identity that is erased by the media. This said, he has a sincere passion for architecture, and he tends to process his thoughts through its idioms. For example, meditating on the radically changed New York skyline after 9/11, he muses, 'a skyline was a collaboration, if an inadvertent one, between generations, seeming no less natural than a mountain range that had shuddered up from the earth' (36). Aspirational yuppie or thoughtful architect – Mo is antithetical to the stereotype of the angry, sexually oppressed Muslim man, visible in *Falling Man*, John Updike's *Terrorist* (2006) and in so many media representations.

But aside from his careerism and passion for architecture, Mo is an enigma – at least until the end of the novel when a more reflective side is revealed – and this makes him inscrutable to Claire. Mo begins to invite this, too, though not because of any sinister propensities to extremism, but because he is undergoing an identity crisis brought on by media hyperbole and the ensuing outrage that followed his announcement as competition winner. Mo's inner turmoil is vivid when he decides to observe Ramadan for the first time in his adult life, amidst the rancour:

> The truth was he didn't know why his first act each day now was abstention, and this uncertainty harbored so many others, even as it was born from them: uncertainty about whether he was right to pursue his memorial, whatever the cost, or right to refuse to explain it. (236)

Mo's refusal to explain his design, or to thank Claire for her initial public support, or to declare his own motivations for entering the competition, is partly down to the uncertainty he describes and partly a form of defiance that grows quickly in response to the identities the media projects on to him. This echoes the way Changez, protagonist of Mohsin Hamid's *The Reluctant Fundamentalist* (discussed in Chapter 2), responds to post-9/11 racism and violent xenophobia: by adopting aspects of the identity created for him. Both cases are reminiscent of the kinds of 'dialogical stereotyping' discussed in Peter Morey and Amina Yaqin's *Framing Muslims: Stereotyping and Representation After 9/11* (2011). Morey and Yaqin note that 'when Muslims see themselves constantly portrayed as having some indefinable propensity to barbarism . . . [i]t is unsurprising if, in the face of such vilification, particular embattled and defensive types of group identity emerge' (31). As a secular man it is telling that amidst the hysterical criticism, Mo begins observing Ramadan and grows his beard, 'merely to assert his right to wear a beard, to play with the assumptions about his religiosity it might create' (146). As the narrative progresses, his inner turmoil is repeatedly manifest as defiance: 'it was exactly because they had nothing to worry about from him that he wanted to let them worry' (99–100).

Though Mo in some ways adopts roles ascribed to him in newspaper articles, and by a society consumed with fear, what we see in *The Submission* is a man thrown into crisis after being vilified by his own nation: Mo's identity fractures along these lines when he begins to 'put psychological distance between himself and the Mohammad Khan who was written and talked about as if that were another man altogether' and, crucially, when he reads accounts that erase his American identity and describe him as 'Pakistani, Saudi, and Qatari' (161). That Mo is living the American Dream in New York and being portrayed as an enemy of America is acutely damaging to his sense of self. He grapples with the question of whether he should defend his design and reassure the American public he is a 'good Muslim' or whether he should demand the benefit of the doubt from his own country. As the Islamophobic reporting escalates, his identity crisis reaches a nadir, and in a fractious exchange with the pernicious Alyssa Spier, he accuses her of making it 'open season on Muslims' (335). When she responds by reversing this and stating that it was he who did this by insisting on his 'right to win, even though it offended so many Americans' – using a tactic we would now call 'gaslighting' – he becomes enraged:

> 'I am an American, too,' he said, continuing to advance on her. 'Put that in your paper. I, Mohammad Khan, am an American, and I have the same rights as every other American.' She peddled backward; he moved toward her. 'I am an American. That's the only quote I'm going to give you. I am an American.' (335)

Here Mo asserts his national identity in the strongest terms possible, but in the final chapter of the book, which takes place twenty years in the future, we learn that he left the United States after the furore and never returned. In this future, he lives in Mumbai, and is 'a global citizen, American only in name' (369). Considering his vociferous assertions of his national identity, the final 'future' chapter reveals just how damaging the ordeal has been.

If such acts of characterisation defy stereotypes and depict acts of stereotyping, then the novel's thematic interest in representation gives this further depth – and enacts a key metafictional dimension. As Catherine Morley notes, *The Submission* addresses a 'central question in post-9/11 art and literature, namely how the artist or writer reconciles the representation of the individual and the collective' (2016, 187). The novel explores this theme in considerable detail. It depicts juries, coalitions, representatives, and various interest groups that vie for space and publicity during the memorial debate. The jury chosen to select the winning memorial design is, ostensibly, the most prominent of these groups, and Claire's central struggle is around her duty to honour her late husband and ethically represent other survivors and the nation. But there are numerous other interest groups in which similar questions are posed. Many of these emerge or gain traction in the wake of the announcement of the competition winner. There are groups in support of Mo (the 'Committee to Defend Mohammad Khan' or the 'Mohammad Khan Protection League') and against him (the 'Memorial Defense Committee'); racist groups against Islam more generally ('Save America from Islam') and groups in advocacy of Islamic people (the 'Muslim American Coordinating Council'). All of these groups, even the ones whose interests seem to align, are shown to differ significantly in their agendas – which are often self-serving and unrelated to the ostensible 'issue'. This preoccupation with groups and representatives functions to first illustrate how they fail to adequately represent the individuals or sections of society they claim to be acting on behalf of, and second, how they demonstrate the complexities that are erased by clash of civilisations rhetoric, which relies on the fantasy that 'cultures and nations are fixed, finished and stable' (Morey and Yaqin 31). The depiction of interest groups in *The Submission* functions as a stern rebuke to such notions.

One of *The Submission*'s groups is of particular interest here, the Muslim American Coordinating Council (MACC). While this group, which supports Khan during the controversy, emphasises the enormous range of interpretations of Islam, the leader, Issam Malik, is driven by the pursuit of power. In this sense, the MACC emphasises the diversity of Islam but also how it can be reduced. Malik is akin to what Morey and Yaqin have described as a 'professional Muslim': a term for 'spokespersons' found 'touring the circuits of think tanks, select committees, and talk shows' as representatives of people of the Muslim faith (94). Malik fits this description well and it is notable that during his first meeting with Mo he mediates between the executive committee members, reminding them that the group should be 'amassing capital' (103). To Mo, he is the 'slick front man for a special interest', and his motivations and ethics are repeatedly questioned. In one scene, a fellow MACC member reproaches Malik, 'we seem to be sending out a lot of emails soliciting donations on the back of this controversy . . . a lot of emails noting how many times the MACC – you – are in the press' (250). Eventually, Mo sees him as an 'unctuous phony', and the emphasis is on just how unrepresentative this representative is (221). Like every dimension of the novel, this strand of the narrative has an antecedent, and we also get some insight into Debbie Dawson, the self-appointed leader of Save America from Islam (SAFI). Of course, there are obvious differences between the MACC and an extremist group build on racism, but like Malik, Dawson's cause is shown to be a ruse for self-interest. SAFI is her main source of income and she thrives on the celebrity status it affords her. While Dawson is a pernicious bigot, both she and Malik are high-profile representatives that are characterised as self-absorbed and shown to make personal gains through their campaigning.

The unrepresentative quality of these representatives is foregrounded in the opening scenes of the novel, which depict the final deliberations of the memorial jury. The chairman, Paul Rubin, has taken the position for professional reasons – 'this chairmanship would lead to others' – and his wife's desire for him to occupy 'prestigious positions' (7). Deliberations narrow to debate between Claire and a prominent sculptor, Ariana, and they become adversarial, both attempting to convince the split jury to vote for their choice. The process becomes personal, and when Claire's choice – Mo's design – wins, it is described as a victory for Claire rather than the design. This image of jurors, meant to represent survivors and the wider public, entrenched in personal rivalries foregrounds the later depictions of Debbie and Malik – all shown to be influenced by private issues or personal aspirations rather than, strictly, the interests of the groups they are representing. But despite the negative portrayal of these forms of representation – which open metafictional reflection on the limits of representation – the novel also uses these structures to challenge crude formations of 'us against them'.

The other function of the novel's depiction of coalitions and groups is to reveal the diversity of belief, opinion and emotion within each 'side'. This is vivid in the depiction of the MACC, which is described as 'striking in its diversity':

> The council was an umbrella organisation for assorted Muslim groups, some political, some theological, others legal. The group was striking in its diversity: South Asians, African Americans, Arabs; bearded men and clean-shaven, in suits and in djellabas; two women in headscarves and one – striking and black-haired in an aubergine suit – without. (179)

The MACC scenes portray nuanced issues within a faith group that is so often subject to homogenising representation. This is powerful given the novel's vision of a sensationalist media. It also drives a consideration of 9/11 that, in some fleeting scenes at least, is multidirectional. For instance, a MACC member, Ansar, insists on a global view:

> where is the memorial to the half million Iraqi children killed by U.S. sanctions? To the thousands of innocent Afghans killed in response to this attack, or the Iraqis killed on the pretext of responding to this attack? Or to all the Muslims slaughtered in Chechnya, or Kashmir, or Palestine, while the U.S. stood by . . . The attack here becomes no less tragic if we acknowledge these other tragedies and demand equal time, equal care for them. (101)

While such comments do not quite model Rothberg's theory of 'multidirectional memory', which argues for what can be gained by moving beyond 'competitive' forms of collective memory in order to engender understanding and solidarity, or 'more supple social logic' (2009, 5), they do begin to resist narrowly national formations and point to a fuller gesture in the novel's final phase. However, despite the forceful critique that comes into view here, and the novel's rejection of clash of civilisations logic, it ultimately privileges Claire's view.

Not only does Claire get much more space than the novel's other 9/11 widow, Asma – which is conspicuous given the narrative strategy of providing a panorama of subject positions – but her story invites sympathy despite the fact that she betrays Mo. Claire's experience of trauma initially engenders sympathy and even as she begins to doubt Mo, this is expressed as self-doubt linked to her experience of trauma. In one scene she likens herself to a matryoshka doll of inner conflict: 'Claire within Claire within Claire within Claire' (302). Here, she has lost a sense of self, and 'every argument, no matter how contradictory, found sympathy'; she is unable 'to find her own core' (302). If our patience with Claire wanes as she ultimately betrays her world view, then it is revived in the conclusion when we learn she is dying.

The Submission's conclusion reinforces the reader's alignment with Claire and a view of 9/11 as a totalising event. As noted, this chapter occurs in the future and begins in Mumbai where Mo now lives. Just before it begins, there is a bridging section where Mo remembers a pre-controversy trip to Kabul. This flashback reveals that Mo had stumbled upon Babur's Garden and had a spiritual experience – as true a 'submission' as possible for a secular man, moved by aesthetic beauty (363). The description of Babur's Garden reveals that it had influenced Mo's memorial design and that in some sense 'The Garden' was an 'Islamic Garden'. This sets up a series of evocative revelations in the final chapter. We learn that Mo has become an internationally celebrated architect and that his departure from America has aligned with accelerations in globalisation and the increasing global influence of China and India in the twenty-first century. This recalls the final chapter of another novel published in 2011, Jennifer Egan's *A Visit From the Goon Squad*, which also features a final chapter set in the future (about fifteen years on) that alludes to the 'shadow' of 9/11 and evokes notions of American declension. In Waldman's novel Mo has thrived, and the global landscape has shifted. His home country, we learn, had 'moved on, self-corrected, as it always did', but Mo remains angry and 'stuck in the past': he 'wanted acknowledgment of the wrong done to him' (370).

The chapter begins with Mo receiving guests in his Mumbai apartment: two young American documentarians, Molly and William, who are making a film about the memorial controversy on its twentieth anniversary; yet another diegetic act of representation and commemoration. Mo is not aware, but William is Claire's son. They interview Mo and discuss the project and some of the other interviews they have conducted. Eventually they show him footage of their interview with Claire. As they watch the video it is clear she is ill and weak and initially regretful: 'I regret so much' (380). But she ultimately has retained a level of suspicion across all these years. When pushed as to why she had not apologised, she responds by stating, 'even though I wanted to apologize I must have felt conflicted' and adds that she was never 'entirely sure I was sorry' (381). The novel ends with the revelation that Mo did in fact get a chance to realise 'The Garden' and William was able to lay symbolically important cairns in memory of his dad. In a reversal of the Mumbai scene, Claire is watching video of William in 'The Garden' laying these stones, and this is the concluding image of the novel – again privileging Claire's perspective and her loss.

The novel's ending, which traces a transatlantic movement from New York to Kabul (in the bridging section) to Mumbai, to Dhaka (a brief passages notes that Molly had visited Asma's son, Abdul, on her way to India) and then back to New York, represents another multidirectional gesture. For Araújo, this final movement engages with 'memory from a place where different urban histories, apparently distinct in their grief, are necessarily interwoven' (43). This is undoubtedly the case, but the circularity concludes with – and therefore prioritises – New York, and Claire and her grief. Moreover, each of the key narrative strands concludes by emphasising the totalising and long-term effect of the attacks and memorial controversy. Mo has had to abandon his homeland after a traumatic period of abuse and vilification. Asma is killed during the peak period of the controversy when hate crimes become rampant. Claire is dying and has never been able to reconcile with Mo or herself. There is hope in the next generation, but the lives of the key characters here have all been inexorably transformed.

Bleeding Edge

Though it belongs squarely in the 9/11 novel genre, Thomas Pynchon's *Bleeding Edge* (2013) challenges the exceptionalisation of 9/11 by positioning this event alongside other moments of historical rupture. Some of these occur around the same turn-of-the-millennium period: the Y2K scare and the bursting of the dotcom bubble in 2000, for example. Others are broader, such as the arrival and transformation of the internet – which the novel depicts as a movement from utopian, democratic possibility to complete corporatisation. Mitchum Huehls argues that *Bleeding Edge* is a novel in which 'technological innovation crests, crashes and leaves a different world in its wake. Everything changes not so much because of 9/11 but because of the Internet' (866). My contention here is that the most important way in which the novel contextualises – and de-exceptionalises – 9/11 is through its depiction of a deeper history of neoliberalism. This strand of the narrative emerges through the characterisation and stories of principal protagonist Maxine Tarnow, a 'decertified fraud investigator', and villain Nicholas Windust, a shadowy agent whom Maxine is magnetically drawn to, despite seeing him as a 'neoliberal terrorist' (108). We learn that Windust's first job was on the ground 'in Santiago, Chile, on 11 September 1973, spotting for the planes that bombed the presidential palace and killed Salvador Allende' (108). This reference to 'the other 9/11' – the CIA-supported coup that installed Augusto Pinochet – is one of the ways the novel binds its interest in turn-of-the-century events and crises with a history of neoliberalism. I argue here that the through these characters, *Bleeding Edge* explores the global violence of neoliberalism. Maxine, a centrist liberal, gradually comes to recognise the ways that she is implicated in the violence committed to secure the hegemony of neoliberalism. Though her experience is one of consumption and immaterial exchange, her relationship with Windust forces her to consider her implication in the violence of neoliberalism outside America. Ultimately, in the final stage of Maxine's recognition of her implication, the September 11 attacks are understood as a kind of blowback against neoliberal terrorism.

Bleeding Edge also approaches new territory in the literature of 9/11, in its depiction of conspiracy, and is somewhat unique in its genre codings. Like Jess Walter's *The Zero* (2006) it is at least partially a detective novel, with Maxine as the detective protagonist, but it also is conspicuous in the way it adopts key tropes of the 9/11 novel genre. For instance, there is a marriage plot and, as in *Falling Man*, an estranged couple – Maxine and her ex-husband Horst – re-establish the marital home after the attacks. It also emphasises their children and, like so many 9/11 novels, depicts parents trying to protect their children in ways that seem pointedly allegorical. I begin analysis of *Bleeding Edge* by considering its depiction of 9/11 conspiracies and conspiracy theories and by reflecting on the significance of the novel's detective novel genre coding through some provisional comparison with *The Zero*. I will then discuss its marriage plot and restoration of post-9/11 order, before focusing on the characterisations of Maxine and Windust which are at the heart of its depiction of neoliberalism.

The conspiracy stories in *Bleeding Edge* quickly move beyond the 'truther narratives' that, as Peter Knight has argued, were 'often underpinned . . . by an ideology of American exceptionalism' just as the 'official narratives' are (157). The narrative begins when Maxine is approached by Reg Despard, who is making a corporate film for an IT security firm, hashslingrz, headed by 'boy billionaire' Gabriel Ice (10). Reg has made observations that open a web of connections between hashslingrz, a mysterious Middle Eastern organisation, and a video depicting training exercises for the launch of Stinger missiles from a New York rooftop. The missile plot is connected to Windust, who may be working for both Ice and the US government. Later, Maxine's husband, a market trader, notices a 'sudden abnormal surge of put options on United Airlines', followed by a similar occurrence with American Airlines, on 8 September (315). When 9/11 happens in the novel, the plot is further complicated by theories introduced from various sources, including Maxine's brother, an ex-Mossad agent, and father, as well as from her friends Heidi Czornak, a professor of popular culture, and March Kelleher, a leftist activist and 'weblogger'. Maxine's father adopts a position on the conspiracy that broadly represents the novel's: 'of course it's possible' (325). *Bleeding Edge* wants readers to register the possibility, or even likelihood, of conspiracy, but it also wants to signal that there are underlying issues at play – specifically, the global structures of neoliberalism – that become visible through the conspiratorial web.

The views of March and Heidi also shape the novel's depiction of conspiracy. Though Maxine is competitive with her friends – an aspect of her character clearly linked to neoliberalism – they are prominent features of her internal world. Maxine continually considers their views at important moments, and they motivate her and play a role in driving the narrative. At one point, their voices converge: March shows Maxine a dollar bill which has an inscription in the margins reading, 'World Trade Center was destroyed by CIA – Bush Senior's CIA is making Bush Jr. Prez for life and a hero' (322). This triggers a memory of a comment Heidi had made: 'these are the places we should be looking, not in newspapers or television but at the margins, graffiti, uncontrolled utterances, bad dreamers who sleep in public and scream in their sleep' (322). The politically engaged ideas of March and Heidi widen Maxine's own views, propel her investigation, and invite her to think critically about the attacks. When Heidi argues that ''11 September infantilized this country. It had a chance to grow up, instead it chose to default back to childhood', Maxine listens (336). Though *Bleeding Edge* does not subscribe to a particular conspiracy theory, these views, as well as an array of voices articulating suspicion from the margins, suggest that some conspiring has occurred and that the 'official narrative' is being used to advance an agenda.

The novel's portrayal of conspiracy is most productively understood in relation to the systems of state and private sector power that converge around the Alden Pyle-esque Windust. Knight's argument for a more productive theorisation of conspiracy is useful here. Knight argues that prevalent 9/11 conspiracy theories are not as 'outrageous' as they seem: 'they share many of the same ideological underpinnings about causality, blame, and American exceptionalism that prop up the orthodox account' and 'often maintain an abiding faith in American innocence and the fundamental soundness of the system of government' (192). Knight contends that these theories generally pointed to a singular evil force (often President G. W. Bush), and in doing so mirrored the Bush administration's own pattern of identifying singular antagonists in the early war on terror. Knight posits a model of conspiracy that shows 'power as decentered and dispersed into a vast network of interlocking vested interests within the wider process of globalization, a picture that cannot easily be pinned down to an evil cabal' (193). This argument has two components: first, conspiracy will inevitably be plural and divergent, involving networks of conspirers with different agendas, rather than an 'evil cabal'; second, entrenched institutional or systemic malaise, rather than fringe actors, should be the subject of scrutiny. In *Bleeding Edge*, the intertwined narratives of 9/11, the internet and neoliberalism portray conspiracy in precisely these terms, and the focus is on systemic malaise, rather than 'the event'.

Occasionally, this focus on systemic collapse is discussed diegetically. For instance, Maxine's therapist, Shawn, articulates an iteration of Chalmers Johnson's 'blowback theory':

> that was the moment, Maxi. Not when everything changed. When everything was revealed ... Showing us exactly what we've become, what we've been all the time ... living on borrowed time. Getting away cheap. Never caring about who's paying for it, who's starving somewhere else all jammed together so we can have cheap food, a house, a yard in the burbs ... planetwide more every day, the payback keeps gathering. (340)

While *Bleeding Edge* is less concerned with blaming globalisation for 9/11 than providing a critique of neoliberalism, Shawn's views are repeatedly endorsed. For example, Maxine meditates on the landscape from a boat in Fresh Kill, 'toxicity central', home to 'everything the city has rejected so it can keep on pretending to be itself' (167):

> for maybe a minute and a half she feels free – at least at the edge of possibilities, like whatever the Europeans who first sailed up the Passaic River must have felt, before the long parable of corporate sins and corruption that overtook it. (169)

Maxine reiterates Shawn's views, begins to reflect on her complicity and, crucially, situates this rhetoric historically. These allusions to 'getting away cheap', 'living on borrowed time', 'corporate sins' and 'corruption' also evoke Knight's ideas about the systems that the network of conspiracies exists within, and this contributes to Maxine's numbness. Moreover, there are echoes of a scene in Jess Walter's earlier and under-discussed 9/11 novel, *The Zero*, where protagonist Remy is looking at the disaster site and sees 'the city's history in garbage': 'Andy Warhol's coffee filters, Ethel Merman's dress shields, Mickey Mantle's chaw. Every gust out here seemed to stink in some new, groundbreaking way' (43). The connections both novels make between consumption and disaster are vivid.

The conspiracy plot and genre coding of *Bleeding Edge* are features it shares with *The Zero*. Both novels use their genre modes to explore conspiracy theories of 9/11, using the detective novel framework to untangle the conspiracies. These novels also share another distinction within the 9/11 novel genre: satire and irony, deployed to critique exceptionalist rhetoric. In *The Zero* post-9/11 exceptionalism is critiqued, and in *Bleeding Edge* the unseen global violence of neoliberalism is brought into view and positioned as a context for 9/11. As the detectives attempt to navigate increasingly inscrutable worlds, the genre modes of these novels allow representations of trauma that move beyond the narrow discourses of victimhood and grief in earlier 9/11 trauma fiction.

The focalising protagonist of *The Zero* is Brian Remy, a traumatised policeman turned counter-terrorism agent. In keeping with the hard-boiled tradition, he is a heavy-drinking divorcee, and when the novel opens, it is the immediate aftermath of 9/11, and he has awoken in a daze after shooting himself. He is disoriented, has gaps in his memory and suffers from blackouts and, as John Duvall has noted, 'the reader is unsure whether Remy's trauma is physical (the gun wound) or psychological (9/11) or a combination' (283). It transpires that Remy has begun working for the 'Office of Liberty and Recovery' (OLR) as a special agent pursuing terror suspects linked to the 9/11 attacks, though he continues to see his ex-partner, Paul Guterak, with whom he patrols 'the zero' (the disaster site). In the early phases of the novel scenes are uncannily repetitive. As Remy and Guterak move through checkpoints at 'the zero', a 'street cop' says each time, 'Fuckin' raghead motherfuckers' and Paul says, 'Yeah. That's right. That's right' (13, 27, 48). This repeated exchange occurs as the two men circle the cite, evoking a sense of traumatic repetition which is compounded by Remy's blackouts. The blackouts come like 'cuts in a movie, or on top of the other, with Remy struggling for breath' or at other times leave him lingering 'in moments that had ended for everyone else' (96). Such passages evoke trauma but also give the novel an interesting formal conceit as the focalising protagonist is impaired and his blackouts leave gaps in time and activity that he has no access to. As Duvall notes, this is a 'Remy we don't have access to' as readers either, a Jack Bauer-style 'ends-justify-the-means man of action' (284). We do know that he is active during these periods, and it transpires that a very different Remy is pursuing the case during these inaccessible moments. When the Remy we do have access to, who is mostly morally upright, is questioned about aspects of the case he is unaware of, he honestly insists that he does not know and frequently asks colleagues what his job actually is. But Remy's questions are received as ironic jokes and dismissed. For instance, when an apparently junior colleague informs him she does not have clearance to access a certain area, he asks, 'do I?', to which she laughs and replies, 'you're funny' and walks away (101).

This conceit opens a sustained discussion of irony that responds critically to the notion of a post-9/11 'end of irony' and motors the subversive, satirical dimension of the novel. Satire, in *The Zero*, centres around the convergence of the rhetoric of heroism and the will to monetise the crisis: from 'First Responder' breakfast cereal to the imperative issued by the mysterious 'Boss' to Remy, the 'two simple words' that will make 'sense of where this leads, of what will save you and me, what will save the entire country: "Private. Sector"' (203, 119). But irony and satire in *The Zero* also mobilises its moral message in the way Remy's inability to remember or know himself actually makes his work more effective. As Duvall notes,

> Remy's inability to remember in no way undercuts his efficacy as a counterterrorism agent; his unknowing thus enacts a post-9/11 ideology that not only allows him to claim a foggy innocence regarding his acts of violence but also actually enhances his abilities as an interrogator. (284)

Irony is an important feature and diegetic topic in *Bleeding Edge*, too, which uses satirical humour towards its social and political critique. In *Bleeding Edge* the alleged 'death of irony' – along with academic debates that addressed this notion – are skewered when Heidi discusses an upcoming academic article, 'Heteronormative Rising Star, Homophobic Dark Companion', which argues that irony,

> assumed to be a key element of urban gay humor and popular through the nineties, has now become another collateral casualty of 11 September because somehow it did not keep the tragedy from happening. 'As if somehow irony,' she recaps for Maxine, 'as practiced by a giggling mincing fifth column, actually brought on the events of 11 September, by keeping the country insufficiently serious – weakening its grip on reality. So all kinds of make-believe – forget the delusional state the country's in already – must suffer as well. Everything has to be literal now.' (335)

One notable diagnosis of the post-9/11 death of irony was Roger Rosenblatt's article in *Time*, published on 24 September 2001. Rosenblatt saw this as a positive outcome of 9/11 stating that 'for some 30 years ... the good folks in charge of America's intellectual life have insisted that nothing was to be believed in or taken seriously.

Nothing was real' (n.p.). While this view was widely contested, there is no doubt that American writers, in particular, were compelled towards sombre tones and realist aesthetics in the wake of 9/11.

The notion of a new post-9/11 'seriousness' was also a central subject of the early 9/11 novel. *The Good Life*, *The Emperor's Children*, *The Writing on the Wall* and *Falling Man* all address this and while *Bleeding Edge* critiques this idea, in certain places it too adopts a form and tone of post-9/11 gravity. Indeed, in some conspicuous – and surprising – ways Pynchon's novel adopts key conceits of the 9/11 novel genre. One way in which it is comparable to *The Emperor's Children* is dramatic irony. Both texts are countdown narratives, and this type of irony is new terrain for Pynchon. The beginning of each novel signals their just-before-9/11 dates, and the reader is invited to anticipate the event and is poised to discover its effects. Another feature *Bleeding Edge* shares with Messud's novel, *Falling Man* and *The Good Life*, is a relationship story as a barometer to measure change. As noted, the relationship between Maxine and her estranged husband Horst is initially similar to that of *Falling Man*'s protagonists, Keith and Lianne. In DeLillo's novel, Keith literally walks out of the burning tower and back into Lianne's apartment. In *Bleeding Edge*, after the attacks, Horst moves his 'sleeping arrangements into Maxine's room, to the inconvenience of neither' (332). The difference between Pynchon's relationship narrative and those in *Falling Man*, *The Good Life* and *The Emperor's Children* is the way the period of post-9/11 re-evaluation and reflection unfolds. While *Bleeding Edge* contains a similar restoration of equilibrium, the ambiguities about whether this is linked to indifference or resilience in previous novels are more complex, because in addition to being shocked by 9/11, Maxine's slow realisation of her own complicity in the violence of neoliberalism (a process that begins before 9/11) becomes the primary narrative focus.

Maxine is initially both critical of neoliberal politics and an archetypal 'homo economicus'. She is a Clinton-era, 'West-Sideliberal' (212) whose wry wit and social liberalism is accompanied by impulsive consumption and 'real-estate envy attack[s]' (4). She embodies what Philip Mirowski calls 'everyday neoliberalism', characterised by the 'entrepreneurial self', by 'promiscuous notions of identity', and where 'competition is the primary virtue' (92). This internalised sense of competitiveness and consumption is pervasive in a world of symbolic and immaterial exchange. The strength with which everyday neoliberalism shapes Maxine's behaviour is emphasised by the novel's extensive cataloguing of her brand obsessions:

Chanel (28), Armani (30), TAG Heuer (31), Hermès (124), Dolce & Gabbana (149), Mikimoto jewellery (150), Officina perfume (201), Coach (212) and Jimmy Choo (305). During one of multiple visits to Saks on Fifth Avenue, Maxine seems magnetically drawn to the famous retailer, and imagines the possibility of seeing the diamond setting she has been 'looking for her whole life' (285). She is captivated by the feeling that 'nothing, nobody on this block is positioned where they are by accident, that saturating the space, invisible as the wavelengths that carry soap operas into the home, dramas of faceted intricacy are teeming all around' (285). Maxine, then, is not an unreflective participant in neoliberal culture, and not only enjoys its material aspects, but also revels in these 'teeming dramas' of transaction and consumption that have pervaded her world.

Just as the diegetic representation of Maxine's entrepreneurial selfhood addresses her implication, the formal properties of the novel align the reader with her perspective. It consistently employs free indirect discourse via Maxine's habit of self-questioning, which is built into ostensibly third-person narration. The novel's opening sentences employ a structure that becomes typical, wherein apparently objective third-person narration slides into Maxine's interior voice as she questions her own actions:

> It's the first day of Spring 2001, and Maxine Tarnow, though some still have her in their system as Loeffler, is walking her boys to school. Yes maybe they're past the age where they need an escort, maybe Maxine doesn't want to let go just yet, it's only a couple of blocks, it's her way to work, she enjoys it, so? (1)

As the narrative proceeds, this device is employed when Maxine makes questionable decisions and almost every time she encounters or considers the 'neoliberal terrorist', Windust (103, 244, 253–4, 258, 411). Moreover, given Maxine's subject position, the use of free indirect discourse in *Bleeding Edge* means the reader is aligned with an implicated subject.

Maxine's patterns of consumerism and competition represent one form of implication in neoliberalism, and this is reinforced through her occupation of the private detective role. Sean McCann connects the classic detective fiction of the late 1800s and early 1900s with the political liberalism of that period, the genre being 'centrally concerned with a fundamental premise of liberal theory – the rule of law – and with the tensions fundamental to democratic societies that constantly threw that principle into doubt' (6). Classic detective fiction was conservative, broadly speaking, because 'civil society produces a stable order that can survive violence and abuse', and the detective's job was to restore stability to this world (16). The politically liberal interpretative quest of the classic detective obscures the economic repercussions of the same system due to its focus on individual crimes and possessions. In contrast, the hard-boiled genre, upon which the characterisation of Maxine – and Remy in *The Zero* – obviously draws, is a response to a crumbling faith in that stable order, itself the product of free market economics. McCann notes that hard-boiled detective fiction emerged from a belief that 'the traditional mystery tale was a political myth, illegitimate because it no longer corresponded to the complex realities of an urban, industrial society' (18). Instead of the detective-protagonist performing a restorative function by re-establishing social stability premised on classic liberal theory, as social tensions mounted in the cities that were the product of this economic model – still within the period of Keynesian compromise and prior to the onset of neoliberalism proper – the detective came to occupy a liminal position, no longer fully aligned with the law or dominant ideology. Consequently, as Patricia Merivale notes, 'the hard-boiled Private Eye often finds himself complicit in the corruption of the world to which he is supposed to bring lucidity and order' (311).

This complicity is apparent in Maxine, whose role extends the critique advanced by the hard-boiled genre into the neoliberal era. Maxine's decertification as a fraud investigator seems to have had no negative impact on her business and, rather, she feels that clients continue to approach her thanks to the way that it provides 'a halo of faded morality, a reliable readiness to step outside the law and share the trade secrets of auditors and tax men' (17). The 2001 of *Bleeding Edge* is a period where, for many characters, distinctions between guilt and innocence have collapsed. In some instances, Maxine's professional conduct invites us to consider her as, in Rothberg's terms, a 'perpetuator', because her actions contribute to rather than rectify a morally bankrupt system that has come unmoored from the principles that once underpinned liberalism (2020, 12). On numerous occasions, Maxine is complicit with bureaucratic and economic systems from which morality and justice have been evacuated. For example, she describes how what she once regarded as the 'no-brainer choice between friendship and super-picky guideline adherence' eventually led to her becoming decertified (18). Later, she evokes a moral grey area when she refers to 'the ancient CFE distinction between being complicit and merely attending to phone calls that should probably be answered'; on this occasion, she answers Gabriel Ice's call, which ultimately furthers her involvement with Windust (136).

For McCann hard-boiled detective fiction emerged when 'the social forces prodding its development threatened to tear the very idea of a liberal society to pieces' and 'the detective story both registered that threat and turned it into a manageable tale' (6). In *Bleeding Edge* Maxine fails to construct a 'manageable tale' from the evidence she gathers regarding Windust, Gabriel Ice or 9/11. This lack of narrative mastery is part of the novel's project of representing neoliberalism as ungraspable, but is also a consequence of Maxine's failure to investigate or interrogate the systems in which she works and thrives.[4] Kostas Kaltsas argues that Maxine is 'self-aware regarding her roles' and that 'she is able to accept or reject them, often treating them ironically as set roles *while* performing their essence sincerely' (41). Similarly, Jennifer Backman suggests she can switch between her role as a detective and the stereotypically feminine modes that are sometimes expected of her (31). Yet this compartmentalisation results in her inability to perform the hermeneutic work on her own life that might enable her to better understand her implication in neoliberalism.

Jodi Melamed argues that neoliberalism 'portrays an ethic of multiculturalism to be the spirit of neoliberalism and, conversely, posits neoliberal restructuring across the globe to be the key to a postracist world of freedom and opportunity' (138). In other words, neoliberalism disguises the adverse effects that it produces, sometimes in socially or political progressive language. Early in the novel, while the routine patterns of consumption made possible by globalisation are evoked with a degree of cynicism, it is not directly linked to suffering and exploitation. For example, Maxine's hairdressers 'are forever going off to Caribbean resorts for intensive tutorial workshops in color weaving' (49) and Eastern philosophy is reduced to Buddhism-as-therapy by Maxine's guru, Shawn, whose first-hand experience of Asia appears to extend to little more than watching Martin Scorsese's *Kundun* (30). At other times, though, the narrative partially but inadequately acknowledges the inequality on which such commodification is predicated, including details that gesture towards potentially violent black market exchanges. For example, a company called Packages Unlimited is guarded by 'chained and padlocked doors ... flanked by Uzi-packing gorillas in uniform, who signed for mysterious shipments and deliveries', while Vyrva McElmo's collection of Beanie Babies is secured via 'a list of retailers on the East Side who get the critters shipped all but directly in from China by way of certain shadowy warehouses adjoining JFK' (4, 39). In both cases, the illegality of these operations is presented as

New York colour rather than evidence of wrongdoing, and Maxine's failure to interrogate the mechanisms by which these exchanges function exemplifies Rothberg's argument that 'the manifold indirect, structural, and collective forms of agency that enable injury, exploitation, and domination . . . frequently remain in the shadows' (2020, 1).

While the destructive effects of neoliberalism hover on the edge of her vision for much of the novel, present but not fully acknowledged, it is with the appearance of Windust that the relationship between the contemporary US economic and political order, and violence perpetrated in the developing world, comes more squarely into view. The arrival of Windust begins to erode Maxine's conception of neoliberalism as a matter of immaterial and symbolic exchange. At first, her conflicted attitude towards him mirrors and brings into sharp relief her conflicted attitude towards neoliberalism. However, as details of his background emerge, the fact that neoliberalism is experienced as material violence by many in the developing world becomes visible. Moreover, the repeated references to Windust's 'innocence' while detailing this history show how implication can overtake individuals, a transformation into complicity and perpetration outstripping any opportunity for reflection or for retreat from this path.

As with Maxine, a history of neoliberalism is embedded in Windust's professional role. It connects the stories of these individuals to a wider history of violence and indicates how such histories operate in a cyclical manner, introducing the potential for the effects of neoliberalism to reverberate back towards their source. Windust is introduced through Maxine's investigation, and initially acts as another locus for her internal conflicts regarding neoliberalism. While she is explicitly critical of his politics (she frequently makes jibes about 'Republicans'), and initially expresses a sense of disgust towards him, professional interest evolves into physical attraction, and just over halfway through the novel she agrees to meet him against her better judgement. After arriving at his flat, she willingly submits to his advances and an unsettling sex scene unfolds:

> His hands, murderer's hands, are gripping her forcefully by the hips, exactly where it matters, exactly where some demonic set of nerve receptors she has been till now only semi-aware of have waited to be found and used like buttons on a game controller . . . impossible to know if it's him moving or if she's doing it herself . . . (258)[5]

Maxine is unsure as to whether to attribute agency to herself or the 'neoliberal terrorist', and the way that she finds herself engaging in actions that she seems to simultaneously recognise as repulsive may be read allegorically, suggesting how individual subjects might participate in activities they know they ought to reject. Maxine's magnetic attraction to things she should disavow is evoked by her admission that she could be tempted to repeat their sexual encounter (260). This imagery connects Maxine's personal attraction to Windust to a wider weakness for the temptations that a market economy offers.

The Windust strand of *Bleeding Edge* also emphasises the violence done by the US across the Global South to secure neoliberal hegemony. While Windust has perpetrated atrocities, the details of these are at first hazy and subject to conjecture. Maxine initially retains the euphemistic language used to justify such actions, her narrative recording that Windust was a specialist in 'interrogation enhancement' and 'noncompliant-subject relocation' (107). When Maxine eventually admits that he is responsible for 'pain and damage applied to various human body parts that might have added up to hundreds – who knows, maybe thousands – of deaths on his karmic ticket' (109), and that he 'can be ticketed with a harvest of innocent souls that puts him easily into the company of more renowned Guinness Book murderers' (244), she begins to acknowledge the extent of his wrongdoing, although the nature of the suffering he has caused still remains abstracted in her figuration.

These limited details are enough to connect Windust to Naomi Klein's popular history of neoliberalism *The Shock Doctrine* (2007), in which Chicago School economic theories attributed to Milton Friedman were violently implemented in South and Central America in the 1970s, before underpinning domestic and foreign policy in the West from the 1980s onwards. The details of his background accord with Klein's thesis that the advance of neoliberalism has been driven by the introduction of policies via shock, during 'malleable moments, when we are psychologically unmoored and physically uprooted' (21). Though Klein's history is meticulously researched, her emphasis on shock or rupture, particularly in the twenty-first century, elides deeper structures of neoliberalism, and it is towards these deeper structures, and their histories, that the stories of Windust and Maxine gesture.[6] Recent scholarship has grappled with the question of how neoliberalism has become the dominant economic mode, and how that mode has in turn created ideological and behavioural norms from within which this system seems difficult or impossible to critique. One notable example is that offered by Huehls and Greenwald Smith, who suggest that neoliberalism has progressed through four phases from the 1970s to the present: 'the economic, the political-ideological, the sociocultural, and the ontological' (8). While this four-phase model has been challenged, with other periodisations locating the beginnings of neoliberalism much earlier, what these narratives have in common is a sense that neoliberalism has evolved from an ideologically implemented set of economic policies to become the social and cultural reality for much of the planet to the extent that it is now a way of being that simply appears natural.[7] This said, those social and cultural realities are very different experiences for people inhabiting different parts of the globe, and it is the relative invisibility of those other worlds that Windust's introduction counteracts.

References to the deeper structures of neoliberalism are mapped onto Windust's backstory, which Maxine accesses in an anonymously delivered dossier. As noted, she learns that his 'first recorded job, as an entry-level gofer, was in Santiago, Chile, on 11 September 1973' and this evocation of 'the other 9/11' binds its interest in turn-of-the-century events and crises with its deeper history of neoliberalism (108).[8] It also reinforces Quinn Slobodian's contention that the neoliberal programme was conceived 'not to liberate markets but to encase them, to inoculate capitalism against the threat of democracy' (2). Moreover, while *Bleeding Edge* alludes to this history of violent interventions in South America (1970s) – discussed again in my analysis of Rachel Kushner's *The Flamethrowers* (2013) in Chapter 4 – and Central America (1980s), it also explores Windust's movement from 'raw ideology' to the actual atrocities with which he is linked (109). In this sense – and again in reference to Huehls and Greenwald Smith's 'four phases' theory – he represents the social and cultural vectors of neoliberalism as much as the political, economic or ideological. We learn he 'was one of the founders of a D.C. think tank known as Toward America's New Global Opportunities (TANGO)' and has a 'thirty-year history of visiting lecturer gigs, including at the infamous School of the Americas' (109). These details are important as they point to the extent to which neoliberal theories circulated institutionally and culturally, via education, building their challenge to Keynesian norms. Windust embodies the violent establishment of neoliberal policies and the slow and sustained cultural dissemination of neoliberal ideology over decades.

A particularly intriguing element of Windust's characterisation, and one that addresses implication, is Maxine's notion that he is a corrupted innocent. This appears to be speculation at first but is corroborated late on by Xiomara, Windust's first wife. This notion also evokes Graham Greene's 1955 novel, *The Quiet American*. In Greene's novel, Alden Pyle, a young American agent, arrives in Indochina in the early 1950s promoting a 'third way' beyond communism or colonialism and influenced by the theories of a fictional author, York Harding. Pyle is brimming with ideological zeal described by his cynical British interlocuter, Fowler, as a 'fanatic gleam' (28). Pyle is repeatedly described as 'innocent', though Fowler understands this innocence as dangerous naivety and even a 'form of insanity', describing the 'innocent' Pyle as a 'dumb leper who has lost his bell, wandering the world, meaning no harm. I never knew a man who had better motives for all the trouble he caused' (36).

The Quiet American is a cautionary tale of how the pursuit of political change or regime change underpinned by theoretical abstraction, and not local cultural knowledge, evolves into complicity with, or the perpetration of, atrocity. In Greene's novel, Pyle funds and supports ruthless militias and terrorist bombings. Maxine's repeated evocation of innocence in her imaginings of the young Windust echo Greene's novel, notably when she can

> [s]omehow see Windust back then, a clean-looking kid, short hair, chinos and button-down shirts, only has to shave once a week, one of a globe-trotting gang of young smart-asses, piling into cities and towns all over the Third World, filling ancient colonial spaces with office copiers and coffee machines, pulling all-nighters, running off neatly bound plans for the total obliteration of target countries and their replacement by free-market fantasies. (109)

This persistent assertion of Windust's innocence is reinforced through his relationship with a local woman, Xiomara (again, echoing *The Quiet American*, in which Pyle pursues a relationship with a Vietnamese woman). Reflecting on their relationship and marriage, Xiomara describes him as an 'entry level kid who didn't know how much trouble his soul was in' (442).

Windust, as this summary of his past indicates, moves rapidly from mere involvement through complicity to full perpetration of atrocity. However, Maxine surmises that

> back in that more innocent day, the damage Windust caused, if any, all stayed safely on paper. But then, at some point, somewhere she thinks of as down in the middle of a vast and unforgiving flatland, he took a step. Hardly measurable in that immensity and yet, like finding and clicking on an invisible link on a screen, transported in the act over to his next life. (110)

Though she can put together the phases of Windust's career, she is unable to gain a sense of mastery over his internal life, and to identify the point at which innocence shaded into complicity and perpetration. Maxine's uncertainty with regard to Windust in fact grows as she comes to learn more about him, and her difficulties in reconciling the idea of corrupted innocence with his brutal professional history are so great that she is finally forced to admit that she 'can't get the two stories to connect' (244). Maxine's difficulty in reconciling the 'two stories' suggests the difficulty of reconciling a way of life in which violence is not generally visible with the knowledge that the same way of life was built upon violent interventions elsewhere. Maxine's struggles to understand Windust mirror her difficulties in recognising her own implication in the violent effects of neoliberalism, and only her encounter with a direct perpetrator of such violence allows this relationship to become visible. The intersection of process and rupture, then, as embodied by the encounters between Maxine and Windust, is what makes visible to Maxine her implication in the violence perpetrated upon these other worlds.

Moreover, in addition to emphasising specific elements of Windust's character, the way that *Bleeding Edge* evokes intertexts represents a search for periodicity, defined by Sharae Deckard and Stephen Shapiro as the attempt to 'ascertain the nature of recurring familiarities across historical cycles of capital's expanded reproduction' (27). The clear echoes of *The Quiet American* suggest a 'cyclical repetition of patterns in American interventions in 'Indochina' in the 1950s and in South America in the 1970s. Initially, the details of Windust's past suggest that these cycles are a matter of repeated US behaviour towards the developing world; however, the 9/11 attacks introduce a new form of cyclicity in which these historical wrongs begin to rebound on the source of their perpetration.

Notes

1. Pankaj Mishra's 2007 article 'The End of Innocence' asked, speaking specifically about Jay McInerney's *The Good Life*, *Falling Man*, *The Emperor's Children* and Ken Kalfus's *A Disorder Peculiar to the Country*, 'Are we meant to think of marital discord . . . as a metaphor for post-9/11 America?' (6). Mishra's article was followed by a review essay by Zadie Smith, published in the *New York Review of Books*, 'Two Paths for the Novel'. Smith questioned the exceptionalisation of 9/11 generally and asked, 'Were there calls, in 1915, for the *Lusitania* novel? In 1985, was the Bhopal novel keenly anticipated?' (72). Mishra's and

Smith's arguments were then advanced in scholarly articles by Richard Gray and Michael Rothberg. Discussing the same novels, Gray argues that they fail to engage with the wider complexities of the crisis and 'simply assimilate the unfamiliar into familiar structures. The crisis is in every way domesticated' (134). The problem with this domestication, he argues, is that 9/11 and contemporary America, as subjects for fiction, demand engagement with difference: 'There is the threat of the terrorist but there is also the fact of a world that is liminal, a proliferating chain of borders, where familiar oppositions – civilized and savage, town and wilderness, "them" and "us" – are continually being challenged, dissolved, and reconfigured' (135). In a special issue of *Modern Fiction Studies*, John Duvall and Robert P. Marzec offer a rejoinder, arguing that they are 'unwilling to look very closely at what 9/11 fiction sets out to do because they are both sure that they know what 9/11 fiction ought to be doing. If one retrospectively applied their perspective to fiction after World War I, one might be forced to say that Virginia Woolf's Mrs. Dalloway and Ernest Hemingway's *The Sun Also Rises* are failures for their oblique treatment of the root cause of historical trauma, since Woolf's Septimus Smith and Hemingway's Jake Barnes only imagine the private traumas of war veterans' (381). Catherine Morley also challenges the prescriptive analysis of Gray and Rothberg, noting that they seem to 'transcend the role of the cultural or literary spectator', and she questions the idea that 'fiction is no more than a political tool, through which writers can understand (and educate readers about) the United States' place in the world' (2011, 720).
2. In *The Terror Dream*, Susan Faludi analyses America's post-9/11 fixation on 'the domestic realm' and on a 'sexualized struggle between depleted masculinity and overbearing womanhood' (9).
3. In *Affect and American Literature in the Age of Neoliberalism*, Greenwald Smith notes that neoliberal hegemony was 'secured' in the 1990s. In the introduction to *Neoliberalism and Contemporary Literary Cultures*, Huehls and Greenwald Smith posit their influential 'four phases' periodisation, in which the third phase occurs in the 1990s when neoliberalism becomes socially and culturally entrenched.
4. One of the leading advocates of neoliberalism anticipated what we might expect to be a critique of it: as Quinn Slobodian notes, 'Hayek began to realize in the 1930s that the dispersal of knowledge throughout an entire market economy was so complete that no individual could ever gain a functional overview of it. The shock of the 1930s brought with it the realization that the world economy was basically unknowable' (18).
5. This seemingly irrational attraction carries echoes of the relationship between Frenesi Gates and Brock Vond in Pynchon's *Vineland* (1990). Frenesi, an independent filmmaker linked to late sixties radicalism, is powerlessly attracted to the Nixonian/Reaganite agent Brock (293).

6. Anna Hartnell argues that Klein's emphasis 'neglects the role of consent' and 'fails to track the progression of neoliberal policies as forms of "slow violence"' (132).
7. Alternative narratives are offered, for example, in Sharae Deckard and Stephen Shapiro, *World Literature, Neoliberalism, and the Culture of Discontent* (2019); and Liam Kennedy and Stephen Shapiro (eds), *Neoliberalism and Contemporary American Literature* (2019).
8. The events of the 'other 9/11' are powerfully portrayed in Ken Loach's contribution to *11'09"01* (2002), a collection of short films broadly about the attacks, produced by Alain Brigand.

Works Cited

Ally, Hamza Karam, 'Mourning in the Age of Terror: Revisiting Don DeLillo's Elusive 9/11 Novel Falling Man', *Canadian Review of American Studies*, 49.3 (2019), 349–71.

Araújo, Susana, *Transatlantic Fictions of 9/11 and the War on Terror: Images of Insecurity, Narratives of Captivity* (London: Bloomsbury, 2015).

Backman, Jennifer, 'From Hard Boiled to Over Easy: Reimagining the Noir Detective in *Inherent Vice* and *Bleeding Edge*', in *Thomas Pynchon, Sex, and Gender*, ed. by Ali Chetwynd, Joanna Freer and Georgios Maragos (Athens: University of Georgia Press, 2018), pp. 19–35.

Baer, Ulrich (ed.), *110 Stories: New York Writes after September 11* (New York: New York University Press, 2002).

Banita, Georgiana, 'Literature After 9/11', in *American Literature in Transition: 2000–2010*, ed. by Rachel Greenwald Smith (Cambridge: Cambridge University Press, 2018), pp. 152–64.

Beigbeder, Frédéric, *Windows on the World*, trans. by Frank Wynne (London: Harper Perennial, 2005).

Bell, Lenore, *The Other in 9/11 Literature: If You See Something, Say Something* (Basingstoke: Palgrave Macmillan, 2017).

Bond, Lucy, '9/11', in *The Routledge Companion to Literature and Trauma*, ed. by Colin Davis and Hanna Meretoja (New York: Routledge, 2020), pp. 407–17.

Bush, George, 'Address to the Joint Session of the 107th Congress', in *Selected Speeches of George W. Bush 2001–2008*, White House Archives <https://georgewbush-whitehouse.archives.gov/infocus/bushrecord/documents/Selected_Speeches_George_W_Bush.pdf> [accessed 31 August 2023].

Carroll, Hamilton, 'Insecurity', in *The Cambridge Companion to Twenty-First Century American Fiction*, ed. by Joshua L. Miller (Cambridge: Cambridge University Press, 2021), pp. 271–88.

Cilano, Cara, *From Solidarity to Schisms: 9/11 and After in Fictions and Film from Outside the US* (New York: Brill, 2009).

Cockley, David, 'Lynn [sic] Sharon Schwartz's *The Writing on the Wall*: Responding to the Media Spectacle', *Studies in American Jewish Literature*, 28.1 (2009), 14–27.

Cowart, David, '"Down on the barroom floor of history": Pynchon's *Bleeding Edge*', *Postmodern Culture*, 24.1 (2013), n.p.

Deckard, Sharae, and Stephen Shapiro, *World Literature, Neoliberalism, and the Culture of Discontent* (Basingstoke: Palgrave Macmillan, 2019).

DeLillo, Don, *Falling Man* (New York: Scribner, 2007).

DeLillo, Don, 'In the Ruins of the Future', *Harper's* (December 2001), 33–40.

DeLillo, Don, *Mao II* (London: Vintage, 1991).

del Pont, Xavier Marcó, 'Metafiction', in *The Routledge Companion to Twenty-First Century Literary Fiction*, ed. by Daniel O'Gorman and Robert Eaglestone (Abingdon: Routledge, 2019), pp. 80–8.

Dufournaud, Daniel, 'Dwelling with(out) Others: Family Dysfunction in Joseph O'Neill's *Netherland*', *Journal of American Studies* (2021), 1–23 <https://doi.org/10.1017/S0021875821001195>.

Duvall, John, 'Homeland Security and the State of (American) Exception(alism): Jess Walter's *The Zero* and the Ethical Possibilities of Postmodern Irony', *Studies in the Novel*, 45.2 (2013), 279–97.

Duvall, John, and Robert P. Marzec, 'Narrating 9/11', *Modern Fiction Studies*, 57.3 (2011), 381–400.

Faludi, Susan, *The Terror Dream: What 9/11 Revealed About America* (London: Atlantic, 2007).

Frank, Michael C., '"Why do they hate us?" Terrorism in American and British Fiction of the Mid-2000s', in *Terrorism and Literature*, ed. by Peter C. Herman (Cambridge: Cambridge University Press, 2018), pp. 340–60.

Gray, Richard, 'Open Doors, Closed Minds: American Prose Writing at a Time of Crisis', *American Literary History*, 28.1 (2009), 128–51.

Greene, Graham, *The Quiet American* (Harmondsworth: Penguin, 1955, 1967).

Greenwald Smith, Rachel, *Affect and American Literature in the Age of Neoliberalism* (Cambridge: Cambridge University Press, 2015).

Greenwald Smith, Rachel, *On Compromise: Art, Politics and the Fate of an American Ideal* (Minneapolis: Graywolf, 2021).

Hartnell, Anna, *After Katrina: Race, Neoliberalism and the End of the American Century* (New York: State University of New York Press, 2017).

Herman, Peter C., *Unspeakable: Literature and Terrorism from the Gunpowder Plot to 9/11* (New York: Routledge, 2021).

Hirsch, Marianne, 'I Took Pictures: September 2001 and Beyond', in *Trauma at Home: After 9/11*, ed. by Judith Greenberg (Lincoln: University of Nebraska Press, 2003), pp. 69–86.

Holloway, David, *9/11 and the War on Terror* (Edinburgh: Edinburgh University Press, 2008).

Houen, Alex, 'Novel Spaces and Taking Places(s) in the Wake of September 11', *Studies in the Novel*, 36.3 (2004), 419–37.

Huehls, Mitchum, 'The Great Flattening', *Contemporary Literature*, 54.4 (2013), 861–71.

Huehls, Mitchum, and Rachel Greenwald Smith (eds), *Neoliberalism and Contemporary Literary Culture* (Baltimore: Johns Hopkins University Press, 2017).

Irom, Bimbisar, 'Alterities in a Time of Terror: Notes on the Subgenre of the American 9/11 Novel', *Contemporary Literature*, 53.3 (2012), 517–47.

James, David, 'A Renaissance for the Crystalline Novel', *Contemporary Literature*, 53.4 (2012), 845–74.

Kaltsas, Kostas, 'Of "Maidens" and Towers: Oedipa Maas, Maxine Tarnow, and the Possibility of Resistance', in *Thomas Pynchon, Sex, and Gender*, ed. by Ali Chetwynd, Joanna Freer and Georgios Maragos (Athens: University of Georgia Press, 2018), pp. 36–51.

Kaufman, Linda S., 'Bodies in Rest and Motion in *Falling Man*', in *Don DeLillo: Mao II, Underworld, Falling Man*, ed. by Stacey Olster (London: Continuum, 2011), pp. 135–51.

Kazdin, Cole, 'Remember "Terror Sex"?', *Salon*, 21 September 2002 <https://www.salon.com/2002/09/11/terror_2_2> [accessed 31 August 2023].

Keeble, Arin, *The 9/11 Novel: Trauma, Politics and Identity* (Jefferson, NC: McFarland, 2014).

Kennedy, Liam, and Stephen Shapiro (eds), *Neoliberalism and Contemporary American Literature* (Hanover, NH: Dartmouth College Press, 2019).

Kirn, Walter, '"Extremely Loud and Incredibly Close": Everything Is Included', *New York Times*, 3 April 2005 <https://www.nytimes.com/2005/04/03/books/review/extremely-loud-and-incredibly-close-everything-is-included.html> [accessed 31 August 2023].

Klein, Naomi, *The Shock Doctrine: The Rise of Disaster Capitalism* (London: Allen Lane, 2007).

Knight, Peter, 'Outrageous Conspiracy Theories: Popular and Official Responses to 9/11 in Germany and the United States', *New German Critique*, 35.3 (2008), 156–93.

Kumar, Deepa, *Islamophobia and the Politics of Empire: Twenty Years After 9/11* (London: Verso, 2020).

Lean, Nathan, *The Islamophobia Industry* (London: Pluto, 2012).

Lorentzen, Christian, 'Shave for Them', *London Review of Books*, 33.18, 22 September 2011 <https://www.lrb.co.uk/the-paper/v33/n18/christian-lorentzen/shave-for-them> [accessed 31 August 2023].

McCann, Sean, *Gumshoe America: Hard-Boiled Crime Fiction and the Rise and Fall of New Deal Liberalism* (Durham, NC: Duke University Press, 2000).

McInerney, Jay, 'Author Q and A', Penguin Random House, n.d. <https://www.penguinrandomhouse.com/books/111755/the-good-life-by-jay-mcinerney/> [accessed 31 August 2023].

McInerney, Jay, *The Good Life* (London: Penguin, 2005).

Melamed, Jodi, *Represent and Destroy: Rationalizing Violence in the New Racial Capitalism* (Minneapolis: University of Minnesota Press, 2011).

Melley, Timothy, 'War on Terror', in *American Literature in Transition: 2000–2010*, ed. by Rachel Greenwald Smith (Cambridge: Cambridge University Press, 2018), pp. 275–90.

Merivale, Patricia, 'Postmodern and Metaphysical Detection', in *A Companion to Crime Fiction*, ed. by Charles Rzepka and Lee Horsley (Chichester: Wiley, 2010), pp. 308–20.

Millard, Kenneth, *Contemporary American Fiction* (Oxford: Oxford University Press, 2000).

Miller, Kristine, 'Breaking the Frame: Amy Waldman's *The Submission* and 9/11 Memorials', *Journal of American Studies*, 54.1 (2020), 212–40.

Mirowski, Philip, *Never Let a Serious Crisis Go to Waste: How Neoliberalism Survived the Financial Meltdown* (London: Verso, 2014).

Mishra, Pankaj, 'The End of Innocence', *The Guardian*, Saturday Review, 19 May 2007, pp. 4–6.

Morey, Peter, and Amina Yaqin, *Framing Muslims: Stereotyping and Representation After 9/11* (Cambridge, MA: Harvard University Press, 2011).

Morley, Catherine, 'The Architecture of Memory and Memorialisation in Amy Waldman's *The Submission*', in *9/11: Topics in Contemporary Literature* (London: Bloomsbury, 2016), pp. 185–200.

Morley, Catherine, '"How do we write about this?": The Domestic and the Glocal in the Post-9/11 Novel', *Journal of American Studies*, 45.4 (2011), 717–31.

New York University Press, 'Description', web page for *110 Stories: New York Writes after September 11*, ed. by Ulrich Baer <https://nyupress.org/9780814799352/110-stories/> [accessed 5 October 2023].

O'Brien, Sarah, *Trauma and Fictions of the War on Terror* (New York: Routledge, 2021).

O'Gorman, Daniel, and Robert Eaglestone, 'Introduction', in *The Routledge Companion to Twenty-First Century Literary Fiction*, ed. by Daniel O'Gorman and Robert Eaglestone (Abingdon: Routledge, 2019), pp. 1–10.

O'Neill, Joseph, *Netherland* (London: Fourth Estate, 2008).

Pease, Donald E., 'The Uncanny Re-worlding of the Post-9/11 American Novel, Joseph O'Neill's *Netherland*; or, The Cultural Fantasy Work of Neoliberalism', in *Neoliberalism and Contemporary American Literature*, ed. by Liam Kennedy and Stephen Shapiro (Hanover, NH: Dartmouth College Press, 2019), pp. 136–40.

Potter, Charlie Lee, *Writing the 9/11 Decade* (London: Bloomsbury, 2016).

Pynchon, Thomas, *Bleeding Edge* (London: Penguin, 2013).

Pynchon, Thomas, *Vineland* (Boston: Little, Brown, 1990).

Rosenblatt, Roger, 'The Age of Irony Comes to an End', *Time*, 24 September 2001 <https://content.time.com/time/subscriber/article/0,33 009,1000893,00.html> [accessed 5 September 2023].

Rothberg, Michael, *The Implicated Subject: Beyond Victims and Perpetrators* (Stanford, CA: Stanford University Press, 2020).

Rothberg, Michael, *Multidirectional Memory: Remembering the Holocaust in the Age of Decolonization* (Stanford, CA: Stanford University Press, 2009).

Safran Foer, Jonathan, *Extremely Loud and Incredibly Close* (London: Penguin, 2005).

Schwartz, Lynne Sharon, *The Writing on the Wall* (New York: Counterpoint, 2005).

Scott, Janny, 'Introduction', in *Portraits 9/11/01: The Collected Portraits of Grief* (New York: Times Books, 2002), p. ix.

Shamsie, Kamila, 'The Submission by Amy Waldman – Review', *The Guardian*, 24 August 2011 <https://www.theguardian.com/books/2011/aug/24/the-submission-amy-waldman-review> [accessed 31 August 2023].

Shostak, Deborah, 'Prosthetic Fictions: Reading Jonathan Safran Foer's *Extremely Loud and Incredibly Close* through Philip Roth's *The Plot Against America*', in *9/11: Topics in Contemporary North American Literature*, ed. by Catherine Morley (London: Bloomsbury, 2016), pp. 21–40.

Simpson, David, *9/11: The Culture of Commemoration* (Chicago: Chicago University Press, 2006).

Simpson, David, 'Telling It Like It Isn't', in *Literature After 9/11*, ed. by Ann Keniston and Jeanne Follansbee Quinn (London: Routledge, 2007), pp. 209–23.

Slobodian, Quinn, *Globalists: The End of Empire and the Birth of Neoliberalism* (Cambridge, MA: Harvard University Press, 2018).

Smith, Zadie, 'Two Paths for the Novel', *New York Review of Books*, 55.18 (20 November 2008), 34–9; repr. as 'Two Directions for the Novel', in *Changing My Mind: Occasional Essays* (London: Penguin, 2009), pp. 71–96.

Strong, Benjamin, 'Last Night: Review of *The Good Life* by Jay McInerney', *Village Voice*, 24 January 2006 <https://www.villagevoice.com/last-night/> [accessed 5 October 2023].

Sykes, Rachel, '"All that howling space": "9/11" and the Aesthetic of Noise in Contemporary American Fiction', *C21 Literature*, 4.1 (2016) <http://doi.org/10.16995/c21.2>.

Updike, John, Jonathan Franzen, Denis Johnson, Roger Angell, Aharon Appelfeld, Rebecca Mead, Susan Sontag, Amitav Ghosh and Donald Antrim, 'The Talk of Town: Tuesday, and After', *The New Yorker*, 16 September 2001 <https://www.newyorker.com/magazine/2001/09/24/tuesday-and-after-talk-of-the-town> [accessed 31 August 2023].

Uytterschout, Sien, and Kristiaan Versluys, 'Desperate Domesticity? Translocating the Political into the Personal in Lynne Sharon Schwartz's *The Writing on the Wall* and Paul Auster's *Man in the Dark*', in *9/11: Topics in Contemporary North American Literature*, ed. by Catherine Morley (London: Bloomsbury, 2016), pp. 125–46.

Versluys, Kristiaan, *Out of the Blue: September 11 and the Novel* (New York: Columbia University Press, 2009).

Walter, Jess, *The Zero* (London: Harper Perennial, 2007).

Wasserman, Sarah, 'Looking Away from 9/11: The Optics of Joseph O'Neill's *Netherland*', *Contemporary Literature*, 55.2 (2014), 249–69.

Waugh, Patricia, *Metafiction: The Theory and Practice of Self-Conscious Fiction* (New York: Routledge, 1984).

Whitehead, Anne, *Trauma Fiction* (Edinburgh: Edinburgh University Press, 2004).

Chapter 2

Writing the 'Clash of Civilizations': Racism, Difference and Terrorism

The Exceptionalisation of 9/11 and the 'Clash of Civilizations'

If the response to 9/11 by America and its allies was, as Richard Jackson has noted, characterised by 'counterproductive overreaction', then a key component of this was the popularisation of Samuel P. Huntington's 'clash of civilizations' thesis (4). The exceptionalisation of 9/11 may have roots in pre-existing forms of American exceptionalism, but it was driven by, and has been sustained by, this formulation or versions of it, like 'Islam versus the West'.[1] As Donald E. Pease has noted, the 9/11 attacks 'supplied the state with a traumatizing event out of which it constructed a spectacle that accomplished several interrelated aims', which for Pease included supplanting the Cold War with the 'war on terror' and the identification of an 'internal enemy' that could 'reinstate the dynamic structure of American exceptionalism as a collectively shared state fantasy' (154). The supposed clash of civilisations was certainly the foundational rhetorical tool and ideological basis of the war on terror, and though it is a crass abstraction at best, its widespread appeal should be understood in relation to the pervasive uncertainty and fear of the time. David Holloway notes in *9/11 and the War on Terror* (2008) that, with 'so many overlapping and unstable factors in play, an abstraction like "clash of civilizations" was attractive because, like all sound bites, it reduced complex and opaque historical forces to a more manageable form' (11). This said, it should also be noted that the 'clash of civilizations' belongs to a tradition of Orientalist and Islamophobic writing that pre-dates 9/11. Huntington originally published 'The Clash of

Civilizations?' in *Foreign Affairs* in 1993, before developing it into a book, with the full title, *The Clash of Civilizations and the Remaking of World Order*, released in 1997; an updated version was rushed in to print in the aftermath of the attacks in 2002. As Holloway notes, after 9/11 Huntington's arguments, previously the topic of academic debate, 'went mainstream' and were frequently reduced to their most base tenets (8). But even in context, Huntington's claims are homogenising and reductive. He defines civilisation as 'culture writ large' and notes that '[o]f all the objective elements which define civilizations . . . the most important usually is religion' (41, 42). Some passages are unambiguously inflammatory, and at one point he contends that 'the underlying problem for the West is not Islamic fundamentalism. It is Islam itself, a different civilization whose people are convinced of the superiority of their culture and are obsessed with the inferiority of their power' (209). Edward Said, long-time critic of Islamophobic rhetoric, noted the danger of the post-9/11 popularisation of the clash of civilisations rhetoric right away and published an article in the *Guardian* just five days after the attacks called 'Islam and the West are Inadequate Banners' (2001). Unfortunately, the force of this rhetoric was seismic, and it became a central part of the exceptionalisation of 9/11 and was perennially linked to that 'event' in its aftermath. It was at the heart of the Manichean rhetoric of 'us against them' or what then President Bush described as a 'monumental struggle of good versus evil' (n.p.).

Whether expressed as 'us against them', 'good versus evil', 'Islam and the West' or the 'clash of civilizations', this rhetoric was profoundly Islamophobic and there was a perceptible shift in the global landscapes of intolerance after the attacks. In America, as Lenore Bell has noted, 'the sudden introduction of a new and menacing "other"' meant that the 'hierarchy of racial stereotypes was shaken in some unpredictable ways' (13). Indeed, just as the clash of civilisations was always an abstraction, the racism it created was based on crude stereotypes – particularly in the Western media where, as Peter Morey and Amina Yaqin have noted, 'Muslims see themselves constantly portrayed as having some indefinable propensity to barbarism' (31). Drawing from Said's *Covering Islam* (1981), and echoing Morey and Yaqin's emphasis on 'framing', Deepa Kumar has identified six Islamophobic 'frames' in which Muslims have often been understood by 'dominant definers' before and, with particular force, after 9/11: Islam as a 'monolithic religion', 'inherently violent', 'uniquely sexist' to the extent that 'Muslim women need to be liberated by the West', 'anti-modern' and unable to separate politics and religion, and 'incapable of democratic self-rule' (70–1). Media stereotyping is just one tenet of post-9/11 Islamophobia, but it is a potent one – which literary texts might be expected to respond to or challenge via 'counter-narratives' of depth or nuance with human stories that cut through crass stereotypes.[2]

In addition to – and as part of – its Islamophobic dimensions, clash of civilisations-driven foreign and domestic policies in America, after 9/11, enacted a shift towards what Brian Massumi has defined as the 'logic of preemption'. This shift has had a 'proliferative effect', creating ceaseless cycles of violent conflict (15). As Massumi shows, the Bush administration responded to what they perceived as an 'unknowable' enemy, and to what Donald Rumsfeld famously characterised as 'unknown unknowns', through pre-emptive strategies that quickly became normative. Crucially, these strategies were 'incitatory' and produced new vectors of conflict and violence:

> you go on the offensive to make the enemy emerge from its state of potential and take actual shape. The exercise of your power is *incitatory*. It contributes to the actual emergence of the threat. In other words, since the threat is proliferative in any case, your best option is to help *make it proliferate more* – that is (hopefully) more on your own terms. The most effective way to fight an unspecified threat is to actively contribute to producing it. (12)

This is a damning diagnosis, and in its interpretation of state violence as 'incitatory', it identifies this state violence as state terrorism, in its emphasis on its rhetorical or symbolic dimensions.[3] Additionally, there is an echo here of a phenomenon identified by Morey and Yaqin, in *Framing Muslims: Stereotyping and Representation After 9/11*, in their discussion of 'dialogic stereotyping', where 'particular embattled and defensive types of group identity emerge' through constant exposure to 'vilification' and negative stereotypes (31). In the aftermath of 9/11, the clash of civilisations rhetoric drove both pre-emptive state terrorism and astonishingly pervasive patterns of media stereotyping with grave consequences.

Yet, it remains important to recognise the deeper histories of clash of civilisations logic, as well as its post-9/11 surge. This is especially true considering the ways that the notion of 9/11 as a world-changing event served certain ideological imperatives. As Holloway has noted, 'the pre-9/11 and post-9/11 worlds were broadly continuous not discontinuous, however much it suited politicians to claim that the attack came out of the blue' (3–4). Echoing this, Ronak Kapadia positions 'the post-9/11 moment not as a radical historical or political rupture, but rather as a continuation of a longer history of US imperialism that has been erased or evaded' (36). It is certainly imperative to keep sight of these continuities, even as we track the consequences of the post-9/11 popularisation of this term, as there is a risk of inadvertently contributing to the exceptionalisation of 9/11, even as one wishes to critique it. Indeed, one strand of my argument here is that the fiction that has critiqued clash of civilisations rhetoric has consistently done this by tracing its deeper histories.

This chapter functions in close conversation with the previous chapter, in that it discusses the ways five novels have grappled with the post-9/11 discourse of this alleged clash of civilisations – a notion emanating largely from America, but quickly becoming globally influential. The novels I analyse here, to varying degrees, challenge this formation – which as I have suggested is closely linked to the exceptionalisation of 9/11 – and begin to decentre this 'defining moment'. As such this chapter begins to move away from the America-centric shape of the previous chapter. I begin in the first section with two further '9/11 novels', Mohsin Hamid's *The Reluctant Fundamentalist* (2007), described by Ambreen Hai as a 'Pakistani postcolonial novel that explicitly makes 9/11 its center-point' (435), and Porochista Khakpour's *Sons and Other Flammable Objects* (2007), a 'clash of generations' story of an Iranian family that flee Tehran to a Los Angeles suburb in the late 1970s, which also centres 9/11. Both novels fit into the 9/11 novel genre in that relationship or family narratives are central and that these domestic formations are used to register the shock of the attacks. Like Amy Waldman's *The Submission* (2011) – analysed in my previous chapter – these novels also depict post-9/11 racism and xenophobia, though they do so with more historical depth and international context, and in ways that destabilise the normative whiteness of the genre. Following this, I look at two novels that seek to understand the inner world of the Islamic terrorist 'other' in the decade following 9/11. I discuss Yasmina Khadra's *The Attack* (2005) and *The Sirens of Baghdad* (2006), which offer inverted perspectives of suicide terrorism: the former depicts the traumatic aftermath of a suicide attack in Tel Aviv and the latter depicts the radicalisation of a young man in Iraq, plotting an attack 'a thousand times more awesome than the attacks of September 11' (11). Though very different, both novels seek to understand the rationale or motivations of the terrorist. In this sense, they are usefully compared with John Updike's 2006 novel *Terrorist*, which also focuses on radicalisation, and the 'Hammad' strand of Don DeLillo's *Falling Man* (2007). I conclude this chapter with a lengthy analysis of Nadeem Aslam's multigenerational novel *The Blind Man's Garden* (2013), which, I argue, powerfully critiques clash of civilisations logic by staging and re-staging various forms of impasse, or clashes, while simultaneously setting up a set of doubles. *The Blind Man's Garden*, I argue, is a complex depiction of post-9/11 state violence – as well as various forms of counter-violence – that can and should be read as a forceful critique of the normative discourse of the war on terror.

Peter Boxall argues that 'an attempt to enter the head of the other' has 'been one of the central tasks of the 9/11 novel' (128). Though the merits of Boxall's analyses of fiction after 9/11 are many, this is not strictly true. None of *Extremely Loud and Incredibly Close*, *Windows on the World*, *The Emperor's Children*, *The Zero*, *The Good Life*, *The Writing on the Wall* or *Bleeding Edge* engages with the inner worlds of the (so often conflated) Islamic or terrorist other. *Falling Man* does include the brief sections focalised by 'Hammad' and *Netherland* deals centrally with some forms of difference, but neither of these novels meaningfully 'enter[s] the head of the other'. The texts under discussion in this chapter – *The Reluctant Fundamentalist*, *Sons and Other Flammable Objects*, *The Attack*, *The Sirens of Baghdad* and *The Blind Man's Garden* – do this, in different ways, and with varying degrees of efficacy. They also track and respond to developments in clash of civilisations discourse that occurred over the course of the 'Bush decade', as the popularity of war on terror policies waned, strategies changed and, eventually, regime change occurred with the election of Barack Obama in 2008. In President Obama's famous speech in Cairo, the next year – 'A New Beginning' – he outlined a new approach to the relationship between the United States and the Muslim world. Despite President Obama's rhetoric here, we can now consider the Obama era as characterised by a specific form of state terrorism – the drone programme – but, as Kumar notes, it also was driven by an emphasis on markets, job growth and diplomacy. Kumar describes it as a shift to 'liberal imperialism and liberal Islamophobia', noting that 'the key characteristics of liberal Islamophobia in the Obama era were the rejection of the "clash of civilizations" thesis, the elevation of "good Muslims" both domestically and internationally, and a concomitant willingness to work with "moderate" (or Pro-American) Islamists' (137). Arun Kundnani also sees continuity in the post-Bush years, noting that while

Obama was elected on a wave of opposition to Bush's war on terror he then failed to take the US in a fundamentally different direction; the administration thereby effectively neutered any remaining opposition and made permanent what had been a 'state of emergency.' (6)

Certainly, domestic events such as the Park51 furore, discussed in the previous chapter, indicate that visceral forms of Islamophobia remained prevalent in America, while the proliferation of the drone programme meant that the emphasis shifted from one form of state terrorism (torture) to another (drone strikes).

The Reluctant Fundamentalist and Sons and Other Flammable Objects

I begin with analysis of two texts that have had very different levels of scholarly response. *The Reluctant Fundamentalist* (2007) – Mohsin Hamid's second novel, following *Moth Smoke* (2000) – was an immediate critical hit and has become the subject of dozens of journal articles and book chapters. It is not an exaggeration to say it is one of the most taught and studied English language novels of the early twenty-first century. It is short, propulsive and accessible but endlessly rich in the questions it poses and symbolic gestures it makes. Porochista Khakpour's *Sons and Other Flammable Objects*, published in the same year, also had favourable critical responses but has had little scholarly attention. It is more than twice the length of Hamid's novel, and while both are immigration narratives, and 'domestic' 9/11 novels, *Sons* is formally very different: irreverent, darkly comic, and partly a revisionary rewriting of Sadegh Hedayat's *The Blind Owl* (1936), replete with lengthy digressions. Though it has some idiosyncratic features, it is difficult to understand the lack of attention to such an evocative debut novel, and this is something I seek to address. I read these works together, as novels of the Bush decade and war on terror era, which centre the subject position of the suspicious 'other' and forcefully address the ways clash of civilisations logic functioned before and after 9/11. I argue that both novels critique this logic by introducing historical contexts and through formal moves that reject the kinds of narrative logic that had quickly come to accommodate and perpetuate it. Here, I offer a new consideration of national allegory in *The Reluctant Fundamentalist*, a feature of the novel that has been frequently seen as purposefully 'overdetermined' (Morey 140; Ilott 581). I consider the novel's vectors of allegory together and in relation to what Hai has described as its 'dangerous ambiguities', and I argue that the allegorical strands of the novel should be understood in relation to these 'ambiguities' (436). Where Hamid's novel immediately engages clash of civilisations logic by staging the narrative as a fraught conversation between a Pakistani and an American man, *Sons* centres the experience of an Iranian family who had fled the Islamic Revolution of 1979 and thus features two moments of seismic rupture. Additionally, in Khakpour's novel, any clash of civilisations is supplanted – in often suggestive ways – by its central focus on a clash of immigrant *generations*.

Much of the richness of *The Reluctant Fundamentalist* derives from tensions between form and content. The story centres on protagonist Changez's youthful immersion in the American Dream and subsequent post-9/11 disenchantment, and as such it in some ways reinforces notions of a precipitous deepening of divisions. Certainly, as the novel nears its conclusion, Changez's position on America's response to the attacks is forceful, and unambiguously combative:

> As a society, you were unwilling to reflect upon the shared pain that united you with those who attacked you. You retreated into myths of your own difference, assumptions of your own superiority. And you acted out these beliefs on the stage of the world, so that the entire planet was rocked by the repercussions of your tantrums, not least my family, now facing war thousands of miles away. Such an America had to be stopped in the interest not only of the rest of humanity, but also in your own. (168)

However, its formal gestures problematise this Manichean logic and hold it up to sustained scrutiny. As Peter Morey argues, its structuring devices amount to a kind of 'deterritorialization of literature which forces readers to think about what lies behind the totalizing categories of East and West, "Them and Us" and so on – those categories continuously insisted upon in "war on terror" discourse' (138). Before analysing this friction between form and content, it is necessary to outline the range of meanings opened by a seemingly uncomplicated story and central narrative device.

The novel is narrated by Changez from a café in Old Anarkali in Lahore, over the course of one evening. It is a dramatic monologue partly in second-person address: Changez tells his story of immigration to America and eventual return to Pakistan, to an unnamed American interlocutor – a 'you' that inevitably, also, interpellates the reader. Though this person does not have any dialogue, Changez frequently registers his demeanour, reactions and comments – which mostly seem to be expressions of unease – over the course of his narrative; at one point Changez notes his bemusement at the man's feeling that the bats flying above the square are 'creepy', a 'delightfully American expression' (62). In any case, it is suggested he is a government agent tracking the narrator, on account of his ostensible, post-9/11 radicalisation. Changez tells this man of his four and a half years in New York, which included an elite education at Princeton, employment at a 'boutique' NYC valuation firm called Underwood Samson upon graduating in 2001, early professional successes, and subsequent post-9/11 experiences of vilification, abuse, heartache and disenchantment (5). A critical part of the story of Changez's immersion in and alienation from America is Erica, whom he meets on a post-graduation holiday, around the same time he is hired by Underwood Samson. He falls in love with Erica, an aspiring novelist and fellow Princetonian, who is dealing with the loss of her boyfriend, Chris, who had died the previous year.

The shape of the story and key formal features come immediately into view. Changez's love of America aligns with his love for Erica, and the narrative of their relationship in some ways maps onto Changez's relationship with his adopted country. This enacts a national allegory that is potent in relation to Erica's post-9/11 decline where she is gripped by a force 'that pulled her within herself' (86). Changez's employer, Underwood Samson, also represents the United States beyond the shared initials (U.S.). This is clear when we are introduced to a corporate value system based on 'meritocracy', 'rankings' and 'efficiency': 'maximum return was the maxim to which we returned, time and again' (37, 38). The company mantra is to '*focus on the fundamentals*', a 'guiding principle' that 'mandated a single-minded attention to financial detail', and it becomes clear that the titular fundamentalism of the novel is not Islamism but neoliberalism (98). Ultimately, as Boxall has noted, the novel 'stages a highly performed and hostile discussion between Pakistan and America' (133), but the shifts between Erica as America and Underwood Samson as the United States, and the ambiguities and misdirections of Changez's dramatic monologue, means it is a multidimensional – if imprecise – allegory.

I will return to this allegory, but there are further formal devices at work in the novel that are important in determining meaning. For instance, it can be read within a tradition of immigration narratives, relationship melodramas, and as a thriller. The generic fluidity of the novel reinforces the unreliability of the narrator, and the thriller frame particularly, as Hai notes, 'predisposes readers towards suspicion' (450). Because of the ambiguities around the addressee's identity and narrator's potential radicalisation, and how their fraught exchange might conclude, suspense builds. As Sarah Ilott observes, 'an overly attentive waiter, the coming of darkness and a mysterious contact who repeatedly texts the American all seem to close in', and a 'language of violence and predation intensifies the sense of unease, with seemingly offhand comments that appear to stand as precursors of what is to follow' (577). Morey, also noting these suspense-creating features, reads the novel as a 'hoax confessional' that responds to a popular genre of war on terror nonfiction, and 'parodies the cultural certainties encouraged by those "true confessions" of former radicals' (136). More importantly, Morey argues, this 'hoax confessional' functions by 'destabilizing the reader's identification through hyperbole, strategic exoticization, allegorical layering and unreliable narration, but also defamiliarizes our relation to literary projects of national identification, forcing us to be the kind of deterritorialized reader demanded by the emerging category of world literature' (136). The genre coding of the novel can certainly be understood as one of the ways it is in tension with the notion of a deepening of division or impasse between East and West, but of equal importance is narrative positionality.

The novel explores positionality at both a formal level and diegetically, as Changez attempts to occupy different subject positions or to adopt identities that are projected onto him. This builds from the novel's first lines, which invite reflection on the reader's own position, via the second-person address and opening question: 'Excuse me, sir, but may I be of assistance? Ah, I see I have alarmed you. Do not be frightened by my beard: I am a lover of America' (1). A few lines later, Changez asks, 'How did I know you were American?' (1). Though the second-person addressee is identified very specifically as an American man, who seems to Changez to be 'on a *mission*', this is also an address to the reader (1). Moreover, as Boxall has noted, 'this interpellation of the reader has an unsettling effect, whereby one becomes peculiarly conscious of one's own skin, one's own clothes, one's bearing, one's nationality' – all things that Changez comments on at various points (133). Boxall argues that the effect of this is 'extraordinarily violent', and a kind of 'assault' in the assumption that 'any member of the global reading public can answer to the call of American citizenship' (133). It soon becomes clear that this unsettling effect is a key element of the novel's social critique, as it also demands reflection on the part of the reader, on the assumptions made about identity and about how assumptions and stereotypes are projected. As Ilott notes, this 'uncomfortable elision of the reader with the American auditor should heighten readers' critical faculties to resist groupings based solely on constructed geopolitical binaries' (581). This elision might also connect to the diegetic instances when identities and narratives are thrust onto him – for instance by his colleague Jim who imagines a class-based affinity between he and Changez, or more potently when Changez assumes the identity of Erica's deceased boyfriend, Chris, a scene I will discuss shortly. But Ilott's argument that this device imbues the reader with a kind of agency, inviting 'active' critique and judgement is persuasive, and illuminates critical dimensions of the novel that cut through binary logics: 'critical onus is placed upon the reader actively to make sense of events and arrive at his/her own conclusions' (572). For Ilott, this gesture also invites the reader to reflect on their own political passivity as it 'not only deconstructs a geographical perpetrator/victim binary that has arisen in the wake of 9/11, but also allows for agency on the part of the reader, thereby challenging a positioning of citizens as passive and unable to effect change' (572). Ultimately, this argument hinges on the unreliability of Changez as a narrator and on the allegorical dimensions of the novel, understood to be deliberately crude and mobilised through 'grossly overdetermined characters' – features that are, in this reading linked. While I agree with Boxall's observations about reader interpellation and Ilott's argument about the creation of an 'active reader', I want to revisit the novel's central allegories, which in my reading remain rich and compelling read together, even if they are individually overdetermined and contingent on Changez's unreliability. I argue here that they are critically important in mitigating some of the narrative's ambiguities that might even, as Hai has noted, reinforce Islamophobic forms of suspicion.

As a novel that constructs a 'first world' national allegory of America via a Pakistani narrator (reversing prevalent positional logic), there is an implicit anti-colonial dimension to the novel. This implicit critique of American empire gains force late on when Changez arrives at the self-realisation that his work in the financial sector with Underwood Samson makes him a 'modern-day janissary' (152). The first world national allegory, however, should first be read in relation to the passage from Fredric Jameson's well-known *Social Text* essay, 'Third-World Literature in the Era of Multinational Capitalism', which famously theorised postcolonial literature as necessarily allegorical:

> Third-world texts, even those which are seemingly private and invested with a properly libidinal dynamic – necessarily project a political dimension in the form of national allegory: *the story of the private individual destiny is always an allegory of the embattled situation of the public third-world culture and society.* (69)

This notion has been robustly critiqued over the years, not least in Aijaz Ahmad's rejoinder, 'Jameson's Rhetoric of Otherness and the "National Allegory"', which critiques the 'binary opposition of what Jameson calls the first and third worlds' and rhetorical moves identified as homogenising and Orientalist. However, Imre Szeman's 2001 recuperation of Jameson's essay, 'Who's Afraid of National Allegory?', points out that Jameson's statements about first world national allegory are often overlooked. Szeman highlights Jameson's statement that 'in the West, conventionally, political commitment is recontained and psychologized or subjectivized by way of the public-private split' (807). Szeman elaborates:

> Jameson believes that in the West, the consequence of the radical separation between the public and the private, 'between the poetic and the political,' is 'the deep cultural conviction that the lived experience of our private existence is somehow incommensurable with the abstractions of economic science and political dynamics.' In terms of literary production, this 'cultural conviction' has the effect of limiting or even negating entirely the political work of literature: in the first world, literature is a matter of the private rather than the public sphere, a matter of individual tastes and solitary meditations rather than public debate and deliberation. (807)

This too is a reductive formulation in that just as 'third world' literature is understood as inevitably allegorical, first world literature is seen as incapable of national allegory or bridging this 'public-private split'. This said, the notion that Western literature is predominantly 'a matter of individual tastes and solitary meditations' certainly resonates with some of the early 9/11 novels discussed in the previous chapter. Here, though, I want to argue that in *The Reluctant Fundamentalist*, the immigrant narrator tells the story of his relationship with an allegorical woman – a first world national allegory that reverses Jameson's logic – and that the 'public-private split' is bridged.

The central allegorical strand of Hamid's novel begins with Changez's relationship with Erica. In his often-cited *Guardian* review, James Lasdun also factored in Erica's recently deceased boyfriend, Chris, in the allegory: 'Erica is America ... and Chris's name has been chosen to represent that nation's fraught moment of European discovery and conquest, while the narrator himself stands for the country's consequent inability to accept, uh, changez' (n.p.). Lasdun's glib comment about Changez presaged the arguments made by Morey and Illot about the deliberate conspicuousness of the novel's allegorical dimensions; but the reading of Chris – whom Morey reads as 'Chris(t)' (140) – also reinforces the richness of this allegory. As an allegorical love triangle, there are intertextual echoes of Graham Greene's allegorical novel of colonial conflict and American intervention in Vietnam, *The Quiet American* (1955) – also discussed in the previous chapter in relation to *Bleeding Edge* (2013) – where a perniciously idealistic American agent and a cynical British reporter vie for an objectified and exoticised Vietnamese woman. The interpretative possibilities introduced by Chris begin to enrich the obvious symbolic dimensions of Erica who is clearly, as Anna Hartnell has noted, a 'personification of American nationalism' that motors the novel's 'compelling exploration of the narrative of American innocence' (346). Erica's turn inwards after 9/11 suggests nationalism or isolationism, as does her nostalgic drift into the past. While Lasdun's reading of Chris smartly hints at the novel's critique of American empire – something I will return to – we might also note the significance of the way Erica's personal loss is compounded by public crisis and tragedy. This is a phenomenon that has been theorised by Irene Kacandes, in her essay '9/11/01 = 1/27/01: The Changed Posttraumatic Self' (2003). Kacandes describes the post-9/11 resurgence of trauma and grief over the personal loss of a loved one, who had died in a violent homicide earlier in 2001. In a passage that is cannily similar to many descriptions of Erica, she notes that her experience of the attacks 'was determined by events that had taken place months earlier' (68).

The allegorical function of Erica becomes evocative through this aggregation of traumas in the surface story. It evokes some of the less-discussed nuances of the social and political climate in America after 9/11 and makes a pointed critique by suggesting that pre-existing, unresolved issues affected America's response to the attacks. This means that as Erica experiences the overlapping of traumas personal and public, her allegorical story neatly engages with the imperative to understand 9/11 in context. Moreover, as she retreats into herself, her entangled traumas relate to other strands of the story. Internationally, the launch of the war on terror and bombing of Afghanistan are watched on television by Changez, and a vicious and rampant xenophobia and nationalism rises to the surface in

New York, affecting him everywhere. Symbols of patriotism and nationalism are ubiquitous: 'flags stuck on toothpicks featured in the shrines; stickers of flags adorned windshields and windows; large flags fluttered from buildings' (79). Changez tries and struggles to understand Erica's decline and simultaneously the changes to his adopted country – in both cases considering whether these are sudden shifts or a surfacing of latent but long-standing issues:

> I never came to know what triggered her decline – was it the trauma of the attack on her city? The act of sending out her book in search of publication? The echoes raised in her by our lovemaking? But I think I knew even that that she was disappearing into a powerful nostalgia. (113)

Changez's attempts to come to terms with Erica's decline are important as the change in Erica mirrors the change in the nation and is closely linked to his own disillusionment. In an interview, Hamid described his protagonist as 'somebody who desperately wanted to succeed in loving the United States but failed to do so', and Erica's decline sheds some light on the national changes that incite his disillusionment (Yaqin 47).

Changez's lingering concerns over his and Erica's 'lovemaking' are important as his descriptions of their sexual encounter are rich with figurative language. After a steadily increasing friendship that is unable to blossom into romance, largely due to Erica's grieving over Chris, Changez and Erica attempt to have sex, just after 9/11. The experience is awkward, and physical intimacy eludes them:

> Mainly she was silent and unmoving, but such was my desire that I overlooked the growing wound this inflicted on my pride and continued. I found it difficult to enter her; it was though she was not aroused. She said nothing while I was inside her, but I could see her discomfort, and so I forced myself to stop. (89–90)

This is, as Hai asserts, an unsettling scene in that there is 'no partnership, no mutuality' (451). After stopping, Changez and Erica speak, and Erica reveals that thoughts of Chris had inhibited her. A few weeks later, though, as they sit speaking of Chris, Erica enters a heightened state of emotion, and Changez suggests that she pretend that he is Chris, and this suggestion leads to physically successful intercourse:

> It was as though we were under a spell, transported to a world where I was Chris and she was with Chris, and we made love with

a physical intimacy that Erica and I had never enjoyed. Her body denied mine no longer; I watched her shut her eyes, and her shut eyes watched him. (105)

These episodes, read together, are highly symbolic and the disturbing language used to describe the sex scene might be understood as an instance where the human surface story is harshly rendered via figurative language. Allegorically, Changez and Erica's initial inability to engage in physical intimacy represents Erica's or 'AmErica's' inability to embrace the perceived 'other'. Indeed, the language of their first attempt at sex might be widely applicable to the immigrant experience. As disturbing as phrases like 'I found it difficult to enter her' or 'she said nothing while I was inside her, but I could see her discomfort' are, in literal terms, they are allegorically suggestive, particularly given the backdrop of rapidly escalating racial tension. Even more potently, the fact that the couple experiences sexual intimacy only by eschewing the realities of their racial/national differences, and imagining they are a white American couple, is indicative of the fallacy of America's 'E pluribus unum', melting-pot claims. After sex, Changez experiences deeply conflicted emotions. He is both exhilarated and ashamed and has difficulty processing the experience. Ultimately, he feels a sense of degradation: 'perhaps by taking on the persona of another, I had diminished myself in my own eyes; perhaps I was humiliated by the continuing dominance in the strange romantic triangle of which I found myself a part' (105).

Changez and Erica's relationship suffers after the attacks, deteriorating with Erica's turn inwards: 'She was struggling with a current that pulled her within herself, and her smile contained the fear that she might slip into her own depths, where she would be trapped, unable to breathe' (86). This is explicitly connected to America's condition, and Changez observes that

> America, too, was increasingly giving itself over to a dangerous nostalgia at that time. There was something undeniably retro about the flags and uniforms, about generals addressing cameras in war rooms and newspaper headlines featuring such words as duty and honor. (115)

Erica's inwards turn, while at odds with this exuberant, flag-waving patriotism, clearly reflects the dangerous side of national nostalgia, and these scenes evoke James Der Derian's description of the 'sepia tones' of American public memory at the time (n.p.).

Though I argue that the first world national allegory in *The Reluctant Fundamentalist* is rich despite its conspicuousness, I agree it engenders active reading. Ilott argues that 'what is most interesting about the mirroring of Changez's relationships with Erica and America . . . is not their clever doubling, but the fact that the reader has to do so little work to make the connection' (577). Ilott reads this as an indication of 'the inadequacy of national allegory and the potential damage that allowing one person to stand in for a nation can do' (577). Here we might consider two things. First, the way Erica's pre-existing trauma allegorically demands that 9/11 be understood on a historical continuum where previous events interact with it is potent and useful. Second, Erica as America should be understood alongside Underwood Samson as the United States – neither is precise (as allegory never is) but both are evocative and together a potent, multivalent critique emerges that might not have been possible without the 'buffer' provided by allegory.

The image of isolationism, nostalgia and nationalism that emerges through Erica is complemented by the neoliberal fundamentalism of Underwood Samson, and they converge powerfully in a critique of American empire. Indeed, Changez's disillusionment reaches a nadir during a business trip to Valparaiso when he has an epiphany about what his work for Underwood Samson means in the context of history and empire. He concludes that he is a 'modern-day janissary, a servant of the American empire at a time when it was invading a country with a kinship to my own and was perhaps even colluding to ensure that my own country faced the threat of war' (152). The significance of Underwood Samson as representing the United States is vivid here: 'I had thrown in my lot with the men of Underwood Samson, with the officers of the empire, when all along I was predisposed to feel compassion for those . . . whose lives the empire thought nothing of overturning for its own gain' (152). Here, Changez monologues about his realisation that he had – eagerly rather than 'reluctantly' – embraced one of America's most virulent strains of fundamentalism: economic. This ironising of the novel's title is one of its several acts of reversal and has particular resonance alongside its reversal of the allegorical logic of what Jameson calls 'third-world' literature. Moreover, the economic fundamentalism represented by Underwood Samson is something that is pervasive beyond just the world of finance and is more than just the 'pragmatic face of American state power' as it has come to shape all facets of American life (Hartnell 340).[4] As such it overlaps with and enriches the story of post-9/11 America presented through Erica.

Over the course of his meeting and discussion with the American man, Changez builds a picture of America's post-9/11 nationalism and suggests it needs to look to its own past to understand its present via Erica, and the novel simultaneously diagnoses a violent form of financial fundamentalism via Underwood Samson that has pervaded everyday life. If the novel's allegorical dimensions are overdetermined – even as they intersect and aggregate – then this mitigates other aspects of the novel that are ambiguous and seem to almost reinforce clash of civilisations logics. As Hai notes, in the

> context of a virulent Islamophobia that is predominantly Western (but not only Western), Hamid's choice to create a central, sustained ambiguity about his narrator-protagonist runs the very high risk of reaffirming readers' pre-existing pernicious negative stereotypes and undermining the apparent goals of the novel itself. (436)

While the novel's allegorical meanings may seem conspicuous, they are critically important in undermining the clash of civilisations discourse and, as I have shown, become more nuanced over the course of the novel.

Just as *The Reluctant Fundamentalist* stages a fraught conversation between two men who occupy either side of an ostensible impasse, *Sons and Other Flammable Objects* begins with a misunderstanding. This misunderstanding occurs between its central protagonists, Darius and Xerxes Adam: an Iranian father and son who, along with Darius's wife (and Xerxes's mother) Lala, fled Tehran to a Los Angeles suburb in 1978, at the beginning of the Islamic Revolution, when Xerxes was two. The pair are introduced in a flash-forward scene depicting one of '*the long line of misunderstandings in their shared history*' which caused them to '*vow to never speak again*' (1). Indeed, it is clear from the beginning that rather than a clash of civilisations, the central drama of *Sons* is a clash of *generations*, though the complex set of issues and emotions that come between father and son are invariably tied to the very different relationships they have with their old and new countries. However, if *The Reluctant Fundamentalist*'s conspicuous presentation of allegory invites questions, then *Sons*, too, metafictionally invites the reader to question its figurative moves. In one early scene describing Darius's formative years, we learn that when his father died, he was frustrated with the idea, presented by his mother, that his father was 'walking with God' (53). Darius's mother elaborately unpacks the 'walking with God' metaphor for the young Darius, and the omniscient narrator connects this scene to Xerxes's views on figurative language: 'it was always easier to render a world literal, since the possibilities of the figurative, rhetorical, and speculative were inanely multitudinous' (53). This is a striking scene given the novel's overt use of symbolism (birds and fire, particularly), character names from ancient Persian history (Xerxes I was the son of Darius the Great), and the ways the novel draws on and alludes to Sadegh Hedayat's *The Blind Owl* (1936). Khakpour's second novel, *The Last Illusion* (2014), similarly invites the reader to question its own figurative dimensions. In that novel, the American scientist Anthony Hendricks recalls sharing the epic poem about Zal, from the *Shanemeh*, with his Iranian wife. When his wife read the text aloud, he had described it as '*the most beautiful allegorical tale*' he had heard; to which his wife responded, '*Allegory . . . Try telling that to any self-respecting Iranian!*' (20). This might be interpreted in different ways, but at the least it invites a cautious reading of the allegorical dimensions of the novel. In *Sons*, as in *The Reluctant Fundamentalist*, such reflexive gestures demand careful and cautious figurative readings.

If Hamid's novel undercuts normative clash of civilisations logics by presenting its story of post-9/11 disenchantment from the perspective of an 'immigrant Muslim other', then *Sons* displaces this discourse with its clash of *generations* narrative. In doing this, it presents the story of a father who is, as Cyrus Amiri and Mahdiyeh Govah argue, obsessed with 'retaining the culture of pre-Islamic Persia' and a son who rejects everything and anything related to 'his father's imaginary world' (445). This is complicated by the fact that, in a narrative that follows Xerxes's childhood in the 1980s and eventual departure from the family home to New York in the 1990s where he eventually survives the 9/11 attacks and meets his 'half Persian' girlfriend Suzanne, each member of the Adam family experiences multiple vectors of pre- and post-9/11 racism and xenophobia (182). This means that instead of, strictly, critiquing the crude abstraction of a clash of civilisations, it displaces it by presenting a vivid story about what it means to be a Middle Eastern immigrant in America before and after 9/11. In this sense it is a novel that has very specific contextual meanings while making universal gestures, too. I argue here that it challenges clash of civilisations logic by refusing to engage with it, an especially potent gesture given that its narrative framework as a 9/11 novel that centres a Middle Eastern family might seem suited to the topic.

Formally, *Sons* fits neatly into the 9/11 novel genre. Like the texts by Jonathan Safran Foer, Jay McInerney, Don DeLillo and Claire Messud, for example, it is very much a family novel that ostensibly measures the impact of the attacks via domestic discord. This said, it unsettles the genre in three ways. First, Khakpour's novel is framed by two traumatic ruptures, not one: the Islamic Revolution of 1979 which drove the Adam family from Iran, and the 9/11 attacks witnessed by Xerxes in New York. While September 11 is a central and pivotal moment in the novel, it is also undoubtedly, as Amiri and Govah note, a novel that is 'haunted by memories of the homeland and allusions to its present and past history', so this event is fundamentally de-exceptionalised (444). Second, these events are understood through the eyes of an Iranian immigrant family and so any telescoping between the domestic as domicile and domestic as national has a different dimension. Finally, the novel's irreverent humour and flawed characters means it is tonally at odds with most of the 9/11 novel canon. These features also mean the story is both universal and specific, even idiosyncratic. Sepideh Saremi observes that it is the 'first work by an Iranian American to transcend some of the unresolved, persistent themes that have dominated contemporary Iranian literature written in English – namely, post-revolutionary Iranian victim status and the longing for an idealized homeland' but also that it addresses 'generational conflicts inherent in all immigrant families and offers a poignant examination of the unsolvable "inbetween-ness" that makes outsiders of immigrant children' (201).

Via these unique formal features, *Sons* tells the story of the growing rifts between Xerxes and Darius, and Lala and Darius, during Xerxes's adolescence, the former culminating in Xerxes leaving the family home suddenly, for college in New York City, aged eighteen. When Darius takes a trip to check in on him in 2000, it is apparent they have only grown further apart, and the trip ends disastrously with the previously mentioned 'misunderstanding', which seems to amount to a terminal fracture of their relationship. However, after 9/11, possibilities of a reconciliation emerge. Initially a sense of existential threat prompts Xerxes to reach out and new forms of discrimination engender forms of familial solidarity, but it is mostly two unexpected personal events that seem destined to create an Adam family reunion. Xerxes meets Suzanne and after sharing the experience of witnessing the attacks, they quickly form a relationship. Crucially, she is interested in his (and her own) Persian/Iranian past and is curious about his estrangement from Darius. Also, Lala hears word of her long-lost brother, Bobak, whom she has not seen since before the Revolution, who is apparently living in New York and suffering from poor mental health. Ultimately, these events build to a stirring denouement which includes a series of flights, missed flights and emergency landings. Xerxes and Suzanne attempt to visit Tehran from New York on separate flights, a trip which Darius attempts to join from Los Angeles, and Lala flies to New York to try to find Bobak.

However, while the novel's conclusion is affecting, much of its sentimentality is short-circuited by characters who make bad choices and who are hard to sympathise with, despite the challenges of immigration and racism they experience. Both Darius and Xerxes are selfish contrarians and, much worse, they are misogynistic and violent. Darius, we learn, was regularly violent with the young Xerxes including a time when the latter was left with '*two black eyes for school*' (210–11). Later, when Suzanne surprises Xerxes for his birthday, with a trip to Tehran, he feels so 'violated' that he slaps her. He quickly feels 'astronomically sorry' and recognises that he has 'become his father', but this single instance of physical abuse follows other forms of psychological abuse that he subjects Suzanne to (286, 291).

Characterising Darius and Xerxes in this way was a risky move on Khakpour's part, given the prevalence – particularly after 9/11 – of Islamophobic stereotypes of Middle Eastern men as violently misogynistic (and here there are similarities to Hamid's characterisation of Changez as 'suspicious'). Indeed, one of the six key frames of Islamophobia, as theorised by Kumar, perpetrated against all kinds of Asian-American and Middle Eastern men (not just Muslims) is the notion that they are 'uniquely sexist' and that 'Muslim women need to be liberated by the West' (70–1). But *Sons* also depicts this kind of stereotyping at work. For instance, Gigi and Marvin, other residents of the Eden Gardens apartment complex where the Adams live, make racist comments and assumptions about Darius and Lala. Lala is described as a 'towelhead' and 'sketchy', and a whole slew of stereotypes are applied to Darius: 'That's how they are with their wives – beat them and shit, put them in veils, they don't care, they'll get the virgins when they're dead!' (226–7). When Marvin finally meets Darius, he observes that he 'had that foreign look and it wasn't Mexican or Indian or anything like that. He looked Middle Eastern and a bit disturbed, the way he had always imagined Lala's husband looking' (342). Additionally, while the novel never asks us to forgive Darius's or Xerxes's violence or misogyny, so many horrible things happen to them that we are invited to still care about them, and particularly Xerxes. Both are haunted by the Revolution, and we learn that Xerxes's first memory is of the sound of choppers and their respective artificially created initial breeze, and moments later a circle of pink lights, spiraling around themselves ... add the tone and vibrations of his mother's sobbing and the echoes of people in the streets, waves of gasps and shouts ... (124)

These vividly rendered memories – which remind us that Khakpour herself, along with her family, fled the Revolution – are not understood by Xerxes until Darius provides context. However, Darius also suggests Xerxes does not have the right to them because of his American upbringing: 'Anti-aircraft missiles. War. Revolution. So what? None of that means anything to you' (125). But while Xerxes is made to feel that he has no right to his traumatic childhood memories, his Middle Eastern-ness means he is subject to much racism and xenophobia as a child. In one episode he receives an 'X-mas card' with simply a picture of a camel from a gleefully racist classmate. Later, the first time Xerxes has a potential romantic interest at his family's apartment – Sam, whose punky sensibilities meant they shared 'something outsiderish' – she notes a photograph of Xerxes as a bewildered and lost child, that sits on one of the shelves (156). The photo depicts Lala, Darius and Xerxes with Mickey Mouse and Donald Duck at 'what was known as the Happiest Place on Earth' and it shows, in Sam's view, a harrowing image of the young Xerxes:

He looked completely out of place, claustrophobic, wanting out, existentially terrorized, as if about to get shot by a gun instead of a camera ... She looked from the portrait to the apartment periphery, to him, and back to the portrait again as if to put it all in context. She looked sick, sad, as if she felt sorry for it all. As if for once she was understanding that he was an altogether *other* type of 'other.' (139)

In this scene Sam sees Xerxes's 'inbetween-ness' and sadness with clarity and begins to understand what has led to his 'compartmentalization instinct' (136).

Perhaps the most evocative way in which *Sons* depicts the experience of immigrant otherness before and after 9/11 is through its engagements with popular culture. One function of this is, as Saremi has noted, to give 'the story a lovely, complex sense of place' (201). We might add time, too, as the references to He-Man and Skeletor, Xerxes's love of Fruity Pebbles, and an Ed McMahon sighting on Rodeo Drive, which Lala believes is a 'street for "the best people"' (132), build a rich sense of 1980s and 90s Southern California. And, indeed, this family name (which Darius insists to the many people who mispronounce it is 'Odd-damn') is itself a potent reference to the classic family sitcom *The Addams Family* (1964–6). This reference is a component of one of the novel's most suggestive formal moves: its consistent citation of classic US sitcoms and appropriation of the framing of so many of these programmes. *Sons* can be read in conversation with both *The Addams Family* and even more so, with *I Dream of Jeanie* (1965–70). Like these shows which draw their comedy from the 'fish out of water' conceit, *Sons* is episodic, dialogue-heavy and draws its irreverent humour from the experience of difference or otherness.

One of the effects of this is that the novel exposes the cruel optimism perpetuated by such shows, with their tidy resolutions, as the characters continually imagine positive outcomes in the most unlikely circumstances. Indeed, the novel maintains a cheerful tone, despite some harrowing moments, at least partly through these allusions, and there are moments of optimism that are particularly fantastical. For instance, as the conclusion nears, Lala imagines that Darius and Xerxes might 'embrace', and that Bobak will be found and might 'preach to Xerxes the merits of everything from letter writing to being-present-for-your-loved-ones' (280). Shortly after, Suzanne imagines her and Xerxes 'holding hands through the bustling streets of Iran', and on the very next page she and Xerxes happily watch *I Dream of Jeannie* (281–2), which seems a pointed evocation of a kind of sitcom-positivity.

TV for Xerxes and for everyone in his generation is a seismic force. The narrator notes that television was 'the icebreaker, the playground unifier – if there was nothing to say there was always TV talk. There were He-Men and She-Ras and sitcom dunces and cartoon villains and commercial quips' (88). But Xerxes quickly develops a deep and abiding obsession with *I Dream of Jeannie*, a show that we learn 'shaped him, his character, his future aesthetic sensibility, his sense of not just world, but its possibilities' (89). Darius and Lala are puzzled and suspicious about this obsession. They debate the possibility that it is linked to some sense of their family's Middle Eastern heritage, which Lala sees as positive in that a 'genie' is a better stereotype than a 'terrorist': 'At first I said, oh, he thinks she is from our country. Genies. Better than terrorists' (91). Darius rejects this notion: 'There are no Persian genies. None! Arabian Nights, got it? No belly dancers either. This Jeannie is just an Arab woman, with low self-esteem, who dyes her hair blonde, with a white man husband she calls "master"' (91). Eventually, they express concern that it might indicate that Xerxes is gay, but they never actually give him the opportunity to explain his interest. Ultimately, it appears that Lala was partly right in her assessment and certainly the titular genie is Persian-speaking, but as the omniscient narrator notes of Xerxes's parents:

> they with their alleged Persian nationalism not even bothering to ask the right questions, not even bothering to probe whether the interest could be, in part, a young boy's investigation into an American rendering of the Middle Eastern myth, the genie – surely there was something to that? It wasn't the whole story, but Xerxes wished, at best, that they could see it that way, if they saw it any way at all, the dullards! – because Jeannie's dog after all was named 'Djinn-Djinn' (Farsi for 'demon-demon') and the enigmatic Chief of All Genies was called Haji (Farsi for something roughly like 'Dude') and Persia was even re-created – poorly – in Episode 2 . . . *what do you make of that, any comment on that, O Iranian progenitors?* (94)

Ultimately, the family dramas of *Sons* – while darkly humorous – are abusive and ultimately violent and upsetting, and this means they spill out of the generic frameworks of the classic US family sitcom. This is especially the case given that the racism and xenophobia they experience is so at odds with the cheerful 'fish out of water' comedy of difference in *The Addams Family* or *I Dream of Jeannie*. Additionally, one of the effects of the allusions to these shows – and to popular culture more generally in *Sons* – is to emphasise the hegemonic whiteness and heteronormativity of such programmes.

Ultimately, the key theme that emerges in *Sons* is the search for meaning and connection across generations and across the other divisions the novel sets up. This is a structuring conceit of the novel: the various scenes and episodes from the lives of the Adam family begin to thematically cohere in particular ways as the wider story arc advances. This is aided by two pronounced and related symbols: fire and birds (and we might include planes and indeed a plane brought down by a bird). The novel's fire imagery is broadly related to death and destruction, and birds to flight and escape – potent symbols given the novel's twin ruptures of the 1979 Revolution in Iran and the 9/11 attacks in New York. It opens with a story about Darius luring the cats of Eden Gardens into the Adam family apartment to attach bells to their collars, so they will not prey on blue jays that have made their home in the complex. This seems to be an innocuously idiosyncratic story until we learn that Darius had been atoning – in an eccentric way – for participating, as an adolescent, in the grotesque practice of applying kerosene to doves, and then setting them alight as they attempt to fly away: 'madly, wildly, desperately, like all hell' (31). This catalyses the fracture in Xerxes's relationship with his father:

> His own devastation shocked him. Was it the birds? No. He didn't care about the birds – at least, not like that. Perhaps it was his father's cruel and unusual past, a world forbidden to be spoken of, that Xerxes had always sensed intrinsically? Another reason, any reason, a final reason, to hate himself and his family? All he knew for sure was that the feeling had familiarity. This was one in a long line of his father's stories that he had unloaded on him, burdened him with, but, as often happens with what is saved deliberately for last, this one would have to be the worst. The past had come full circle; this story had pulled with it every other story; history had become theirs, just theirs. (34)

Here, the burning birds augur the falling out at the centre of the novel; and throughout the narrative, images of birds and flames recur. Fire, which, in Darius's Zoroastrianism represents God's wisdom, is particularly potent. In one scene, Darius takes Lala and a nine-year-old Xerxes to a protest including speeches about 'the tyranny of the ayatollahs, about Islam gone bad, American indifference, about revolution', where they witness at close range a gruesome act of self-immolation. Indeed, we learn that 'those seconds so thoroughly pierced themselves a slot in the easy mold of a child's mind that off and on for years he could not escape the thought of the man, his impassioned auto-cannibalistic *tada!*' (131). This episode helps the reader better understand the power of Darius's burning birds story and is one example of the way the novel's symbols aggregate. Images of birds recur, too, and as noted, the novel builds towards a conclusion where each key character boards a flight and Xerxes's is forced to emergency land due to a bird disabling an engine. Ultimately, these linked symbols connect, in broad ways, the novel's two very different moments of rupture – the Islamic Revolution in Iran and the 9/11 attacks – in the characters' lives.

Though its clash of *generations* narrative supplants and comments on the prevalence of clash of civilisations rhetoric and logic, September 11 is a central part of *Sons* and it draws on certain myths of the post-9/11 period in New York. For instance, Xerxes and Suzanne's relationship begins in the aftermath of 9/11 as the two young people feel a need for intimacy and human contact and are magnetically drawn to each other in the aftermath. Xerxes even seems to recognise his participation in 'terror sex', the much-discussed notion that, faced with 'anxiety and uncertainty' and a feeling that life is 'precious and civilization is precarious', people were urgently seeking sexual intimacy (Kazdin n.p.). In *Sons*, this phenomenon is presented in more nuanced terms, though the logic remains similar:

> It had spread through the city like a most desired virus: singles haunting bars to find not just flings but companions, the heyday's speed-dating sextravaganzas suddenly morphing into support-group-style coupling, fuck-buddies being fine but replaced by the finer and fewer who could play monogamy if not marriage, the desired dating being the dating that verged on holy matrimony, that said *constant*, that said *forever*, that said *life* not just *love*. (177)

This is certainly the case for Xerxes and Suzanne, though when they run into relationship trouble and Suzanne starts feeling nostalgia for the immediate aftermath of 9/11, these sentiments feel flimsier. Ultimately, *Sons* scrutinises notions of post-9/11 profundity and re-evaluation. Xerxes feels that the solemn gestures of truth and connection after the attacks amounted to a kind of 'surface melodrama', and the pervasive feeling after the attacks is certainly a sadness but it is based more on the 'sad disappointing truth that nothing had really changed, had it – they were all different and all alone and would live and die, alone, even if all together, with one another, in a warningless blast, in a crumbling staircase in a flame, in a fall' (179). Xerxes's suspicions about notions of post-9/11 change and re-evaluation thus seem oddly juxtaposed with the very real amplification of racism and xenophobia that he, Lala and Darius experience after the attacks. Yet, *Sons* carefully builds lines of continuity between pre-9/11 and post-9/11 forms of discrimination and violence through Xerxes's experiences at school, and the suspicion aimed at the Adam family by other Eden Gardens residents and members of the wider community. Even when, at the novel's conclusion, Xerxes is profiled and detained at an airport, this scene is presented as consistent with a lifetime of experience, not as an example of the zealousness of post-9/11 securitisation. Ultimately, by foregrounding a clash of generations story within the framework of a 9/11 novel, *Sons* implicitly critiques clash of civilisations logics while also drawing attention to the long-standing tribulations of immigrant families in America, and long-standing forms of bigotry and discrimination.

The Attack and The Sirens of Bagdad

The Reluctant Fundamentalist and *Sons and Other Flammable Objects* disrupt the dominant narrative positionality of the 9/11 novel and depict post-9/11 racism and xenophobia with more historical depth and international context than most other iterations of the genre. But while they destabilise the normative whiteness of this body of work, and include significant transnational dimensions, they remain America-focused. This section continues to focus on literary engagement with clash of civilisations rhetoric but moves away from America-centred narratives, broadly aligning with the movement away from event-based narratives of terrorism that I am tracing over the course of this book. This said, the novels under discussion in this section – Yasmina Khadra's *The Attack* (2005) and *The Sirens of Baghdad* (2006), both translated from the French by John Cullen, in 2007 and 2008, respectively – respond to the aftermath of an attack, in the former, and the possibility of one, in the latter. *The Attack* explores the impact of a suicide attack in Tel Aviv, and *Sirens* is a 'radicalisation narrative' that unfolds in Iraq after the 2003 invasion, building towards a potential attack 'a thousand times more awesome than the attacks of September 11' (11). But while the 'events' in these novels are important parts of the narratives, both books are focused on contextualising the events historically and internationally, on attempting to understand the 'unimaginable' interior worlds of terrorists and to understand the material and human conditions that make the events possible. Consequently, I argue that these novels should be understood as articulating a direct challenge to clash of civilisations logics.

Khadra's career has included some extraordinary turns. He has been lauded as subversive, critiqued for being formulaic, and questioned for opportunism and disingenuous claims to authenticity. His early writing, under his real name Mohammed Moulessehou, coincided with his career as an officer in the Algerian military, and he was forced to adopt the pseudonym Yasmina Khadra in 1988, to continue writing. Subsequently, his Inspector Llob detective novels became increasingly critical of the Algerian government and finally he was forced into exile in France in 2000. As Sharae Deckard has noted, Khadra was initially 'feted in France as an Arab woman writer with special feminist insight into the masculinist, fundamentalist violence characterizing Algeria's civil war' and for 'colonizing a genre seen previously as the domain of men' (75). When Khadra revealed his identity in *Le Monde*, he received a backlash from the literary establishment, and the 'sexist and homophobic hard-boiled cliches in his noir detective fiction' were suddenly interpreted in different ways (Deckard 75). As Deckard notes, Khadra's journey as a writer might be understood as

> a salutary lesson not only in the perils of modes of literary criticism which distort texts to 'fit' pre-existing theoretical models, but also in the dynamics of . . . 'consecration' within the French literary field . . . So long as Khadra's fictions seemed to enshrine the exotic difference of francophone North Africa and to assimilate comfortably to French liberal anti-Islamist perspectives, they were rewarded with recognition and literary capital. However, not long after his public declarations in support of the Algerian military, Khadra was stripped of his funding by the IPW [International Parliament of Writers] and subjected to a series of delegitimations, entering into a more ambivalent, defensive relationship with the French media. (75)

Khadra's post-9/11 move into 'serious' or 'literary' fiction with *The Swallows of Kabul* (2002), *The Attack* and *Sirens* – often referred to as his 'fundamentalism trilogy' – saw a shift in his relationship with the literary press and media, as these texts were celebrated for offering an authentic, Arab Muslim perspective on the war on terror. However, some reviewers questioned Khadra's knowledge of the nations, cultures and people featured in these novels, and some scholarly assessments have been critical of the way Khadra positioned himself in the post-9/11 literary marketplace as an expert on the wider Muslim world. Karl Ågerup argues that 'Khadra's aesthetics is based largely on the illusion of authenticity' and that an implied (and in Ågerup's view, false) 'anchorage in historical reality is essential to Khadra's realism' (188). Ågerup notes that Khadra had never visited Afghanistan before writing *The Swallows of Kabul*, or Israel before writing *The Attack*, or Iraq before writing *The Sirens of Baghdad*, stating flatly that '[t]hese are works of fiction, inventions, just like his name' (184). This critique suggests that Khadra's novels reproduce the very logic he has sought to break down. Outlining Khadra's combative media engagements and divisive literary status during the 2000s, Ågerup contends that '[t]here was a polarizing aspect to Khadra's appeal: he challenged his readers to pick sides – you were either with him or against him' (183). Deckard is also critical, noting that Khadra's fundamentalism trilogy 'represent[s] terrorism . . . in two-dimensional stereotypes uneasily reminiscent of American neoconservativism' (76).

I am indebted to the detailed contextual work in both of these compelling essays. However, focusing particularly on *The Attack* and *Sirens*, I argue that whatever the extent of Khadra's political manoeuvring or market opportunism, and however thin his implied claims to authenticity might be, these novels function as compelling counternarratives to the clash-driven media formulations of Islamism and terrorism of the time, and of today. They are formulaic novels, but their depictions of terrorism and terrorists are not reductive or 'two-dimensional' and, in fact, the genre modes they adopt have a multidirectional function: they provide a route into the 'unfamiliar' worlds of terrorists while they simultaneously resist the stereotypes of terrorists and terrorism. These are works of the imagination that think beyond binaries and Islamophobic abstractions. Moreover, their formulaic generic dimensions leave space for some compelling innovations – and particularly the depiction of focalising protagonists who move in and out of reader alignment and sympathy. These works have much to offer in the way they insist on nuance, ambiguity and historical context in depicting 'terrorism'. As Robert Spencer argues, writing specifically about *The Attack*, Khadra's writing 'reveals that it is possible for novels to discourage the habit of applying labels like "fundamentalist" and "terrorist" in ways that are hypocritical, inconsistent or merely unselfconscious' and demonstrates 'fiction's capacity to puncture the ideological conceit that fuels such campaigns' (403).

In their depictions of terrorists and terrorism, *The Attack* and *Sirens* seek to make new and long-standing structures of geopolitical conflict and state terrorism, elided by clash logics, visible. This begins at the level of form. *The Attack* functions as a detective narrative, Khadra's primary genre in the 1980s and 1990s, in which Dr. Amin Jaafari, a talented surgeon and settled Arab-Israeli, is thrown into chaos when his wife's suicide attack kills nineteen citizens, including several children, at a Tel Aviv restaurant. Amin quickly slips into a detective persona, as he seeks to understand how his wife had become radicalised and how he had been blind to this radicalisation. Just as Khadra's Llob novels 'expose occluded social conditions and explore ideological contradictions', in *The Attack* the detective fiction frame emphasises the act of making facts visible and unravelling complex plots: potent pursuits in the context of the complex historical conflict between Palestine and Israel and common understandings of terrorism as 'unspeakable' (Deckard 75). In surprising ways, it can be read alongside other detective novels of terrorism such as *Bleeding Edge* and *The Zero*, discussed in the previous chapter, and certainly the novels by Attica Locke, Ausma Zehanat Khan and Percival Everett discussed in my final chapter. *Sirens* can also be read within familiar genre frameworks. It belongs to the tragedy tradition in its depiction of the tragic but flawed anti-hero whose world is thrown into chaos and crisis, and functions as a kind of first-person bildungsroman, too. The tragedy tropes – and other elements of the novel – mean it is usefully compared with Kamila Shamsie's *Home Fire* (2017), discussed in the next chapter. Shamsie's novel uses the narrative architecture of *Antigone* and both feature young men radicalised through experiences of state violence and state terrorism.

As noted, generic familiarity provides a point of entry into the unfamiliar, but both novels can also be read as early iterations of a genre that works not to understand the unfamiliar, but to unsettle or dismantle too familiar stereotypes. This is a genre that has proliferated in the second decade of the twenty-first century: the literary 'radicalisation narrative'. Jago Morrison outlines the stereotypes of radicalisation, demonstrating the ways they inform and reinforce the policy logic of programmes such as the UK's 'Prevent' through images of 'vulnerable' young Muslims susceptible to manipulation.[5] Morrison cites a set of Western-set novels that invite the reader to 'question what we think we know about radicalisation, jihadis and the counterterrorist response to them' (570). *The Attack* and *Sirens* both do this, too, in the global context of the war on terror, and they also challenge dominant, Islamophobic media narratives of radicalisation, which ignore state violence and 'elide or obscure the historical and political context within which anti-Western sentiment takes form' (Morrison 569). Indeed, while the flash-forward prologue of *Sirens* evokes the violent event that may or may not conclude the novel, from the opening chapter the unnamed protagonist is characterised as sensitive and affable, and its opening phases focus on ordinary familial dramas. This is an image not of a vulnerable young man exploited by pernicious militants, but of a thoughtful and intelligent person with agency and social vision. This characterisation emphasises the magnitude of his subsequent experiences: a series of escalating instances of state violence and, crucially, the American military's belligerent treatment of his family and village – Kafr Karam – which is characterised by a lack of care and knowledge of local traditions and values.

As noted, in both *The Attack* and *Sirens*, the familiarity of genre helps the novels to both engage with unfamiliar phenomena and challenge stereotypes that are all too familiar. Though Khadra's canny manoeuvring in the post-9/11 literary marketplace may have helped frame these novels as 'literary', their formal features create the kind of tensions and ambiguities often considered the hallmarks of literary fiction. Ågerup critiques Khadra's 'didafiction' – a term coined to describe 'interdiscursive play that integrates historical fact and fantasy' – because it is not rooted in the expert knowledge or first-hand experience that may be implied or assumed (181). However, one important part of both *The Attack* and *Sirens* that is grounded in knowledge and experience is that the protagonists of both novels are Bedouin. Khadra's mother came from a nomadic North African tribe, and he self-identifies as Bedouin: 'my roots are Bedouin. I was born into a desert tribe, and I'm North African, Arab-Berber and Muslim' (Adam n.p.). Bedouin cultures have specific traditions that are important features of both novels – particularly *Sirens*, where a belligerent lack of knowledge or care about these traditions on the part of American soldiers is instrumental; but also in *The Attack*, where the protagonist's Bedouin roots are juxtaposed with what he ultimately recognises as a life of privilege that has created a 'blindness' to the 'desolation' of his own people (227). We might also note that Bedouin culture and identity has historically been nomadic and not necessarily adherent to national borders. This seems resonant and conspicuous in the context of Khadra's 'fundamentalism trilogy' and these two novels, particularly. Though they have specific national contexts of conflict, they are oriented by characters with a cultural identity that has historically transcended nation states while being repeatedly impinged upon by them. This speaks to the desire of these novels to address broader vectors of Arab and Muslim experience while meaningfully addressing specific contexts.

The Attack has a framing device that immediately evokes DeLillo's *Falling Man*, published in the same year as the English translation of Khadra's novel. Both novels end where they begin, circling back to and repeating images from their opening scenes. For DeLillo this is in the burning towers of the World Trade Center, and for Khadra it is the aftermath of an Israeli rocket attack outside a crowded mosque in Jenin. Both scenes are impressionistic and evoke immediacy and emergency, and there are some powerful echoes across the texts. For instance, this image in *The Attack* echoes the opening passage of *Falling Man*, quoted at length in my previous chapter (though the French language publication of *The Attack* preceded *Falling Man*):

> In a fraction of a second, the sky collapses, and the street, fraught with the fervor of the multitude a moment ago, turns upside town.

> The body of a man, or perhaps a boy, hurtles across my vertiginous sight like a dark flash. (254)

Though this framing device is similar, it serves different thematic functions. In *Falling Man* Keith walks out of the burning towers, and as his story concludes with a descent into the circular repetitions of trauma, the novel's ultimate return to this scene explicitly evokes the return to the originary traumatic event. In *The Attack* this repetition adds formal emphasis to the novel's narrative engagement with the cyclical violence and counter-violence that have characterised the Palestine–Israel conflict. Any comparisons between these novels ends there, and in *The Attack* the prologue gives way to a brief introduction to Dr. Jaafari – as a prominent surgeon in Tel Aviv and settled Arab-Israeli. In the first chapter, shortly after the prologue, Jaafari is rushed into crisis mode when dozens of victims of a terror attack (which, it will soon be revealed, has been committed by his own wife) are brought into his hospital.

When evidence shows that it was his wife, Sihem, who committed the atrocity, Jaafari enters a period of intense denial before launching a belligerent investigation into how his wife became militant and who was responsible for her 'indoctrination' (102). As his investigation unfolds, a staged series of shifts occur. The narrative begins by inviting the reader to sympathise with the innocent victims of the restaurant attack, and to align with Jaafari as a focalising protagonist. He is a dedicated husband who has been betrayed by his true love, and possibly also by some family members and part of his former community in Nazareth, who apparently have helped facilitate the attack in Tel Aviv. He is also devoted to his profession, presented as an almost religious calling to heal and save lives. However, as Jaafari visits Bethlehem, Jerusalem and Jenin, and speaks to family members – places and people he had left behind – he starts to realise the extent of the violence of Israeli occupation, and a form of political awakening begins. And, as Jaafari uncovers more about how his 'wife was indoctrinated', a fuller picture of the conflict emerges, and the reader is invited to reorient their sympathies (102).

This process of realisation coincides with Jaafari's precipitous physical and mental deterioration, which manifests in a hard-boiled persona with increasingly erratic patterns. Jaafari drinks, rejects kind gestures from friends, and reacts violently to any form of reproach. By the middle of the novel, he is 'naked, and suicidal' (125). He embarks on a series of visits across the border and back, echoing and reversing the narrative structure of Hany Abu-Assad's famous film about two would-be Palestinian suicide terrorists, *Paradise Now* (2005), which also features multiple crossings and checkpoints. These movements also echo Edward Said's famous comment that the 'truest reality' of Palestinian lives 'is expressed in the way we cross over from one place to another ... This is the deepest continuity of our lives as a nation in exile and constantly on the move' (1999, 164). Certainly, for Jaafari this process is critical to his eventual awakening as he visits places and people from a previous life. His visits to Palestine also feature a series of adversarial interviews with his 'suspects', who, despite his rage, begin to turn his attention from the injustice of his own personal 'case' to the impoverished condition of Palestinians under the yoke of occupation. As his desperation reaches a nadir, his hard-boiled persona begins to sound like the stereotypical desperation of a terrorist, and when Kim, his closest friend and confidant, asks him to stop playing detective, he states, 'I'm not a cop or an investigative journalist. I'm angry, and my anger would eat me alive if I didn't take some action' (143). Just pages later, Jaafari again performs the stereotypes of the desperate terrorist whose only choice is violence: 'The only thing I want to hear is what's already in my head, dragging me willy-nilly toward the only tunnel that offers a glimmer of light now that all the other exits are closed' (147). When a few pages later Jaafari admits that he is 'totally blinded by hatred', the point is overdetermined (153).

In conspicuous ways, Jaafari's behaviour suggests the ways humiliation and betrayal can lead to hatred and violence, and the narrative cleverly invites the reader to consider their alignment to a character who has adopted the ostensible traits of a terrorist. However, the interviews Jaafari undertakes also, for the most part, emphasise the clarity of thought of his interlocutors; and ultimately, it becomes clear that the horrific attack committed by his wife was undertaken not from a place of belligerent rage but careful consideration. The conversations he has – with, first, a taxi driver and his Uncle Yasser in Bethlehem (116–19, 126–30), then the Imam at the Great Mosque (148–50), then unnamed 'commanders' in Bethlehem (155–62) and Jenin (217–20), and finally his cousin Adel (221–32) – rehearse similar arguments about the validity of Sihem's martyrdom. In one sense these repetitions reinforce the point made by the novel's narrative structure, about the un-ending and cyclical nature of violence and the unbridgeable impasse at the heart of the conflict. Most of his interlocutors echo the sentiments of the commander who refutes Jaafari's accusations of extremism: 'We're not Islamists, Dr. Jaafari, and we're not fundamentalists, either. We are only the children of a ravaged, despised people. Fighting with whatever means we can to recover our homeland and our dignity. Nothing more, nothing less' (158). This repeated sentiment draws from Frantz Fanon's logic of violence, in *The Wretched of the Earth*, as the only way to respond to the dehumanisation of occupation or colonisation: 'that this narrow world, strewn with prohibitions, can only be called in question by absolute violence' (29).[6] The interviews also build in context, and they are crucial components of the novel's subversive message that the 'terrorist' and her conspirators were rational and thoughtful people: not craven murderers. This is particularly the case in the image of Sihem that emphasises a considered revolutionary commitment:

> No one joins our ranks for the pleasure of it, Doctor. All the young men you've seen, the ones with slingshots as well as the ones with rocket launchers, loathe war unspeakably. Because every day, enemy fire carries off one of them. They'd like to be respectable, too; they'd like to be surgeons or pop singers or film actors, ride around in fine cars and live their dreams every day. The problem, Doctor, is that other people deny them those dreams. Other people are trying to confine them to ghettos until they're trapped in them for good. And that's the reason why they prefer to die. When dreams are turned away, death becomes the ultimate salvation. Sihem understood this, Doctor. You must respect her choice and let her rest in peace. (220)

Jaafari's cousin, Adel, suggests that the luxury that life in Tel Aviv afforded was felt by Sihem to be excessive and ugly in the face of the suffering of their people:

> that wasn't the happiness she wanted to see in you; she found it a little indecent, a bit incongruous. It was as if you were firing up a barbecue in a burned-out yard. You only saw the barbecue; she saw the rest, the desolation all around, spoiling all delight. It wasn't your fault; all the same, she couldn't bear sharing your blindness anymore. (227)

Jaafari begins to hear his interlocutors and to witness the devastation of occupation. Even before the interviews, he travels through Jenin and sees a landscape decimated by state violence and occupation: 'small villages in a state of siege; checkpoints on every access road; larger roads littered with charred vehicles blasted by drones; cohorts of the damned lined up and waiting their turn to be checked' (200). He even concedes that 'in Tel Aviv, I was on another planet. My blinders shield me from taking in much of the tragedy devasting my country' (201). Nevertheless, he remains fixated on his wife's betrayal. This is one of the ways the novel retains its genre coding within the hard-boiled tradition, while asking readers to question the received binaries of good and evil, victim and perpetrator. It also means that Jaafari's realisations are mitigated by his stubborn misogyny and failure to imagine his wife's agency. He becomes aware of his 'blindness' and the ways he has neglected his old community and family, but his suspicions of betrayal and interpretation of his wife's martyrdom as cuckolding persist; he simply fails to believe she could have agency even when it is revealed she was the architect of the operation. In his exchange with the first 'commander', Jaafari makes repeated statements about his wife's 'obligations' and makes chauvinistic comments like 'a wife can't deceive her husband like that' (220). Even in his final interview with Adel, who he believes has had an affair with Sihem, he cannot fathom his late wife's agency. Adel refutes Jaafari's suspicion of an affair and insists Sihem was 'the daughter of people known for resistance' and that 'she was in a very good position to know exactly what she was doing' (228).

Here, another dimension of the novel and of Jaafari's characterisation comes into view: his role as a doctor. Just when it appears that his sympathies have shifted, he reorients himself by returning to the ostensibly neutral ethics of a surgeon. Listening to Adel, he had reasoned to himself that Sihem 'grew up among the oppressed, as an orphan and an Arab in a world that pardons neither', and that she was 'carrying around a wound so awful, so hideous, that she was too ashamed to show it to me' (228–9). But his understanding stops abruptly: 'Adel's talking, talking and smoking . . . I realize I'm not listing to him anymore. I don't want to hear anything else. I don't fit in the world he's describing. There, death is an end in itself. For a physician, that's too much to swallow' (229). Jaafari grasps this idea as way to regain ballast and, in doing so, he effectively returns to the values that were foregrounded in the first chapter, completing another kind of cycle that fits just inside the framing device that bookends the novel. Indeed, at the end of the penultimate chapter, he insists, 'the only battle I believe in, the only one that really deserves bleeding for, is the battle the surgeon fights, which consists in recreating life in the place where death has chosen to conduct its manoeuvrers' (234). Ultimately, the novel combines some striking shifts and changes within this circular return to neutrality, which is structurally folded just inside its circular framing 'event' – a clear depiction of cyclical violence. As readers we follow the crossing back and forth of borders physical and psychological, and are invited to question our assumptions and orientation as new information and different viewpoints accumulate.

As Ågerup has noted, this layering and accumulation of perspectives is carefully constructed:

> Not only does Khadra present many different types of Israelis and Palestinians in *The Attack*, but he also times their appearances to maintain a perfectly neutral balance. For example, just after showing the violent, racist rage of the Arab hero's Jewish neighbours, Khadra introduces a pacifist and Palestine-friendly Jew. (186)

This sense of balance is amplified by the novel's frequent meditations on the nature of terrorism as a broadly pervasive phenomenon, and the notion that radicalisation 'can happen to anyone' (93). In one sense this is a reductive notion and the analogy that appears twice is particularly lacking in nuance: 'it falls on your head like a roof tile or it attaches itself to your insides like a tapeworm. Afterward, you no longer see the world in the same way. You've got only one thing on your mind' (93, 228). This said, the novel offers a counterpoint to this through the story of Dr. Jaafari and Sihem. As noted, in his immediate anger and sense of betrayal, Jaafari quickly adopts the stereotypical blind rage of the terrorist. But this is eventually contrasted with the clarity of thought and vision Sihem is described as having. These are less examples of the two analogies – tile and tapeworm – and more an insistence that a terrorist might be irrational or belligerent but might also be careful and thoughtful. The layers of balance and returns to neutrality in *The Attack* mean that it is not two-dimensional, and nor does it reinforce 'us against them' logics. Rather, it combines unsparing critique of Israeli state and colonial violence – rare in the immediate aftermath of 9/11 – with forms of ambiguity and neutrality that remain potent in the enduring shadow of clash logics.

The Sirens of Baghdad is more explicit in the way it addresses reductive clash logics. A memorable scene halfway through the narrative exemplifies its awareness of the absurdity of such abstractions and simultaneously insists on taking them seriously, urging a better understanding of their appeal. The nameless protagonist, newly arrived in Baghdad, witnesses the bombast of two young men – Sayed and Yaseen – who come from his home village, Kafr Karam. Sayed states, with a conspicuous use of 'clash':

> our streets are going to witness the greatest duel of all time, the clash of titans: Babylon against Disneyland, the Tower of Babel against the Empire State Building, the Hanging Gardens against the Golden

Gate Bridge, Scheherazade against Bonnie Parker, Sinbad against the Terminator . . . (176)

Though the protagonist is inexperienced, he is intuitive, and immediately registers the absurdity of these formations and performativity of his home villagers. He even reflects that listening to these arguments was like being 'in the thick of a farce' or a 'play rehearsal' with 'mediocre actors who'd learned their roles but didn't have the talent the text deserved' (176). But despite this, he also feels inspired, and reflects that 'under different conditions' such rhetoric 'would have made me laugh out loud, but now it gave me great relief' (176). Considered in the context of the Bush-era war on terror, which often featured clumsy forms of Hollywood posturing (from wanted posters of Osama bin Laden to the President cosplaying in an Air Force flight suit), this is a potent engagement with the theatrical posturing (mostly by the Bush administration) of this period. Crucially though, it exemplifies the way the novel combines critique of clash logics while taking seriously the way they gain traction, but without mobilising stereotypes of impressionable young men.

Though *Sirens* features a more explicit critique, there are several similarities to *The Attack*. Just as Dr. Jaafari unravels over the course of his 'investigation' and in relation to a series of adversarial interviews, the nameless protagonist of *Sirens* is radicalised in stages and through experiences of different forms of US state violence. In both cases, the protagonists are unmoored and consumed by anger, but they are also characterised in ways that resist stereotypes. As noted, the novels use genre frameworks – with their stock tropes and narrative architectures – to open out nuanced depictions of radicalisation that critique clash logics just as they show how these formations work. However, their settings are very different, and *Sirens* is distinct in the way it reverses the usual dynamics and point of view in narratives of the war on terror, as here it is the American military that is shown to be barbaric and 'uncivilised'. This said, Khadra again emphasises balance. Certain aspects of the nameless protagonist's value system are shown to be rigid and intractable, and his comments about the American 'GIs' rely on caricature. However, if this ostensibly pits a barbaric US occupying force against an intractable or anti-modern Bedouin villager, staging a clash of civilisations, then other elements of the story build in layers of complexity.

There is again an emphasis on medicine via the protagonist's sister, who left the patriarchal home in Kafr Karam to become a doctor in Baghdad, and who abhors all forms of violence. When the protagonist finds she has been living with a man out of wedlock, and asks if she has given up on God, she replies simply, 'I believe in what I do, that's enough for me' (140). The secular humanism of the protagonist's sister is similar to Dr. Jaafari's in *The Attack* and is reinforced by other characters. Omar, another fellow Bedouin from Kafr Karam, living in Baghdad, helps the protagonist find work and accommodation upon his arrival. Omar is sympathetic to his suffering but concerned about his need for revenge. Eventually, Omar is brutally murdered by the militants the protagonist joins, partly for an alleged betrayal but mostly because they discover he is gay, and guilt adds a new dimension to the protagonist's inner turmoil. Finally, there is Dr. Jalal and a novelist called Mohammed Seen, who undertake a fierce debate about the clash of civilisations that is witnessed by the protagonist in the novel's final phase.

Dr. Jalal is introduced in the novel's prologue and then reappears with Seen in its conclusion. Like the circular framing device of *The Attack*, *Sirens* also includes a set piece opening that it returns to for its conclusion. In *Sirens*, this take the form of a prologue in Beirut, the staging place for the final preparations for a viral attack in London that will 'decimate a good part of the population', to be carried out by the protagonist (5). This means we begin near the end of the story with the protagonist on the precipice of committing an atrocity before the narrative flashes back to cover his journey up to this point and finally reveals the ultimate choice he makes. Dr. Jalal and Mohammed Seen are thus important characters in the way they influence him in this final phase. Dr. Jalal is an intellectual elite and expert on the Muslim world who functions as a kind of interlocutor for the protagonist. He had built a career in the West as a cultural commentator akin to what Morey and Yaqin describe as a 'professional Muslim', before turning his back on Western intellectual circles and 'taking a side' in the clash of civilisations.[7] The novelist, Seen, is dismayed by Jalal's turn, and challenges him in a potent scene directly addressing clash logic and referencing DeLillo's famous idea of a 'zero-sum game between novelists and terrorists', discussed in the Introduction to this book. I will return to this debate shortly.

In addition to the characterisation of these peripheral figures, the novel's genre coding collapses the clash discourse it sets up. As a tragedy, the 'peripitea' moment which launches the protagonist's inexorable trajectory is related to an avoidable deficit in the American GIs' cultural awareness. Equally, the 'hamartia' element, the protagonist's own self-diagnosed 'sensitivity', is richly dramatised. He initially detests violence and describes himself as an 'emotional person' who finds 'other people's sorrows devastating' (96). Because of these traits, the magnitude of his experiences of state violence is amplified. Yet, his radicalisation is never something depicted as a stereotypical vulnerability to indoctrination.

Within the bookends of the novel's framing scenes in Beirut are two halves. It begins in the village of Kafr Karam, after the protagonist has returned home from university in Baghdad at the onset of the invasion, when the 'sirens echoed in the silence of the night, buildings started to explode in smoke, and from one day to the next, the most passionate love affairs dissolved in tears and blood' (19). In the second half he returns to Baghdad to find purpose as an insurgent after a series of escalating instances of military and state terrorism. The three key events of the first half of the novel represent a staged trajectory towards this departure, the final one proving decisive. The first of the three events occurs when a local child, Sulayman, who has a disability, is brutally shot by an American soldier. The protagonist, Sulayman and his father are travelling to a nearby health clinic when they encounter Iraqi and American soldiers. Sulayman's father tries to explain that the child may behave unpredictably but they do not listen, and when he bolts out of fear, they execute him. The protagonist witnesses it all and vomits violently before passing out, his body having 'lost its power to react' (58). When the situation calms and the American soldiers realise their mistake, they apologise to the elders of Kafr Karam, and the war on terror momentarily returns to a subject of village debate and discussion, rather than visceral reality. However, before long the second event occurs, and in this case Khadra draws on real-world source material. In the novel, a rocket attack kills dozens of innocents at a wedding party outside of Kafr Karam.[8] After the rocket attack, the protagonist works through the night to help the injured and grieving, amidst the rising anger of the people of Kafr Karam. When the media arrive, he witnesses a distraught father speaking to the cameras: 'The real terrorists are the bastards who fired the missile at us', and he walks home 'like a man stumbling through a fog' (95). Again, the Americans apologise for their mistake (which they did not do in the aftermath of the wedding massacre in Mukaradeeb, Iraq, in 2004) and a semblance of normal life resumes in Kafr Karam. At this point, the protagonist is suffering from what he has witnessed and meditates on his sensitivity: 'I wasn't a weakling, I simply hated violence' (97). Around him, village debates about the war and occupation intensify and a heightened unrest develops. Finally, the protagonist's own family is violently impacted when American soldiers manhandle his father, knocking the old man to the floor in his own home. Their ignorance of Bedouin cultural values means they commit an unspeakable offence:

> while my family's honor lay stricken on the floor, I saw what it was forbidden to see, what a worthy, respectable son, an authentic Bedouin, must never see: that flaccid, hideous, degrading thing, that forbidden, unspoken-of, sacrilegious object, my father's penis, rolling to one side as his testicles flopped up over his ass. This sight was the edge of the abyss, and beyond it, there was nothing but the infinite void, an interminable fall, nothingness. (101)

Khadra lingers on the impact of this episode for several pages, drawing on his knowledge of Bedouin culture, and emphasising the way this moment hinges on a knowledge deficit. The protagonist's internal monologue is devastating: 'A Westerner can't understand, can't suspect the dimensions of the disaster. For me, to see my father's sex was to reduce my entire existence, my values and my scruples, my pride and my singularity, to a coarse, pornographic flash' (102).

Soon after this event, the protagonist packs for Baghdad to find an outlet for his rage, and this second half of the novel continues its staged trajectory, moving from a desire to join the resistance to a willingness to commit atrocity. However, the flashpoints that punctuate both halves of the novel occur amid contextual elements that provide nuance to the cause-and-effect, terror-and-counter-terror logic of the novel's clash of civilisations frame. A key part of this is its metatextual registering of clash logic, and the scene I began with, in which a 'clash of titans' is evoked by one of the protagonist's associates, and understood as both farce and destiny, is foreshadowed by an exchange he has with a driver taking him to Baghdad. The driver, who reveals he had worked as a 'collaborator' with the US military, informs the protagonist that Hollywood sanitises and glorifies American soldiers: 'Real American GIs having nothing to do with the Hollywood marketing version. That's just loud demagoguery. The truth is, they don't have any more scruples than a pack of hyenas let loose in a sheep barn' (127). Presaging Sayeed and Yaseen's imagery, the driver suggests that in contrast Americans see Arabs as 'retarded':

> 'We taught the world table manners; we taught the world hygiene and cooking and mathematics and medicine. And what to these degenerates of modernity remember of all that? A camel caravan crossing the dunes at sunset? Some fat guy in a white robe and a keffiyeh flashing his millions a gambling casino on the Côte d'Azur? Clichés, caricatures . . .' (128)

These two moments show how attuned the novel is to the clichés that it seems, in some ways, to be reinforcing. The driver's rhetoric urges the protagonist to look for the reality behind the caricature or propaganda, but the reality that is determined by such crude formations is all around them. Later, when Sayeed and Yaseen's arguments about the inevitability of a 'clash of titans' register it as both farcical and something that is magnetically appealing, the position the novel takes is clear: the clash of civilisation is a reductive and inflammatory formation built on flimsy caricatures, but it is also powerfully alluring in ways that demand more attention. It adds a further dimension of critique in its acts of reversal, as readers are invited to think about the appeal of these abstractions to Iraqi citizens under occupation in comparison with the way Americans adopted them after 9/11.

The novel continues this critical mode up until the final section, set in Beirut. As the protagonist becomes entrenched with a militant group, and is groomed for his ultimate mission, we learn that he is given DVDs of the 'various atrocities committed by coalition forces' (198). He even describes this using one of the most clichéd metaphors of indoctrination: 'It was as if I were downloading into my brain all the possible and imaginable reasons I'd need to blow up the fucking world' (198). But alongside such clichés are moments where the protagonist is shown to be a complex character whose capacities for witnessing and experiencing violence have been overwhelmed. He even reflects that 'the sirens of Baghdad no longer reached me', using this titular phrase to evoke his own change and the changes Baghdad has experienced (199). He also describes his condition using the metaphor of matryoshka dolls, as Amy Waldman does in *The Submission* (2011) in a scene discussed in the previous chapter where the protagonist is struggling to orient herself. For the protagonist of *Sirens*, this is more about entrapment and claustrophobia: he feels like 'the smallest in a set of Russian nesting dolls' and needs to 'come unglued, to explode like a bomb, to be useful somehow' (206). The killing of Omar is perhaps the final straw for him and leads to his volunteering for the viral attack. But his feelings about Omar are despair, regret and self-disgust over allowing his fellow militants to needlessly kill this young man who had been so kind. The passages describing his feelings for Omar are in sharp contrast to the clichéd depictions of 'downloading' propaganda videos:

> Omar's ghost had become my companion animal, my walking grief, my intoxication, and my madness. All I had to do was to lower my

eyelids and he it would fill my mind . . . There was nothing left in the world except Omar's ghost and me. We *were* the world. (234)

It is in this state that the young man volunteers to be a host for a viral attack, travels to Beirut for preparations, meets Dr. Jalal, and witnesses a bitter debate between Jalal an old friend of his, the novelist Mohammed Seen – who seems to be a stand-in for Khadra in the political arguments he makes.

The final section of the novel comprises sixty-two pages in which the protagonist is prepared for his journey to London where he will spread a mutating virus that he will be injected with in Beirut. Upon arrival in Beirut, he takes up residence at a nice hotel and is given tickets, by his handler, Sayed, to see Dr. Jalal speak. He describes Dr. Jalal's 'about face', noting that he had heard of him in high school and read his books, including *Why Are Muslims Angry?*, and that for 'the ordinary devout Muslim, Dr. Jalal was nothing but a mountebank, a Western lackey in the pay of factions hostile to Islam in general and to Arabs in particular' (249). He was, we learn,

> one of the most repulsive examples of those traitors who proliferated like rats in European media and academic circles, fully prepared to exchange their souls for the privilege of seeing their photographs in a newspaper and hearing themselves talked about. (249)

These views have changed, since Jalal renounced the West; and after hearing him speak at a packed auditorium, the protagonist is in awe of his proficiency and intellect:

> The accuracy of his analyses and the effectiveness of his arguments are a joy to consider. No imam can match him; no speaker is better at turning a murmur into a cry. He's hypersensitive and exceptionally intelligent, a mentor of rare charisma. (251)

The protagonist seems appreciative of the evolution of Jalal's thinking and perhaps sees his own journey reflected in this. Ultimately, Jalal reinforces his convictions and it is clear Sayed has intentionally placed the protagonist in his orbit as he prepares for his attack. Indeed, the young man seeks out Dr. Jalal in a moment of doubt near the very end of the novel at a point where it switches to the first-person present tense: 'I feel all alone. I try to get a hold of myself. I need Jalal's anger to fill my blank spots' (268).

In this moment the protagonist witnesses the debate between Dr. Jalal and Mohammed Seen, who were friends before the former renounced his alignment with Western intellectual spheres. After a cordial greeting the two sit down, as the protagonist listens in, and Seen admonishes him for his lecture and his political 'about face'. Seen is aggrieved by the way Dr. Jalal has adopted clash logic and taken the side of those who use violence to stand up to the West. What ensues is a debate about the nature of binary logic, that reifies the larger arguments of the book and establishes Seen, at least partially, as a stand-in for Khadra. One intriguing aspect of this is the way it references DeLillo's 'curious knot between novelists and terrorists', posited by the protagonist of *Mao II* (1991, 41). In DeLillo's novel, the writer Bill Gray repeatedly argues that writers and terrorists are playing a 'zero-sum game' for the 'inner life of the culture'. This is recalibrated by Seen, who insists to Jalal that Muslim intellectuals must compete with insurgents to 'represent' Muslim people:

> Muslims are on the side of the person who can project their voice, the Muslim voice, as far as possible. They don't care whether he's a terrorist or an artist, an imposter or a righteous man, an obscure genius or an elder statesman. They need a myth, an idol. Someone capable of representing them, of expressing them in their complexity, of defending them in some way. Whether with the pen or with bombs, it makes little difference to them. (275)

Putting aside the contradictions in the imperative to represent the 'complexity' of Muslim lives while purporting to know what 'they need' in very homogenising terms, this is a reconfiguring of DeLillo's 'zero-sum game' between terrorists and artists, the 'pen and the bomb' for the specific context of the Muslim world. This evolves into a debate about the clash of civilisations, which Seen describes as 'pseudomodernity against pseudobarbarity' (276). Dr. Jalal first agrees with this notion and seems to refute clash logic by undercutting its core assumptions: '"The West isn't modern; it's rich. And the 'barbarians' aren't barbarians; they're poor people who don't have the wherewithal to modernize"' (276). Ultimately, though, as the two men's tempers boil over, and their debate turns ugly and personal, Dr. Jalal implores Seen to take a side in the clash: '"You're caught between two worlds, Mohammed. It's a very uncomfortable position to be in. We're in the midst of a clash of civilizations. You're going to have to decide which camp you're in"' (281).

This debate has a serious impact on Dr. Jalal, who cancels his lectures and appointments and halts progress on his scholarly work. By extension it impacts the protagonist, who has been inspired by Dr. Jalal and who is disheartened that he has been 'flustered by a servile scribbler', and tension grows between them (282). Eventually,

Dr. Jalal finds out about the terror plot and reproaches him in terms that again exemplify the novel's argument on clash logic. Dr. Jalal is incredulous and angry asks, '"Where are we, in a Spielberg film?"' (294). This echoes other already cited moments in the novel that reference Hollywood and US popular culture. It critiques the crass nature of clash logic, while also inviting the reader to compare the ways it has been adopted by a young Bedouin with its prevalence in post-9/11 America. It both critiques it and insists that it be taken seriously, as a few lines after suggesting the young man is living in a fantasy world of revenge, Dr. Jalal insists, '"what you're going to do. Very, very, very serious. Unthinkable. Unimaginable . . ."' (294). Ultimately, the young man cannot bring himself to board his flight to London and is assassinated after aborting the mission, in tragic circumstances. His last thoughts are meditations on wasted life: 'I'm only twenty-one years old and all I have is the certainty that I've wrecked my life twenty-one times over' (306).

Khadra's novels address clash logic via genre, using their familiar formulas and frameworks to address topics that, for Western readers, were and are unfamiliar while simultaneously resisting stereotypes of radicalisation that remain very common. In the next section, I conclude this chapter with analysis of Nadeem Aslam's *The Blind Man's Garden* (2013) – a novel that is loosely connected to his previous novel, *The Wasted Vigil* (2008), but which addresses an earlier period, directly after 9/11. Though Aslam's novel is much longer, is much wider in scope, and might be more obviously 'literary' than Khadra's novels, I identify some surprising connections in the formal dimensions of these works. Ultimately, I argue that *The Blind Man's Garden* repeatedly stages instances of binary thinking just as it deals in a set of compelling doubles, all while attending to the more subtle and entrenched ideological currents that underpin clash logics.

The Blind Man's Garden

Though *The Blind Man's Garden* shares elements of the tragedy genre with *Sirens of Baghdad*, it is ostensibly more 'literary' than the novels by Khadra. It features a labyrinthine, multi-generational plot that unfolds over 462 pages, it is conspicuous in its mobilisation of metaphor and allegory (blindness/the titular garden), and it is much more poetic in terms of sentence-level style. The novel is organised in four sections and begins with the declarative opening line: 'History is the third parent' (1). This signals its emphasis on familial relationships, its imbrication of the personal and political, and its challenge to Western narratives of the war on terror. It begins in the fictional town of Heer, Pakistan, in October 2001. Its significant characters are Pakistani, though much of the action occurs in Afghanistan, which is facing yet another period of violence and invasion in the aftermath of 9/11. Jeo, a medical student, decides to cross the border to help the wounded, and is joined by his mercurial adopted brother, Mikal. Jeo and Mikal are soon captured by Taliban fighters and left to die in the facility they are held in when it is attacked by another militant faction allied to the US Army. Mikal survives (barely) as a prisoner of a warlord and is sold for $5,000 as a terror suspect to the American military forces, who torture him over several weeks. Jeo had been married to a young woman called Naheed, following an arrangement between his father, Rohan, and Naheed's mother, Tara, who was imprisoned for adultery under Sharia law after being raped because there were not 'four male witnesses' to corroborate her story (118). Rohan agreed to the marriage to ensure Naheed's wellbeing, for Tara's piece of mind. Jeo was not aware, until near the end of his life, that before his marriage, Naheed and Mikal had fallen in love. Rohan, an ageing schoolmaster, leaves Naheed and his daughter Yasmin, and travels to Peshawar, on the border, to find his sons, but is too late. The loss of Jeo, and presumed loss of Mikal, compounds his decades-old guilt over the death of his wife, Sofia, nearly twenty years earlier, who died – in Rohan's view – an 'apostate'. The rigidly devout Rohan had quarrelled bitterly with Sofia, a painter and humanist who had disavowed religion, and who had stopped speaking to him when he expelled a young student whose mother was a prostitute, and he has spent decades worrying about the fate of her soul and reflecting on his actions. Rohan formerly owned the school where he and Sofia worked, Ardent Spirit, but had signed it over to a former student, Ahmed the Moth, 'because money carried the devil's taint', staying on as a modestly salaried headmaster (32). However, when Ahmed dies in the days after 9/11, it is inherited by his militant brother, Major Kyra. These various plot strands begin to cohere in the second half of the novel, which moves towards the outcomes and permutations of two events: the reunion of Mikal and Naheed, and Kyra and his followers' terrorist attack on a Christian school where Rohan's daughter Yasmin and Mikal's brother Basie – who are married – both teach. This complex plot unfolds through Aslam's poetic and symbolically rich prose.

In a review of the novel, Nina Martyris celebrates Aslam's 'lyrical style' while noting his 'weakness for metaphor' and his tendency to combine and juxtapose images of beauty and violence. For Martyris, also given to figurative language, he is 'a writer who can bend barbed wire into calligraphy' (n.p.). Pankaj Mishra also notes the distinctiveness of Aslam's prose and narrative style, which he describes as a 'premodernist fusion of the individual and the historical more reminiscent of *The Charterhouse of Parma* than of any contemporary literary novel' (n.p.). However, if there are some conspicuous ways in which we might understand Aslam's writing as 'literary', there are, as noted, some formal similarities with Khadra's novels too, and crucially, like *The Sirens of Baghdad* and *The Attack*, *The Blind Man's Garden* mobilises certain genre frameworks as entry points into the unfamiliar. For instance, the story of Mikal, as Gen'ichiro Itakura notes, 'takes its narrative drive not only from its realism and "action-adventure thriller" elements, but also from its appropriation of elements of romance or melodrama' (358). This is an astute observation. *The Blind Man's Garden* is a sweeping story that, for all its complexity, includes several improbable coincidences and symmetries, and is built around melodramatic plot turns: brothers in love with the same person, the possibility of forced marriage, wrongful detention and unlikely escape, and a lifetime of guilt and regret. Mishra connects these features to the 'fairy tale' genre, pointing to the '[d]ramatic partings and reunions, stories of betrayal, captivity, exile and rescue, historical legends, Islamic folklore, rumours' and 'superstition' (n.p.). What is significant, though, is the way these familiar narrative frames allow access to ideas that may be unfamiliar to Western readers. As Itakura argues, 'Aslam's text facilitates affective, emotional engagement with "unfamiliar" feelings of pain specific to a postcolonial, post-9/11 context' and does this via the 'transfer of affect from familiar scripts to specific emotions' (361, 366). As is the case in Khadra's novels, these scripts represent entry points for Western readers but also enable the novel to challenge stereotypes of Afghan and Pakistani people that remain prevalent, and the clash logics which continue to perpetuate them.

The Blind Man's Garden has received a fair amount of scholarly attention, most addressing its response to 9/11 and the war on terror and to early 9/11 fiction, though there is growing interest in the novel's depictions of nature. Margaret Scanlan, eminent scholar of literature and terrorism, reads the novel as a direct response to 9/11 fiction but also to larger structures of clash logic, arguing that it 'evokes the difficulties of interpretation, areas of mutual ignorance and distortions of propaganda and mass-produced popular culture that fill up the empty space where Samuel P. Huntington sees civilisations clashing' (103). Sarah O'Brien makes a similar claim, arguing that Aslam's novel gives 'voice to those marginalised by post-9/11 rhetorics' (99). Both Scanlan's and O'Brien's analyses align with Itakura's argument about the formal dimensions of the novel, and particularly the 'romantic, sensational' story of Mikal and Naheed, which 'helps us engage emotionally with characters caught up in the chaotic situation of contemporary Pakistan and Afghanistan' (358). Given the symbolism of the titular garden, the pervasive ornithological imagery, a snow leopard cub adopted at different points by both Mikal and an American soldier – who functions as his double – as well as the general emphasis on the natural world, it is unsurprising that recent scholarship has focused on nature in *The Blind Man's Garden*. Shazia Rahman argues that the novel's obsession with nature and animals works in relation to a theme that has been prevalent in all of Aslam's writing: misogyny. Rahman notes that it 'explores and occupies the intersections of masculinity, contemporary imperialism, and our multispecies world' (199). Rahman identifies significance in the novel's depiction of 'the interconnections between the human and nonhuman' worlds, and points to the way it sees potential for 'egalitarian' relationships, while also noting that some characters fail to make these connections; in particular, Rohan (though he becomes less rigid) and the American soldier paired with Mikal in the novel's final phase (208). Saba Pirzadeh also focuses on the novel's engagement with nature but is more interested in the way it shows how the Afghan landscape is subjected to a kind of militarised othering which 'codifies it as a hostile space' (900).

I argue that Aslam's stirring novel functions as a multivalent rejoinder to the alleged clash of civilisations. I show how it attends to the crudest formations of clash logic as well as the more subtle currents that underpin them. I argue that in addition to its use of genre 'scripts', the novel's depiction of the natural world is central to its critique of what Aslam has described as a clash between 'an incomplete understanding of the East and an incomplete understanding of the West' (Khalid n.p.). The novel's substantial cast of characters, ornithological leitmotif, its titular – and allegorical – garden, animal imagery and animal characters, and landscapes both beautiful and harsh mean that it locates a specific moment of geopolitical conflict, terrorism and counter-terrorism in broader and yet sometimes idiosyncratic terms, inviting the reader to orient themselves and reorient themselves in unexpected ways, and to adopt new coordinates for a conflict that has often been understood in simplistic terms. Though I agree with Pirzadeh that the novel shows how the Afghan landscape has become 'othered' and codified as 'hostile', and how it 'depicts the consequences of incessant warfare, ethnic in-fighting, and socio-political conflict on both the local population and the landscape', the novel undoubtedly also emphasises the natural beauty of this nation and region (893). Equally, and while an emphasis on the natural world invites us to question socially and politically constructed borders, the distinctions that do become visible between Pakistan and Afghanistan respond to the crude conflations imposed upon these nations – such as the term 'AfPak', coined by Richard Holbrooke, a special adviser to President Obama. The term is one of many devised to impose a sense of order or mastery. As Ronak Kapadia has noted, the term offered a 'vision of a single battlefield of military operations to disrupt the transnational presence of Al-Qaeda' and it 'speaks volumes about the imagined geographies of US empire' (67). Ultimately, Aslam's novel's vision of the natural world as dynamic, unsparing and rich with internal difference and dramatic juxtaposition mirrors the internal tensions of the social and cultural formations that are violently homogenised by clash logics. Simultaneously, the distinct visions of Afghanistan and Pakistan resist the clumsy and reductive thinking behind terms such as 'AfPak'.

The novel's response to the post-9/11 clash of civilisations is introduced immediately. We learn, via the omniscient narrator, that 'The Battle of the World Trade Center and Pentagon is what some people here in Pakistan have named September's terrorist attacks' (6). This emphasis on a different name for '9/11', which might be unfamiliar to Western readers – an unsubtle reframing – is given nuance by the omniscient narrator's qualifier, 'some people', and more familiar descriptor: 'terrorist attacks'. It also opens the novel's sustained interest in positionality, and its insistence that world events are understood differently in different contexts. This emphasis on positionality and context is sustained via comments from minor – but usually important – characters, who rehearse and reframe the conflict in several ways.

One of the most evocative instances of this comes when an aged local fakir evokes binary logic in broad philosophical terms during an intense discussion with Rohan. Referred to also as a 'djinn' and a 'mendicant', this recurring character carries heavy chains linked between a metal ring on his neck and wrists (386). Like Rohan, and roughly the same age, he is burdened, and this connection is affirmed when we learn that Basie and Mikal believed he was their lost father when they were children; actually their parents were communists, and their father was arrested around the time of Mikal's birth and never seen again (17). Rohan, Basie and Yasmin encounter the fakir just after a Christian church has been bombed. The narrator notes that 'those claiming responsibility had said that since Western Christians were bombing and destroying mosques in Afghanistan, they were beginning a campaign to annihilate churches in Pakistan', setting up the exchange between the fakir's comments (94). The fakir is moving slowly under the weight of his chains while watching the distant flames. The trio stop to see if they can help him and Rohan initiates the discussion, asking, 'How can anyone explain the world?', to which the fakir replies '[w]ith great care, as though writing the words instead of uttering them' (97):

> 'It can be done. *Ahl-e-Dil* and *Ahl-e-Havas*. We all are divided into these two groups. The first are the People of the Heart. The second are the People of Greed, the deal makers and the men of lust and the hucksters . . . The first people will not trample anyone to obtain what they desire. The second will. Here lies this world. (97)

This is a very different kind of binary, and though it might be tempting to map the 'People of Greed, the deal makers' onto 'the Americans', the novel's depiction of internal division in Pakistan and Afghanistan refutes this, and instead the fakir's comments provide an alternative set of binaries that contextualises other diegetic evocations of the clash of civilisations. In one sense, the latter abstraction is displaced by the fakir's broader abstraction, but the novel's repeated patterns of doubling or emphasising connections between characters – Rohan and the fakir, Mikal and Jeo, Mikal and the US soldier, and finally Naheed and Yasmin – troubles this binary logic. Indeed, shortly after this scene with the fakir, another highly symbolic character, the bird pardoner, with whom the novel opens, espouses a kind of binary logic that reveals a connection between him and Rohan. The bird pardoner snares birds and takes payment from anyone willing to pay to free a bird, which will then 'say a prayer for the person who has bought its freedom' (7). Rohan is suspicious of this man and becomes angered when he leaves several birds to die in his garden, but is forgiving when he learns that his son, at fourteen years old, had fled to Peshawar to fight, and that the bird pardoner had gone after him to try to stop him. This is a conspicuous link as both men's sons have fled to the battlefield, albeit with different objectives. The bird pardoner laments to Rohan, emphasising another kind of binary logic:

'All I can say is if September's terrorist attacks had to happen, I am sorry that they happened in my lifetime. They have destroyed me. And I live so far from where they took place. What does Heer know about New York, or New York about Heer? They are two different worlds.' (133)

That these symbolic characters, the fakir and the bird pardoner, make these statements to Rohan is evocative, as he is a character who is deeply divided between a rigidly pious and patriarchal value system and his empathy towards several women whose experiences represent a rebuttal of that system. The great love of his life, his late wife, was a secular humanist, and in addition to witnessing and perpetuating her suffering, he witnesses the humiliation and persecution of his daughter-in-law Naheed, his daughter Yasmin, and Tara, imprisoned for being raped. Rohan is defined by internal conflict but also clearly sympathetic as he is blinded, widowed and soon bereaved by the loss of his son. The novel invites us to align with and occupy his uncertain and conflicted world, and to read and interpret these various iterations of binary logic while also considering the intense connections between him and the fakir and bird pardoner, and the other doubles the narrative sets up. It is a world of meaningful doublings, and violent binaries, that cautiously, and with some qualification, begins to favour connection and solidarity over conflict and division.

There are many other instances, within the diegetic world of the novel, where characters address binary logic or positionality directly. For example, early on, the militants who contrive to have Jeo and Mikal captured – at Ahmed the Moth's instruction – discuss the violence unfolding around them. As they stop for water, one hears explosions and gunfire in the distance and comments wearily, 'it's the world', to which another replies, 'The world sounds like this all the time, we just don't hear it. Then sometimes in some places we do' (57). This is an elliptical exchange that simultaneously suggests the world is defined by conflict while also insisting that some places are immune – at least for periods. It resonates in a novel intent on rethinking assumptions about geopolitical connections and divisions.

Ultimately, though Rohan is at the heart of the novel, Mikal's story drives the novel's re-staging and reframing of clash logics, as well as its most compelling instance of doubling. This begins during Mikal's time in American captivity, and the scenes in which he is tortured are among the most discussed in *The Blind Man's Garden*. These are undoubtedly key moments, but they should be understood in the context of the novel's developing vision of binaries and doubling. One of the most striking moments in the sequence of torture scenes comes when the interrogator, David Town – a crossover character from *The Wasted Vigil* – points to a poster of the twin towers of the World Trade Center and asks how Mikal felt about the attacks. When Mikal informs him that he believes it was a 'disgusting crime', David insists, 'Most of your people didn't think so. They were pleased' (216). Mikal questions David's recourse to homogenising 'his people' and asserts, 'Now you know we don't all think alike', adding the question, 'How many of my people have you met anyway?' (216). Finally, when David replies unconvincingly that he has met 'enough', Mikal reverses his logic: 'Do you want me to base my opinion of *your* people on the ones I have met here?' (216). This conversation comes after sustained scenes of torture, and the repeated insistence – by the Americans – that they do not torture because it is 'barbaric and uncivilised' (208). This scene depicts the exceptionalist underpinnings of the war on terror and entrenched Islamophobia – and certainly the first of Deepa Kumar's six frames of Islamophobia, the perception that Islam is 'monolithic', is vividly rendered (70). However, it also relies a bit too much on caricature and bears some similarity to scenes from popular counter-terrorism television shows like *24* (2001–10) and *Homeland* (2011–20). Yet, understood in relation to the novel's broader set of doublings and binaries, and uses of genre frames, it is more complex.

Mikal is reflective and his acts of questioning and self-questioning are at the heart of the novel. In one memorable scene, he catches himself making assumptions. He is watching from a distance as figures on a hillside search the 'network of caves' (373). He assumes they are 'looking for terrorists' and as he witnesses an encounter between the searchers, assumed to be Americans and the sought, he questions his own assumptions just as he applies his own kind of binary logic: 'The Americans, if they are Americans, are completely silent as though their words and sounds are incapable of travelling through the air of this land' (374), again reinforcing the notion that understanding is impossible. He then notes that actually 'the searchers are Pakistani soldiers' because he 'hears them begin to talk in Urdu, Punjabi, Pashto and Hindko' (374). Not only, then, does Mikal realise the inaccuracies of his assumptions, he notes the multiplicity of languages and voices – and differences – of the searchers. Another small detail is relevant here. A few pages earlier, when the novel establishes the setting – Mikal in the outskirts of a small town in the Afghan desert – it poetically describes 'the open wild desert to the west' (369), using language that evokes the American 'wild west'. This foreshadows events to come, where Mikal is paired with an American soldier, but also connects what Pirzadeh describes as a landscape codified as 'hostile space' to an American landscape that was often envisioned in similar terms.

Eventually, Mikal is released from captivity. Traumatised and fearing for his life, he shoots two American soldiers and goes on the run. With some assistance from Afghan militants – particularly a man called Akbar – he returns to Heer and is reunited with Naheed. However, driven by an obligation to help Akbar, he returns to Afghanistan and this leads – in a most unlikely eventuality – to Mikal's discovery of an American soldier, alone and collapsed in the desert, who is the brother of one of the soldiers he killed. They are instantly connected. Both the American and Mikal have lost their brothers in the conflict. They both subsequently find themselves in solitary and perilous situations in the desert, using their skills to 'navigate by the stars' (377, 386). Their connection is strengthened by a snow leopard cub, in the possession of the American, that had previously befriended and captivated Mikal. But what makes this doubling so potent is that despite Mikal's attempts to connect with, protect and save the solider, their coming together ends in tragedy. As Rahman notes, 'there is no way to get past the gulf of differences between them even though they have this love for the snow leopard in common' (205). However, Mikal's own convictions are strengthened during the encounter, even as he is increasingly imperilled, and this happens through powerful connections with the cub and with other aspects of the natural world. During the initial encounter, unsure what to do, the cub inspires him towards empathy. He provides water and care to the soldier just as he reflects on the cub: 'astonished at the power the animal's eyes have over him, the gaze captivating within an instant, a radiant dreamlike effect on his mind' (396). Later, near the end of their fraught time together, Mikal breaks down after witnessing the simple natural beauty of a firefly:

> He looks away from the miraculous sight and back at the American, wondering if there are fireflies in his country. Looking through the broken window between them he is suddenly overwhelmed, not by an emotion he knows, suddenly feeling himself unequal to so wide a chase, so remorseless a life. He is shocked to find himself close to weeping, a few initial sobs escaping. (431)

Mikal goes on to tell the American soldier his life story, concluding with an apology for killing his 'countrymen', but, of course, we know this goes unheard because of the language barrier (431). While Mikal's empathy grows, the US soldier remains hostile. As Rahman notes, his 'connection with animal others does not rid him of his racism and hegemonic masculinity which continue to lead him to dehumanize other humans' (205). Mikal recognises the suffering of the American, and through their contrived and melodramatic encounter, his own empathy is widened and, for the reader at least, some forms of connection come into view. As Itakura notes, 'the injured American soldier's eyes serve for Mikal as a "doorway" to the suffering of a man who belongs to an ethnic group he has never sympathized with' (366). Moreover, *The Blind Man's Garden* 'serves for its readers as a portal taking them to the locations of suffering, not through magic or technology, but through a transfer of affect from familiar scripts to specific emotions' (366).

At every stage of Mikal's story, the same binaries that Rohan confronts are prevalent, and particularly so as he is doubled with the American soldier. Nearing the end of their journey, Mikal discusses the fate of the American with the servant of an Afghan family who have detained them. Mikal wants to help the American soldier even though everyone he encounters urges him to kill him or sell him. The servant recalls his own history with 'Westerners', how he fought 'when they were here in the 1930s' (441). The old man echoes the bird pardoner and numerous other characters in emphasising the impossibility of understanding the motivations of the 'other', and near the novel's end this strikes a maudlin note:

> 'We can't know what the Westerners want,' the old man says. 'To know what they want you have to eat what they eat, wear what they wear, breathe the air they breathe. You have to be born where they are born.' (441)

This scene's poignancy derives from its place, late on in the novel, and the way it reframes comments from other older characters including the bird pardoner, the fakir and Rohan. Ultimately, Mikal dies trying to deliver the American to safety, and his death is doubled by the death of his brother, Basie, who dies in the brutal terrorist attacks at the Christian school where he and Yasmin work. Through these eventualities, the narrative ends with the blind Rohan, his daughter-in-law Naheed and daughter Yasmin.

I have not discussed the school terror attack in depth, and it is worth noting that it provides the most conventional vision of terrorism in the novel in depictions of Major Kyra and militants who 'want the birth of a new world, and will take death and repeat it and repeat it and repeat it until that birth results' (312). This sounds like a meta-statement on the nature of terrorism, and this episode also results in serious trauma for the survivors. In a later scene, Yasmin, unable to sleep, 'sees again and again the thirsty children drinking urine at St Joseph's on the second day of the siege' (353). This terrorist attack, perpetrated by Major Kyra's Taliban militants, also operates within the novel's layers of binaries. As Alex Houen notes, Major Kyra's rhetoric of 'sacrificial militancy' is interesting in that the idea of 'sacrifice' was a common part of President Bush's rhetoric during the war on terror (507, 508), and in that 'sacrifice' might normally be distinct from martyrdom. When Major Kyra argues for the killing of innocents, by claiming that 'Allah is asking us to sacrifice them', the choice of language is conspicuous (286). But this episode is woven into a story that includes many other forms of terrorism and violence – including the torture experienced by Mikal – and if the novel has any overarching statement on the nature of terrorism, it might be its depiction of Rohan, for whom terror is not contingent on sectarian, paramilitary or state loyalties; instead, '[t]error is not knowing where the pain is coming from' (282). Ultimately, Rohan survives, and despite the deaths of Jeo, Mikal, the American soldier and Basie, there is some hope in the final allegorical image of the titular blind man's garden – replete with a rope with which Rohan can navigate and orient himself. The rope 'connects all the different plants and locations Rohan likes to visit' and we learn that the children want it to reach out into the community, to the 'mosque, the bazaars, the houses of acquaintances' (460). This vision of connection, provided by the next generation, concludes a novel obsessed with forms of division and possibilities of connection. It is fitting that an image of nature concludes this 462-page novel of binaries and doublings. Images of the natural and animal worlds have driven its strongest refutations of clash logics, and though it remains uncertain about the possibilities of collapsing this reductive abstraction, it is fiercely critical of those who seek to uphold it.

Notes

1. Marita Sturken, discussing the origins of '9/11 exceptionalism', describes American exceptionalism as 'a national narrative that defines the United States as an exemplary nation that not only stands apart from other nations but also imagines itself as outside of international and global norms' (8).
2. The idea of the literary 'counter-narrative' of 9/11 emerged from DeLillo's essay 'In the Ruins of the Future' (2001). DeLillo did

not emphasise responses to Islamophobia, but an idea of literary sophistication redressing simplistic formations does feature.
3. State terrorism is defined in the Introduction to this book. I refer to instances of torture, drone strikes and other forms of state violence as state terrorism throughout.
4. In recent studies of 'homo economicus' and periodisations of neoliberalism (Huehls and Greenwald Smith 2017; Deckard and Shapiro 2019) there is some consensus that market logic pervaded social and cultural life in Western capitalist democracies in the 1990s. Huehls and Greenwald Smith's notion that it subsequently became 'ontological' is contested.
5. As Morrison shows, the logic of the Prevent programme in the UK has leaned on ideas of 'vulnerability' and a set of Islamophobic assumptions. Preti Taneja's comments in *Aftermath* aptly summarise these: 'it has proved damaging, sowing distrust, disillusionment and a dangerous isolation and affecting the opposite of what it says it wants to achieve' (126).
6. The Fanonian logic of violence we see in *The Attack* also appears in Hany Abu-Assad's wonderful 2005 film, *Paradise Now*. Protagonist Said gives an impassioned monologue: 'A life without dignity is worthless. Especially when it reminds you day after day of humiliation and weakness. And the world watches cowardly, indifferently. If you're all alone, faced with this oppression you have to find a way to stop the injustice. They must understand that if there is no security for us, there'll be none for them either. It's not about power. Their power doesn't help them. I tried to deliver this message to them but I couldn't find another way. Even worse they've convinced the world and themselves that they are the victims. How can that be? How can the occupier be the victim? If they take on the role of oppressor and victim then I have no other choice but to also be a victim and a murderer as well.'
7. Morey and Yaqin discuss the phenomenon of the 'professional Muslim' which emerged in the early war on terror era: 'particular voices representing certain recognized and accommodated strands within Islam have been cultivated and brought to the fore, while others have been downplayed and marginalized as "less representative"' (80).
8. This echoes the Mukaradeeb, Iraq, wedding massacre of 2004, in which 42 civilians were murdered by the occupying forces, and the wedding massacre in Uruzgan province, Afghanistan, in 2002, when over 30 celebrating villagers were killed by a US bomber (BBC News).

Works Cited

Adam, Loraine, 'Yasmina Khadra: "Fiction keeps me safe from the hardships of real life"', *Afrique* (November 2015) <https://afriquemagazine.

com/fiction-keeps-me-safe-hardships-real-life#:~:text=Yasmina%20 Khadra%2C%20whose%20real%20name,in%20the%20choice%20 of%20themes> [accessed 5 October 2023].

Ågerup, Karl, 'Knowing an Arab: Yasmina Khadra and the Aesthetics of Didactic Fiction', *Critique: Studies in Contemporary Fiction*, 59.2 (2018), 180–90.

Ahmad, Aijaz, 'Jameson's Rhetoric of Otherness and the "National Allegory"', *Social Text*, 17 (1987), 3–25.

Amiri, Cyrus, and Mahdiyeh Govah, 'Hedayat's Rebellious Child: Multicultural Rewriting of *The Blind Owl* in Porochista Khakpour's *Sons and Other Flammable Objects*', *British Journal of Middle Eastern Studies*, 50.2 (2023), 436–49 <https://doi.org/10.1080/13530194.2021.1978279>.

Aslam, Nadeem, *The Blind Man's Garden* (London: Faber, 2013).

BBC News, '"Scores killed" in US Afghan Raid', *BBC News*, 1 July 2002 <http://news.bbc.co.uk/1/hi/world/south_asia/2079565.stm> [accessed 5 October 2023].

Bell, Lenore, *The "Other" in 9/11 Literature: If You See Something, Say Something* (Basingstoke: Palgrave Macmillan, 2017).

Boxall, Peter, *Twenty-First-Century Fiction: A Critical Introduction* (Cambridge: Cambridge University Press, 2013).

Bush, George W., 'Remarks by the President in Photo Opportunity with the National Security Team', The White House Archive, 12 September 2001 <https://georgewbush-whitehouse.archives.gov/news/releases/2001/09/20010912-4.html> [accessed 5 October 2023].

Deckard, Sharae, '"Nothing is truly hidden": Visibility, Aesthetics and Yasmina Khadra's Detective Fiction', *Journal of Postcolonial Writing*, 49.1 (2013), 74–86.

Deckard, Sharae, and Stephen Shapiro, *World Literature, Neoliberalism, and the Culture of Discontent* (Basingstoke: Palgrave Macmillan, 2019).

DeLillo, Don, 'In the Ruins of the Future', *Harper's* (December 2001), 33–40.

DeLillo, Don, *Mao II* (London: Vintage, 1991).

Der Derian, James, Der Derian, James, '9/11: Before, After, and in Between', Social Science Research Council, 1 November 2001 <https://items.ssrc.org/after-september-11/9-11-before-after-and-in-between/> [accessed 5 October 2023].

Fanon, Frantz, *The Wretched of the Earth* (London: Penguin, 1963).

Hai, Ambreen, 'Pitfalls of Ambiguity in Contexts of Islamophobia: Mohsin Hamid's *The Reluctant Fundamentalist*', *Studies in the Novel*, 52.4 (2020), 434–58.

Hamid, Mohsin, *The Reluctant Fundamentalist* (London: Hamish Hamilton, 2007).

Hartnell, Anna, 'Moving through American: Race, Place and Resistance in Mohsin Hamid's *The Reluctant Fundamentalist*', *Journal of Postcolonial Writing*, 46.3 (2010), 336–48.

Holloway, David, *9/11 and the War on Terror* (Edinburgh: Edinburgh University Press, 2008).
Houen, Alex, 'Afterword', in *Terrorism and Literature*, ed. by Peter C. Herman (Cambridge: Cambridge University Press, 2018), pp. 505–14.
Huehls, Mitchum, and Rachel Greenwald Smith (eds), *Neoliberalism and Contemporary Literary Culture* (Baltimore: Johns Hopkins University Press, 2017).
Huntington, Samuel P., *The Clash of Civilizations and the Remaking of World Order* (London: Simon and Schuster, 2002).
Ilott, Sarah, 'Generic Frameworks and Active Readership in *The Reluctant Fundamentalist*', *Journal of Postcolonial Writing*, 50.5 (2014), 571–83.
Itakura, Gen'ichiro, 'Screams and Laughter: Transfer of Affect in Nadeem Aslam's *The Blind Man's Garden*', *Journal of Postcolonial Writing*, 56.3 (2016), 356–69.
Jackson, Richard, 'Introduction: A Decade of Critical Terrorism Studies', in *Routledge Handbook of Critical Terrorism Studies*, ed. by Richard Jackson (Abingdon: Routledge, 2016), pp. 1–13.
Jameson, Fredric, 'Third-World Literature in the Era of Multinational Capitalism', *Social Text*, 15 (1986), 65–88.
Kacandes, Irene, '9/11/01 = 1/27/01: The Changed Posttraumatic Self', in *Trauma at Home After 9/11*, ed. by Judith Greenberg (Lincoln: University of Nebraska Press, 2003), pp. 168–83.
Kapadia, Ronak, *Insurgent Aesthetics: Security and the Queer Life of the Forever War* (Durham, NC: Duke University Press, 2019).
Kazdin, Cole, 'Remember "Terror Sex"?', *Salon*, 21 September 2002 <https://www.salon.com/2002/09/11/terror_2_2> [accessed 31 August 2023].
Khadra, Yasmina, *The Attack*, trans. by John Cullen (London: Vintage, 2007).
Khadra, Yasmina, *The Sirens of Baghdad*, trans. by John Cullen (London: Vintage, 2008).
Khakpour, Porochista, *The Last Illusion* (London: Faber, 2014).
Khakpour, Porochista, *Sons and Other Flammable Objects* (New York: Grove, 2007).
Khalid, Nauman, 'From Jaipur with Love: Nadeem Aslam's "The Blind Man's Garden" (part one)', *Huffington Post*, 1 June 2013 <https://www.huffingtonpost.co.uk/nauman-khalid/post-4565_b_2961323.html> [accessed 5 October 2023].
Kumar, Deepa, *Islamophobia and the Politics of Empire*, 2nd edn (London: Verso, 2021).
Kundnani, Arun, *The Muslims Are Coming: Islamophobia, Extremism and the Domestic War on Terror* (London: Verso, 2014).
Lasdun, James, 'The Empire Strikes Back', *The Guardian*, 3 March 2007 <https://www.theguardian.com/books/2007/mar/03/featuresreviews.guardianreview20> [accessed 31 August 2023].

Martyris, Nina, 'Of Pomegranates and Grenades: Nadeem Aslam's "The Blind Man's Garden"', *Los Angeles Review of Books*, 16 November 2013 <https://lareviewofbooks.org/article/of-pomegranates-and-grenades/> [accessed 5 October 2023].

Massumi, Brian, *Ontopower: War, Powers, and the State of Perception* (Durham, NC: Duke University Press, 2015).

Mishra, Pankaj, 'Postcolonial Disenchantment: *The Blind Man's Garden* by Nadeem Aslam', *London Review of Books*, 35.3, 7 February 2013 <https://www.lrb.co.uk/the-paper/v35/n03/pankaj-mishra/postcolonial-enchantment> [accessed 31 August 2023].

Morey, Peter, '"The rules of the game have changed": Mohsin Hamid's *The Reluctant Fundamentalist* and Post-9/11 Fiction', *Journal of Postcolonial Writing*, 47.2 (2011), 135–46.

Morey, Peter, and Amina Yaqin, *Framing Muslims: Stereotyping and Representation After 9/11* (Cambridge, MA: Harvard University Press, 2011).

Morrison, Jago, 'Jihadi Fiction: Radicalisation Narratives in the Contemporary Novel', *Textual Practice*, 31.3 (2017), 567–84.

O'Brien, Sarah, *Trauma and Fictions of the War on Terror* (New York: Routledge, 2021).

Pease, Donald E., *The New American Exceptionalism* (Minneapolis: University of Minnesota Press, 2009).

Pirzadeh, Saba, 'Topographies of Fear: War and Environmental Othering in Mirza Waheed's *The Collaborator* and Nadeem Aslam's *The Blind Man's Garden*', *Interventions*, 21.6 (2018), 892–907.

Rahman, Shazia, 'Animals, Others, and Postcolonial Ecomasculinities: Nadeem Aslam's *The Blind Man's Garden*', *Journal of Commonwealth Literature*, 58.1 (2023), 197–212 <https://doi.org/10.1177/0021989420952125>.

Said, Edward, *After the Last Sky: Palestinian Lives* (New York: Columbia University Press, 1999).

Said, Edward, 'Islam and the West are Inadequate Banners', *The Guardian*, 16 September 2001 <https://www.theguardian.com/world/2001/sep/16/september11.terrorism3> [accessed 31 August 2023].

Saremi, Sepideh, 'Review of *Sons and Other Flammable Objects*', *MELUS*, 33.2 (2008), 201–2.

Scanlan, Margaret, 'Transparency into Opacity: Nadeem Aslam's Alternative to the 9/11 Novel', *European Journal of English Studies*, 22.2 (2018), 103–14.

Spencer, Robert, 'Reading *Lolita* in Tel Aviv: Terrorism, Fundamentalism and the Novel', *Textual Practice*, 27.3 (2013), 399–417.

Sturken, Marita, *Terrorism in American Memory: Memorials, Museums, and Architecture in the Post-9/11 Era* (New York: New York University Press, 2022).

Szeman, Imre, 'Who's Afraid of National Allegory? Jameson, Literary Criticism, Globalization', *South Atlantic Quarterly*, 100.3 (2001), 803–27.

Taneja, Preti, *Aftermath* (Oakland, CA: Transit Books, 2021).

Yaqin, Amina, 'Mohsin Hamid in Conversation', *Wasafiri*, 23.2 (2008), 44–49.

Chapter 3

The Novel of Terrorism and the War on Terror

This chapter examines the contemporary novel of terrorism in relation to the ongoing 'war on terror'. It builds on analysis of texts discussed in the previous chapter – and particularly Yasmina Khadra's *The Sirens of Baghdad* (2006) and Nadeem Aslam's *The Blind Man's Garden* (2013) – which I discussed as novels of the alleged 'clash of civilizations'. Here, I analyse four very different novels, whose innovations respond to the narrow ways terrorism has been defined via clash logics during the war on terror. As Arun Kundnani shows, this conflict has seen terrorism defined via 'ideological projection and fantasy'; and even as the war on terror has advanced through multiple phases, 'the assumption remains that the term "terrorist" is reserved for acts of political violence carried out by Muslims' (17, 23). The novels discussed in this chapter all challenge this phenomenon by emphasising state terrorism and the kinds of contexts that such narrow definitions have eschewed: long-standing colonial and imperial structures, historical conflicts and global patterns of rising neoliberalism. In this way they redress common narratives and approaches that, as Kundnani puts it, 'eschew the role of social and political circumstances in shaping how people make sense of the world and then act upon it' (10). In this chapter, as elsewhere in the book, I provide some contextual commentary on the nature of the war on terror, drawing on scholarly work that has revealed the disturbing extent of its catastrophe. In the previous chapters I emphasised the exceptionalisation of 9/11 and argued that we should stop periodising by this event and properly recognise that it has been America and its allies' disproportionate response to 9/11 that has caused the seismic changes of the early twenty-first century – not '9/11' as a singular defining moment. Having said this, in-depth commentary on the war on terror is not the focus of this book or this chapter, and my aim here is to focus on how four exemplary novels have portrayed terrorism or the effects of it in the context(s) of this conflict.

The novels under discussion here depict different theatres and phases of the war on terror and focus on four different national contexts. This is the most formally disparate set of texts discussed in any of the chapters in the book, and this perhaps reflects the need for narrative innovation in depicting an unruly and tentacular conflict built on dubious premises. I begin with Ahmed Saadawi's *Frankenstein in Baghdad*, first published in Arabic in 2013 and in an English translation, by Jonathan Wright, in 2018. Saadawi's novel offers a nuanced portrait of conflict in Baghdad in 2005, following the US invasion and occupation, and as the country leans towards civil war. Its use of the Frankenstein story explores and interrogates the nature of 'terror' and the 'terrorist other', against the backdrop of a conflict where imperial and state violence overlaps with sectarian conflict; in this sense, it resonates with Anna Burns's *Milkman* (2018), discussed in the next chapter. I then discuss Karan Mahajan's *The Association of Small Bombs* (2016), a novel that follows the aftershocks of a deadly 'small bomb' that devastates two families in 1996 during a period of upheaval in India that includes the 2002 anti-Muslim riots in Gujarat, described by many as a state-sponsored pogrom.[1] Mahajan's novel builds in layers of context and a panoramic range of perspectives including that of the terrorists, and its depictions of radicalisation and terror sharply contrast typical war on terror-era representations. I then turn to Kamila Shamsie's *Home Fire* (2017), which uses the narrative architecture of *Antigone* to tell the story of a London-based family torn apart by state violence and inequality under neoliberalism. I focus on its devastating critique of what Jodi Melamed calls 'neoliberal multiculturalism', in which dishonest visions of freedom and meritocracy posited by politicians and the media elide structural inequality. This aspect of Shamsie's novel has sometimes been overlooked because of its striking formal features and well-known prescience in 'predicting' the rise of Sajid Javid and its resonance with the Shamima Begum case.[2] I conclude this chapter with discussion of another transatlantic post-2016 narrative: Ayad Akhtar's autofictional 'novel' *Homeland Elegies* (2020), which radically critiques the discourse of terrorism from 9/11 to the Trump era. In each of these very different novels, I argue, formal innovation works to rethink the deeply troubling and Islamophobic frames in which terrorism has been defined in the war on terror era.

Frankenstein in Baghdad

Ahmed Saadawi's novel has quickly accrued a substantial scholarly response, whose divergences are a testament to its richness. Much of this work has focused on the vectors and limits of the text's figurative dimensions. Marwa Essam Eldin Fahmy Alkhayat reads the novel as 'postcolonial gothic', attending to the way it depicts the 'effects of neo-colonial practices, economic disenfranchisement, and warfare' via its gothic formal features (47). The creature in Saadawi's novel, the Whatsitsname – translated from the Arabic 'shesmeh', a combination of 'shinu' and 'ismu', or 'what's' and 'his name' – is combined of body parts from victims of various religions, ethnicities and heritages. Alkhayat explores the way this represents multiculturalism in Baghdad, or the way different identity formations are 'sewed into one whole to symbolize the Iraqi national unity' (47). Netty Mattar reads the novel within the zombie tradition, noting how zombies 'are radical figures of unbelonging' whose 'attachments to place' are 'severed' even as they 'are bound to the lands they are no longer a part of' (159). Mattar notes that popular contemporary depictions of the 'enslaved-style zombie' are 'based on stories connected to Haitian vodou and folklore', and shows how the Whatsitsname is both a 'conscious attempt to express Iraqi solidarity with the Haitian oppressed' and a character that carries 'particular histories and memories that differentiate experiences and trouble assumptions about the other' (160, 62). Jinan F. B. Al-Hajaj discusses the magical realist elements of the novel and its depictions of mysticism and the 'oracular'. Al-Hajaj emphasises the novel's allegorical dimensions, arguing that it is a 'parable of a world that is on the verge of total collapse' but that it 'can by no means be dismissed as unrealistic' (465). Annie Webster's biopolitical reading argues for a moving away from the figurative dimensions of the novel and contends that by 'mirroring and inverting narratives of biomedical salvation, Saadawi's novel destabilises their narrative logic and brings into question the ways in which the human consequences of the Iraq War have been imagined by the international community' (439). While Webster notes that prevalence of reading 'the Whatsitsname as a national allegory follows a long tradition of reading Frankenstein's creature as a social metaphor', such interpretations overlook 'the visceral, biological significance of the Whatsitsname's anatomy', which is made up of parts of bodies that have been discarded without care, as rubbish. In this context, Webster argues that an allegorical reading

> risks reproducing the logic of medical metaphors and allegories deployed by coalition forces during the Iraq War to frame military operations as if they were medical procedures, and therefore part of a humanitarian intervention. These metaphors, which shaped how the international community perceived the human consequences of this conflict, abstracted the violence enacted upon individual bodies by referring to a collective body politic. (441)

Webster makes a strong case, and apart from the potential to reproduce such pernicious logics, one can understand the call for caution in relation to the conspicuousness of the figurative elements of the novel – which, as in *The Reluctant Fundamentalist*, discussed in the previous chapter, are in some ways overdetermined. This said, and like Mohsin Hamid's novel, *Frankenstein in Baghdad* is not singular in its allegorical strands, and instead offers a compelling set of symbolic meanings that intersect and enrich each other. A cautious approach to interpreting these allegorical strands might also relate to a general caution invited by the novel's diegetic patterns of second- and third-hand storytelling that are staged alongside numerous metafictional flourishes that emphasise misrepresentation – such as the journalist, and central protagonist, Mahmoud's magazine article, 'Frankenstein in Baghdad' (133) published with a photograph of Robert De Niro as the creature in Kenneth Branagh's *Mary Shelley's Frankenstein* (1994). These prominent metafictional dimensions mean the reader is continually invited to 'question the construction of meaning, narrative and truth' in specific relation to notions of terror and terrorism (del Pont 86).

I follow Dominic Davies's logic that an 'outright rejection of the novel's allegorical implications risks eliding its critical and resistant potential' and that we can read 'Saadawi's body parts as both literal and metaphoric simultaneously' (924). Indeed, I draw from and build on these readings to consider *Frankenstein in Baghdad* as a novel of terrorism. The Whatsitsname is created in the aftermath of three separate terrorist attacks, two of which occur in the opening pages of the novel and are multiply revisited in relation to different focalising characters, and another that had occurred months before the action of the novel and is narrated via flashback much later. The novel opens with a car bomb explosion near Tayaran Square, witnessed first by Elishva, the 'mad old woman' who lives alone with her cat hoping for the return of her son, Daniel, missing since the Iraq–Iran war (1980–8). The streets are littered with body parts, and Elishva's neighbour and eccentric junk dealer, Hadi, known at the local coffee shop for his wild stories, collects a nose and places it in a canvas bag. Later, in his squat, he sews it to a corpse comprised of various 'body parts that had been left in the street like rubbish' (25). In the next chapter, Hasib Mohamed Jaafar, a twenty-one-year-old security guard at the Sadeer Novotel, attempts to stop a suicide bomber charging the hotel gates in a 'dynamite-laden rubbish truck' (33). Jaafar's body is eviscerated but his soul watches the scene from above, drifts around the city, and eventually 'sinks' into the 'strange and horrible' corpse at Hadi's squat: 'it didn't have a soul, while he was a soul without a body' (38). Later we hear the full story of the death of Hadi's former business partner, Nahem, and it is suggested that the Whatsitsname's creation is also related to the terror attack in which he died. When Hadi is introduced, we learn that Nahem died 'several months' before from a 'car bomb that had exploded in front of the office of a religious party in Karrada', and that it had been 'hard to separate Nahem's flesh from that of his horse' (23). Much later, Aziz the coffee shop owner reveals that the corpse Hadi completed with the nose was intended to in some way represent Nahem, even if the body parts were from numerous different victims:

> Hadi had gone to the mortuary to collect the body because Nahem didn't have any family other than his wife and young daughter. Hadi was shocked to see that the bodies of explosion victims were all mixed up together and to hear the mortuary worker tell him to put a body together and carry it off – take this leg and this arm and so on. (214)

As Alkhayat notes, the assembling of the corpse is intended to 'memorialise the death of his close friend' (53). The origins of the Whatsitsname are thus related to three terrorist attacks, and when the corpse rises, animated with a soul, he then begins to avenge various victims of terror attacks and other violence, and then becomes a kind of 'terrorist' himself. He is thus perennially associated with 'terrorism', and a compelling figurative exploration of what constitutes 'terror' and 'terrorism' is enacted in relation to his other symbolic dimensions.

Three other features of the novel's depiction of violence in Baghdad in 2005 reinforce its depiction and interrogation of the nature of terrorism, and each relates in certain ways to Peter C. Herman's theorisation of the 'speakable/unspeakable' paradigm. In Herman's formation, terrorism is defined by the fact that it always intends to convey a message but that the message goes unheard because as an atrocity it is 'unspeakable'. The Whatsitsname's first narrated attack in the novel is a highly symbolic one, as four individuals are found in a kind of circle each with their arms around another's neck 'like some weird tableau or theatrical scene' (66). We learn that the 'file' on this event, perused by Brigadier Sorour Mohamed Majid, Director General of the Tracking and Pursuit Department of the Iraqi government, reveals that it 'was meant to send a message' (74). Crucially, the message does the work of terrorism in creating fear as everyone 'in the area had heard the story, and the local people were afraid, and on the lookout' (75). This gruesome display seems to symbolise the circularity or cyclical nature of violence. However, when the Whatsitsname begins to articulate his message, it is even more general. He states that he is 'the only justice there is in this country' and later that he is 'the answer to the call of the poor', but as we will see, his 'noble' moral crusade 'decomposes' (130, 136). The message or symbolism of his killing is also contextualised by a landscape of escalating terrorist attacks committed by both sides of the sectarian divide and by the state, which also resonates alongside Herman's theorisation. Herman argues that

> to attract and to maintain attention, terrorists need to conceive of acts that reach beyond anything that has been previously accomplished, something that breaks all previous limits and conventions, thus rendering the audience speechless because they lack the terms to comprehend what has just happened. (2020, 6)

This aligns with the novel's depiction of escalating attacks that nevertheless sustain a kind of impasse. The opening attack in Tayaran Square is described in gruesome terms, and we learn that it 'might have been the neighbourhood's biggest explosion' (8). Later when the threat and fear of a suicide attack leads to several people jumping from the Imams Bridge, it is described as 'the biggest disaster that had struck Iraq so far' (116). Near the end of the novel, 'the largest explosion that had ever taken place in Bataween' occurs, in similarly devastating terms (225). But as Herman theorises, despite the increasing devastation, an impasse is retained. Additionally, the novel is explicitly engaged with the ways in which the term 'terrorist' has been misused during the war on terror, aligning with Herman's notion that, particularly for American commentators, 'terrorism is always the work of another' and that the term approximates 'violence you don't like by people you don't like' (2020, 5). This is something that Saadawi has been explicitly interested in, noting in an interview that people 'tend to view themselves as saints seeking justice, and others as terrorists. In truth, no one's innocent' (Hankir n.p.).

Two areas of the novel drive its resistance to the kinds of definitions of terror and terrorism associated with the war on terror.

First, is its insistence that terrorism is a tactic used by both sides of the sectarian conflict, the state and the occupying forces; it is consistently depicted as a component of contemporary warfare. Second, is the novel's metafictional depiction of writing and storytelling, and the specific ways that *Frankenstein in Baghdad* places writing in dialogue with terrorism. The novel emphasises a climate of pervasive and cyclical violence from the outset. In chapter 1 we are told that death 'stalked the city like the plague', that it was an 'unsettled and confused time' and a 'time when people disappeared' (6, 80, 83). American Apache helicopters are omnipresent, and at one point Hadi assumes 'a car bomb or some other explosive might go off' as 'no day passed without at least one car bomb' (100). The novel also historicises this phase of the war in Iraq with some conspicuous references to previous conflicts. In fact, a further facet of the Whatsitsname's identity is shaped by the Iraq–Iran war. In addition to having the body parts of various citizens killed in terror attacks, the soul of the young man killed in a terror attack, and a symbolic relation to Hadi's friend, Nahem, who died in a different attack, the Whatsitsname stumbles in to Elishva's home where she immediately welcomes him as her lost son, Daniel. This means his identity is connected to the Iraq–Iran war, from which the real Daniel never returned after being aggressively recruited by the Baathist Abu Zaidoun. The memory of Daniel is frequently discussed through different focalising characters, and in relation to people who had left for different wars and eventually returned. In one passage we learn of people who had returned from imprisonment in Iran as well many who had returned from 'the war over Kuwait' in the 'middle of the 1990s' (60). Moreover, the novel's omniscient narrator frequently remarks on the nation's history of conflict and observes at one point that there were people 'who survived many deaths in the time of the dictatorship only to find themselves face-to-face with a pointless death in the age of democracy' (227).

The climate of death and violence, which is both new and rooted in historical conflicts, is also frequently generalised. There are numerous explosions that occur – including some I have already discussed – that are not named as Shiite or Sunni, attached to any sectarian militia, the state or occupying forces. The politics of the narrative is also somewhat deterritorialised via the novel's magical realism. Fictional entities like the secret Tracking and Pursuit Department, led by Brigadier Majid, employ 'analysts in parapsychology, astrologers, people who specialize in communication with spirits and with the djinn, and soothsayers', and the political affiliations of key players in the novel are perennially abstracted (73). For instance, when Mahmoud, the most consistent focalising protagonist of the novel, goes with his editor Saidi to visit Majid – they are old friends – he puzzles over their political affiliations, and how their positions relate to ongoing 'fronts' in the conflict. He reflects that Saidi is 'an Islamist, and his friend's a Baathist. But Saidi's a lapsed Islamist. His ideas changed while he was living abroad. And his brigadier friend is a lapsed Baathist' (75). Reflecting further, he tries to contextualise his own questions by simplifying the conflict in his head: 'there were two fronts now, Mahmoud said to himself – the Americans and the government on one side, the terrorists and the various anti-government militias on the other' (77). However, he quickly self-corrects, noting that actually '"terrorist" was the term used for everyone who was against the government and the Americans', and the complexity of the novel's depiction of ongoing sectarian conflict collapses any notion of 'two fronts' (77). The novel's many depictions of terrorist explosions that are not assigned a 'side' strangely align it with one of the narrative strategies of Anna Burns's *Milkman*, which eschews the use of proper names, replacing ideologically loaded signifiers with a more general language of conflict. In *Frankenstein in Baghdad* – as in *Milkman* – this is far from a depoliticising gesture, and instead works to emphasise the complex intersections of violence perpetrated by the state, sectarian militia fighters and occupying forces. In fact, the one entity that is repeatedly named is the American military, who operate with 'considerable independence': 'no one could hold them to account for what they did' (66). Indeed, in one of the few references to sectarian conflict that name Shiite and Sunni forces, a theory about the American occupation perpetuating cyclical violence is proffered – by the increasingly (at this point) untrustworthy editor, Saidi, who reveals that Majid is actually 'carrying out the policy of the American ambassador to create an equilibrium of violence on the streets between the Sunni and Shiite militias' (171).

Whether or not it is the case that the Americans are creating an 'equivalence of violence' to aid their 'political process', Saidi's theory aptly describes the violence, counter-violence and impasse the novel depicts (171). The cyclical nature and oxymoronic banality of daily violent explosions are also rendered at the level of the form. The omniscient narrator of Wright's English language translation uses functional prose and is often flat and minimally emotional. This reinforces the depiction of a city in which violence has 'brought life to a standstill' (112). The flatness of tone is also consistent as scenes are repeated from the perspectives of different focalising characters – particularly Mahmoud, Hadi, the Whatsitsname and Elishva, but other peripheral characters too. This enhances the novel's depiction of circular patterns of violence as the reader begins to wonder if the latest explosion being depicted is a new one, or one that is being seen from a different vantage point. Moreover, time passes in strange ways in the novel – as it must for citizens under occupation and subject to sectarian violence – sometimes moving slowly and elsewhere lurching forwards precipitously. The consistency of the narrative voice across different focalising characters, and movements back and forth in time, also affects a narrative in which storytelling is key: stories are told and retold, recontextualised with new information and questioned, throughout (and I will come to the novel's metafictional dimensions shortly).

The novel's consistency of tone and narrative voice connects the lives of a disparate cast of characters, meticulously and without fuss noting their national, ethnic or religious identities. Moreover, it is a narrative style that is also adopted by the Whatsitsname – an apparent embodiment of Baghdad's multiculture. When he records his story on Mahmoud's voice recorder it is narrated in a 'calm' voice that has depth and intelligence but is not overly emotional, in spite of the violence of his story (158, 215). These are the formal elements that 'stitch' the novel together: the 'calm', functional narrative, the ubiquitous violence it describes, and the diverse citizenry whose lives are affected daily by violence. The novel's vision of diversity includes Elishva, an Assyrian Christian, Aziz the Egyptian coffee shop proprietor, Luqman the Algerian, and Abu Anmar's Armenian partner. We learn that Elishva's daughters live in Melbourne and one of Hadi's clients moves to Russia to be with his girlfriend; and this depiction of a globalised Baghdad is, of course, also affected by the occupation. In addition to the American imperial forces, in the opening pages we encounter a German journalist and a Palestinian photographer (17). In this landscape, the figurative dimensions of the Whatsitsname – which as I have noted are multivalent – come into view.

That the Whatsitsname symbolises Iraqi national identity is a notion articulated diegetically, by the young madman, an 'assistant' to the Whatshisname, late in the narrative. This disciple argues that Hadi's creation represents the 'impossible mix that never was achieved in the past' and that he is the 'first true Iraqi citizen' (140). The author echoes this, noting that he was conceived as 'a truly Iraqi figure who is made up of all of these different identities' (Hankir n.p.). Yet, while the disparate identities of the people whose body parts are brought together are important, the author was also moved by the way these parts were discarded. He has described witnessing the same scene Hadi does in a morgue filled with body parts, in which the mortician tells a bereaved brother to simply 'take what you want, and make yourself a body' (Hankir n.p.). The significance of this moment, for Saadawi, is reinforced by the novel's emphasis on bodies and body parts as rubbish. Therefore, if the creature symbolises Iraq's diversity, it unifies this via an image of biopolitical disposability that seems to broadly affect the 'poor' and the 'innocent', whom the Whatsitsname initially claims to stand for. One question we might ask of this stretched symbol, then, is how it squares with an inevitable intertextual reading that draws on Mary Shelley's vision of 'otherness' – also emphasised in many of her novel's adaptations. I suggest that we do so by considering how the Whatsitsname functions as a 'terrorist other', who complicates reductive notions of what a terrorist is, while also committing acts of terror. In some ways the Whatsitsname is a stereotypical war on terror-era 'terrorist other' in the way he creates fear, and lives in the imagination as unknowable. Ultimately, he also embarks on a pattern of killing to survive that in some ways embodies the cyclical forms of terrorism that have formed the backdrop for the novel.

He is established as a monstrous other in terms that recall Shelley's *Frankenstein*. We hear of his 'mouth like a gash right across the jaw, the horrible face, the stitches across the forehead and down the cheeks, the big nose' (83). We also eventually learn that the first killing of the four beggars, theatrically arranged, was not a symbol of violence and counter-violence, but actually happened because of the way these people responded to the Whatsitsname's appearance:

> His horrible face was an incentive for them to attack him. They didn't know anything about him but they were driven by that latent hatred that can suddenly come to the surface when people meet someone who doesn't fit in. (125)

This revelation reveals contradictions as the Whatsitsname has also made claims to being a protector of the poor. Such contradictions in his rhetoric escalate and as this happens, his figurative meanings shift. Indeed, as he learns that he needs to keep replacing body parts, which causes him to kill to keep going, he becomes an allegory not just of a diverse body politic but of cyclical violence. This is centrally important; we might note some of the powerful passages in the aftermath of the Imams Bridge disaster, at which the threat of a potential suicide bomber causes nearly a thousand deaths. The disaster is interpreted in numerous ways – including as a successful aversion of a terrorist threat – but Mahmoud's colleague, Farid, makes a powerful comment about the power of fear that the author has echoed in his comments about complicity.[3] Farid monologues:

> all the security incidents and tragedies we're seeing stem from one thing – fear. The people on the bridge died because they were frightened of dying. Every day we're dying from the same fear of dying. The groups that have given shelter and support to al-Qaeda have done some because they are frightened of another group, and this other group has created and mobilized militias to protect itself from al-Qaeda. It has created a death machine working in the other direction because its afraid of the Other. (118)

The capitalisation of 'Other' here seems pointed, and there are certainly ways in which the Whatsitsname comes to embody the kinds of circular violence Farid is describing. Moreover, the Whatsitsname's escalating violence takes on other features and stereotypes of terrorists. He moves from an ostensibly moral crusader, fighting for the oppressed, to a 'criminal' and consequently goes through phases of self-questioning and self-aggrandising. At one point, he states:

> They have turned me into a criminal and a monster, and in this way they have equated me with those I seek to exact revenge on. This is a grave injustice. In fact there is a moral and humanitarian obligation to back me, to bring about justice in this world, which has been totally ravaged by greed, ambition, megalomania, and insatiable bloodlust. (137)

As he continues his campaign of terror, the Whatsitsname begins combining acts of revenge with less justifiable killings, some of which are carried out simply to keep him alive. Nevertheless, even as the 'nobility' of his work diminishes, his mythos increases, and he amasses various disciples who assist his causes and who have their own followers, meaning something of a terror network emerges. We learn that each of them 'promoted his own idea of [the Whatsitsname] to his clique, amassing followers who were fed up with what they saw around them' (147). Eventually, some even run for office, and an image of the way terrorism exists in larger political landscapes, conflicts and histories emerges.

A final dimension of *Frankenstein in Baghdad* cements it as a novel of terrorism: its perennial interest in storytelling. From details like the first volume of al-Sayyab's collected poems among Hasib Mohamed Jaafar's scant belongings, Farid's passion project of producing an anthology of 'the one hundred strangest Iraqi stories' or Abu Anmar's passion for 'books about astrology and fortune telling, his favourite genre', to structural acts of storytelling by Hadi, the Whatsitsname and then 'the author', literature and storytelling are the fabric of the novel; and this, of course, echoes the storytelling frames of Shelley's novel. Hadi and Mahmoud are both established storytellers, too. Hadi's exaggerated and eccentric stories – usually told at Aziz's coffee shop – are known around the area, and Mahmoud, as an ambitious journalist and editor, offers an ostensibly more 'objective' voice. However, the emphasis is on their exchanges and how the story of the Whatsitsname evolves through them. When Mahmoud records himself recounting the story, he is 'aware he was paraphrasing the words that Hadi had attributed to the Whatsitsname and that he was adding his own personal gloss' (126). The questionable attributions, 'paraphrasing' and 'personal gloss', to emphasise the slippages between reality and representation. More metafictional layers emerge to bring this out further. For instance, on the one hand Mahmoud is an ambitious journalist who aspires to the life and lifestyle of his mentor, Saidi, a slick neoliberal subject and author of *Conditions of Democracy in Rentier States* (219). However, we also learn that Mahmoud is living in exile in Baghdad after a story that got him in trouble for 'inciting violence' in his hometown of Amara (162). This is a potent example of the novel's portrayal of relations between textual representation and violence, and between the power of violent acts and written words; and the potential violence of misrepresentation in storytelling. Indeed, the only writing or storytelling within the novel that is 'truthful' is that which was recorded in Mahmoud's father's journals. He was a prolific diarist who had completed 'twenty-seven notebooks of one hundred pages each' by the time he died (113). But when Mahmoud and his brother read the journals, they were shocked by the nakedly honest entries about 'the times his father had masturbated when he was married' and 'about the women he dreamed of sleeping with, some of them old women from the neighbourhood', and more presciently about their family's invented origins (114). The diaries are then burned – the truth being apparently too dangerous. Ultimately, after patterns of deliberate misrepresentation, myth-making, exaggeration and deception in storytelling, the penultimate chapter, 'The Writer', switches to a first-person narrative in which an unnamed writer describes meeting Mahmoud and being given the recordings and story. He reveals that Mahmoud tells him that a writer of his quality 'could use it to write a great novel' (251). This is very different to the 9/11 metafiction discussed in my first chapter, which laboured over the problem of representing 9/11, and instead more closely resembles the patterns of metafiction described by Margaret Scanlan in relation to the novel of terrorism in the 1980s and 1990s, which explore the 'the influence of fiction on history and politics, the relation between language and violence, the nature of power, and the impetus to resist' (14). Ultimately, the vision of sectarian conflict overlapping with imperial and state violence is powerfully rendered in *Frankenstein in Baghdad*, and the kinds of terror and terrorism usually attached to this conflict are radically re-visioned.

The Association of Small Bombs

Karan Mahajan's second novel, *The Association of Small Bombs* (2016), traces the aftermath of the 1996 Lajpat Nagar Market bombing in Delhi, in which thirteen people died. It focuses on the entangled fates of a set of fictional survivors, family members, terrorists and their accomplices, and activists. As such, it functions in some obvious ways as an 'event-based narrative'. However, as a novel that seeks to understand the nature and impact of an act of terrorism from every possible position, including oppositional views, it is very different to the usual event-based narratives of terrorism that eschew context and history. Though the event, in a sense, is totalising for the characters, profoundly shaping all their lives, the novel is at pains to emphasise that this 'small' bomb attack occurred within a context of ongoing, violent political conflict. As Amanda Lagji has noted, the attack is situated in a 'specific regional conflict, albeit one produced in concert with the colonial partitioning of India and Pakistan and the politicization of religious difference' (405). At the heart of the novel, I argue, is a probing exploration of the nature of 'events' or 'bombs' that resonates powerfully in the war on terror era.

Mahajan has noted that the novel was conceived when one historical event triggered his memory of another. The first was the '26/11' attack in 2008 in which 164 people were killed mostly at the Taj Hotel in Mumbai; an event described by some as 'India's 9/11'.[4] The second was the bombing at Lajpat Nagar market, a personal haunt of the author's youth:

> Soon after the 26/11 attacks in Mumbai, memories of this blast in Lajpat Nagar market in 1996 began flashing through my mind. I don't know why. It had been in the deep freeze for years. My grandmother had visited the market a day before the blasts – to buy

yarn, I think – and perhaps the possibility that a family member might have perished in the attack stuck with me. It was a market I knew well. It was where I went to shop for my school uniform. (Ruiz-Camacho n.p.)

The novel's chronology covers a period between 1996 and 2003, and two further events within this timeline are significant: the election of the Hindu nationalist Bharatiya Janata Party (BJP) days before the Delhi bombing in May 1996, and the Gujarat massacre of 2002, in which more than 1,000 people, mostly Muslims, were killed during a period of Hindu supremacist rioting and violence. Indian Prime Minister Narendra Modi, who was Chief Minister of Gujarat during this time, has been widely condemned for allowing the massacre to happen, to the extent that many commentators refer to it as a pogrom, in which Modi was 'able to mobilize city residents psychologically for violence while, at the same time, extricating the political from the event' (Ghassem-Fachandi 3). Modi's impact on India beyond this is also a key subtext of *The Association*, which was published after he had become Prime Minister. The September 11 attacks also happen in the middle of the novel and are central, in this sense, but mostly decentred in the importance the event plays. This is potentially quite evocative for Western readers accustomed to encountering representations of September 11 as a central marker of before and after. The novel spends about six pages in America, and the attacks are consequential, but mostly in how they give existing structures of conflict new inflections. Ultimately, the novel is interested in what one character, Vikas, a documentary filmmaker and father of the novel's two young fictional victims of the Lajpat Nagar bombing, calls the 'connective tissue' between such events (97). This is often antithetical to the logic of 'events', taking the form of structural phenomena like Hindu supremacism, corruption and the legacies of colonialism. Indeed, some of the novel's most brutal images of violence are depictions of state terrorism, torture and wrongful incarceration. The latter feature is particularly notable given the eventuality, in 2019, of the release of Ali Mohammad Bhat, twenty-three years after he was wrongly jailed for involvement in the Lajpat Nagar attack.[5]

If the timeline of *The Association* places 9/11 at the chronological centre of its narrative only to decentre and de-exceptionalise this moment in minimising its global importance, its interest in 'small bombs' also resists the gravitational pull of the early theatres of the war on terror: Afghanistan and Iraq. Yet, it remains potent as a narrative of war on terror-era terrorism as it both draws attention to lesser-known conflicts in which terrorism is integral and considers the question of continuity and discontinuity from a vantage point that is not America-centred. While Ronak Kapadia has shown that the launch of the war on terror should be understood 'not as a radical historical or political rupture, but rather as a continuation of a longer history of US imperialism that has been erased or evaded', other histories cone into view in *The Association* (36). And yet, while the novel deals directly with specific regional and national conflicts – Kashmiri separatism and rising Hindu nationalism – in its philosophical dimensions it responds specifically to broader war on terror-era concerns. First, it insists on moving beyond narrow formations of victims and perpetrators, including emphases on the wrongly accused and on people Michael Rothberg might describe as 'implicated subjects' (1). Mahajan's novel seeks to adopt as many vantage points as possible, and in doing so challenges reductive notions of radicalisation and extremism that eschew context.

Though *The Association* was initially critically neglected, numerous scholarly articles have discussed it in depth in recent years, and some divergences in the interpretation of its local and global resonances can be identified. Lagji argues that the novel focuses on a 'specific regional conflict' and that it 'interrogates terror in ways inclusive of but not reducible to the aftermath of 9/11' (405, 409). This said, Lagji certainly reads it as a post-9/11, war on terror-era novel in which 'the outpouring of sympathy for the victims from that "large" terrorist event is juxtaposed with the lack of sympathy for or limited memory of the victims of "small" bombs' (405). Daniel O'Gorman also points to the novel's global resonances, arguing that it is exemplary of a 'growing and vital body of literary writing that is working to resist global terror by generating a "feeling" of globality, and in doing so contributing toward a collective reimagination of the very "globe" of which it is part' (466). Though Sangeeta Ray agrees that the novel can usefully be read as a 'postcolonial post-9/11 novel' or 'the genre of fiction that can loosely be gathered under depictions of the "war on terror"', she focuses attention on the novel's realism, and its depiction of terror within specific regional and national conflicts (22). For Ray, *The Association* is a novel in which Kashmir is 'ever present on the horizon as the place destroyed by military oppression, its population made militant as a result' (22). Babli Sinha turns focus to another phenomenon often discussed in relation to India's now Prime Minister, Narendra Modi: neoliberalism. Sinha argues that *The Association* is a novel of neoliberalism whose large cast of characters means it can depict a larger 'breakdown in society and state' that 'produces a collective experience of depression' (293). In the analysis that follows, I build on these accounts and on Melanie R. Wattenberger's discussion of the ways the novel collapses distinctions between victims and perpetrators within the context of cyclical violence. Wattenberger usefully points out that the novel does this while taking up the 'issue of who is outside of the state's compassion, and certainly its protection' in relation to moments of tragedy (685). I read *The Association* as a contemporary novel of terrorism that seeks to understand an act of terror from as many vantage points as possible. In doing so I show how its depictions of radicalisation, and movement from nonviolent to violent forms of resistance – including terrorism – resonate with particular force in the context of war on terror logics and rhetoric.

The Association begins with a 'blast' and works chronologically through a set of overlapping subject positions, its omniscient narrator building in backstory and 'connective tissue' between characters. Two middle-class Delhi families are at the heart of the novel: the Muslim Ahmeds: Afsheen, Sharif and son Mansoor; and the Hindu Khuranas: Deepa, Vikas and sons Nakul and Tushar. The latter family are 'cut-and-dried secularists and liberals' who are 'inordinately proud' of their Muslim friends (72). The Ahmeds are also privileged liberals, and both families employ servants and live in relative affluence. The three boys visit the Lajpat Nagar Market and the two Khurana children are killed while Mansoor escapes with minor injuries. The terror attack is carried out by Shaukaut 'Shockie' Guru, the 'leading bomb maker of the Jammu and Kashmir Islamic Force' (33). Despite the group's name, Shockie is secular and motivated politically, by revenge, and by some delusions of grandeur. Shockie is not apprehended for the attack but his nonviolent best friend Malik, who writes revolutionary pamphlets and propaganda for the group, is arrested, tortured for ten days and incarcerated indefinitely. Malik had previously been tortured, too, including having had his penis 'burned and electrocuted' (54). In the years after the attack the Khuranas' marriage collapses, and Mansoor experiences psychological trauma and a debilitating injury in his wrist that he traces back to the bombing. At age seventeen, Mansoor leaves for America where he studies IT, and becomes obsessed with porn and individual achievement (a slightly clunky detail sees him reading Ayn Rand's *The Fountainhead* obsessively). However, after little more than a year studying in Santa Clara, California, he returns when his wrist injury intensifies to the point he can no longer type, an unexplained phenomenon that happens in the aftermath of the 9/11 attacks. Eventually, back in Delhi, Mansoor befriends Ayub and Tara who run an NGO called Peace For All. Formed in the wake of Gujarat, Peace For All works with wrongly convicted prisoners, including those incarcerated for the Lajpat Nagar Market bombing, and Ayub and Tara recruit Mansoor for the weight his testimony and position might carry as an educated, middle-class Muslim victim. Later, the NGO's attention returns focus to Gujarat, demanding the country 'own up to what Modi had done in Gujarat: massacre scores of Muslims in public view, with the police standing by and watching, even helping' (176). Tara and Ayub organise a large-scale protest but when it fails to make an impact, Ayub becomes depressed, Tara leaves him, and he begins his drift towards violence. Eventually Ayub falls into Shockie's orbit, and he uses Mansoor to carry out a devastating bombing attack of his own, resulting in the wrongful incarceration of Mansoor, who under torture pleads guilty. This completes a looping narrative that connects victims and perpetrators and formally reinforces the novel's depiction of circular patterns of violence and counter-violence.

The opaque language of the section titles in *The Association* is instructive: 'Blast May 1996'; 'Victims May 1996'; 'Terrorists May 1996'; 'Mr. and Mrs. Khurana's Response to Terror 1996–1997'; 'Mansoor Ahmed's Response to Terror May 1996–March 2003'; 'Ayub Azmi's Response to Terror March 2003–October 2003'; 'The Association of Small Bombs October 2003–'. These titles emphasise the key vantage points from the which the original blast and its impacts are traced, but also have figurative and aggregative possibilities. The titular 'Association' is the shorthand for a survivors group set up by the Khuranas. Officially it is the 'Association of Terror Victims' and is designed to support victims of attacks that are quickly forgotten, vanishing into 'a morgue of memories, overshadowed by bigger events' (238). Though the Khuranas begin endorsing the views of George W. Bush and discover eventually that they 'were no longer liberals', the group name and emphasis on small or forgotten moments of rupture overshadowed by larger events is evocative. Moreover, just as 'bomb' becomes metaphorical for that which causes turmoil and upheaval, 'association' does not just refer to the group, but to a broader sense of connection or the 'connective tissue' evoked by Vikas. As Peter C. Herman points out, this 'illustrates the ongoing "associations" of a terrorist bombing, how the effects ripple outward with many overlapping, unintended consequences' (2023, 118). This section title and indeed the novel's title also address the connection between different bombs – how, precisely they are 'associated' with each other. In both senses this term works against the singularity of event-based logic. Equally notable are the three uses of 'Response to Terror'. Not only does this signal the different vantage points or 'responses' the novel explores, but the non-specificity of 'Terror' invites us to think beyond the initial bombing. For the Khuranas this might mean the bombing or the terror of married life without children. For Mansoor this means the original bombing he escapes, the 9/11 attacks that occur during his time in America, and the state terror committed at Gujarat that Peace For All is protesting. For Ayub, too, it means Gujarat, and 9/11, but also his own failed and successful acts of terrorism.

The novel's depictions of these different kinds of terror and responses to terror begin and end with philosophical musings on the nature of a 'bomb', and over the course of the narrative *The Association* considers explosions in affective terms, as moments of rupture in individual lives, and as symbols or metaphors. The novel's opening chapter '0' describes the market blast as a 'flat percussive event' and a page later as 'deafening', and it repeatedly describes 'the texture of the bomb' (3, 27, 106). In one memorable scene, Vikas, having decided to make a documentary about the nature of bombs, considers his approach:

> he didn't want to make a film about the aftermath; he was living the aftermath . . . [H]e wanted to make a film about the moment itself, when there was a hush as the bomb shut off humans and machines in the vicinity and then viciously rearranged everything. (76)

This notion of wanting to return to before the 'aftermath' evokes Don DeLillo's discussion of the 'writer's task', in 'In the Ruins of the Future'. DeLillo famously noted that the event 'has no purchase on the mercies of analogy or simile' and that 'the writer 'begins in the towers, trying to imagine the moment, desperately. Before politics, before history and religion, there is the primal terror . . . human beauty in the crush of meshed steel' (39). But while Vikas too wants to focus on the material reality of the moment, and not the aftermath, his phrasing is irresistibly figurative in ways that evoke the aftermath. In particular, the notion that the bomb had 'rearranged everything' suggests the kind of personal disorder his family experiences.

There are other evocations of the trace effects of the bomb, and the notion of a 'defining moment' soon becomes conspicuously over-determined. For Mansoor the bomb has the effect of 'cleaving his life into before and after'; a line that again evokes DeLillo (117).⁶ Later in the novel the bomb remains 'sitting vastly on the horizon of his past, like a furious private sun' (165). Later still, Ayub tells Shockie that Mansoor's 'entire personality can be extrapolated from that one incident' (224). Even when Mansoor faces other life events, they are described like explosions. For instance, when a doctor tells him he may never type again because of his wrist injury, he 'walked out of the office with his hands in his pockets and the world wild and broken around him – dust in the air; haze against the eye; telephone and electric wires stretching around the colony like a noose' (160). For Vikas, too, it seems that 'everywhere he turned, his past was detonated', and he and Deepa dwell painfully on the 'what ifs' (70). Even as they move forwards to focus on the many incidents of unnoticed 'small bombs' – directly engaging with the idea that ruptures are many and overlapping – they remain fixated on the notion that their lives have been determined by a single moment. When they become pregnant and have a daughter, named Anusha, she is perceived as 'the daughter of the bomb' (124). In this respect their understanding of the bomb aligns with Shockie's, who believes that a 'blast reveals the truth about places' (223). And yet, textures are built in that explicitly question the notion of a totalising event. Deepa and Vikas's backstories reveal pre-existing problems that might have imperilled their marriage, and Mansoor finds ways of working through his trauma – via yoga, exercise and religion – only to have his fate sealed by the structural violence of prejudiced policing. Moreover, in a highly reflexive moment, Mansoor remembers that the 'bomb survived through the living, not the dead' (139). Here, the suggestion is that forms of representation – storytelling and myth-making – perpetuate the idea of a defining moment, conferring importance to the representation of events, rather than the events themselves.

Vikas and Deepa quickly begin focusing on revenge and this, too, turns attention from the event itself. For instance, Deepa becomes 'aware, suddenly, that the death of her children was not a metaphysical event, but a *crime*' (68). Eventually, Deepa and Vikas's political activism – though conservative in its quest to punish terrorists – consolidates the novel's emphasis on structural violence and the banality of 'small bombs'. As Wattenberger notes, the novel's depiction of the 'invasion of terrorist violence into the mundane' is particularly potent, and allows connections to emerge between 'small bombs', systemic Hindu supremacism and state violence, and historical conflicts (683). This is also motored by *The Association*'s philosophical musings on the nature of bombs, which move away simply from notions of a 'defining moment'. At the outset we are presented with the curious notion that 'a good bombing begins everywhere at once' (3). We are then told, by the omniscient narrator, that 'a crowded market also begins everywhere at once', that it is an ever-shifting 'Heisenbergian nightmare of motion and ambiguity' (3). This is a curious and potent opening that at once suggests the totalising nature of the bomb or event, while also comparing it to dynamic and ubiquitous social formation, exemplary of capitalist democracy.

But if the bomb is 'everywhere at once', and somehow like a sprawling market, it is also linked closely to individuals. In one memorable passage, Mansoor, trying to work through his trauma, has the epiphany that 'if you carried rage against your parents and sexual fury against women in your head, as he had – how could you be healthy, happy? Your body imploded. You became the bomb' (170). This is an evocative description in which an encompassing set of destructive energies and obsessions are 'the bomb'. Though in this scene Mansoor's new friend Ayub is counselling him, it is he who ultimately – in a surrealist fever dream – becomes the bomb. After committing an atrocity and using the trust of Mansoor and the Ahmed family to escape capture, Ayub unravels and hallucinates a medical procedure where a bomb is surgically implanted inside him: 'You are the bomb', he is told by an imagined 'doctor', who reveals it is a new kind that 'goes off when you move your body in a particular way' (267). In his hallucination he keeps imagining the explosion:

> how it might gush out of him like a white star, pelting the ocean with soft embers and pieces of his skin. What was a bomb, really? A means of separation, of opening. A factory of undoing. It took the violent forces of civilization and applied them to the very opposite aims with a childlike glee. A bomb was a child. A tantrum directed at all things. (267)

This passage does quite a bit of work. As a moment of delirium shortly followed by Ayub's death by dehydration on a beach, it recycles some of the novel's musings on the nature of a bomb, only to undercut them as craven and fanciful. As Lagji argues, it is 'certainly a hallucination' and 'the surrealist mode allows Mahajan to explicitly address the ways characters are weaponised, or internalise the terror in the aftermath' (412). Moreover, because Ayub does not know when his imagined implant will detonate, this surrealist moment depicts a scenario that separates the material effect of a 'bomb' from the ostensible 'act of terror', defined by its symbolic potential or message. As Lagji points out, 'given the unpredictability of this internal bomb, Ayub is unable to "send a message" in the way the other bombings are designed, when they are timed to coincide with election in Kashmir, for example, or to affect the Indian economy' (412). Ultimately, in *The Association* the overly conspicuous rhetoric of the 'defining moment' calls into question this very idea, and the philosophical musing on the nature of bombs collapses, returning the reader's attention to structural phenomena. This is where the novel most forcefully critiques the rhetoric of the war on terror, and I turn now to its depictions of terrorism, terrorists and radicalisation in the context of systemic violence and historical conflict.

The Association cleverly constructs clichés of terrorists and radicalisation only to 'explode' them. In early scenes Shockie and his accomplices are caricatures that evoke satirical literary terrorists from those in Joseph Conrad's *The Secret Agent* (1907) to Doris Lessing's *The Good Terrorist* (1985). They are sexually repressed, compulsive masturbators with disturbingly violent fantasies: at a restaurant Shockie stares at women and imagines 'pinning the dhaba owner's wife on a table and ripping of her kurta' (45). They are also repeatedly shown to be incompetent slobs. On the journey to execute the first bombing, Shockie's accomplice Meraj picked 'dandruff off his hair and sniffed his fingers', and when he falls asleep on the bus, he 'drenched his shoulder with drool' (37). Mahajan also lampoons the mythos of terrorists, and we learn that Shockie has encyclopaedic knowledge of 'the greats' (46). He aspires to be like Ramzi Yousef, who had orchestrated the 1993 attack on the World Trade Center in New York, musing on this 'genius of terror' who had 'shocked America' (47). Nevertheless, these stereotypes are mitigated by other factors: the novel's gruesome depictions of state violence and torture, the picture it builds of Hindu supremacism, and the emphasis it places on the historical conflict in Kashmir.

Shockie's friend Malik, slovenly accomplice Meraj, and eventually Mansoor are all brutally tortured. The nonviolent Malik had his penis burned and electrocuted even before he was wrongly arrested, and after that he is tortured for ten straight days, and we also learn that Meraj too had been 'beaten and tortured by the Jammu and Kashmir police' (40). Terrorism in *The Association* is always part of an ongoing cyclical narrative of violence and counter-violence. That the novel concludes with Mansoor, wrongly arrested and tortured, emphasises just how pernicious the state's approach to 'counter-terrorism' is. Moreover, the terrorists are never characterised as religious zealots and Shockie considers religion 'the crutch of the weak' (57). He is also politically committed and 'dislikes all aspects of the job that make him feel like a common criminal' (44). The novel's attention to the context of Kashmiri separatism and anti-Muslim violence in India also builds slowly but forcefully. This first comes through a kind of aggregation of passing comments including Sharif's insistence, in an early passage, that while 'in this country, they're always accusing Muslims of terrorism', the 'most dangerous terrorists have been Hindus and Sikhs' (18). But it is also the case that while 9/11 is chronologically at the centre of the novel, the main political backdrop is the issue of systemic Hindu supremacism, manifest in the 2002 Gujarat riots and exemplified by the rise of Narendra Modi, who has become Prime Minister by the time of the novel's publication. When Mansoor joins Peace For All, formed in response to this event, the novel's critique gathers force. The group is described as a disparate, and much space is given to cataloguing the atrocities in response to which it formed:

> They had witnessed what Narendra Modi, the chief minister of Gujarat, had done in his state in March, how he and his administration had stood by, in localities like Naroda Patiya, Meghaninagar, and Bapunagar, as violent Hindu mobs, armed with swords, tridents, and water pistols to spray fuel, had set upon Muslims, burning them alive, tearing infants from mothers and fetuses from wombs, raping women, killing a thousand. (144)

This damning imagery of the riots is repeated and gathers force over the course of the novel as it is considered from different vantage points. Though Gujarat and systemic Hindu supremacism is at the political centre of the novel, decentring 9/11, the novel does attend to the residual effects of that attack. Indeed, Ayub directly connects the riots to post-9/11 xenophobia in America: 'thousands of innocent Muslims are being killed in plain sight' while 'innocent Muslims are being harassed in America for a crime they didn't commit' (220). The rhetoric of the war on terror also strengthens the Khuranas' anti-terror (which increasingly approximates an anti-Muslim) position, as they recycle the rhetoric of the Bush administration in America: 'passivity doesn't work' (246). But while the political backdrop of *The Association*, which attends to Shockie and his group's Kashmiri separatism, systemic Hindu supremacism, and the ways anti-Muslim sentiment was inflamed by the war on terror, is complex, its depiction of radicalisation is perhaps the sternest rebuttal it offers to the uncomplicated ways terror and terrorism have been understood in the early twenty-first century.

Just as the novel begins with a set of near-caricature terrorists only to complicate this depiction, it introduces some of the clichés of radicalisation only to add depth and complexity. The story of Ayub becomes a potent depiction of the slide from nonviolent resistance to terrorism, in that it shows a set of overlapping factors that aggregate and gather. Certain conspicuous lines evoke the arch clichés of radicalisation. Ayub's disposition becomes a state of 'normal uncontrolled anger', and he develops fantasies of grandeur about killing Narendra Modi and becoming a hero: 'he imagined books being written about his heroism, his humble background, his idealism, the world he carried within him' (186, 192). Such moments are driven by the clichés of radicalisation: perceived impotence, self-aggrandisement, delusion and uncontrollable rage. Yet, a more sophisticated picture emerges when we think of Ayub's defining characteristics – his erudition and eloquence, which are repeatedly emphasised. Additionally, his movement to violence is fraught with missteps, failures and reconsiderations, and is driven by overlapping factors: his despair at being left by Tara, the failure of the nonviolent protest he had planned and his genuine outrage at systemic prejudice. His experience with the failed protest also attends to the media's disinterest in nonviolent protest. Ayub eventually reflects that 'nonviolence, with its graying temples and wise posture', could never have the impact of atrocity (185). Ayub is also an educated, essentially middle-class twenty-seven-year-old, and this cuts against the stereotype of the poverty-stricken teenager made vulnerable to extreme ideology. This was a clearly stated concern of Mahajan's:

> I didn't feel that modern literature – fiction or nonfiction – had done an honest job describing so-called 'radicalization.' There was a widespread belief in liberal circles that terrorism was caused by poverty, when in fact most well-known terrorists in modern times have come from middle-class families, have degrees – often multiple degrees – and have lived between cultures. (Ruiz-Camacho n.p.)

In *The Association of Small Bombs*, war on terror-era stereotypes of terrorism and radicalisation are defused. Eventually, a picture of the association between 'bombs' – the 'connective tissue' of forms of systemic and institutional violence – emerges with clarity, and at every turn the reductive nature of war on terror rhetoric and logics is dismantled.

Home Fire

Kamila Shamsie's writing – both as a novelist and critic – has been a significant driver in the movement away from event-centred narratives of terrorism. Her celebrated novel *Burnt Shadows* (2009) is an important postcolonial response to the war on terror whose epic and multivalent historical narrative contextualised 9/11 in new ways. As a critic, Shamsie has also addressed the fictional response to 9/11 and the war on terror in several settings. For instance, Shamsie praised Amy Waldman's *The Submission* (discussed in my first chapter) in *The Guardian* for 'tearing up the contract' that had seen novelists focus on the narrowly domestic (2011 n.p.). Like Waldman's novel, *Home Fire* is organised in a way that moves through different subject positions and points of view. But *Home Fire*'s reflexivity has a further dimension as it invites readers to consider the characters to which they align – moving from an archetypal 'good Muslim' to a 'radicalised subject'. Crucially, it does this through the narrative architecture of *Antigone*, and in doing so it 'draws not only on Sophocles' tragedy, but also on the postcolonial legacy it has built' (Pishotti 350). Indeed, as Naomi Weiss notes, 'as a novel focused on Muslim identity, Islamophobia, and citizenship rights in contemporary Britain' it 'fits within this long tradition of politically resonant Antigones' (242). The contemporary potential of the *Antigone* story has also been a subject of Shamsie's criticism. Reviewing Joydeep Roy-Bhattacharya's *The Watch* (2012), also for *The Guardian*, she described it as 'another interpretation of the 9/11 wars as Greek myth' and a 'novel set in Afghanistan that has an opening chapter entitled "Antigone"' (2012 n.p.). As Urszula Rutkowska notes, there is a 'substantial overlap between Shamsie's writing in *The Guardian* and *Home Fire*' and 'the novel can be read as an extension of Shamsie's journalist work' (877). This ostensible 'overlap' has, of course, become particularly visible in the ways *Home Fire* is said to have 'predicted' the real case of Shamima Begum, who was stripped of her British citizenship by Sajid Javid, after she left the country to join ISIS as a child.

Like Tabish Khair's *Just Another Jihadi Jane* (2017), *Home Fire* is a British novel that responds to a new phase of the war on terror in which ISIS, not al-Qaeda, is the focus of the West, drone strikes and not torture are the main forms of state terrorism, and the violence of neoliberalism is increasingly decisive. Ostensibly, like Khair's novel, *Home Fire* addresses rising instances of disillusionment and radicalisation in Western, and particularly British and European, citizens. But *Home Fire* is not simply the story of a vulnerable or exploited young person who becomes 'radicalised'. It is very much a post-2016 novel that registers the hostility of the post-Brexit climate in the UK, broader vectors of rising, authoritarian populism and the stark division of wealth under neoliberalism. In other words, it addresses the reasons why extremism gains traction. Indeed, here I read Shamsie's novel as a response to the forms of state violence underpinned by the infamous 'hostile environment' created by the UK's Conservative government of this period. Though the violence of inequality under neoliberalism might ostensibly be less visible, it too can be understood as terroristic; and as Charlotte Heath-Kelly, Christopher Baker-Beall and Lee Jarvis show, neoliberalism 'creates economic terror for citizens deemed losers in the neoliberal society (through the hollowing out of the welfare state and the removal of economic support)' (3).

Home Fire tells the story of a young British man, Parvaiz Pasha, who leaves the UK to join ISIS in a non-combatant media technician role, after becoming alienated by the limited opportunities available to him in neoliberal Britain, in a culture of competition and transaction that does not suit his sensitive, thoughtful demeanour. He leaves behind his twin sister Aneeka, and older sister Isma, a de facto parent, fatally fracturing their relationship. Parvaiz quickly comes to regret his decision and wants to return home but is unable to in a climate of zero tolerance for 'terrorists'. The novel tells the story of Aneeka's attempt to get Parvaiz home through her burgeoning relationship with Eamonn Lone, son of Home Secretary Karamat Lone. The novel is structured in five acts, which are focalised by the five key characters built into the *Antigone* framework: Isma Pasha (Ismene), Eamonn Lone (Haemon), Parvaiz Pasha (Polyneices), Aneeka Pasha (Antigone) and Karamat Lone (Creon). As such it features a similar 'panoramic' narrative organisation to *The Association* and to Waldman's *The Submission*. The *Antigone* framework gives weight and resonance to the story of Lone's stripping of Parvaiz's and eventually Aneeka's citizenship, but the way the five acts are ordered is crucial. We begin with Isma, who is sharply critical of Islamophobia, but also a 'voice of compromise and accommodation' who reported her brother following his radicalisation, to protect the rest of her family (Haynes n.p.). Through free indirect discourse the opening section 'enables an emotional transaction between the reader and a young observant Muslim woman' (Ahmed 1151). But Isma slips out of focus and the narrative quickly privileges Aneeka, who is not compromising and who feels betrayed by Isma. As Rutkowska notes, by letting Isma recede from focus, Shamsie 'refuses to satisfy the cosmopolitan reader's desire to see her rewarded' (877). Instead, the reader is invited to consider the situations and perspectives of Parvaiz, a radicalised subject, and his uncompromising and justifiably enraged sister, Aneeka, both subjected to forms of state violence and terror.

Moreover, while Aneeka's story is privileged, it is 'rendered at a distance, through layers of mediation' (Ahmed 1151). This 'distance' is present in each of the sections but especially her own, which is constructed with fragments of dehumanising tabloid newspaper articles, tweets and interviews – approximating a particularly British iteration of what Nathan Lean calls the 'Islamophobia industry' – along with fragments of verse. The Aneeka section can, as such, be 'understood as performing the role of Chorus in a Greek tragedy, guiding the audience to a certain reading of events' (Ahmed 1151). So while Aneeka is central and displaces the moderate Isma, the mediation and misrepresentation of her emphasises Aneeka's powerlessness and erasure and is the moral heart of the novel. Ultimately, *Home Fire* ends in violence and tragedy, offering a pessimistic depiction of neoliberal multiculturalism and a damning indictment of British state violence.

In some guises, the rhetoric of positive multiculturalism has persisted in the UK, alongside the pernicious rises and spikes in post-9/11 and post-7/7 Islamophobia. However, this usually has been presented less as a social ideal, and more as an expression of the benefits of capitalist democracy and globalisation. The London Olympics of 2012, marketed via then Mayor Ken Livingstone's strapline 'one city containing all the world', is a paradigmatic example of how a vision of multiculturalism was sustained in this way; despite then Prime Minister David Cameron's indictment of 'state multiculturalism' in 2011, in a speech where, as Paul Gilroy has noted, Cameron 'instrumentalised the theme of failed, corrupting plurality' (2012, 385). From Danny Boyle's opening ceremony to the promotion of key athletes, the London 2012 Olympics celebrated Britain's national identity as multicultural; though mostly in ways that actually aligned with Cameron's evolving rhetoric, soon to cohere around the idea of an 'aspiration nation'. The London 2012 brand, and other such articulations of multiculturalism, relied fundamentally on the notions of relative equality of opportunity and meritocracy (the latter, of course, particularly resonant in the context of elite sport) that are memorably espoused by *Home Fire*'s

Conservative Home Secretary, Karamat Lone. Such notions are based on false premises. As Jo Littler has noted, meritocracy has been actively used to marketise the idea of equality despite the ways it functions 'as a mechanism to both perpetuate, and create, social and cultural inequality' (53). In Littler's terms, the rhetoric of multiculturalism persists alongside the continued, post-financial crisis rise of neoliberalism, despite the conspicuous closing and tightening of national borders and increasingly uneven distribution of wealth. Indeed, neoliberalisation has often been enabled by the aspirational myths of meritocracy and 'global connectivity' that accompany (and sometimes rely on) the rhetoric of multiculturalism. As Jodi Melamed has shown, neoliberal notions of 'freedom' have helped forge a contemporary era of 'neoliberal multiculturalism', described as a 'market ideology turned social philosophy': 'It portrays an ethic of multiculturalism to be the spirit of neoliberalism and, conversely, posits neoliberal restructuring across the globe to be the key to a postracist world of freedom and opportunity' (138). This all said, the ideals of a generative plurality, global human solidarity and cultural exchange should obviously not be discarded, and I hope my position on this is unambiguous. I embrace Gilroy's enduring belief in 'tolerance, peace, and mutual regard' (2004, 2). However, the inequalities that characterise contemporary multicultural societies are often elided in the public discourses of multiculturalism.

I argue that the forceful pessimism of *Home Fire*, and the links it explores between neoliberal multiculturalism, and terrorism and violence, confronts the realities of a multiculturalism that is hamstrung by structural inequality. I read *Home Fire* as a critique of the neoliberal rhetoric of meritocracy, the unbending violence of the British class system, and the unevenness of globalism and the contemporary world-system. I show how its critique is aimed at precisely the antagonists that Gilroy identifies in *Postcolonial Melancholia* (2004), when he was addressing earlier war on terror-era attacks on multiculturalism: 'institutional indifference and political resentment' that have been fed by 'the destruction of welfare states and the evacuation of public good, by privatization and marketization' (1). In *Home Fire*, multiculturalism is violently short-circuited by precisely such practices.

When we are first introduced to Isma Pasha, she is entering airport security at Heathrow where, inevitably, she is profiled and interrogated for hours about her 'Britishness'. Isma provides a series of rehearsed responses that open some of the political questions the novel explores. For example, launching the novel's sustained critique of the hypocrisies and double standards that characterise Britain's foreign policies and attitudes towards Muslim citizens, she points out that '[k]illing civilians is sinful – that's equally true if the manner of killing is a suicide vest or aerial bombardments or drone strikes' (5). Soon after this, we learn that Isma is writing about this particular social and political landscape, and it is hard not to make connections between her project and the novel's. Having left the family home in London, where she had raised her younger siblings, to continue the doctoral studies that were interrupted by the death of her mother when the twins were children, Isma is researching the 'sociological impact of the War on Terror' (39). We learn that she is co-authoring a research paper called 'Insecurity State: Britain and the Instrumentalisation of Fear' with her doctoral supervisor, too (39). Though the power of fiction is, of course, to 'go beyond the narrowly political', Isma's subject is Shamsie's subject (Morley 720). This metafictional impulse means that the novel implicates itself in its own pessimism. Not only does it dramatise the unevenness and cracks in British multicultural society, which lead to violence, it extends that sense of futility to the potential for literary or academic 'representations' to make any kind of difference.

This reflexivity girds a depiction of British multiculturalism where the benefits of plurality are qualified by a perennial, and often stark, inequality. Many scenes in the novel include visions of diversity that emphasise vibrancy and cultural exchange in ways that resonate with the 'one city containing all the world' rhetoric and which reveal the positive potential for multiculturalism. For instance, in the grocery store where Parvaiz works, the diversity of patrons and products is emphasised: 'Pakistanis, West Indians, Albanians – they were all fine by Nat. His shelves bursting with freshness and colour, the promise of family meals and welcoming neighbours' (140). Similarly, the siblings' Aunty Naseem notes that where her generation of Muslim women were divided by those who were veiled and those who wore make-up, '[n]ow everyone is everything at the same time' (64). The novel's extensive cast of minor characters embellish this too; Claire Chambers points to the Iranian neighbour, Scottish political assistant and Latin American bodyguard in her reading of the novel's depiction of a 'convivial diversity' (208). Other moments point to the realities that underpin this positive image of diversity and multiculturalism. For instance, Eamonn's friends perform a series of microaggressions in discussing his suspicious or 'rapidly altered behaviour', which they jokingly relate to his 'Muslim background' (82). Or, more pointedly, the spelling of his name, which as Isma (and later Aneeka) notes is 'an Irish spelling to disguise a Muslim name – Ayman became Eamonn so that people would know the father had integrated' (15–16, 64). However, it is the characterisation of Eamonn's father, Home Secretary Karamat Lone, that most vividly and explicitly depicts this qualified multiculturalism.

Lone is an archetypal, aspirational Tory, whose strident, Thatcherite individualism has crystallised in the neoliberal, multicultural present. He is a voice of assimilation, modernisation, meritocracy and individual responsibility who has been embraced by the Conservative party and abandoned by the Muslim community from which he emerged. As one newspaper hatchet job has it, he 'used his identity as a Muslim to win, then jettisoned it when it started to damage him' (247). Crucially, he repeatedly argues that Britain celebrates and embraces all of its citizens as long as they conform to certain expectations and codes of Britishness. In a rousing speech to schoolchildren in Bradford at a 'predominantly Muslim school which counted among its alumni Karamat Lone himself and two twenty-year olds who had been killed by American airstrikes in Syria earlier in the year', he states, 'There is nothing this country won't allow you to achieve – Olympic medals, captaincy of the cricket team, pop stardom, reality TV crowns. And if none of that works out you can settle for being Home Secretary' (87). Lone's rhetoric of meritocracy in multicultural Britain is quickly qualified, however. He goes on to note:

> You are, we are, British. Britain accepts this. So do most of you. But for those of you who are in doubt about it, let me say this: don't set yourselves apart in the way you dress, the way you think, the outdated codes of behaviour you cling to, the ideologies to which you attach your loyalties. (88)

Finally, Lone concludes his mandate to conform with an alarming oxymoron. He warns that if they insist on their 'difference from everybody else', then they will miss out on all that is on offer in this 'multiethnic, multi-religious, multitudinous United Kingdom of ours' (88). For Lone, the UK's multiculture is to be celebrated, via the lens of aspiration, but contained and controlled – particularly in terms of how people think, what they believe and how they dress. As noted, this kind of neoliberal authoritarianism has been persuasively figured as terroristic. Heath-Kelly, Baker-Beall and Jarvis, in a special issue of *Critical Terrorism Studies* on 'neoliberalism as/and terror', point specifically to the 'economic terror' experienced by 'citizens deemed losers in neoliberal society' but also to a 'growing form of political terror . . . characterised by the militarisation of public space at home and the suppression of dissent' (3)

This depiction of Lone reveals the acumen and prescience of Shamsie's novel in two ways. First, *Home Fire* famously 'predicted' the rise of Britain's first Muslim Home Secretary, Sajid Javid, who was appointed under Prime Minister Teresa May in 2018. Like Lone, Javid was born in Northern England (Rochdale) to Pakistani migrants; and like Lone, he was inspired by Thatcherite calls for individual responsibility. Javid's world view is often expressed in terms of meritocracy. He is a vocal champion of neoliberal policies, has sat on free market think tanks such as the Institute of Economic Affairs, and has been a regular participant at the American Enterprise Institute. Shamsie addressed this 'prediction' in a *Guardian* article in 2018, following Javid's appointment and after being referred to as 'NostraShamsie' on Twitter. She describes wanting to create a fictional Home Secretary who, like the Pasha siblings, is a child of Pakistani Muslim migrants in the first instance. Following this impulse, she felt emboldened to go ahead with what she initially felt was implausible, by three emerging politicians who were children of 'Pakistani-British bus drivers: Sajid Javid, Sadiq Khan and Sayeeda Warsi' (2018 n.p.). So while Lone is not based strictly on Javid, he was something of an inspiration. Second, and more pertinently, one of Lone's key policies is to give the Home Secretary the power to rescind British citizenship. In *Home Fire*, Parvaiz's and (for all intents and purposes) Aneeka's citizenships are stripped from them in a context that is particularly potent in the light of the Shamima Begum case. Begum was a so-called 'IS bride' who left the UK for Syria 2014 as a fifteen-year-old child. Her citizenship was eventually revoked in February 2019 by Sajid Javid amidst a sustained and toxic attack on Begum from the Conservative media. In both the novel and in the Begum case, the Home Secretary refused to listen to the pleading of these citizens (and their families), who were labelled 'enemies of Britain'.

Acts of listening and, indeed, not listening provide another way of considering *Home Fire*'s depiction of multiculturalism as something that is qualified and arbitrary. The significance of sound and listening in the novel has been meticulously analysed by Claire Chambers, whose discussion of these preoccupations begins by considering the novel's invitation to 'listen to – while simultaneously refusing to condone – jihadists' (202). For Chambers, this is where the novel's power lies: in its willingness to listen to 'individuals who are usually unattended to: most notably, radicalized subjects' (202).

It is undoubtedly the case that the novel is particularly attentive to the aural. Soundscapes are woven into the texture of the narrative, and they are important to the diegetic action, too. Of particular importance are the home field recordings made by Parvaiz, part of the way the novel depicts him as a sensitive, creative and thoughtful young person. Parvaiz sits on the roof of the garden shed, which gives him a 'clear view of the trains pulling in and out of Preston Road' and 'snapshots of life passing by', and he records the sounds of his neighbourhood in Alperton for a project he has called *Preston Road Station Heard from the Garden Shed* (217). We learn that Parvaiz has spent two years recording a minute of random ambient sound from this space, which he plans as a 1,440 minute audio track that 'his ideal listener would play between midnight of one day and the next – a soundscape of every minute of a day from this perch, recorded over 1,440 days' (131). But Parvaiz's recordings do not ever find a listener, much less an 'ideal listener', and this has powerful metaphorical traction. Crucially, as Chambers points out, neither does he:

> Parvaiz is not listened to by his own sisters, and instead Farooq lends a sympathetic ear outside the family. More broadly, those seeking to return home from Islamic State are not given a second chance, nor are their families granted an empathetic hearing. (217)

In *Home Fire*, the consequences of these acts of not listening are grave, and lead, as Chambers has observed, to 'fury' and 'violence'. We might also note, however, that there are moments where people are listened to, and this is particularly clear in the first section oriented by Isma's perspective. As Eamonn sits with Isma, who, initially balks at his gestures of friendship and is suspicious of him (knowing his father is the Conservative Home Secretary Lone), he listens attentively: 'he was careful not to dominate the conversation – listening with interest' (19). Later, as they share music with each other, he 'listened, eyes closed' to the track she shares (29). Eamonn listens to Isma and, of course later, to Aneeka. Even Lone gives Isma something of hearing as the novel nears its tragic conclusion, though of course, while he listens, he is uninterested in her case. This is not to challenge Chambers, so much as to point out that the novel's tragic conclusion is a result of both acts of 'not listening' and a failure to listen thoroughly or respectfully.

Home Fire's vision of multicultural London is coextensive with its depiction of globalism and the contemporary world-system. Just as it meticulously constructs a vision of 'convivial' multicultural

London only to tragically reveal its inequalities, it also defines its international perspective – London, Amherst, Raqqa, Istanbul and Karachi – through inequality, both in terms of the differential wealth of nations, and with regard to the freedoms to move freely from place to place. Indeed, in some compelling ways, the global structure of the novel mirrors its vision of London – which has its own core–semiperiphery–periphery dynamics: the Kensington flat where Eamonn lives, or centres of political and financial power in which Karamat circulates represent the core, and the Preston Road area, the periphery. This narrative architecture dramatises the assertion made by Sharae Deckard and Stephen Shapiro that the world-system comprised of core–semiperiphery–periphery relations 'operate[s] on multiple scales, rather than strictly national spheres', which might include 'house-hold, city, region, nation or macro-area' (9). The pessimism of *Home Fire* is first of all located in its critiques of the persistence of global neoliberalisation – particularly in relation to the ways neoliberalism has, as Mitchum Huehls and Rachel Greenwald Smith note, expanded 'granularly into the sociocultural and ontological fabric of everyday life' and in the hollow rhetoric of meritocracy that has facilitated this expansion (3). In *Home Fire*, neoliberalism is a defining cause of radicalisation but also is itself terroristic.

Homeland Elegies: A Novel

Like *Home Fire*, Ayad Akhtar's *Homeland Elegies: A Novel* (2020) is also very much a post-2016 text. It begins with a preface that traces its origins to a 'fever dream' in which the author's father and his nation (America) are 'starting to show signs of decline', prompting a desire 'to remember' (front matter) and trace a history leading to the present. The preface concludes with a short statement clarifying the fictionality of the text – as if the '*A Novel*' part of the title is not enough: 'As the sort of writer who has always felt the need to deform actual events enough to be able to see them clearly, I have not resisted the temptation here. This is a novel' (front matter). There are reasons for this emphasis. Fictional characters and events are described by a first-person narrator who shares a name with the author and who describes several events that are a matter of public record in the author's life – his winning the Pulitzer Prize for a play, for instance, and publishing a play in which a Pakistani American character experiences a 'blush of pride' at the 9/11 attacks, causing much controversy and gaining much attention (24). Because of this, *Homeland Elegies* is best described as autofiction and it uses some of the hallmarks of this genre to useful effect in its depiction of the war on terror era in America and beyond. For instance, the reader's curiosity or 'suspicion' at what parts of the novel are 'real' overlap with the various forms of Islamophobic suspicion its protagonist and other characters experience during several key episodes in the novel. Given that the narrator/protagonist is a writer, who has caused shock and controversy and has sought to make sense of war on terror-era racism in America, this results in another unique recalibration of DeLillo's 'curious knot'. In a profile for the *New Yorker*, Alexandra Schwartz notes that Akhtar's novel 'entic[es] readers with the promise of personal disclosure without ever revealing whether or not they have glimpsed actual flesh. The effect can be salacious, even inflammatory' (n.p.).

But if *Homeland Elegies* formally plays with one of its key themes – a culture of suspicion – it also uses the tools of autofiction to address what Akhtar sees as a post-2016 devaluing of 'truth'. Akhtar notes to Schwartz that he sought to address 'something about the audience and the decay of their relationship with reality, and the collapse of truth into entertainment' and that he tried to construct 'a strategy that was going to make its peace with this, not as a critique but as a seduction' (n.p.). In doing this, with a first-person narrator who is a writer, who frequently addresses the 'reader', *Homeland Elegies* evokes a particular dimension of DeLillo's 'curious knot', its notion that the immediacy of mass media has displaced depth and some notion of 'the literary'. As DeLillo's novelist character Bill Gray states in *Mao II* (1991), 'we're giving way to terror, to news of terror, to tape recorders and cameras, to radios, to bombs stashed in radios. News of disaster is the only narrative people need. The darker the news, the grander the narrative. News is the last addiction before – what? I don't know' (42). In Akhtar's novel, America's attention is consumed by the 'theatre' of the Trump era, 'in thrall to our own stupidity', and US politics in this era is 'just dramaturgy' (288). Given that *Homeland Elegies* traces a narrative broadly between the early 1990s, when *Mao II* was published and when the protagonist was at college reading 'the postmodernists' and 'magic realism', Akhtar's framing of his autofictional strategy as a method designed to address a 'collapse of truth into entertainment' carries some powerful echoes of this 'literature'/'media' aspect of the 'curious knot' (64).

But this narrative of the 1990s to the Trump era in America is also a narrative of neoliberalisation and – again, like *Home Fire* – neoliberal terrorism. The narrator protagonist meditates at length on his realisation that the 'market had seeped into our language', that 'we were now customers first and foremost, and to buy was our privileged act', and that there was 'no way to turn back the tide' (240). This is sharply aligned with contemporary theories of 'homo economicus' and the emergence of social and cultural forms of neoliberalism in the 1990s and their continued growth in the twenty-first century. For Akhtar, in *Homeland Elegies*, this market logic of everyday life is crystallised by the election as US President of Donald Trump, who is a 'human mirror in which to see all we'd allowed ourselves to become' (242).[7] *Homeland Elegies* begins with the narrator tracing his Pakistani father's interest in and 'friendship' with Donald Trump, whom he treated in the 1990s as a heart specialist. What ensues is a meandering exploration of the narrator's parents' relationships with their homeland and adopted country, which emphasises the seismic impact of partition and the conflict between Russia- and US-backed forces in Afghanistan. This unfolds alongside an exploration of the narrator/protagonist's relationship with both his home and heritage, with his writing about 9/11 at the centre. This personal history is brought explicitly into the realms of public political discourse, and the novel's international dimensions and attention to various frictions and tensions within spheres of the Pakistani Muslim community in America are uniquely powerful. At its heart is an insistence that these characters and citizens are 'real', in that they evolve and grow in surprising and contradictory ways. This is certainly the case with the narrator, whose self-questioning captures what Hywel Dyx identifies as one 'of the key insights of autofiction':

> that a person's sense of selfhood is partly constituted through interaction with a social landscape, which can change. In other words the point of autofiction is not to portray a person's existing subjectivity for all time, but to recognize that subjectivity is elusive and hence to place the subject of narrative endlessly in question. (6)

Though *Homeland Elegies* is not a novel about terrorism, I argue that at its heart is a project not about resisting stereotypes, but about how the process of resisting stereotypes can form new stereotypes and clichés. The ranging and loving depiction of (a) variously flawed ordinary Muslim lives navigating a hostile climate, (b) the narrator's attempts to write about variously flawed ordinary Muslims' lives, and (c) grappling with various arguments about the need for positive representation addresses this phenomenon head on. In what follows I focus on the novel's family stories, and its metafictional devices, elements of the novel that inevitably overlap.

As well as resisting the stereotypical ways of resisting stereotypes, the novel's deeper family story attends to histories and historical ruptures that mitigate an impulse to see 9/11 as a totalising moment of rupture. In a prologue entitled 'Overture: To America' that precedes the first of three sections, 'Family Politics', the narrator begins by evoking that 'terrifying day in September that changed Muslim lives in America forever' (xvi). References to the attacks and their aftermath are ubiquitous. At the beginning of the third section, 'Pox Americana', the narrator recalls telling a new lover, Asha, about his experience of the day of the attacks, when he was living in Manhattan, narrating his tale over ten pages. The 9/11 attacks are also a key part of the novel's metafiction, as the protagonist's writing about 9/11, and the controversy and acclaim it has garnered, comes in and out of view and ultimately drives the scene that concludes the narrative. But yet, family stories and 'family politics' demand that the attack is contextualised by deeper histories of conflict and terror. In one potent scene, at the dinner table of his Aunt Ruxana's home in Abbottabad, Pakistan, in 2008, the narrator's 'first time back in Pakistan since 9/11', he and his father, Sikander (Ruxana's brother), listen as her husband, Naseem, monologues at length about the 9/11 attacks, describing them as 'tactical *genius*' from a '*military* point of view' (70). In the preamble to this scene the narrator, from a position of retrospect, connects the climate in Pakistan in 2008 to the climate in America in 2016, reversing the logic of 'Islam versus the West' in a potent comparison. He muses:

> I see now the broad outlines of the same dilemmas that would lead America into the era of Trump: seething anger; open hostility to strangers and those with views opposing one's own; a contempt for news delivered by allegedly reputable sources; an embrace of reactionary moral posturing; civic and governmental corruption that no longer needed hiding; and married to all this, the ever-hastening redistribution of wealth to those who had it at the continued expense of those who didn't. (70)

When Naseem monologues on the tactical genius of the 9/11 attacks and how they 'changed the history of how war will be fought', the narrator's father objects, decrying 'the chaos it started' (73). Naseem replies, 'who truly started the chaos we might not agree' (74). Though many of Naseem's claims are absurd, this emphasis on America's response to the attacks as the true cause of 'chaos', and not the singular moment itself, has an important resonance here and aligns with the narrator's own views about the war on terror as a 'new era of unending American vengeance' (71). The episode closes with the narrator noting that after a heart-rending and tearful goodbye between Sikander and Ruxana, father and son pass 'the dirt-road entrance that led to the compound where, at that very moment, Osama bin Laden was residing' (78).

The 9/11 attacks and the war on terror, too, are contextualised by the deeper historical narrative of the protagonist's parents, Sikander and Fatima, and their move to the US in the 1960s, after the childhood trauma of partition. The narrator comes to see this experience as the heart of his mother's struggles with life in America before and after 9/11, and thinking about it through his mother's eyes and her 'earliest memories' of 'Lahore station the summer of the bloodshed, when fifteen million people were uprooted', he connects it to the other violent historical episodes the novel discusses, including the Afghan struggle against Russia and the 'war on terror' (30). Ultimately, thinking about his parents' experience of partition enables him to 'educe ... the contours of the deepest fault line, I believe, separating so much of the so-called Muslim world from the so-called West' (26). In one trenchant passage he argues that 'Pakistan's late-twentieth and early twenty-first century obsession with terror-as-tactic – learned of course from the CIA – was the paranoid calculus born of partition's trauma' (26).

This 'fault line' is examined and challenged over the course of a divergent set of family stories and conflicts. One particularly potent one is the story of Latif, Sikander's best friend and the man of Fatima's dreams. When, during medical school, she finds out he is betrothed to another woman, she decides to settle for Sikander but remains in love with Latif and connected to him as he is recruited to an American hospital around the same time Sikander is and eventually has a family in the US, too. But Latif changes as the conflict with the Soviets in Afghanistan intensifies in the early 1980s, for him 'shedding a new light on a more frivolous life in the West than perhaps he'd expected' (37). In 1983 Latif moved his family to Lahore and set up a medical practice. His clinic was funded by the CIA on the condition it was used to treat wounded mujahideen fighters from across the Afghan border. But when, 'to much of the world's surprise', the 'mujahideen prevailed' in 1989, it did not take long for America to move its focus to Iraq. Here, this family story – and the story of Latif – becomes directly didactic:

> The straight line from the American-backed mujahideen to Al Qaeda is still a story little told, little understood; in his way, Latif's fate

is emblematic of it. For once the American money dried up, like everyone else who'd depended on that cash, Latif pivoted ... The abandonment of Afghanistan and the first war in Iraq sent a clear message: whatever the Americans said meant nothing; whatever they promised was a lie. (45)

Ultimately, we learn that Latif's family was torn apart by the opium trade and fundamentalism. At the end of June in 1998, Latif was murdered as a 'terrorist spy', and the protagonist watches on CNN as a special report shows images from his clinic with photographs of the holy mosque in Mecca alongside one of Osama bin Laden, failing 'to mention that Latif was an American citizen' (47). Though this detail functions as another reference to 9/11, it also insists – in very didactic terms – on understanding a tragic pre-history to 9/11.

In the many episodes of family life and the narrator's wider and evolving networks of Pakistani Americans, there is a constant attention to the bad choices, mistakes and moral failures of these characters. This includes the shady mogul Riaz Rind, who helps the protagonist become rich; Asha, whom he falls in love with but who doesn't reciprocate; and any number of family members, not least his father, who cheats, gambles, drinks excessively and harbours an unhealthy fixation on Donald Trump. The protagonist, too, is guilty of multiple moral failings, which he willingly and repeatedly admits to. This means that just as the reader is appalled by the racism he experiences, particularly after 9/11, his evolution into a 'neoliberal courtier', and particularly his 'season of sexual fecklessness', means he is not a moral hero of any kind. This appears to be the point as he is repeatedly critical of the cliché of the 'good Muslim' and hostile to the critical clamour for 'a Muslim character driven to valiant ends by unimpeachable motives' and 'not the tortured, vindictive antihero' of one of his plays (228, 264). Several debates over his writing's avoidance of the 'good Muslim' cliché are staged in the novel. The lengthiest of these debates is with Riaz Rind, to whom he defends his 'artistic procedure' and its emphasis on 'trying to show people as they are, no better, no worse' (140). Rind is fundamentally opposed to this, as his plan for the elevation of Muslims in America is to mimic white Christian American culture: 'they push the minority of their best in our faces and then pretend that's the whole picture. We need to do the same. Shove the best of our minority down their throats' (140). But this is one issue on which the protagonist is consistent, and he doubles down with reference to Edward Said's *Orientalism* (1977):

Said writes a book about how wrong they've been about us, and it becomes our bible, a high road to self-knowledge. But that's not what it is. Not remotely. Constantly defining yourself in opposition to what others say about you is not self-knowledge. It's confusion. (141)

Again, and again the narrator is challenged on his insistence to portray morally ambiguous characters. His father's dear friend, Sultan, questions him, too. When he posits his well-rehearsed argument, Sultan responds, 'we're under attack in this country now. We have to stick together' (316). This part of the metafictional, autofictional project of *Homeland Elegies* is strengthened by other features. It is a book in dialogue with other books and with the creative process, beginning and ending with anecdotes featuring the protagonist's beloved literature professor, Mary Moroni, and using three of Leo Tolstoy's novellas, *The Kreutzer Sonata* (1889), *Hadji Murad* (1912) and *The Death of Ivan Ilyich* (1886), as inspiration for particular sections.[8] Akhtar's probing depiction of various acts of challenging the 'good Muslim' trope and resisting the stereotypes associated with resisting stereotypes is a rich and important addition to the literature of the war on terror, and to the overlapping post-2016 era. Nevertheless, this too is something the novel remains uncertain of, and even while the protagonist's rationale for not defining characters strictly through their rejection of racism is persuasive, he admits early on that one of the novel's most discussed depictions of Islamophobia was an episode that led to a 'new unwillingness to pretend' he is 'not conflicted' about his country or 'place in it', and to finally finding his way as a writer (121).

Notes

1. The description of the 2002 Gujarat massacre as a 'pogrom' is common. Parvis Ghassem-Fachandi makes a particularly compelling case for this in *Pogrom in Gujarat: Hindu Nationalism and Anti-Muslim Violence in India* (2012).
2. Shamsie wrote a short essay for *The Guardian* ('True Story') about how *Home Fire* 'predicted' the rise of Sajid Javid, the horrific case of Shamima Begum, and the overlaps between her fiction and reality.
3. In an interview with Zahra Hankir for *Literary Hub*, Saadawi discusses his interest in 'complicity'. Hankir describes their discussion: 'Saadawi's not so subtle intention here is to emphasize what he refers to as the "complicity" of all those involved in the conflict. In his mind, everybody has blood on their hands: American soldiers; foreign mercenaries;

Al-Qaeda fighters; warlords; journalists; and corrupt Iraqi officers' (n.p.).
4. Arundhati Roy rejected the popular notion of 'India's 9/11', perpetuated by various parties, in a short piece in *The Guardian* entitled 'The Monster in the Mirror': 'we should reclaim our tragedy and pick through the debris with our own brains and our own broken hearts so that we can arrive at our own conclusions'. In a scholarly article entitled 'India's 9/11: Accidents of a Moveable Metaphor', Tania Roy argues that 'the reference to 9/11 effects a quasi-theological "conversion" by cancelling history'.
5. *The Association*'s emphasis on the stories of the wrongly accused proved prophetic when Mohammed Bhat, wrongly jailed for involvement in the Lajpat Nagar blast, was released and cleared in 2019.
6. This line in *The Association* recalls a passage from Don DeLillo's *Falling Man* (2007), when the omniscient narrator states, 'everything now is measured by after' (138).
7. In the introduction to *Neoliberalism and Contemporary Literary Culture*, Huehls and Greenwald Smith posit their influential four phases theory, in which the third phase occurs in the 1990s when neoliberalism becomes socially and culturally entrenched.
8. Akhtar notes to Schwartz that *The Kreutzer Sonata* is inspiration for a sequence on 'sex and rage'; *Hadji Murad*, 'for the bravura middle section about a Muslim hedge-funder who deploys an ingenious financing scheme to avenge himself on American Islamophobia'; and a final passage dealing with the decline of Akhtar's father is inspired by *The Death of Ivan Ilych*.

Works Cited

Ahmed, Rehana 'Towards an Ethics of Reading Muslims: Encountering Difference in Kamila Shamsie's *Home Fire*', *Textual Practice*, 35.7 (2021), 1145–61.

Akhtar, Ayad, *Homeland Elegies: A Novel* (New York: Little, Brown, 2020).

Al-Hajaj, Jinan F. B., 'Magic Realism, the Oracular, Mysticism and Belief Legacy in Ahmed Saadawi's *Frankenstein in Baghdad*', *Critique: Studies in Contemporary Fiction*, 64.4 (2020), 453–67.

Alkhayat, Marwa Essam Eldin Fahmy, 'Gothic Politics in Ahmed Saadawi's *Frankenstein in Baghdad*', *Arab Studies Quarterly*, 44.2 (2022), 45–67.

Chambers, Claire, 'Sound and Fury: Kamila Shamsie's *Home Fire*', *The Massachusetts Review*, 59. 2 (2018), 202–19.

Davies, Dominic, 'Concrete Stories, Decomposing Fictions: Body Parts and Body Politics in Ahmed Saadawi's *Frankenstein in Baghdad*', *Interventions: International Journal of Postcolonial Studies*, 23.6 (2021), 922–40.

Deckard, Sharae, and Stephen Shapiro, *World Literature, Neoliberalism, and the Culture of Discontent* (Basingstoke: Palgrave Macmillan, 2019).
DeLillo, Don, *Falling Man* (New York: Scribner, 2007).
DeLillo, Don, 'In the Ruins of the Future', *Harper's* (December 2001), 33–40.
DeLillo, Don, *Mao II* (London: Vintage, 1991).
del Pont, Xavier Marcó, 'Metafiction', in *The Routledge Companion to Twenty-First Century Literary Fiction*, ed. by Daniel O'Gorman and Robert Eaglestone (Abingdon: Routledge, 2019), pp. 80–8.
Dyx, Hywel (ed.), *Autofiction in English* (Basingstoke: Palgrave Macmillan, 2018).
Ghassem-Fachandi, Parvis, *Pogrom in Gujarat: Hindu Nationalism and Anti-Muslim Violence in India* (Princeton, NJ: Princeton University Press, 2012).
Gilroy, Paul, '"My Britain is fuck all": Zombie Multiculturalism and the Race Politics of Citizenship', *Identities: Global Studies in Culture and Power*, 19.4 (2012), 380–97.
Gilroy, Paul, *Postcolonial Melancholia* (New York: Columbia University Press, 2004).
Hankir, Zahra, 'Ahmed Saadawi Wants to Tell a New Story about the War in Iraq', *Literary Hub*, 19 June 2018 <https://lithub.com/ahmed-saadawi-wants-to-tell-a-new-story-about-the-war-in-iraq/> [accessed 31 August 2023].
Haynes, Natalie, 'Home Fire by Kamila Shamsie Review – A Contemporary Reworking of Sophocles', *The Guardian*, 10 August 2017 <https://www.theguardian.com/books/2017/aug/10/home-fire-kamila-shamsie-review> [accessed 5 October 2023].
Heath-Kelly, Charlotte, Christopher Baker-Beall and Lee Jarvis, 'Editors' Introduction: Neoliberalism and/as Terror', *Critical Studies on Terrorism*, 8.1 (2015), 1–14.
Herman, Peter C., '"Nothing terroristic about him": The Figure of the Terrorist in Karan Mahajan's *The Association of Small Bombs*', in *The Figure of the Terrorist in Literature and Visual Culture*, ed. by Maria Flood and Michael Frank (Edinburgh: Edinburgh University Press, 2023).
Herman, Peter C., *Unspeakable: Literature and Terrorism from the Gunpowder Plot to 9/11* (Abingdon: Routledge, 2020).
Huehls, Mitchum, and Rachel Greenwald Smith, 'Four Phases of Neoliberalism and Literature: An Introduction', in *Neoliberalism and Contemporary Literary Culture*, ed. by Mitchum Huehls and Rachel Greenwald Smith (Baltimore: Johns Hopkins University Press, 2017), pp. 1–18.
Kapadia, Ronak, *Insurgent Aesthetics: Security and the Queer Life of the Forever War* (Durham, NC: Duke University Press, 2019).
Kundnani, Arun, *The Muslims Are Coming: Islamophobia, Extremism, and the Domestic War on Terror* (London: Verso, 2015).

Lagji, Amanda, 'Terrorist Plots: Temporality, the Politics of Preemption, and the Postcolonial Novel', *Studies in the Novel*, 52.4 (2020), 403–18.

Lean, Nathan, *The Islamophobia Industry* (London: Pluto, 2012).

Littler, Jo, 'Meritocracy as Plutocracy: The Marketising of "Equality" Under Neoliberalism', *New Formations*, 80/81 (2013), 52–72.

Livingstone, Ken, 'One City Containing All the World', *Financial Times*, 12 July 2005 <https://www.ft.com/content/08676d34-f302-11d9-843f-00000e2511c8> [accessed 31 August 2023].

Mahajan, Karan, *The Association of Small Bombs* (London: Vintage, 2016).

Mattar, Netty, 'Zombies, Placelessness, and Transcultural Entanglement: Ahmed Saadawi's *Frankenstein in Baghdad*', in *Decolonizing the Undead: Rethinking Zombies in World-Literature, Film and Media*, ed. by Giulia Champion, Roxanne Douglas and Stephen Shapiro (London: Bloomsbury, 2023), pp. 159–78.

Melamed, Jodi, *Represent and Destroy: Rationalizing Violence in the New Racial Capitalism* (London: University of Minnesota Press, 2011).

Morley, Catherine, '"How do we write about this?": The Domestic and the Global in the Post-9/11 Novel', *Journal of American Studies*, 45.5 (2011), 717–31.

O'Gorman, Daniel, 'Global Terror, Global Literature', in *Terrorism and Literature*, ed. by Peter C. Herman (Cambridge: Cambridge University Press, 2018), pp. 446–68.

Pishotti, Gabriella, 'Materializing Grief: The Reclamation of Loss in Kamila Shamsie's *Home Fire*', *Journal of Postcolonial Writing*, 58.3 (2022), 349–60.

Ray, Sangeeta, 'Bombs and Bomb Makers: Realism, *The Association of Small Bombs*, and the Post-9/11 Novel', *Studies in the Novel*, 53.1 (2021), 20–35.

Rothberg, Michael, *The Implicated Subject: Beyond Victims and Perpetrators* (Stanford, CA: Stanford University Press, 2019).

Roy, Arundhati, 'The Monster in the Mirror', *The Guardian*, 13 December 2008 <https://www.theguardian.com/world/2008/dec/12/mumbai-arundhati-roy> [accessed 31 August 2023].

Roy, Tania, 'India's 9/11: Accidents of a Moveable Metaphor', *Theory, Culture & Society*, 26.7 (2009), 314–28.

Ruiz-Camacho, Antonio, 'I Want Complete Freedom When I Write', *The Millions*, 22 March 2016 <https://themillions.com/2016/03/i-want-complete-freedom-when-i-write.html> [accessed 31 August 2023].

Rutkowska, Urszula, 'The Political Novel in Our Still-Evolving Reality: Kamila Shamsie's *Home Fire* and the Shamima Begum Case', *Textual Practice*, 36.6 (2022), 871–88.

Saadawi, Ahmed, *Frankenstein in Baghdad*, trans. by Jonathan Wright (London: Oneworld, 2018).

Scanlan, Margaret, *Plotting Terror: Novelists and Terrorists in Contemporary Fiction* (Charlottesville: University of Virginia Press, 2001).

Schwartz, Alexandra, 'An American Writer for an Age of Division', *The New Yorker*, 14 September 2020 <https://www.newyorker.com/magazine/2020/09/21/an-american-writer-for-an-age-of-division> [accessed 31 August 2023].

Shamsie, Kamila, *Home Fire* (London: Bloomsbury, 2017).

Shamsie, Kamila, 'The Submission by Amy Waldman – Review', *The Guardian*, 24 August 2011 <https://www.theguardian.com/books/2011/aug/24/the-submission-amy-waldman-review> [accessed 31 August 2023].

Shamsie, Kamila, 'True Story: Kamila Shamsie on Predicting the Rise of Sajid Javid', *The Guardian*, 3 May 2018 <https://www.theguardian.com/books/booksblog/2018/may/03/true-story-kamila-shamsie-on-predicting-the-rise-of-sajid-javid> [accessed 31 August 2023].

Shamsie, Kamila, '*The Watch* by Joydeep Roy-Bhattacharya – Review', *The Guardian*, 15 June 2012 <https://www.theguardian.com/books/2012/jun/15/the-watch-joydeep-roy-bhattacharya-review> [accessed 31 August 2023].

Sinha, Babli, 'Collective Suffering and the Possibility of Empathy in Karan Mahajan's *The Association of Small Bombs* and Kiran Desai's *The Inheritance of Loss*', *Journal of Commonwealth Literature*, 54.2 (2019), 292–302.

Wattenberger, Melanie R., 'When Person Becomes Problem', *Interventions: International Journal of Postcolonial Studies*, 20.5 (2018), 682–96.

Webster, Annie, 'Ahmed Saadawi's *Frankenstein in Baghdad*: A Tale of Biomedical Salvation?', *Literature and Medicine*, 36.2 (2018), 439–63.

Weiss, Naomi, 'Tragic Form in Kamila Shamsie's *Home Fire*', *Classical Receptions Journal*, 14.2 (2022), 240–63.

Chapter 4

Contemporary Historical Novels of Terrorism

In contrast to the previous chapters, this one discusses just two novels: Rachel Kushner's *The Flamethrowers* (2013) and Anna Burns's *Milkman* (2018). These formally inventive works depict terrorism in the late twentieth century in the context of other forms of violence, and within complex histories of conflict.

Both novels feature first-person retrospective narratives in which young women protagonists are pursued by much older men. They are both set in the 1970s, and address acute forms of misogyny in particular historical moments, while resonating in the contemporary political contexts in which they were published.[1] This said, they are also very different in terms of scope and narrative style. *The Flamethrowers* is a global novel and work of world-literature, which traces a multigenerational and transnational history that unfolds over a century.[2] It connects the lives of three principal characters. The central protagonist is a young, nameless, working-class art graduate from Nevada who moves to New York after college, aged twenty-one, 'shopping for experience' and wanting to meet other artists and be 'part of something' (44, 313). She is nicknamed 'Reno' by one of the scenesters she meets, accepts this moniker without protest, and soon becomes romantically involved with Sandro, a celebrated artist fourteen years her senior. Sandro is a player on the scene, and the scion of the Valera motorcycle and tyre empire. The story of his father, Pietro 'TP' Valera, provides the historical and global scope of the novel. Pietro is raised in Alexandria at the beginning of the century, becomes involved in the Futurist movement in Rome as a student, fights in WWI, builds a construction empire in 'newly industrialised Milan', develops a motorcycle company and then a rubber business via slave labour in Brazil during WWII, and becomes influential to the Italian government during the 'new Italy' of the 1950s (38). These three characters are connected to overlapping and contrasting revolutionary currents, leading ultimately to Reno's involvement in a Brigate Rosse (Red Brigades) terrorist plot.

In stark contrast to the global scope of *The Flamethrowers*, *Milkman* is set entirely in what is usually read as the Ardoyne district of north Belfast (though it is never explicitly named) and its immediate environs over a period of weeks in 1979, though centuries of conflict simmer beneath the surface setting of the novel and there are repeated references to the 'eight hundred years of the political problems still to be sorted' (254). It is focalised by eighteen-year-old 'middle sister' and, as with Reno, but to different effects, we never know her proper name. Unlike the global web of connected characters that Reno encounters, middle sister attempts to navigate the perils of predation by the titular antagonist, Milkman, a forty-one-year-old paramilitary 'terrorist', in a densely populated community in which suspicion and gossip are pervasive, including within her own family, during a period of violent conflict. While Reno covers thousands of miles, crosses international borders, oceans and mountain passes, middle sister does not venture far past the local reservoir around which she runs; though her routine travels around Belfast cross sectarian borders and boundaries. Her circumscribed life and heavily surveilled movements contribute to the novel's sometimes claustrophobic affective quality, which is in contrast to the expansive, panoramic aesthetics of *The Flamethrowers*.

Both novels have well-known but very different formal conceits relating to their first-person narrators. Though the vivid prose of *The Flamethrowers* has been repeatedly praised, the characters can feel 'flat', and this part of Kushner's writing has been critiqued in the same ways that her mentor and friend Don DeLillo's writing has occasionally been: in its stylish but seemingly emotionless emphasis on surface.[3] Reno, in particular, has repeatedly been read as a 'passive' character, whose silence is conspicuous, and whose life is governed by 'chance' (Greenwald Smith 293).

Milkman is equally stylish and its central device of withholding proper names is deceptively simple as it places the novel in productive conversation with canonical Troubles texts, while also marking it as unique. Like Brian Friel's play *Translations* (1979), it grapples with both philosophical and context-specific issues of naming and language, and like Seamus Heaney's 'Whatever You Say Say Nothing', from *North* (1975), it addresses the binaries of speaking and silence. Yet its formal innovations remain distinctive.

Claire Hutton has taxonomised its 'system of naming' into three strands: first, 'descriptions which are unique to the perspective of "middle sister" such as "Somebody McSomebody"'; second, 'words, phrases, and syntactical structures which record, play with, and build upon the particular linguistic features of Hiberno-English'; and third, 'words and descriptions which more neutrally model the features of the frighteningly dysfunctional and violent world in which the action takes place' (358–9). In contrast to Reno, middle sister has a distinctive narrative voice, and her inner monologues have even been misread as a 'stream of consciousness' (Garner n.p.). *Milkman* is better understood as a 'novel of voice', and while the novel tells the story of middle sister's traumatic experience of predation, surveillance and 'loose tongues', it is thoughtfully and stylishly narrated in a voice that, as Siân White notes, is both 'authentic and idiosyncratic' (121). As such, she is very different to Reno, who is often silent, content to listen and observe.

These works have garnered substantial bodies of scholarship, most of which has focused on their formal innovations and the way these respond to the histories the novels depict. *The Flamethrowers* has frequently been read as a historical narrative of the emergence of neoliberalism or post-Fordism in the 1970s, and *Milkman* as a new kind of Troubles novel that gives representation to the 'complexity of life as lived under prolonged and extreme conditions of terror' (Malone 2022b, 1144). However, the scholarship on these works has rarely discussed them in depth, as novels of terrorism. I argue that they are usefully compared in this way, and I focus on how they depict terrorism in a set of interlinked circumstances, attending to the specificities of terrorism and its effects, while insisting on its proper contextualisation beyond reductive binaries. Discussing terrorism of the 'long twentieth century', John Bew, Alexander Meleagrou-Hitchens and Martyn Frampton note that in the late twentieth century, terrorism in Europe 'invariably emerged as the violent iteration of some pre-existing socio-political movement or claimed to embody a particular community' (126). They also remind us that it should be understood in relation to the other forms of violence – from the devastating consequences of two world wars to various 'civil wars, and episodes of brutal state repression' – that shaped the twentieth century (115). In what follows I discuss the ways these novels disrupt and complicate Peter C. Herman's 'speakable/unspeakable' paradigm in evocative ways, and ultimately make terrorism 'speakable'. I connect this to their depictions of artistic expression, returning again to DeLillo's notion of the 'curious knot between novelists and terrorists', and considering the ways that art and literature relates to violence in both texts. Kushner has noted that art 'has complex ties to violence', and the two are undoubtedly linked via *The Flamethrowers*' dual interest in artistic expression and revolutionary violence (Cotton n.p.). In *Milkman* one of middle sister's defining idiosyncrasies is her habit of 'reading-while-walking', which gives her a small 'bit of power' in a 'disempowering world' (205). Finally, I argue that the novels squarely resist the conventions of event-based narratives of terrorism, and the kinds of trauma narrative that emerged in response to 9/11, in ways that are instructive and revealing in the contemporary contexts in which they were published. They usefully remind us in the era of the unending 'war on terror', that, as Luis De la Calle and Ignacio Sánchez-Cuenca have argued, 'terrorism is a European innovation' and Europe was 'the cradle of terrorism' (543).

Though neither of these novels is an 'event-based' narrative of terrorism, *The Flamethrowers* features two 'crashes' that might be understood as central events. Reno literally crashes on her advance edition 1977 Moto Valera motorcycle in the Bonneville Salt Flats in Utah during a time trial/art project early in the novel, and this is an event that sets certain things indelibly in motion. Reno's crash occurs in the immediate aftermath of another more public crash, the fiscal crisis in New York City of 1974–5; and it also evokes a third contemporary 'crash', the financial crisis of 2008–11, which occurred during the writing of the novel. Kushner has endorsed the idea that the novel addresses the 'collapse and disappearance of the manufacturing era' in America and points to the 'link between the 1973 recession and oil crisis, the decay of urban America, and this very productive discourse that sprang up in the art world in New York in the early and mid-1970s' (Hart and Rocca 199, 208). Yet despite this emphasis on moments of change and turmoil, the novel's depiction of terrorism, which is crucial to its plot and thematic meanings, does not emphasise traumatic rupture or the before and after of events, but instead shows how terrorism emerges from and around other political, cultural and subcultural phenomena. This is partly because Reno moves discursively into and out of different scenes and movements, observing their internal contradictions, including eventually the world of Autonomist activism in Rome, where she becomes involved with Red Brigades terrorists. Ultimately, she is an unwitting accessory to an act of terror – the political assassination of Roberto Valero, head of Moto Valera and Sandro's brother. In the novel's historical chronology, this event occurs just before the real kidnapping and eventual murder of Aldo Moro, former Italian Prime Minister and eminent political figure, an event that, Daniela Irrera argues, 'made the Italian government and public realise the veritable threat that the group represented to the democratic political institution of the country' (19). However, the nonlinear narrative of *The Flamethrowers*, and its emphasis on deeper histories of violence, and various revolutionary energies and movements, complicate any sense of rupture, and the novel's movements back and forth in time mean that information about Reno's final experiences with the group are revealed sporadically. Additionally, the Red Brigades are compared to Up Against the Wall Motherfucker (UAW/MF) an anarchist group that evolved out of the Black Mask art collective in New York, whose various (and sometimes violent) actions are given a whole chapter, and whose former members and residual mythos enter Reno's orbit early in the narrative. What is significant here is the contrasting – sometimes antithetical – ideological coordinates of these movements. As Reno observes, in relation to the militants and activists she becomes involved with in Rome:

> There were a lot of gray areas with these people. Roberto and Sandro, despite their political differences, both had presented the issues as stark and tidy, as if there were exactly two groups that opposed the state, as distinct from each other as black and white: the Red Brigades – armed, underground militants. And the leftist youths – open, public, more or less nonviolent. But nothing was simple or stark, I was beginning to see. (288)

These observations invite comparisons to Reno's previous interactions with Burdmoore Model, a former member of UAW/MF – described in the novel as a 'political street gang' – and are contextualised by the narrative's lurches from the 1970s back to moments of wartime, colonial and state violence (153). These contexts strengthen its vision of terrorism, reminding us that it is not as reducible as post-9/11 logics suggest.

In *Milkman*, event-based logics are addressed with equal force. There are certainly unspeakable violent incidents, some of which have a strong symbolic dimension, and the canicide scene, in which middle sister recalls the murdering of the dogs of her neighbourhood when she was only nine, is a powerful example of the traumatic impact of acts of terrorism. Yet, what makes *Milkman* an unusual Troubles novel is that it resists the sometimes reductive discourses of trauma and the rhetoric of terrorism – which as we have seen can be divisive and homogenising. Unlike many Troubles narratives in which, as Caroline Magennis notes, 'the violent act is the main narrative catalyst', *Milkman* offers layers of context and insists on giving narrative and voice to trauma (2021, 139). As Patricia Malone notes, middle sister's narrative mounts a 'radical challenge to the received wisdom of trauma as "unspeakable"' (2022b, 1145). Indeed, *Milkman* eschews the logic of traumatic rupture, in favour of an affecting depiction of the atmosphere of fear created by prolonged patterns of state, paramilitary and patriarchal terrorism. One of the effects of this is to offer a vision of terrorism that is not assigned to an evil enemy other, but which, instead, depicts it as a pernicious tactic employed by different forces or 'sides' within the conflict.

The Flamethrowers

The Flamethrowers follows two narrative strands which overlap: Reno's nonlinear first-person narrative, and an episodic third-person narrative of key moments in the life of Pietro Valera. Chronologically, the first is the story of Valera, but while this covers six decades and bears profoundly on Reno's and Sandro's lives, Reno's narrative gets much more space. Pietro is introduced in combat in north-eastern Italy in 1917 in the novel's short first chapter. He parks his motorcycle when a compatriot crashes, only to be attacked by a German whom he fights and kills with a motorcycle part. The episode ends with the single sentence: 'Valera brained him with the headlamp' (2). This scene introduces threads that connect most of the novel, and notably Valera's character is established through violence and in relation to motorcycles. We then flash back to his privileged childhood in Alexandria, Egypt, where his adolescent sexual desires are embroiled in his first encounter with an early motorcycle. His story then moves precipitously to his struggle to adjust to the 'noise and chaos' of Milan in his adolescence, and to his time as a student in Rome where he becomes involved in a group that are coded partly as bohemians who want 'change' from 'lives structured around tradition, custom, sameness', but who turn out to be early, motorcycle-riding Futurists (38). Valero is intoxicated by the group's spirit and senses something 'coalescing, an energy transfer from the cyclists to his own spirit. Life is here, he thought. It is happening now' (41). But Valera's story tracks the evolution of this movement which valorised violence and war as 'the world's hygiene', and he is soon unambiguously aligned with the far right.[4] After fighting in WWI, he develops a motorcycle company which expands into tyres, and during WWII it becomes globalised with rubber plantations in Brazil run through slave labour. Valera's brutal 'overseer', we learn, has the key ability to 'recognize what was within human limits, but just barely' (127). Ultimately, Valera becomes an associate of Mussolini and adviser to the government as his industrialism embodies the 'postwar miracle, everyone in his own little auto, put-putting around well enough paid from their jobs at Valera to buy a Valera, and tires for it, and gas' (266). He dies in 1958 before the social unrest and labour disputes that plague the Moto Valera company in the contemporary 1970s world of the novel, and 'Years of Lead' in Italy more generally.[5]

Sandro Valera, we learn, did not have a great affinity for his father when he was alive, even if it was he who insisted Sandro become an artist. Sandro is introduced as a revered player in the New York art scene – Kushner often cites the 'Pictures Generation' particularly – and the novel's allusions to artists of this period are numerous.[6] Sandro is immersed in this counter-cultural scene even while he enjoys the benefits of his family's exploitation-gained wealth, and he avoids talk of his privileged upbringing or his family's political orientation which are not compatible with his rebellious posturing. Reno comes from a working-class family in Nevada, where she was raised by her mother and uncle, alongside her cousins, Andy and Scott. She describes her background unequivocally: 'I come from reckless, unsentimental people' (5). But while Reno's imagery of the 'slag-heap world of the West' she grew up in suggests few opportunities, she was able to ski in the sierras, develop her passions for speed, motorcycles and art, and find her way onto an art programme at the University of Nevada, Reno, where she begins making films, taking photographs and becomes interested in land art. When she moves to New York and is pursued by Sandro, she becomes romantically involved with him, and immerses herself in the scene, absorbing debates about performance, authenticity, life and art as they are staged in various loft gatherings, gallery openings and dinner parties across the city. The final phase of Reno's story sees her travel to Italy with Sandro, where she is betrayed by him, and where she comes to know a group of activists including members of the Red Brigades.

Scholarly discussion of *The Flamethrowers* has focused on interpreting Reno, the question of what exactly the novel is saying about the histories it traces, and how these elements connect; or do not, as some argue for reading *The Flamethrowers* 'against Reno' (Tucker-Abramson 75).[7] Several comparative gestures emerge in its historical narrative, but so do many contradictions and notably within the revolutionary currents it depicts. The contradictions of its divergent strands are ostensibly compounded by a narrator frequently read as depthless or a 'neutral, passive observer' (Greenwald Smith 300). Rachel Greenwald Smith is not critiquing the novel here, but reads Reno's passivity as part of the novel's political commentary, arguing that it is crucial to its 'formal model for how a populace that, in the name of liberal values of individual freedom, withdraws from participation in the intentional distribution and management of power – that is, democracy' only to support violent and/or authoritarian forces (302). In other words, Reno's apparent lack of political engagement is incongruous with the violent emergence of neoliberalism. Similarly, Nicholas Dames refers to Reno's 'enigmatic depthlessness' (n.p.) and Matthew Hart and Alexander Rocca cite her 'attractively unfinished, almost liquid, quality' (197), suggesting the metaphorical potential of her passivity. These are insightful readings, and Reno is undoubtedly guided partially by entrenched ideological notions of individual freedom. However, the idea that she is swept along, 'governed by chance' and stumbling into various situations without purpose is not entirely accurate, nor is it the case that she is apolitical (Tucker-Abramson 79). While Reno valorises 'chance' and 'risk', and is often silent in social situations, she is not strictly disengaged. For instance, after riding alone to the Bonneville Salt Flats to carry out her project of filming the lines her motorcycle makes in the earth, and after crashing at 140 mph, breaking a time trial record, and winning the regard of the Valero racing team, she is invited to Italy for a publicity tour as part of the team. Sandro is against the idea insisting she will be simply a 'calendar girl', but Reno quietly persists, and is sure she will get what she wants: 'I didn't push things with Sandro. I simply knew privately that I was going, and hoped he would eventually see things my way' (139). Though Reno repeatedly discusses the value she places in 'chance', which for her has 'a kind of absolute logic', this is not the only instance where her quietness is underpinned by purpose (125). She is also highly reflexive in relation to the choices she makes and ways she is led. Meditating on her first encounter with people on the art scene in New York, she notes:

> What occurred did so because I was open to it, and not because fate and I met at a certain angle. I had plenty of time to think about this later. I thought about it so much that the events of that evening sometimes ran along under my mood like a secret river, in the way that all buried truths rushed along quietly in some hidden place. (49)

This image of a 'secret river' of 'truth' is almost overdetermined in suggesting she is being carried along; but the opening declaration of wilfulness mitigates this. The liquid imagery recurs later in the scene with equally contradictory inflections:

> I was in the stream that had moved around me and not let me in and suddenly here I was, at this table, plunged into a world, everything moving swiftly but not passing me by. I was with the current, part of it, regardless of whether I understood the codes, the shorthand, of the people around me. (65)

Here, Reno insists she is 'with the current', and though she does not understand its complex flow, she is absorbing everything. Moreover, at the end of this scene, which marks her entrance into a new world, she again reflects on her choices: 'I had followed the signs with care and diligence: from Nina Simone's voice, to the motorcycle, to the Marsden Hartley shirt' (70). Her reference to the music that drew her into the bar that night is freighted with an old familiarity – Nina Simone is associated in her mind with an artist she had been infatuated with in college – and the motorcycle and shirt also trigger feelings relating to her passions. When Reno follows these 'signs', she is making instinctive but deliberate decisions based on familiarity, desire and excitement, in quite conventional ways – and with 'care and diligence'.

An emphasis on Reno's passivity can also elide the views she expresses and while Tucker-Abramson rightly notes her tendency to 'flatten, commodify, fragment, and misread the political and artistic world of the 1970s', she is an intuitive and, in places, highly reflective young person (75).[8] She certainly reflects critically about the ways she was led and how drifting without aim can be a false pretence. Recalling early experiences with Sandro, she notes, 'He had a way of leading, I later understood, by not stating we were going anywhere in particular. By seeming to wander when he wasn't, we weren't' (97). The reader never knows exactly know how much time has elapsed between the action of the novel and the moment of narration, but this is an insightful observation and an instructive comment on how the novel works. Its images of drifting or stumbling along can obscure its carefully crafted narrative architecture as well as its protagonist's own convictions. Ultimately, Reno strongly disavows Sandro and the 'humiliations of his fabulous moneyed stupid world' and is moved by the political energies and demonstrations in Rome (268). Even before this, as a guest of Sandro's at the Valera villa in Lake Como, she is embarrassed around the groundskeeper (whom she comes to know as Gianni, and eventually discovers is a Brigadist), feeling more affinity with him than with the Valeras: 'I was self-conscious, in his presence, of being the lover of someone both older and very bourgeois . . . I felt a desire for him to understand that I was not with my own people' (258).

It is unsurprising that much attention has been given to Reno's 'depthlessness' or quietness, as several motifs and symbols reinforce this. For instance, she works for film producers in New York as a 'China Girl', modelling for still images used on film leaders for colour corrections. Her image thus appears widely but is mostly unseen, used only by technicians and left 'in the margin' to 'establish and maintain a correct standard of appearance' (92). In this role Reno is both an unseen everywoman and an embodiment of anonymity or consensus white normativity, appearing in 'many films' but so briefly as to be undetectable and without story or history (92). This said, Reno's internal musings on the power of such images are wryly reflexive. She describes holding the colour chart for the images 'lovingly like it was the answer to a television game show question' and smiling 'in a tentative but friendly way, as if some vaguely intimate possibility might exist between me and whoever caught a glimpse of me on film' (140). The novel's US cover image – a photograph of a young woman wearing face paint with two strips of tape over her mouth like an 'X' – is also highly suggestive. This image, originally published on the cover of a 1980 issue of the Roman leftist newspaper *I Volsci*, resonates with Reno's silence and youth, and suggests the possibility she is *being silenced*; a notion several reviews proposed.[9] The worlds Reno inhabits are certainly violently misogynistic, leaving little space for her voice. However, Kushner's comments on the cover image point to a richer reading of how it does and does not relate to Reno. She describes the cover photo, the 'inspiration' for the novel, not as an image of silencing, but as an image of refusal that symbolises the 'insurrectionary foment that overtook' Italy in the 1970s, the Autonomist movement. Kushner associates it with a person linked to 'the most shadowy, clandestine, and violent (and paradoxically, the most visible and sensational)' arm of the movement, 'the Red Brigades' (2022b, 114). In her essay 'Made to Burn' (2020), whose title is also a slogan appearing variously in *The Flamethrowers* like a refrain, Kushner connects the photograph to a woman she interviewed during research for the novel:

> The Italian seventies had seemed a logical subject for fiction, on account of the fact that I kept stumbling upon its lore. It all began when I met a mysterious and magnetic woman who didn't say much, and who, when I naively asked her what she did, what she was

interested in, stared at me and said: '*Niente*.' She had been the girl-friend of a 'third-wave' Red Brigades terrorist, I learned. Her '*niente*' did not mean 'nothing.' It meant, I don't engage in what you'd call work. Or interests. (2022b, 114)

In this light, the photograph of the mouth-taped woman is not one of patriarchal oppression, but one of rebellion.

Kushner's interest in silence as an act of refusal relates to the value she places on listening, something she has returned to in interviews and essays. Discussing this quietness with Matthew Hart and Alexander Rocca, Kushner suggests it was a part of Reno's characterisation, if not quite a revolutionary act of refusal:

> There are moments when she says nothing for many pages, which is, in my experience, how life sometimes is. It's not always worth it to expend a bunch of energy in a social situation where other people are hungrier to speak. (Hart and Rocca 203)

Kushner's emphasis on listening and absorbing rather than passivity is borne out by decisions Reno makes and positions she articulates after listening. It also explains how she assimilates into the Autonomist house she briefly resides in with Gianni and others. However, as Kushner continues, she also seems to partially position Reno in alignment with readings emphasising her passiveness or political ignorance:

> The narrator of *The Flamethrowers* wasn't on a journey of self knowledge. Being young, at least in my conception of what it means to be young, is not to be on a journey that leads inward – What do I want? How do I feel? – but to experience a massive desire to annex your small world and make it bigger. (Hart and Rocca 204)

That Reno is seeking to expand the horizons of her experience but not gain 'self knowledge' seems contradictory as there is usually a correlation between these pursuits. In any case, Reno is certainly eager to learn about the worlds she inhabits and frequently asks questions, particularly about the Red Brigades. She asks Burdmoore Model, formerly of UAW/MF, Sandro and Tonino, the Valera team doctor, numerous questions about the group. As she witnesses the 'insurrectionary foment' unfolding in Rome, she understands that the movement is different in nature to what she had been told, that there is no 'stark and tidy' or 'black and white' division between nonviolent and violent groups: 'nothing was simple or stark, I was beginning to see' (288). The cover image in this light is not meant

Figure 4.1 The American cover for Rachel Kushner's *The Flamethrowers* (2013). Cover design © Scribner.

to depict a part of Reno's character, but a political position towards which she begins to gravitate.

Reno's move to New York, her idea to return to the West to race in the time trial as an art project, and her decision to go to Italy are deliberate choices. Even if she leaves Sandro impulsively, after being betrayed, her decision to help the activists she meets through Gianni – who provides her escape route to Rome – is shaped by weeks of intimate experiences learning about the 'the movement', and her steadily growing disgust at the excesses of the Valeras (271). At the level of form, too, the novel's propulsive plot reflects Reno's aims and desires, even if her quietness invites allegorical readings of her journey. For instance, her obsession with speed and desire for action aligns with the 'ascendancy' of 'US-led global capitalism', as Myka Tucker-Abramson has pointed out (74), and her obsession with 'risk' aligns in abstract ways with neoliberal ideologies of speculation. But this is only one of a set of figurative possibilities that emerge and overlap. Pietro's story, for instance, which provides the international and historical scope of the novel, allegorises twentieth-century capitalist world-systems, and the motorcycle itself, as an object, is highly symbolic, even if it has 'shifting associations' and traces a history that, for Andrew Strombeck, 'refuses to cohere' (472). Ultimately, the novel's lurches and jumps are driven by Reno, and though these are often exploratory, or influenced by the magnetic forces in her life, it is neither the case that there is a singular allegorical meaning that her movements decipher, nor that she simply stumbles discursively from one episode to the next.

While Reno is sometimes swept along by currents she does not understand, like many young people are, in other moments she is quietly purposeful. I read her quietness as the practice of observation, listening and reflection, and contend that these characteristics invite the reader to inhabit her subject position as she enters new, subcultural, or 'foreign' environments that need to be decoded. This is also key to the novel's formal moves – and specifically the historical and international connections it suggests, partly via the 'meandering path' of the motorcycle (Strombeck 454). As Reno observes and tries to understand the worlds she enters, the reader attempts to understand the connections that are suggested. For this reason, I argue for reading the novel with Reno, even if her narrative lacks certainty. This is important in relation to the novel's depictions of terrorism, particularly as it explores the ways different revolutionary or political energies intersect. Indeed, Reno's (and our) process of decoding aids the novel's project of demystifying a notoriously contested phase of terrorism. Though Reno is ultimately exploited as an asset in the political kidnapping – and eventual assassination – of Sandro's brother, she has become aligned with the perpetrators in meaningful ways. Reno draws the reader into the movement and explores the 'gray areas' and intersections between 'armed, underground militants' and nonviolent 'leftist youths' (288). These observations about what Kushner has described as the 'multiple layers' of 'insurrectionary foment' come after Reno has spent time in Rome, but she had long sought to understand the movement's complexities (2022b, 114). After crashing at the time trials in the first third of the novel, Reno spends time with the Valera racing team workers, who are on a 'work to rule strike' in solidarity with factory workers in Milan (118). Reno is naturally curious about this and about the unrest she has read about in newspapers and heard about – through limited interpretations – from Sandro. She asks the team doctor, Tonino, about the situation and the Red Brigades, and he emphasises complexity:

> 'That's just one group. The most visible one. There are so many groups at this point. Many of them come together only after an action, to give those who committed the action a name, and then they disband, disappear. You can't know who is part of what. They don't know either. They might not know they are in a group until the action is done and the group claims it.' (121)

When Reno witnesses the interactions of nonviolent activists and terrorists, she is building on knowledge she has pieced together from newspaper and artistic representations of the Red Brigades, Sandro's views and Tonino's comments.

As Irrera notes, the 'ideology and actions' of the Red Brigades have 'sparked animated scholarly debate', addressing the importance of the labour disputes of the 1960s – notably at Fiat and Pirelli factories – the international leftist student movement that gained force in the late 1960s (Red Brigades founders Renato Curcio and Margherita Cagol met at the University of Trento), and the Italian Communist Party (16). Some accounts have attempted to impose a guiding logic to better frame or understand this history, including Alessandro Orsini's controversial history *Anatomy of the Red Brigades: The Religious Mind-Set of Modern Terrorists* (2011). Orsini argues that the group amounted to a 'political movement operating with the typical words, thoughts, and dogmas of a religious sect' (6). Though this notion broadly aligns with the 'made to burn' mantra in *The Flamethrowers*, the real emphases in its depiction of the Red Brigades are the 'gray areas' and complexities seen by Reno. These reflect historical and scholarly accounts that emphasise 'disproportionate state repression' as well as an escalation and 'more violent repertoire' emerging around the time Reno is in Rome – 1977 (Bosi 150, 153). Though it is the case, as Emma Bond notes, that in her first days in Rome Reno 'fuses her sadness over her break-up with Sandro with the angry chants of the women protestors' (99), she begins to articulate a class- and gender-based political position. She has repressed feelings of disgust at the Valera family's excesses, and her experiences inspire nostalgic reflection on her working-class upbringing. In the aftermath of the violent demonstration in Rome, the smell of gasoline reminds her of her youthful companions, cousins Scott and Andy, who 'loved the smells of gas and oil and carburetor cleaner, soaking into their hands', which were 'permanently black' (284). But her meditation ends with another contradictory thought that seems at least on the precipice of class-based solidarity: 'That I could draw no connection between that world and this one, the people who stank of gasoline in the Piazza del Popolo, and Scott and Andy who loved its smell, made me sad for Scott and Andy in a way I could not explain' (284). Though Reno can draw 'no connection' and cannot explain her feelings, this disconnect is a lament for the fact that Reno's people – of the 'slag-heap world of the West' from which she hails – are not politically minded like her new Roman companions, and her sadness for Scott and Andy relates to their inability to see what she has witnessed (8). As Treasa De Loughry argues, this sadness is 'for the lack of political ignition in Scott and Andy's petro-urban upbringing. Cut off from the sinews linking Nevada and Rome, they are unable to imagine the alternate uses and abuses of gasoline beyond summer chores' (184). This is not a failure of political vision, even if Reno remains searching for connections, but a young person sensing political articulation that is just out of reach, and in this way, it is redolent of a key affective dimension of the novel: a pathos at the vastness and inscrutability of world-systems compounded by the elusiveness of the connections that are repeatedly suggested.

Ultimately, Reno's actions in Rome and later in the Alps as she readily helps Gianni (even if she is unaware of the terrorist act she is facilitating) punctuate the questions of complicity and proximity that permeate the novel: how connected to the Red Brigades is Reno and how culpable is she for the assassination of Roberto Valera? How should Sandro respond to the facts of his father's slaveholding and fascism? Moreover, what does the novel's depiction of violent world-systems say about the roles of radical political groups? What are the connections between the various revolutionaries: the Futurists and Autonomists, the radicals of the NYC art scene, UAW/MF or 'The Motherfuckers' who are all in some sense 'made to burn'? Is there a broader philosophical vision of the need to live urgently or differently that binds these strands together?

The Futurists wanted 'speed and change', the Autonomists wanted to dismantle capitalism, and the 'Motherfuckers' and affiliates were more broadly anti-authority. The connections and contrasts between the art scenesters who had been members of Black Mask or participant in UAW/MF actions and the Italian Autonomists and Red Brigades are richly staged. Both are the subject of various instances of storytelling which emphasises their mythos; and the romantic refrain of 'made to burn', also appearing in the Latin '*FAC UT ARDEAT*', embellishes this (224). As noted, Reno pieces together information about the Red Brigades before becoming personally involved with members. Equally, she has multiple encounters with former 'Motherfucker', Burdmoore Model, who is regarded as a 'formidable' legend of the movement (158). UAW/MF get a full chapter in which an omniscient narrator recounts 'a few choice cuts' – twenty-one short episodes over ten pages – from their 'potent five-year run' from 1966 to 1971 (186). Though this is described as an effort to 'defend a new and total freedom from Amerikan capitalism and its wars, its deadening effects, its slaveries', the actions described such as bank robberies and concert hall riots are mostly just in broad advocacy of individual liberty and against the police/authorities (186). Reno is eager to hear Burdmoore's stories, and when they meet at an art scene party, he tells her that the Lower East Side – a former UAW/MF territory – is 'dead now' (157). When Reno contends that there is 'all kinds of stuff going on there', he responds:

> 'I'm talking,' he said, 'about insurrection. There isn't shit going on in that regard. It was armed struggle, and the cops . . . had come in with tanks, and dirtier methods, informants, heroin.' (157)

But Burdmoore draws ideological distinctions between UAW/MF and the Red Brigades on multiple occasions: 'Our trip was not about rigor and self-sacrifice . . . those people are Leninists. We were more like libertines' (171). Later, after Roberto Valera is kidnapped, Burdmoore visits Reno and they discuss the events. She imagines a 'silent sympathy for my involvement with Gianni' owing to Burdmoore's revolutionary past, but he speaks in impersonal terms (319). He makes broad comparisons regarding the shared belief that for revolutionaries, the 'means they use' are 'the same, morally as those of their enemy. In other words, no less justified' (319).[10] But while this common defence of terrorism connects the groups, he distinguishes the Red Brigades for their anti-capitalist politics: 'To them, the capitalist . . . isn't a marionette serving some other, larger system of evil. He is power himself. Evil itself' (319). The historical narrative of the collapse of Fordism in *The Flamethrowers*, which is fundamentally international, certainly suggests connections between the revolutionary energies in New York and Italy in the 1970s. And yet the novel distinguishes between the anti-capitalism of the Autonomists/Red Brigades and the focus on individual liberty of UAW/MF.

In even starker contrast to the activists of Rome are the New York artists. Guns are in heavily circulation in both groups, but they are props or abstractions for the artists. This is emphasised from the outset when we learn Sandro keeps a photo of himself above his desk 'looking cool and aloof, holding a raised, loaded shotgun' (5). Guns appear in nearly every art scene episode, from Nadine and Thurman – 'the people with the gun' – shooting each other with blanks as a game at a loft party, to Sandro showing off an old 'cap and ball pistol' that he later uses to shoot a mugger (168). But when Reno arrives in Rome and briefly resides in an activist house, she notes that for these people guns are 'a tool like a screwdriver was a tool, and they all carried them' (288). The Roman activists, with 'guns jammed here and there in their pockets, no concern for make or model', starkly contrast with Sandro's interest in 'manufacture, protocol, history, the weapon as almost a work of art' (288). This is a vivid juxtaposition of the 'wild Italian Autonomist movement and the far more complacent, and underclass-ignoring, art of downtown New York' (Strombeck 464). Indeed, this juxtaposition, connected by the path of the motorcycle, is understood by oppositional evocations of the factory floor. In New York the 'largely apolitical artists' occupy abandoned factories; in Italy 'highly political activists are activated by factories with tightened shop-floor rules' (Strombeck 465).

Reno's captivation at the demonstrations she attends is never explicitly contrasted with the ironic cadences of the NYC art scene, but this juxtaposition is potent and driven by the pattern of the novel's final chapters, which move back and forth between Italy and New York. This device means that the reader encounters further 'gray areas' and layers of revolutionary posturing: the performed rebelliousness of the NY artists along with the nonviolent and violent protestors in Italy whose arguments are diverse. The Roman protest scenes repeatedly emphasise diversity and 'sections':

> The women's sections, the high schools, the various representatives from factories – Valera, Fiat, SIT-Siemens, Magneti Marelli ... There were the students from the university, bespectacled and grave, their faces masked with scarves. The Bologna Contingent, here to avenge the death of the young radical who had been gunned down by police yesterday. (275)

And yet, the range of revolutionary energies depicted in the novel is made even wider by Pietro's backstory and the deeper historical currents of the novel, a recurring reference point that contextualises the depiction of the Autonomist movement. Indeed, the story of Pietro, Futurist-turned-soldier-turned-magnate-turned-fascist, provides yet another vector of juxtaposition in the novel's depiction of revolutionary zeal.

The Flamethrowers presents revolutionary terrorism as part of the violent fabric of twentieth-century history. The motto 'made to burn', 'chiseled into the flagstone above the hearth' at the Valera family home in Italy, seems only to make the novel's multifaceted vision of 'insurrectionary foment' more opaque. It is an irresistibly figurative term, and one late chapter in which Sandro reflects on his father's burning 'ardor', the force that made him 'dash into war, toward death, and then toward money and power', is explicit about this, describing it as a 'phrase that could not be reduced to its imprisonment in the literal' (365). This refrain also echoes Kushner's depiction of revolution in *Telex from Cuba* (2008), in which, the idea that '[r]evolutions start with fires' is repeatedly posited and depicted (187).[11] If this opens out interpretive possibilities, these are exacerbated by another of the novel's preoccupations, and one which connects Pietro to Sandro and his artist friend Ronnie Fontaine, and to Reno: the idea of living urgently and authentically. This is an obsession that pervades Kushner's writing and is often explored through characters who desire to live intensely in the present but hover between participation and observation. In 'The Hard Crowd' Kushner meditates on her own experiences of moving between these positions and discusses a formative idea that 'real meaning lay with the most brightly alive people, those who were free to wreck themselves' (2022a, 248). In the previously cited 'Made to Burn' – which appears in the same collection – Kushner recycles this logic in relation to Anna in *The Flamethrowers*, a homeless, pregnant, drug-addicted teen whom Reno encounters in Rome. Inspired by the titular protagonist of Alberto Grifi and Massimo Sarchielli's film *Anna* (1975), Kushner is almost celebratory of this desperate figure: 'The people I've known like Anna – and I've known many – they live in the present tense of their lives, not the past. Caught up, mired, and possessed by real time instead of nostalgia' (2022b, 133). These ideas are clearly at work in the characterisation of Reno, and though much is made of her musings on 'chance', she is equally obsessed with the idea of 'risk' as a value that represents urgency and intensity of experience. Recalling her early years of motorcycle riding with cousins Scott and Andy, she reflects, 'I trusted the need for risk, the importance of honoring it' (12). She also attaches this value to art: 'I thought art came from a brooding solitude. I felt it had to involve risk, some genuine risk' (10). The multiple applications of what seems to be the novel's mantra, 'made to burn', as well as these abstract ideas of embracing risk to live urgently, and the sometimes pretentious posturing of the allegedly 'radical' artists Reno mixes with, seem at odds with the clear political arguments of the novel in their opaqueness.

How, ultimately, can we interpret its various strands, some of which seem divergent and internally contradictory: Reno's simultaneous quietness and propulsive drive; the 'made to burn' mantra and emphasis on risk that seems applicable to revolutionaries of the left and right; the vivid depiction of the complexity and diversity of the Autonomist movement and Red Brigades in Italy, which seem to inspire awe and a provisional political awakening in Reno; the juxtaposition of this movement with the other forms of revolutionary energy and activism the novel depicts; and finally Reno's conclusion that she'd been 'drawn in by three different men, Ronnie, Sandro, Gianni' but that she ultimately 'knew nothing about any of them', which seems to reinforce readings of her passivity (345)? The difficulty of answering this question reinforces James Wood's often-cited comments about the Red Brigades plot in *The Flamethrowers*, which he reads as an 'overloading of the novel's thematic circuits, a wrongheaded desire to make everything signify' (2013 n.p.). I argue that while the novel is ranging and even unwieldy, the terrorist plot is meaningfully positioned in relation to a larger narrative of violence in the twentieth century.

That the novel concludes with Reno waiting for Gianni – and not in the chronological aftermath of this, which takes place in earlier chapters – is telling. The novel ends with Reno's final involvement with the Red Brigades, and in doing so it concludes the longest narrative arc, the story of Pietro Valera that begins the novel.

The Flamethrowers begins with Pietro's youth and concludes with a scene that signals the death of his son – by the hands of terrorists protesting against his company. This also means the novel concludes by emphasising an act of terror within a story of globalisation and multinational capitalism. Indeed, the Pietro Valera chapters of *The Flamethrowers* present an unambiguous critique of the modern capitalist world-system, depicting it as violent and brutal, and they provide the broader historical scaffolding for this story. Pietro's violence permeates the novel even outside of the chapters in which he is the focalising character. For instance, in a chapter that chronologically comes after the death of Sandro's brother at the hands of the Red Brigades, Sandro reflects on his father's global empire while waiting to leave New York to be with his mother. At the airport, waiting for his flight from 'New York to Milan via London' – one of many allusions to globalisation – Sandro meditates on the airport design and thinks of Brasília, the federal capital in Brazil that in the world of the novel is created via profits from the Valera rubber factories (365). Sandro's artist's eye notes the 'same white concrete parabolas and huge glass bays' that were 'born of the same idea, a proscriptive lie about progress and utopias' (366). From here he veers into reflection on the real violence of this part of his father's empire as he imagines 'one wretched Indian walking some godawful distance in dire heat with a basket of grain or laundry on her head, casting a shadow on a blank and baking concrete wall two hundred feet high' (366). From here his reflections fill in the detail:

> His father's rubber-harvesting operations in the Amazon had made the Brazilian government enough money to build an all-inclusive concrete utopia, a brand-new capital. The money had poured in. The rubber workers were still there – they were still there now, in 1977 – and there were many more for them because their children were all tappers as well. Neither Sandro's father nor the Brazilian overseers and middlemen ever bothered to tell the rubber workers the war was over ... They believed that someday there would be an enormous payment, if not to their children, maybe to their children's children. (367)

These are Sandro's thoughts as he prepares to fly home to comfort his mother after the death of his brother, who had been running the Valera empire. It is one of many moments emphasising the violence of the development and sustainment of this empire, and the Red Brigades plot that ends in Roberto Valera's death is a kind of conclusion for this story.

This is not an 'overload' of the novel's thematic circuits. The story of T. P. Valera is the novel's historical narrative spine and the way it connects the characters is clear. Moreover, the reader is invited to consider these connections from the beginning of the novel. In the second chapter, which follows the short first chapter, Reno's first-person narrative establishes some backstory and the key dimensions of her relationship with Sandro before shifting suddenly, to directly address the reader on page 23, stating that this is 'where the lines begin to cross ... Sandro is Sandro Valera, of Valera Tires and Moto Valera motorcycles' (23). This clarifies the connection between the three principal protagonists and to the subject of the previous chapter which had taken place fifty years earlier. It is a prominent metafictional flourish in a novel that is perennially interested in the slippage between performance or representation and reality. If the novel begins by showing us where 'the lines begin to cross', and by establishing the deeper history in which Reno's story is to be contextualised, these two strands conclude together, too. It is the end of Reno's story and the end of Pietro's story and as such we should note that the act of terrorism is contextualised in some important ways. First, via the different vectors of activism in Rome – the 'gray areas' and diversity discussed previously – as well as the novel's other images of 'insurrectionary foment'; and second, within a wider history of corporate, state and colonial violence.

The novel's depiction of terrorism in the context of the violence of modern capitalist world-systems asks the reader to follow the lines as they cross. The connected world it builds is also partly constructed by a web of cultural allusion – to art, music, literature and cinema. References include Nina Simone, The Stooges and Lou Reed; Ginsberg and Plath; films from *Wanda* (1970), *Anna* (1975), *Red Desert* (1964), *Klute* (1971) and *Zabriskie Point* (1970) to *Behind the Green Door* (1972); and artists from Robert Smithson to Rothko and Warhol. This tapestry of artists real and fictional not only characterises the New York milieu that Reno inhabits, but it expands the novel's depiction of the violence of world-systems. In one scene after leaving an exhibition of 'drawings of the Red Brigades victims', Sandro, clearly wrestling with the contradictions in his own pretences to subversion and rebellion and his family's history of violent exploitation, begins telling Reno about his Argentine friend M., whose father was part of the junta, and the 'notorious new military dictatorship in Argentina' (122). Sandro and M. are connected through their fathers' shared enemies, as 'leftist guerrillas' had 'torched a Valera plant in Buenos Aires', and through their ostensible political alignment with these shared enemies (123). We learn that M. is an artist, a 'Marxist, and also gay, and hated his own father' but also that, like Sandro, 'he didn't want to atone for it to anyone else' (123). Sandro's unwillingness to accept his own complicity in his family's pernicious practices is part of a broader pattern established early in the novel. This reference to Argentina, one of the 'laboratories' of neoliberalism in the 1970s – a history that is also explored in Pynchon's *Bleeding Edge* – is potent. There are other moments that expand the story of the Valera empire. In Reno's first encounter with Ronnie Fontaine, he riffs on the contradictions of the VW 'folks wagon', associated with 'flower power' but 'created by Hitler' and tied to a history of 'genocide and forced labor camps' (61). In this early scene, Ronnie connects this history to Sandro, whom Reno has not met yet:

> They pretend this name, Valera, is about firm Italian tits and desmodromic valves, but actually, they used Polish slave labor to make killing machines for the Nazis. Perhaps not specifically. Not exactly. But they used some kind of X to make a Y; fill in your human cost and slick modern contraption of choice. (61)

These episodes broaden the novel's story of Pietro's rise in the twentieth century, and crucially they show how thin layers of remove elide complicity and culpability. Ronnie's comment about the 'human cost' of the 'slick modern contraption of choice' also connects the artists to the industrialists. As Christian Lorentzen points out, the novel is 'about machines (motorcycles and guns, but also cameras) and the way they revolutionized the last century (its politics and violence, but also its art)', and it should be noted that Reno is as attached to her camera as she is to her motorcycle (n.p.). Ultimately, neither Sandro, Ronnie nor M. is interested in interrogating or properly acknowledging their own privilege or complicity.

In addition to the vast network of allusion in *The Flamethrowers* – which I have only glossed – the novel is usefully understood in relation to a set of extra-diegetic intertexts that illuminate its musings on the relationships between art and violence, representation and reality. For example, it was written and published in the immediate years after the release of two relatively high-profile cinematic portrayals of leftist terrorism in Europe: Uli Edel's *The Baader Meinhof Complex* (2008), a depiction of the Red Army Faction (RAF) and titular subgroup, and Olivier Assayas's *Carlos* (2010), released both cinematically and as an extended mini-series, which focuses on the life of Ramírez Sánchez, aka Carlos the Jackal. Both works are stylish and reflexively attuned to the aesthetics and styles of the terrorists they portray; like *The Flamethrowers*, they depict leftist terrorism in Europe at a historical moment in which terrorism has become synonymous with jihadi terrorism. Another intertext for *The Flamethrowers* – and these two films – is Don DeLillo's short story 'Baader-Meinhof', in which two strangers meet at MoMA in 2002, where Gerhard Richter's famous Baader-Meinhof paintings, a cycle called *October 18, 1977*, is being shown; DeLillo would also include oblique references to the Baader-Meinhof group and Red Army Faction in *Falling Man*, as discussed in my first chapter. Not only do these works look back to a period of leftist terrorism in the late twentieth century that had been somewhat buried by the war on terror's focus on Islamism, but they also variously evoke DeLillo's famous notion of a 'curious knot that binds novelists and terrorists' (41).

The Flamethrowers and DeLillo's *Mao II* (1991) – from which that idea came – are very different novels but there are some intriguing continuities between their interests in global networks, crowds, and most importantly the relationship between the violent reality of terrorism and the impact of art, literary or otherwise. DeLillo's notion that the 'future belongs to crowds' (16) and to mass culture finds a strange echo in one of the scenes in Rome where Reno is captivated by the crowds and meditating on questions of human connection. Reno recalls, 'It repeated in my head as more and more people packed in the enormous square. The "we" of it: people lost in the vast thickets of the world. People lost among people, since there wasn't anything else' (277). This is different from *Mao II*'s consideration of how people both find meaning and lose individuality via different forms of collectivity, but there is an affective resonance with DeLillo's novel in the way this image of the crowd is contextualised by the inscrutability of the global, and of world-systems. Moreover, while Kushner's depiction of terrorism and art is not a restaging of DeLillo's 'curious knot', which is both a 'zero-sum game between novelists and terrorists' and an alignment between terrorist and literary 'plotting' (156–7), a vivid juxtaposition between the violent realities of terrorism and the circular discussions about performance, art and life occurs throughout the novel. Reno's rising suspicion of such abstractions, which thanks to the nonlinearity of the narrative, overlaps with her experiences with activists and terrorists in Rome, is one way in which she begins to grow. She is frustrated by Ronnie's insistence that 'surviving the human condition' requires '*eye-ron-eee*' and '*Diss-sim-you-lay-shon*. Giving the false appearance that you are not some thing' (315). This is particularly clear when he reveals all of

Sandro's infidelities to show Reno 'the uselessness of the truth' (342). She is equally disappointed with her friend Giddle – one of Sandro's catalogue of infidelities. Apart from this betrayal, Giddle's practice of treating life like art and 'playing the part' of 'girl working in a diner' becomes less interesting to Reno over the course of the novel, and this is mostly because of Reno's growing alertness to the violence the novel portrays. Ultimately, *The Flamethrowers* depicts an act of terrorism that is contextualised and de-exceptionalised by a history of the violence of capitalist world-systems, and by other forms of 'insurrectionary foment'.

Milkman

Like *The Flamethrowers*, *Milkman* resists event-based narrative logics. It also seeks to interrogate the meanings of 'terrorism' and to properly contextualise the acts of violence that are described as terrorism within the diegetic world of the novel. It meticulously portrays a 'hair-trigger society', a 'psycho-political atmosphere' with 'rules of allegiance, of tribal identification, of what was allowed and not allowed' and of the ever-present threat of violence – some of which is unambiguously terrorism (6, 24). Part of this project is dealing with trauma, but as Malone argues, *Milkman* challenges 'the received wisdom of trauma as "unspeakable"', and instead of an event-based model, of rupture, aftermath and working through, it renders inherited and entrenched colonial trauma (2022b, 1145). Crucially, this comes through middle sister's testimony, which, contrary to some readings, is not unreliable or a form of traumatic realism characterised by gaps and fragmentation. Middle sister narrates her experience of encroachment and trauma from a retrospective position of authority and care. Building on Malone's analysis of *Milkman* as a 'novel of voice' that resists conventional paradigms of trauma narrative, I read it in relation to Herman's notion of terrorism as a phenomenon characterised by the 'speakable/unspeakable' binary. In this formation, terrorism is a form of violence that always carries a 'message', but one that 'often goes unheard because, to those on the receiving end, terrorism is unspeakable' (6). Herman draws on the language of trauma here, but the notion of terrorism's rhetoric means this formation more specifically relates to terrorism studies. On the surface, Herman's notion of impasse seems ideally suited for a consideration of the Troubles and its representation in fiction. However, in *Milkman* the range of violent acts that can be usefully understood as 'terrorism', and the use of terrorism as a tactic by 'the state' as well as pro-state and anti-state paramilitary groups, challenges this formation. Moreover, the length of the conflict in which the acts of terror occur, and the novel's emphasis on a climate characterised by entrenched relations as well as unpredictable patterns of development, problematises the application of this paradigm. Some textual clues suggest the moment of narration is in the early 2010s, and the action occurs when 'the political problems of eleven years were going on' – meaning 1979 if we accept the convention that the Troubles began in 1968. Incidentally, this means the eighteen-year-old middle sister is roughly the same age that Burns, born in 1962, was at this time; and around the same age as Amelia Lovett, the protagonist of her first novel, *No Bones* (2001), who is seventeen in 1979. However, while middle sister repeatedly refers to 'these present troubles' or 'our troubled times', the current climate is also understood in relation to 'eight hundred years of political problems . . . still to be sorted' (136, 187, 254). Though middle sister describes the experience of traumatic disorientation – including a bodily response to the predation of her by the titular antagonist of the novel – her experiences of trauma are given articulation in her retrospective narration. The 'precision' of her narrative, I argue, extends to that term and phenomenon which is so imprecisely defined: terrorism (Malone 2022b, 1151).

The novel's central narrative device – of withholding proper names in favour of what Hutton has taxonomised as 'words, names, and descriptions which are unique to the perspective of "middle sister"'; 'words, phrases, and syntactical structures which record, play with, and build upon the particular linguistic features of Hiberno-English'; and 'words and descriptions which more neutrally model the features of the frighteningly dysfunctional and violent world in which the action takes place', has been the central focus of most of the already substantial body of scholarship it has accrued (358–9). Here again, I follow Malone's argument that this device ultimately 'troubles language' and I consider this in specific relation to the ways it interrogates acts of 'terrorism' and the nature of 'terrorists' – terms used liberally in the novel. I argue that the novel's depiction of a deeply rooted violent conflict resists the 'speakable/unspeakable' paradigm and, like *The Flamethrowers*, it insists that terrorism be understood in context, and not exceptionalised or removed from the other forms of violence and resistance in which it inevitably occurs. Additionally, I focus on the novel's interest in art and literature, and middle sister's apparently eccentric habit of 'reading-while-walking' (5). This habit is given much attention and ostensibly represents a form of escapism from the 'bombs and guns and death and maiming' (21). However, it also evokes and recalibrates DeLillo's formation of a 'zero-sum game between writers and terrorists', in specific relation to the entrenched conventions and norms of middle sister's world, when she questions the notion that her reading-while-walking is somehow 'beyond the pale', while violence is ordinary. In a memorable scene with 'longest friend', she laments a situation where 'it's okay for him to go around with Semtex but not okay for me to read *Jane Eyre* in public?' (200). I argue that in *Milkman*, the depiction of terrorism as part of ongoing conflict, and the relations between literature, art and violence offer a potent alternative to event-based narratives of violence and terrorism – within both the canon of 'Troubles fiction' and the contemporary novel of terrorism more generally.

That the novel 'troubles language' and reflects on the relations between art, reading and violence, ostensibly locates it in a tradition of Northern Irish writing. As Tom Walker notes, twentieth-century novels about the early Troubles included an 'array of artistic strategies redolent of transnational postmodernism' including poststructuralist interrogations of the limits of language, as well as more context-specific language play that went 'beyond questions of language' alone and were also responding to 'other writing on the Troubles and by other writing about writing of the Troubles' (304). *Milkman*'s innovations and strategies are not simply a response to the 'unspeakable' and neither is it interested in the kinds of metafictional circularity described by Walker. *Milkman* is also distinct in relation to contemporary Northern Irish writing, and while it certainly participates in what Magennis identifies as a 'turn to the intimate' (Magennis 2019, 191), its unique narrative devices mean it is both a vivid rendering of middle sister's affective responses to predation and systemic violence, and also similar to the 'big ambitious', 'encyclopaedic' or 'maximalist' fictions in its 'comparably immersive world-building and epistemological exploration' (White 114). As White notes, this is made possible by the narrative voice which continually and reflexively negotiates 'between her powerlessness to speak then and her power to tell now. As a result, her narrative is both explanatory and exploratory, spontaneous and unguarded, but also grounded and assertive' (118). White's emphasis on middle sister's retrospective authority and power – her mastery over her own story – is similar to Malone's emphasis on the way the novel formally urges us to trust middle sister. As Malone notes, reading the novel in relation to Felskian theories of the post-critical, middle sister's narrative 'establishes a relationship of solidarity between teller and listener as part of a turn away from the hermeneutics of suspicion and towards the "willingness to listen"' (2022b, 1149). Such formal reinforcements of the novel's story of predation, in which nobody listens to middle sister, are partly why the novel was so resonant in the immediate context of the #MeToo movement. Similarly, White notes how the novel's challenge to narrative omniscience implicitly critiques abusive structures of power. White takes this further, arguing for *Milkman* as a novel that has just as viable a claim to being a novel of the world as some of the big novels of globalisation:

> By linking narrative omniscience to storyworld omnipotence, the novel implicitly critiques the problematic claims to certainty and authority that bolster abuses of power – by state actors, paramilitaries, sexual harassers, even community gossips and bullies – in the real world. Driven by these big ambitions, *Milkman* foregrounds a single feeling human by letting that human speak for herself. (119)

I focus on the novel's use and depictions of language and voice in particular relation to terrorism, its contextualisation of terrorism in relation to other forms of violence, and its consideration of the ostensible opposition between art and violence.

The effect and role of the novel's central device has been a subject of debate, and the divergence of scholarly readings is acute because of the necessity, in many of these works, to clarify common misreadings. These relate to the period of middle sister's story and retrospective narration, the notion that her narrative is a stream of consciousness, and to the related idea the novel is 'difficult'. As noted, the novel is almost certainly set in 1979. We learn of 'the political problems of eleven years were going on' and early references to a 'catlike' Kate Bush and to Sigourney Weaver 'killing the creature in that new film when none of the men in that film had been able to' (58, 8), echoing a passage in *No Bones* that dates 1978 via 'that film starring Robert De Niro, the one that had the Russian Roulette in' (87). Slightly more elusive is the time of narration. Also early on, middle sister describes not understanding Milkman's methods of predation 'until later, and I don't mean an hour later. I mean twenty years later' (6). This has prompted some readers to identify the time of narration as the late 1990s, just post-Good Friday Agreement. However, as White notes, textual clues including a reference to a 2013 film and 2012 advertisement, indicate that while middle sister's understanding may have crystallised 'twenty years later', the time of narration is likely more than thirty years later (130). The claims made about middle sister's 'stream of consciousness' narrative mostly refer to patterns of digression, which can be long and meandering, but do not constitute a stream of consciousness.[12] They are important, though, as they are moments where background information is supplied, and in places they bridge the distance between the narrative action of 1979 and the present time of narration in the 2010s. In a broader sense, these misreadings relate to the narrative device at the heart of the novel: middle sister's present voice of precision and authority which describes a past experience of traumatic disorientation unfolding in 'hair-trigger' conditions.

In *Milkman*, the backdrop is of a prolonged violent conflict between 'the state' and 'defenders of the state', and 'renouncers of the state' and 'the country over the water'; and citizens like middle sister, whose large family includes members who have taken up arms for and betrayed the cause, occupy shaky and changeable relationships to their 'side' (22). These sides and the familiar groups and phenomena attached to them are defamiliarised, and this invites the reader to interrogate the rhetorical power of the language of this conflict. For Malone, these terms are nonetheless 'precise' and 'name things as they are' even if they are clearly more 'general' (2022b, 1151). The careful reader will quickly identify which 'side' of the conflict is being referred to but might also reflect on the connotations and resonances of the terms ordinarily used and what is laid bare by omitting them. It is a 'deterritorialization by which those terms and phrases seen as "unique" to "the Troubles" – the Six Counties, the Orange Order, the border question, the peace wall, the Loyalists, the Provos, the Republicans – are reterritorialized with a more general language of conflict' (Malone 2022b, 1151). Another term that is not changed – which ostensibly is already part of a 'general language of conflict' – is 'terrorist' and variants including 'terrorism' and the more unusual 'terroristic'. Within the deterritorialisation and reterritorialisation of language in *Milkman*, this term, already malleable, emotive and imprecise, is conspicuous. One example of its suggestiveness comes late in the novel, as middle sister is recovering from being poisoned by 'tablets girl', the 'district poisoner' and self-confessed '*Faithful Terror Of Other People And Not Just On Difficult Days*' (266). Recovering in bed, middle sister overhears a phone call to her mother alerting her to the shooting of 'real milkman', an actual milkman who has been supportive to middle sister's family and others including the 'issues women', a marginalised feminist group, and who stands up to the 'renouncers' for trying to use his residence to store arms. Middle sister's mother, who is in love with real milkman, learns that a 'state killer squad' had shot him as a terror suspect, and exclaims incredulously, 'Can you imagine? *Real milkman! . . . a terrorist!*' (247). She leaves frantically for the hospital, telling middle sister, 'They're saying he was a terrorist. They're searching his house right now, digging up his backyard, trying to find things terroristic' (248). Here 'terrorism' is at the centre of the novel's language games as via 'counter-terrorist' operations, the state has mistaken the actual milkman, one of the few people to stand up to their 'terrorist' antagonists, for the titular paramilitary Milkman. This episode thus includes a cycle of violence involving the actual ostensible terrorist, Milkman, and the real milkman who is an antiterrorist, and the state counter-terrorist squad committing an act that genuinely inspires terror. Such eventualities border on farce, particularly when we consider that this all happens while middle sister recovers from her poisoning at the hands of the '*Faithful Terror Of Other People And Not Just On Difficult Days*', tablets girl. Such episodes mobilise a proper interrogation of the term, which is sustained throughout the novel. This includes depictions of the perennial misapplication and misuse of the term, and misidentification of citizens as terrorists, which occurs as incompetence, gaslighting and also through extreme forms of suspicion. For instance, middle sister recalls how the renouncers suspect that one of the issue women, from another district, might 'not be an issue woman really, a women's libber really, but instead some slippery *agent provocateur* for the state' (157). More potently, when 'the state' finally kills Milkman, it is only after 'six false starts' in which they 'shot a binman, two bus-drivers, a road sweeper, a real milkman who was our milkman, then another person who didn't have any blue-collar or service-industry connections – all in mistake for Milkman' (303).

Though there is much emphasis on such misuses of the term, and misidentification of terrorists, *Milkman* does not shy away from depicting forms of violence that can clearly be defined as terrorism. However, its depiction of false and real terrorists is further complicated by a repeated emphasis on the evolving nature of the profile of terrorists, and nature of terrorism, during the conflict:

> In our district the renouncers-of-the-state were assumed the good guys, the heroes, the men of honour, the dauntless, legendary warriors, outnumbered, risking their lives, standing up for our rights, guerrilla-fashion, against all the odds. They were viewed this way by most if not all in the district, at least initially, before the idealistic type ended up dead, with growing reservations setting in over the new type, those tending towards the gangster style of renouncer

instead. Along with this sea change in personnel came the moral dilemma for the 'our side of the road' non-renouncer and not very politicised person. (118–19)

In this rich passage, middle sister is sarcastic ('legendary warriors') but also attuned to a 'sea change' from the 'men of honour' renouncers to the 'gangster style'. Such observations build her authority as a narrator – supporting Malone's and White's readings – and even if she is narrating in retrospect, they refute the accusations levelled by other characters of a lack of knowledge of the 'political problems'. Such observations also add complexity to the novel's depiction of terrorism and the debates about definition and categorisation it stages. She points to the grey areas, and to the 'inner contraries, the moral ambiguities' faced by ordinary citizens when considering the escalations of violence and death, and particularly the kinds of violence meted out on subjects of suspicion within the renouncers' own community (119). The gruesome acts of violence described – symbolic, designed to instil fear – are also acts of terror: 'beatings, brandings, tar and featherings, disappearances, black-eyed, multi-bruised people walking about with missing digits who most certainly had those digits only the day before' (119). This movement from 'honour' to gangsterism, or from a corruption of ideals, also locates the novel's depiction of terrorism in more universal contexts as this is a common trope in Troubles narratives but also a recognised phenomenon in post-1968 leftist terror groups in Europe, including the Red Brigades.[13] This evolution is also depicted in films like *The Baader Meinhof Complex* or *Carlos*.

The novel's real emphasis, in terms of terrorism, however, is twofold – it portrays the 'day-to-day' forms it takes, cutting against event-based logics, and it builds a potent connection between this climate and violent, misogynistic predation, exploring the ways these forms of violence interact while attending to their distinctions. While much attention has been given to the novel's central formal device, it is full of subtle but potent flourishes, too. For instance, when middle sister recounts the death of the brother of Somebody McSomebody and 'nuclear boy' – another of the district's 'beyond the pales' – her repetitions are evocative: 'his favourite brother's head got blown off in the middle of the week, in the middle of the afternoon, in the middle of the street, right there in front of him' (62). This repetition of 'middle' emphasises the centrality and day-to-day-ness of this violent act, its being in the middle of everything, just as 'middle sister' is. One of the effects of the centrality of violence in middle sister's world is to strengthen her initial sense of Milkman's encroachment as insignificant:

> how could I open my mouth and threaten the widespread disintegration of the current status quo? Especially this would be impossible in the context of the political problems, where huge things, physical, noisy things, were most certainly, on a daily basis, an hourly basis, on a television newsround-by-newsround basis, going on? (64–5)

This is not a backdrop of sporadic violence, not a community making the best of a difficult period, but a state of all-encompassing conflict. In *Milkman* pervasive violence is somewhat mitigated by humour, but it is repeated and forceful. Middle sister looks back in some agony at 'those extreme, awful crowd days, and on those streets too, which were the battlefield which were the streets' (112). The complexities and gradations and the centrality of violence, as well as the liberal use of the terms 'terrorism' and 'terrorist', make it difficult to identify the novel's articulation of what 'terrorism' is, and the connection it builds between Milkman's predation and his terrorism further complicates this.

If *Milkman*'s central device is both unique and part of an identifiable tradition of Troubles literature that raises and addresses questions of language and naming, then its convergence of personal and public experiences of terror also represents a uniquely potent iteration of an established conceit. This starts with Milkman's stalking of middle sister as she moves through public spaces – while she runs, while she walks around the district, and in the third instance, waiting for her outside her 'adult evening French class', which occurs 'downtown' (69). Middle sister's experiences are not, strictly, personal traumas that are psychologically connected to the political conflict. They are, instead, experiences of predatory sexual harassment by a violent paramilitary, whose established potential for violence is used to threaten and coerce her into a sexual relationship. This, too, is a form of terrorism. As Arun Kundnani argues, 'the daily reality of gender-based violence . . . ought also to be labelled terrorism' as it is a shocking form of political violence that carries a message; and as Kundnani reminds us, 'the maintenance of patriarchy is eminently political' (21). Milkman's gender-based violence is particularly terroristic given the forms of subterfuge he employs, using the deference and fear he inspires in the community, and a process of indirectness that middle sister describes as 'constant hints, symbolisms, representations, metaphors' (181). For instance, he makes an indirect threat to 'maybe boyfriend', the mechanic that middle sister had been dating for a year, by casually noting that a 'car bomb blows up and out', in relation to a different topic within the same conversation (109). Here, his paramilitary credentials come to bear and relate to his terrorising of middle sister. As White notes, 'he wields power by maintaining a plausible deniability – a tactic no doubt important to his political work – which sows in her self-doubt and silence' (124). However, while this tactical alignment is evocative, the convergence of private and public in *Milkman* is not a metaphorical linking of personal and collective traumas, it is a linking of different forms of terrorism. And yet, middle sister's narrative inevitably emphasises the connections between her personal bodily and psychological experiences, and the ongoing conflict. As Magennis notes, there is a triangulation between embodied experience, personal feelings and the 'collective affective mood' of the community (2021, 141). The novel is certainly as attuned to embodied experience as it is psychological violence, and middle sister's physical response to Milkman's stalking seems to exemplify the experience of 'terror'. Long passages in six different scenes describe the 'strange bodily sensation' middle sister experiences in Milkman's presence or thinking about his presence (79, 102, 139, 159, 214, 342). These passages emphasise disorientation, and the threat of sexual violence. The first instance is particularly vivid:

> an omen of warning, originating in the coccyx, with its vibration then setting off ripples – ugly, rapid, threatening ripples – travelling into my buttocks, gathering speed into my hamstrings from where, inside a movement, they sped to the dark recesses behind my knees and disappeared ... my first thought, unbidden, unchecked – was that this was the underside of an orgasm, how one might imagine some creepy, back-of-body, partially convulsive shadow of an orgasm – an anti-orgasm. (79)

This is an unsettling scene and it gains power in the next episode, in which the distance between the time of narration and the experience being described is bridged by ongoing trauma. This is conspicuous in a novel where the retrospective authority of the narrator is clear, even as she describes disorienting experiences. As noted, *Milkman* 'records the voice of someone who has struggled to find that voice', and as I have argued, following Malone and White, middle sister's narrative voice is authoritative and renders a persuasive vision of her community, and a compelling story of her experiences of trauma (367). However, middle sister does occasionally reflect on the ongoing impact of this experience in the present and this is clear when she describes the physical reaction 'then, as now' when relating her attempts to defend maybe boyfriend to Milkman, from accusations of disloyalty. She reflects: 'I felt then, as now, the losing of my step. I was falling over, slipping in' (107). This is conspicuous in a novel in which one of the subtexts is the emergence of the language and discourse of trauma during the gap between the main events of the narrative in 1979 and the time of narration in the early 2010s. Ultimately, after Milkman is killed, middle sister does begin to understand his impact, and her reflections on this are devastating: 'it was, while standing in our kitchen digesting this bit of consequence, that I came to understand how much I'd been closed down, how much I'd been thwarted into a carefully constructed nothingness by that man' (303).

The subtle sense of 'lightness' – both literal and metaphorical – that emerges in places in the novel, and particularly at the end with Milkman's demise, never quite means that middle sister's trauma is being resolved or worked through. Instead, as Magennis notes, middle sister is returned to a condition of living which includes 'moments of possibility and pleasure that live alongside the worst days' (2021, 167). This lightness, and the imagery of light that closes the novel, relates to its ongoing discussions of art and literature, which, I argue, are also critically important to its depiction of terrorism. The closing image of middle sister heading out on a run returns her to a beloved activity curtailed by Milkman, and calls back to an earlier moment in the novel – two earlier moments in fact – of viewing sunsets. Middle sister closes her narrative: 'I inhaled the early evening light and realised this was softening, what others might term a little softening' (348). The sunset scene(s) open chapter 3 with a 'literary passage', from a French novel that the class is reading with their eccentric teacher. Middle sister seems to have liked the fact that the class 'had surprising things', and that it occurred downtown with learners from 'both sides' including people 'who really did have the names Nigel and Jason' (71). She recalls how the class collectively took issue with this literary passage in which the sky is 'not blue' (69). First, they dispute the 'confusion of subjects' on the grounds that French class should be about learning a language and not 'taking things apart which are in the same language', or 'figures of speech and rhetorical flourishes, with one thing representing another thing', the domain of the 'English Literature' class – 'the weirdos down the hall' (70). They are also unwilling to admit that there are more 'colours than the acceptable three in the sky – blue (the day sky), black (the night sky) and white (clouds)' (70). When their protestations are curtailed by the teacher, who insists they all move to the window, middle sister describes this and her first ever viewing of a sunset, a few days prior with maybe boyfriend:

> It had changed colours during our short trip along the corridor and before our eyes was changing colours yet. An emerging gold above the mauve was moving towards a slip of silver, with a different mauve in a corner drifting in from the side. Then there was a further pinking. Then more lilac. Then a layer of turquoise that pressed clouds – not white – out of its way. Layers were mixing and blending, forming and transforming . . . (73)

She reflects on this experience and particularly the earlier viewing of this spectacle recalling an epiphany. She describes being befuddled by the spectacle to the extent that she begins questioning her relationship with maybe boyfriend amongst a host of the other 'irreconcilables' and 'uncontrollable irrationalities' that she references periodically (76). But then something becomes clear just as she is wondering what she and the other sunset watchers around them are doing:

> something out there – or something in me – then changed. It fell into place because now, instead of blue, blue and more blue – the official blue everyone understood and thought was up there – the truth hit my sense. It became clear that there was no blue out there at all. For the first time I saw colours. On both occasions, these colours were blending and mixing, sliding and extending, new colours arriving, all colours combining, colours going on forever. (76–7)

This is an evocative scene. As middle sister sees the horizon – something she has seen her whole life – in a new way, noting that the 'official blue everyone understood' was not actually blue at all, the passage reinforces the novel's formal strategy of defamiliarisation. There is a satisfying echo here of a scene in *No Bones*, in which one character is seen 'ignoring, as he'd always done, the ordinary things – his neighbours, the sky, the pink early-evening light, the breeze from the end of summer upon his arm' (93). Here, two quiet but profound moments of shared beauty, first between middle sister and maybe boyfriend, and then between members of the French class from 'both sides', model a way of seeing beyond the codes of an intractable ideological impasse. The experience allows the participants to transcend the 'consensus thinking that shows how people can come to accept the tacitly unacceptable' (Malone 2022a n.p.). It also suggests that aesthetic beauty, art – and indeed literature – can enable this kind of vision. The emphases on mutability and transformation are particularly potent. They resonate with the novel's depiction of an evolving backdrop of conflict, but also – without excessive sentimentality – they point to the possibility of change. Finally, the emphasis on reading metaphors or symbols is important, too, in a situation where Milkman's strategies of predation involve misdirection, 'symbolisms, representations, metaphors' (181).

The novel is also, of course, invested in the role of literature in the life of its protagonist, whose defining hobbies are running and 'reading-while-walking', which Burns has revealed was also her own habit. Middle sister's bookishness is an element of characterisation that results in her ostracisation and yet it simultaneously reinforces her persuasiveness as a narrator; especially when we learn that her reading-while-walking includes 'taking notes, checking footnotes' and 'underlining passages' (200). Her erudition makes her linguistic and stylistic flourishes as a narrator convincing. It does two other things, also. First, it eventually aligns her with the other community outcasts like real milkman, tablets girl, nuclear boy and the issues women, when longest friend reveals to her that because of her reading-while-walking, she was also 'considered a community beyond the pale' (199). Second, it is at these moments, when middle sister is under scrutiny by her allies for reading-while-walking, that she is at her most defiant.

We learn immediately that books have been a form of escape for middle sister. She reads only novels from the nineteenth century or earlier, noting that she does not like twentieth-century books because she does not like the twentieth century (5). Over the course of the novel, she reads or references *Ivanhoe* (1819), *Jane Eyre* (1847), *Vanity Fair* (1848), *Madame Bovary* (1857), *Martin Chuzzlewit* (1844), *Castle Rackrent* (1800), *Persian Letters* (1721) and *The Overcoat* (1842) and mentions reading Hardy, Conrad and Kafka to her 'wee sisters'. Middle sister hints at the perceived 'beyond the pale-ness' of her reading-while-walking when she notes on page 3 that it was 'something else to be added as further proof against me', and in the first quarter of the novel has an extended debate with her running partner and ally, third brother-in-law (3, 57–67). The debate is intriguing as she had thought that they shared a mutual disinterest in 'the political problems' and is surprised when he critiques her practice first for being risky and anti-social, and then disengaged. He warns her of being vulnerable 'amongst the lions and the tigers', and the 'cunning and unruly dark forces' – but also for contravening convention and withdrawing from the community (58). This opens a discussion about their knowledge of and engagement with the political landscape – which third brother-in-law surprises middle sister by naming as 'the sorrows, the losses, the troubles, the sadnesses' and alerting her to the fact that the 'political problems' were now being referred to in these terms (61). Ultimately, middle sister is unapologetic about this perceived lack of political engagement, stating that she 'paid at least the minimum' attention and was aware through 'osmosis' of the 'very noticeable social and political upheaval of the time and the place' (59). Though it is surprising that middle sister does not know the new name of the conflict, she obviously knows it intimately, and this enacts another echo of the novel's strategy of defamiliarisation and scrutiny of language. Ultimately, middle sister recalls her conclusion at the end of this debate with third brother-in-law, as the conviction that there was 'no way I'd stop reading-while-walking' and that her 'mind was already made up' (67).

Middle sister's defiance reaches a peak when she is finally reproached by longest friend for reading-while-walking, and informed that she has become a 'community beyond the pale'. She is both hurt and perplexed because she was presuming longest friend wanted to discuss the rumour of her involvement with Milkman, not her eccentric but harmless reading practices. Longest friend echoes and extends third brother-in-law's comments. She describes the practice as 'creepy, perverse, obstinately determined', and then as 'disturbed', 'deviant' and 'Not public spirited' or 'Not self-preservation' (200). This inspires a rejoinder, and a debate about 'difference' ensues in which middle sister bravely argues that conventions or consensus does not always represent a strong moral position. She first interrogates longest friend's logic: '"Hold on a minute," I said. "Are you saying it's okay for him to go around with Semtex but not okay for me to read *Jane Eyre* in public?"' But longest friend returns to her argument about convention, noting that in this place at this time, 'Semtex isn't unusual' and that 'it's not *not* to be expected' and so ultimately, 'it is okay for him and it's not okay for you' (201). This debate escalates and its nadir is reached when longest friend becomes exasperated with what she sees as a wilful lack of understanding of the politics of the community, what is acceptable and what the consequences could be. Here, middle sister admits that her reading-while-walking is defiant, but also empowering: 'I needed my silence, my unaccommodation, to shield me from pawing and from molestations by questions' (205). She continues, describing the practice as her 'one bit of power in a disempowering world' (205). This is more than escapism or refusal, as reading gives her joy and a small bit of power. When she regretfully resigns herself to not reading-and-walking, she recognises that she will miss 'the experience of relaxing into it' (206). Ultimately, though she returns to her running, she does not return to reading-while-walking. This might be a necessary accommodation or survival tactic, a consequence of the damage done by Milkman, or even a need to be more 'alert' to the ever-changing political landscape. In any case, there is no doubt that her reading and engagement with literature and art has been a force of opposition to the landscape of terror.

In this sense, *Milkman*, too, recalibrates DeLillo's 'curious knot that binds writers and terrorists' (1991, 41). In *Mao II*, DeLillo's protagonist Bill Gray is a reclusive novelist, and his characterisation suggests similarities between writers and terrorists, and posits a notion that there is a 'zero-sum game' between writers and terrorists over who can 'influence mass consciousness' (1991, 157). As Margaret Scanlan has shown, *Mao II* was part of a wave of novels in the 1980s and 1990s in which the terrorist is the writer's 'rival, double, or secret sharer' (15). In *Milkman* middle sister is not doubled by anyone but there is a 'curious knot' or doubling set up between her reading and her associations (alleged and actual) with the terrorist, Milkman. As noted, she expects to be reproached by longest friend over Milkman rumours and is astonished to find it is her reading that has made her 'beyond the pale'. She even sets up a comparison between his possession of Semtex and her public reading of *Jane Eyre*. Even more compelling is the way her practices of reading seem to allow her simultaneously to block out or temporarily escape the fraught politics of her time and place, while also building skills in decoding metaphors, symbols and plots. Such skills surely enable her to better 'read', interpret and ultimately narrate Milkman's terrorism. Finally, her practice of reading-while-walking, which lands her amongst the community outcasts, means she is made to experience a position of otherness, and this gives emotional weight to the novel's depiction of what it means to break with convention or resist entrenched consensus.

The Flamethrowers and *Milkman* are historical narratives that clearly resonated in their political presents of publication. Kushner's novel was partly written during the initial unfolding of the Occupy movement and she has noted how events from the present began to 'echo those in the book':

> While I wrote about ultraleft subversives, *The Coming Insurrection*, a book written by an anonymous French collective, was published in the United States, and its authors were arrested in France. As I wrote

about riots, they were exploding in Greece. As I wrote about looting, it was rampant in London. The Occupy movement was born on the University of California campuses, and then reborn as a worldwide phenomenon, and by the time I needed to describe the effects of tear gas for a novel about the 1970s, all I had to do was watch live feeds from Oakland, California. (2022b, 121)

Milkman was even more explicitly resonant in its time of publication, something addressed by many of the scholarly works that discuss it. Though it was completed in 2014, its publication in 2018 meant it was contextualised by the post-2016 landscape of rising nationalism and the #MeToo movement. The Brexit vote, which renewed debates about the borders between Europe and the United Kingdom, and therefore Ireland and Northern Ireland, inevitably raised the spectre of the Troubles, too. As White notes:

> The novel's implied narrative present also coincides with unfolding revelations about abuses of sexual power and sexual predation in the United Kingdom, Ireland, and beyond, and with growing pressure and agitation – including a rise in nationalist and xenophobic responses to immigration – in the UK about its relationship to the European Union. The significance of those developments coalesces in the near coincident 2016 Brexit referendum and 2017 launch of the #MeToo movement. (113)

As I have argued, these novels also depict historical instances of terrorism that resonate in the present. Burns's contextualisation of terrorism within other forms of violence attends to both its distinctions and overlaps, and Kushner's depiction of the 'gray areas' between violent insurrection and youthful activism are potent. It is worth noting, too, that Kushner's little-discussed depiction of the Red Brigades has real comparative value in the present. As Dareen Al-Khoury has observed in a study of the rhetoric and methods of the Red Brigades between 1970 and 1984, and the Islamic State (ISIS) group between 2014 and 2019, comparative analysis can reveal biases and productively illuminate strategies. Al-Khoury notes that the processes of establishing 'legitimacy and building social capital' of these two groups are usefully comparable, and they reveal four strands of connection in relation to the rationales and justifications 'within which both movements identified their enemies, along with social and political struggles; ideology; violence; and organisation' (882). Similarly, in *Milkman* middle sister's grappling with patterns of suspicion, prejudice and rigid ideological conventions means that it resonates universally. These sophisticated novels of historical instances of terrorism – and much more – offer profoundly valuable perspectives on our present in the early twenty-first century.

Notes

1. *The Flamethrowers*' depiction of the emergence of neoliberalism resonated in the immediate aftermath of the 2008–11 financial crisis – something Kushner discusses in 'Made to Burn', and *Milkman* was published in a post-Brexit moment in which the Irish border had become acutely politicised in new ways.
2. The Warwick Research Collective (WReC) define 'world-literature' as 'the literature of the world-system – of the modern capitalist world-system' and suggest that 'world-literature be conceived precisely through its mediation by and registration of the modern world-system' (8, 9).
3. Tom LeClair was one of the first to comment on this, noting in 1987 that 'DeLillo maintains an elusive or ironic detachment from his narrators or characters' (27). More recently, James Wood (2001) has argued that DeLillo's emphasis on complex world-building has come at the expense of characterisation and interior depth.
4. Anne Bowler notes, in an article entitled 'Politics as Art: Italian Futurism and Fascism', that in 'The Founding and Manifesto of Futurism' of 1909, F. T. Marinetti 'upheld the glory of war, "the world's only hygiene," as an announcement of the imminent crisis that would reveal the radical foundation of a new social and aesthetic world order' (763).
5. Federica Rossi describes the 'Years of Lead' as spanning the 1970s into the early 1980s: a 'prolongation of political and social unrest that many Western countries experienced during the late 1960s. The decade saw the multiplication of far-left *extra-parliamentary* organizations, the presence of a militant far right movement, and an upsurge in the use of politically motivated violence and state repressive measures' (381).
6. Kushner has written extensively and knowledgeably about various forms of art, often in *Art Forum*, where she also held an editorial role before her first novel was published in 2008.
7. Notable readings 'against Reno' include those by Myka Tucker-Abramson and Rachel Greenwald Smith. The latter argues that in *The Flamethrowers*, Reno's lack of political engagement or awareness should be something the reader is critical of, and that 'the dynamics of depoliticization and authority are worked out through the figure of the novel's passive first-person narrator' (293).
8. Reno's reflections on the record-holding land racer Flip Farmer, a childhood hero, show critical acumen particularly in relation to a hero of her past and in relation to the recent (in the world of the novel) political flashpoint. She notes wryly that Farmer lamented cancelled races because of the Watts riots one year and early rainfall in another, noting

that for him 'riots and rain were presented in the book as misfortunes of the same order' (23).
9. Laura Miller's *Salon* review, 'Rachel Kushner's Ambitious New Novel Scares Male Critics', focused on its feminism, as did Nicholas Miriello's *LARB* review.
10. The character Burdmoore Model's comments about violent means being 'the same, morally as those of their enemy' and 'no less justified' align with common defences of terrorism/revolutionary violence but also specifically echo the comments of one of the ex-Red Brigades terrorists interviewed by Alessandro Orsini in his book *Anatomy of the Red Brigades: The Religious Mind-Set of Modern Terrorists* (2011), who notes that 'we see politics as indivisible from the use of force' (3).
11. The most vivid connections between *Telex from Cuba* and *The Flamethrowers* come in their images of revolution and burning passion as multivalent and inscrutable. In *Telex from Cuba*, one of the revolutionaries, the conflicted and complicit La Mazière, emphasises the symbolic power of fire, which for him is 'alchemical', and that even 'long after it's extinguished, a fire may continue to burn and corrode' (240). He later comments on the idea of 'burning passion' in relation to revolution, again seeing it as abstraction: 'True revolution was attitude and passion, not ideas and ideology, something Castro seemed to understand well' (290).
12. The term 'stream of consciousness' does not accurately describe the narrative style of *Milkman*. As Malone notes, there is 'no continuous flow of thought or feeling for a reader or for a narrator' (2022b, 1144). There are digressions where an episode is paused and layers of backstory are filled in over several pages, though. As White observes, these digressions 'build out context not extradiegetically but as mental associations prompted by something in the young character's immediate present . . . . [T]hey signal the volume of underlying information and the pressure she feels to explain the context' (130).
13. As Lorenzo Bosi notes in reference to a general trend in post-1968 leftist terror groups in Europe, but with particular reference to the Red Brigades, there was a 'movement of the BR toward adopting a more violent repertoire' (153).

Works Cited

Al-Khoury, Dareen, 'Radicalisation: Old and New a Comparative Analysis of the Red Brigades and the Islamic State', *Quality and Quantity*, 54 (2020), 867–85.
Bew, John, Alexander Meleagrou-Hitchens and Martyn Frampton, 'The Long Twentieth Century', in *The Oxford Handbook of Terrorism*,

ed. by Erica Chenoweth, Richard English, Andreas Gofas and Stathis N. Kalyvas (Oxford: Oxford University Press, 2019), pp. 115–30.

Bond, Emma, 'Looking Sideways to Italy in Contemporary World Literature', *Italian Culture*, 40.2 (2022), 95–111.

Bosi, Lorenzo, 'Social-Revolutionary Violence in Western Europe: The Case of the Red Brigades' Trajectory during the 1970s and Early 1980s', in *Terrorism and Modern Literature*, ed. by Peter C. Herman (Cambridge: Cambridge University Press, 2018), pp. 148–74.

Bowler, Anne, 'Politics as Art: Italian Futurism and Fascism', *Theory and Society*, 20.6 (1991), 763–94.

Burns, Anna, *Milkman* (London: Faber, 2018).

Burns, Anna, *No Bones* (London: HarperCollins, 2002).

Cotton, Jess, 'Voiceless Voices: An Interview with Rachel Kushner', *The Quietus*, 3 February 2014 <https://thequietus.com/articles/14407-rachel-kushner-the-flamethrowers-interview> [accessed 31 August 2023].

Dames, Nicholas, 'Seventies Throwback Fiction: A Decade in Review', *N+1*, 21 (Winter 2015) <https://www.nplusonemag.com/issue-21/reviews/seventies-throwback-fiction/> [accessed 31 August 2023].

De la Calle, Luis, and Ignacio Sánchez-Cuenca, 'Terrorism in Western Europe: A Homegrown Trademark', in *The Oxford Handbook of Terrorism*, ed. by Erica Chenoweth, Richard English, Andreas Gofas and Stathis N. Kalyvas (Oxford: Oxford University Press, 2019), pp. 543–58.

DeLillo, Don, *Mao II* (London: Vintage, 1991).

De Loughry, Treasa, *The Global Novel and Capitalism in Crisis* (New York: Palgrave Macmillan, 2020).

Garner, Dwight, '"Milkman" Slogs through Political and Cultural Tension in Northern Ireland', *The New York Times*, 3 December 2018 <https://www.nytimes.com/2018/12/03/books/review-milkman-anna-burns-man-booker-prize-winner.html> [accessed 31 August 2023].

Greenwald Smith, Rachel, 'The Contemporary Novel and Postdemocratic Form', *Novel: A Forum on Fiction*, 51.2 (2018), 292–307.

Hart, Matthew, and Alexander Rocca, 'An Interview with Rachel Kushner', *Contemporary Literature*, 56.2 (2015), 192–215.

Heaney, Seamus, *North* (London: Faber, 1975).

Herman, Peter C., *Unspeakable: Literature and Terrorism from the Gunpowder Plot to 9/11* (Abingdon: Routledge, 2020).

Hutton, Claire, 'The Moment and Technique of *Milkman*', *Essays in Criticism*, 69.3 (2019), 349–71.

Irrera, Daniela, 'Learning from the Past: Case of the Red Brigades in Italy', *Counter Terrorist Trends and Analyses*, 6.6 (2014), 16–20.

Kundnani, Arun, *The Muslims Are Coming: Islamophobia, Extremism and the Domestic War on Terror* (London: Verso, 2014).

Kushner, Rachel, *The Flamethrowers* (London: Vintage, 2013).

Kushner, Rachel, 'The Hard Crowd', in *The Hard Crowd: Collected Essays 2000–2020* (London: Vintage, 2022a), pp. 229–52.

Kushner, Rachel, 'Made to Burn', in *The Hard Crowd: Collected Essays 2000–2020* (London: Vintage, 2022b), pp. 114–36.

Kushner, Rachel, *Telex from Cuba* (London: Scribner, 2009).

LeClair, Tom, *In The Loop: Don DeLillo and the Systems Novel* (Champagne: University of Illinois Press, 1988).

Lorentzen, Christian, 'The Wild Bunch', *Book Forum* (April/May 2013) <https://www.bookforum.com/print/2001/politics-art-and-betrayal-collide-in-rachel-kushner-s-new-novel-11212> [accessed 31 August 2023].

Magennis, Caroline, 'Northern Irish Fiction', in *The Routledge Companion to Twenty-First Century Literary Fiction*, ed. by Daniel O'Gorman and Robert Eaglestone (Abingdon: Routledge, 2019), pp. 190–8.

Magennis, Caroline, *Northern Irish Writing After the Troubles: Intimacies, Affects, Pleasures* (London: Bloomsbury, 2021).

Malone, Patricia, 'Breathing Lessons', *Post45Contemporaries*, 27 October 2022a <https://post45.org/2022/10/breathing-lessons/> [accessed 31 August 2023].

Malone, Patricia, 'Measures of Obliviousness and Disarming Obliqueness in Anna Burns' *Milkman*', *Textual Practice*, 36.7 (2022b), 1143–74.

Miller, Laura, 'Rachel Kushner's Ambitious New Novel Scares Male Critics', *Salon*, 5 June 2013 <https://www.salon.com/2013/06/05/rachel_kushners_ambitious_new_novel_scares_male_critics/> [accessed 31 August 2023].

Miriello, Nicholas, 'What Is This Review Interested In?: On Frederick Seidel's Review of Rachel Kushner's "The Flamethrowers"', *Los Angeles Review of Books*, 20 July 2013 <https://lareviewofbooks.org/article/what-is-this-review-interested-in-on-frederick-seidels-review-of-rachel-kushners-the-flamethrowers/> [accessed 31 August 2023].

Orsini, Alessandro, *Anatomy of the Red Brigades: The Religious Mind-Set of Modern Terrorists* (Ithaca, NY: Cornell University Press, 2011).

Rossi, Federica, 'The Failed Amnesty of the "Years of Lead" in Italy: Continuity and Transformations between (De)politicization and Punitiveness', *European Journal of Criminology*, 20.2 (2023), 381–400.

Scanlan, Margaret, *Plotting Terror: Novelists and Terrorists in Contemporary Fiction* (Charlottesville: University Press of Virginia, 2001).

Strombeck, Andrew, 'The Post-Fordist Motorcycle: Rachel Kushner's *The Flamethrowers* and the 1970s Crisis in Fordist Capitalism', *Contemporary Literature*, 56.3 (2015), 450–75.

Tucker-Abramson, Myka, '*The Flamethrowers* and the Making of Modern Art', in *Neoliberalism and Contemporary American Literature*, ed. by Liam Kennedy and Stephen Shapiro (Hanover, NH: Dartmouth College Press, 2019), pp. 73–91.

Walker, Tom, '"Something in the making": The Troubles and the Singularity of Northern Irish Literature', in *Terrorism and Literature*, ed. by Peter C. Herman (Cambridge: Cambridge University Press, 2018), pp. 303–19.

White, Siân, 'A "Hair-Trigger Society" and the Woman Who Felt Something in Anna Burns's *Milkman*', *Genre*, 54.1 (2021), 111–37.
Wood, James, 'Youth in Revolt', *The New Yorker*, 1 April 2013 <https://www.newyorker.com/magazine/2013/04/08/youth-in-revolt> [accessed 31 August 2023].
Wood, James, 'Tell Me How Does It Feel?', *The Guardian*, 6 October 2001, <https://www.theguardian.com/books/2001/oct/06/fiction> [accessed 31 August 2023].
WReC (Warwick Research Collective), *Combined and Uneven Development: Towards a New Theory of World-Literature* (Liverpool: Liverpool University Press, 2015).

Chapter 5

Genre, Policing and Terrorism

In Preti Taneja's *Aftermath* (2021), a powerful personal narrative of the 2019 Fishmonger's Hall terror attack in London and meditation on systemic and institutional violence, the author attends to the implications of terms like 'neo-Nazi terrorism' or 'white nationalist terrorism'. As Taneja observes, the use of qualifying language in formations like this reinforces the common practice of assuming 'jihadi' or 'Islamist' terrorism as normative. Taneja points to the case of Harry Vaughan in the UK, who made headlines after pleading guilty to fourteen terror offences at age eighteen, noting that he was described 'not a *terrorist* but qualified as *neo-Nazi terrorist, far-right terrorist* as if the *terrorist* is not normally those things' (134). I proceed in this chapter with this normative logic squarely in mind, as I analyse three novels that emphasise the point that 'white nationalist terrorism' is far from an outlying form in the global, and particularly North American, landscapes of violent extremism. In what follows, I discuss Attica Locke's *Heaven, My Home* (2019), Ausma Zehanat Khan's *A Deadly Divide* (2019) and Percival Everett's *The Trees* (2021), novels that all deal centrally with terrorism, and which emphasise its historical pervasiveness, and institutional entrenchment. Because the novels by Khan and Locke are each part of a series of detective novels, and because the novel by Everett has compelling connections to several of his other novels dealing with neo-Nazi violence and terrorism, this emphasis on institutional entrenchment is particularly pronounced: the scope provided by seriality and intertextuality meeting the subject of systemic violence. Indeed, this chapter will consider the seriality of Locke's and Kahn's writing, and Everett's intertextual moves, and argue that these novels position terrorism in relation to and as part of structural and historical forms of white supremacism.

Though white nationalist terrorism is clearly the oldest and most pervasive form of domestic terrorism in America – exemplified by the heinous but widespread practice of lynching – this history of violence is rarely described as terrorism. In one sense this is baffling given the obvious ways it fits with common definitions, until we recognise that acknowledging this is, as Marita Sturken notes, to 'understand terrorism as an integral active force in the origins of the United States and its very social fabric' (18), it becomes easier to see how this history has been elided or effaced by those invested in sanitised visions of America. Additionally, and as *The Trees* emphasises, police shootings are also a form of lynching – and terrorism – and there are other new forms of white supremacist terrorism emerging at alarming rates globally and in North America particularly. It is also the case that this kind of terrorism is under-studied, despite the overwhelming evidence that it is the most prominent and dangerous terrorist threat in the world today. Three recent independent reports have made this clear. The European Union's Terrorism Situation and Trend report (TE-SAT) 2020, the US-based Soufan Center's 2019 report on *White Supremacy Extremism: The Transnational Rise of the Violent White Supremacist Movement* and the Center for Strategic and International Studies' (CSIS) 2020 report on 'The Escalating Terrorism Problem in the United States'. The latter shows that 'far-right terrorism has significantly outpaced terrorism from other types of perpetrators, including from far-left networks and individuals inspired by the Islamic State and al-Qaeda' (n.p.). This is echoed by the Soufan Center report:

> By nearly every metric, white supremacy extremism has become one of the single most dangerous terrorist threats facing the United States, if not the single most dangerous. Yet despite this, and despite numerous public overtures by intelligence and law enforcement officials, there is a significant disparity in the amount of funds, personnel, and law-enforcement tools that America devotes to combatting Islamist versus white nationalist terrorism. (9)

This body of research – along with numerous other studies – shows unequivocally that white nationalist terrorism is the biggest terrorist threat in the world today, but that resources remain disproportionately allocated to combatting or preventing Islamist terrorism. This discrepancy is perpetuated by certain forms of framing. For instance, as Aurelien Mondon and Aaron Winter have shown, the early twenty-first century has seen 'an increasing emphasis on the individual' in cases of white nationalist extremism, which has 'contrasted with a persistent focus on Islam when terrorist attacks are caried out in its name, in which the perpetrator – however loose their adherence to or knowledge of the religion might be – is attached to a global threat' (19–20). Mondon and Winter point to the 'lone wolf' trope, which does much work in disconnecting terrorist attacks from entrenched, and sometimes quite mainstream ideological currents.

Here it must also be noted that the fiction of terrorism has, until recently, disproportionately focused on Islamist terror, too. The celebrated novels discussed in the previous chapter, Rachel Kushner's *The Flamethrowers* (2013) and Anna Burns's *Milkman* (2018), along with some of the works discussed in my third chapter – which emphasise state terrorism – are among a small set of twenty-first century novels of terrorism that do not focus on the aftermaths or perceived threat of Islamist attacks. Yet, the recent fictional depictions of white nationalist terrorism under discussion in this chapter are a key part of the movement away from event-based narratives of terrorism that this book has sought to examine. It is, of course, significant that these three representations of white nationalist terrorism are all crime or detective novels. This said, I am not interested here in setting up any kind of crude split between the 'literary' fiction of the 'war on terror' or of historical instances of terrorism on the one hand, and the crime fiction of white nationalism on the other. A cursory look back at the previous chapters – which have discussed 9/11 genre novels like *Bleeding Edge* (2013) and *The Zero* (2006), clash of civilisations genre novels like *The Attack* (2005), and war on terror genre novels like *Frankenstein in Baghdad* (2013) – refutes this notion. Moreover, the formal innovation and intellectual sophistication of Everett's *The Trees* mean it is as 'literary' as anything discussed in this book, even if some of these innovations can be understood as forms of genre play. What *is* interesting about the genre frameworks of these novels is the way they persuasively position white nationalist terrorism not as rogue criminal activity, but as a form of systemic white supremacy which is institutionally entrenched in structures of law enforcement and government. This is especially notable given the ways hegemonic ideological currents move through genre and how, as Maureen T. Reddy has shown, American crime genres and subgenres tend to reinforce the notion that 'the white/male heterosexual consciousness is sacred' (2003, 27). Quite aside from this point, a feature of my approach throughout this book has been to collapse the value hierarchies that remain associated to 'literary' and genre fiction, and to consider the formulas and innovations in all kinds of fiction, recognising, as Jeremy

Rosen has pointed out, that often 'genre fiction' equates automatically to 'popular fiction' and not literary fiction.[1]

As noted in the Introduction to this book, the social sciences-oriented discipline of Critical Terrorism Studies has begun to question the prevalence of event-centred narratives of and critical approaches to terrorism. For instance, as Bart Schuurman notes, 'event-driven critiques' have 'served to prioritize particular subjects ... while others, such as state-terrorism or right-wing extremist violence, are by this same logic left un- or under-examined' (464). With this in mind, it is useful to again reflect on the potential applications or uses of the interpretive frames theorised by Peter C. Herman and Alex Houen, whose work I have drawn on throughout this study. Houen's 2002 monograph *Terrorism and Modern Literature* focuses on interaction between the 'symbolic and real', noting that 'the figurative has been imbricated in terrorism's events and history in complex, material ways' and that the 'terrifying effects of terrorism are produced and exacerbated by such interactions' (6). For Houen, the symbolic dimension of terror – which is the heart of its rhetoric or message, compounds the 'real' violence, or material impacts of the event. These two components together create terrorism's 'terrifying effects'. Herman reframes this using the language of trauma and moving from the 'symbolic and the real' to the 'speakable and unspeakable'. Herman argues that 'terrorism's perpetrators always mean to convey some sort of message', but that 'theorists of terrorism have not sufficiently noted that the message terrorism means to send often goes unheard because, to those on the receiving end, terrorism is unspeakable' (6). For Herman, this means that cycles of terrorism continue because the grievances of the terrorists go unheard – the symbolic effectively short-circuited by the material horrors.

Despite the contradictions here, and despite the ways that the previous chapter has demonstrated how texts such as Anna Burns's *Milkman* have unsettled these formations, they remain useful theoretical frames that help us make sense of a violent phenomenon and a contested, misused and overused term; and, they are particularly useful in relation to literatures of the nineteenth, twentieth and early twenty-first centuries, which are the primary focus of these respective monographs. However, as interpretive tools they have some limitations in relation to contemporary texts that represent terrorism in the context of entrenched systemic phenomena, historical patterns of violence and/or slow violence. In some cases, the limits of applying Houen's or Herman's arguments are because of the particular narrative strategies of texts that decentre 'events' or ruptures in favour of stories about the conditions that make terrorism possible. This said, these theories are also less useful in relation to historical narratives that look back at instances of terrorism that were both spectacle and routine, shocking and ordinary – a key emphasis of Everett's depiction of lynching in *The Trees*, for example. There are other problems of application here, too. For instance, the symbolic dimensions of some forms of terrorism – like lynching or police shootings – are very different in the 'messages' they carry. Where some instances of 'terrorism' are atrocities committed in the name of broadly supportable causes or understandable grievances, racist terrorism is obviously not. This means that the interplay between the 'symbolic and real' has a different texture, and the task a novel might undertake, to 'enter the mind of the terrorist', takes on a different dimension (Boxall 131). Herman reflects on this late in his monograph, almost as a footnote. He usefully reminds us that since the early 9/11 novel debates, scholars have 'argued that novelists should not depict terrorists as "caricatures and stereotypical human monsters," but instead present the reader with "understandable, rational human beings"' (203). The problem here, as Herman notes, is that this only works 'when the author or film-maker has some degree of sympathy or agreement with the terrorists' perspective' (203). More recently, Richard Jackson has reflected on his long-time 'opposition to the demonisation and dehumanisation of terrorists' which has 'always excluded white supremacist terrorists' (270). For Jackson, the disturbing rise in this form of terrorism raises a series of ethical questions about representation, including whether an 'empathetic humanised depiction of the white terrorist' is 'necessary or needed' (270). Nevertheless, and despite this aporia, novels like the ones discussed here by Khan, Locke and Everett can show how this form of terrorism relates to institutional violence. They are less interested in entering the mind of the white supremacist terrorist than exploring the ways this form of terrorism has operated, and continues to operate, in relation to mainstream ideological currents. This is critically important given that white nationalist terrorism often functions as 'pro-state' terrorism. Indeed, Jeff Goodwin theorises 'what we might call conservative terrorism or what some have termed "pro-state" terrorism' as 'non-state terrorism in defense of the status quo' (259). Goodwin goes on to cite the 'Ku Klux Klan in the United States, which for many decades used terror tactics to reinforce white supremacy', as an exemplar (259).

In this chapter I analyse the novels by Locke, Khan and Everett in their serial and intertextual contexts. *Heaven, My Home* is the second of Locke's Darren Mathews mysteries, in which Mathews, a Black Texas Ranger, investigates crimes linked to deeper regional histories of slavery, lynching and racism. In *Heaven, My Home* this history is connected to the activities of the Aryan Brotherhood of Texas – a notorious white supremacist terror group – as well as the more genteel and suited forms of white supremacism that are endemic in the American South. *A Deadly Divide* is the fifth of Khan's Rachel Getty and Esa Khattak mysteries, in which the Toronto-based duo – Getty a white Canadian woman and Khattak a first-generation Pakistani-Canadian man – run a Community Policing programme installed to deal with rising hate crimes. Khan's series begins by exploring the legacies of war crimes in Bosnia – figuring these as acts of terror – and then moves through a jihadi terror plot, a geopolitically inflected heist and abduction case in Iran, another abduction case in Lesvos, at a refugee camp during the peak of the so-called migrant crisis, and, in *A Deadly Divide*, a mass shooting in a mosque in a small town in Quebec. *The Trees*, Everett's thirty-first book and twenty-third novel, explores the legacies of lynching – America's most gruesome and pervasive form of domestic terrorism. Through its crime-genre framework, it connects this form of historical violence to contemporary police shootings and to an imagined form of revolutionary counter-violence. The spectacles, ideological dimensions, and shock caused by these three forms of violence mean they are each figured as terrorism. *The Trees* is not part of a serial narrative but can be usefully read alongside Everett's recent novels that deal with white nationalist extremism, such as *Wounded* (2005), *Assumption* (2011) and *Telephone* (2020) as well as earlier novels of radical resistance to white supremacism, like *Watershed* (1996).

The procedural form of these novels, and the seriality of the works by Khan and Locke, allows the narrative capacity to explore both the practices of policing terrorism and the terroristic practices of policing – at a structural level. There is scope for in-depth accounts of the bureaucracy, managerial hierarchies, internal departmental prejudices and the ideologically inflected relationships between police and local and national governments. This means the revelation in *A Deadly Divide* that 'all levels of law enforcement have been infiltrated by the far right' carries a particular potency as the fifth novel in the series, because of the range and scope of the first four books (228). First, each of these series (and I include Everett's twenty-first century novels linked by depictions of violent white nationalism) begins before and then moves into the Trump era, exploring the ways certain forms of racial hatred became suddenly more socially acceptable again; and in each case this shift is registered alongside deeper historical gestures. For instance, in *Heaven, My Home*, set just after the election, Mathews's work-based friend group, 'five men – three black, two Latino – and one white woman', note that 'something had shifted . . . in the world at large but on the job too':

> They were dealing with things they'd never seen in their lifetimes, stories they'd only heard from the older men in the department: church burnings; the defacement of a mosque in Bryan; black and brown kids shoved in lunchrooms, spit on in gym class; a Mexican woman currently in critical condition after she was attacked in front of her husband and three kinds in the parking lot of a Kroger in Fort Worth. (25)

Khan's novels have a different national context – Canadian – and are, in fact, international in scope, but they also register the global changes that have been understood in the West mostly in relation to Trump and Brexit. Though these novels focus on authoritarianism in Iran and the plight of refugees after the Syrian genocide, they also are attuned to the global scope of 'creeping anti-Muslim' sentiment and the ways the refugee crisis has stoked the 'voices of the extremist right' (Khan 2017, 141). In one scene in *A Deadly Divide*, right-wing protesters descend on the small town with 'bamboo torches', all wearing 'white polo shirts and dark slacks, the torchlight flickering across their clean-cut faces' (207). These images evoke the Trump-era extremism of the infamous and deadly 'Unite the Right' rally in Charlottesville, NC, in 2017. These novels also discuss white nationalist terrorism comparatively, both in the sense that they position terrorism alongside other forms of crime and by addressing different forms of terrorism. Khan's series does this with real latitude. The first novel, *The Unquiet Dead*, deals with the death of a war criminal in contemporary Toronto whose brutalities in Bosnia are described as acts of terror. The second novel, *The Language of Secrets*, is about an Islamist terror plot in Toronto. The third and fourth, *Among the Ruins* and *No Place of Refuge*, depict forms of state terrorism alongside more conventional kinds of crime like kidnapping and theft. Finally, in the fifth book, *A Deadly Divide*, after building a substantial cast of peripheral characters in law enforcement and government, the series tackles white supremacist terror. This trajectory allows the novel substantial comparative possibilities, including insight into the different ways in which Islamist and white nationalist terrorism are policed. Because of the ways other forms of terrorism have been approached over the course of the series, there is real weight behind the scenes where Khattak and Getty work to secure a 'terrorism' charge for the perpetrators.

Locke's books also offer evocative comparisons. In *Bluebird, Bluebird*, when Mathews explains his reason for returning to East Texas to become a Texas Ranger, he cites the horrific murder of James Byrd Junior, who was dragged to death in Jasper, Texas, in 1998. He says flatly, 'that was my September eleventh' (243). In *Heaven, My Home*, discussing the appeal of Aryan Brotherhood of Texas culture and processes of indoctrination into violent white supremacism, Mathews comments, '"Sounds like some ISIS shit . . . Mix an unhappy home life with few legal economic opportunities, shake and stir, then let ferment . . . in a few years, you got a home-grown terrorist"' (111).

But while the novels I am considering here work comparatively in understanding white nationalist terrorism, and operate historically, bridging the before and after of a visible 2016 shift, they also share another feature: a lead investigator of colour. This means that their depictions of policing white nationalist violence are particularly powerful, and that their interest in figuring policing as terrorism is complicated. It also means that policing is fraught with the perils of institutional bias and a sense of conflict that has different vectors in each of the novels. In Locke's Darren Mathews books, this is articulated through the protagonist's simultaneous 'impulse to police crimes against black life and to protect black life from police' (2019: 49–50) – something Mathews feels he can do best as a Texas Ranger (his other potential career path was in law). But these impulses continually imperil Mathews, particularly through an underlying story arc that connects both novels, where his career and family are threatened by actions driven by this conflictedness. In Everett's *The Trees*, the two lead investigators, Jim Davis and Ed Morgan, describe the self-loathing they feel as Mississippi Bureau of Investigation agents of colour in terms that move from jesting to deadly serious. In Khan's novels, Inspector Khattak, a devout Muslim, is questioned about his loyalty from every angle and he sees policing and truth-seeking as ultimate forms of neutrality. On one of several occasions when asked which 'side he is on', in *A Deadly Divide*, his revulsion over this 'construction of binaries' is explicit' (91). But often Khattak's neutrality is performed, too, and in *Among the Ruins* we learn that '[c]areful and measured consideration was the only way he knew to answer the assumption of Muslim rage' (290).

Heaven, My Home

Heaven, My Home is set in the anxious weeks between the election of Donald Trump as US President in November 2016 and when he took office in January 2017. It pays close attention to the subtle and sometimes unsubtle shifts in Texan – and American – race relations in this period. As a sequel to *Bluebird, Bluebird*, this means the wider Darren Mathews narrative offers a 'before and after' perspective. However, we learn early in the first novel that while Mathews had hoped that 'change might trickle down from the White House' in the Obama era, 'the opposite had been true', and in fact 'America had told on itself' (17). So, while *Heaven, My Home* is clearly interested in tracing the rise of 'Make America Great Again', or 'MAGA', culture, something it repeatedly references, its primary protagonist – and other characters – had seen it coming long before 2016. In any case, what comes across most vividly in *Heaven, My Home*, and what I focus on here, is a tension between what the novel is at pains to identify as emergent forms of white supremacism in the early twenty-first century, and an emphasis on its deeper and far-reaching histories of violence. Indeed, as with many of Locke's novels – and *The Cutting Season* (2012) is a rich example – a present-day crime is linked to histories of slavery and Jim Crow-era forms of structural white supremacism. In fact, the Darren Mathews novels are exemplars of an emergent body of historical crime fiction discussed in a special issue of *Crime Fiction Studies* on 'Crime Fiction and the Past'. In the introduction to this issue, Eric Sandberg notes that as a genre, 'crime fiction engages with the past in structural terms', pointing to the different ways the genre invites readers to function as detectives, in order to relive, retrace or uncover the past (154). For Sandberg, a key strand of this is fiction, like all the novels discussed in this chapter, that is 'engaging with and critiquing our contested and complex histories' (155). In this section, I argue that *Heaven, My Home*'s dual project of depicting historic forms of structural white supremacism as well as emergent 'MAGA-era' forms is fruitful, and that ultimately this convergence strengthens the novel's vision of institutionally entrenched violent racism in America, and the impact this has on Black, non-white and indigenous lives.

Heaven, My Home is Locke's fifth novel, though her oeuvre also features screen-writing credits and writing room roles on Ava DuVernay's *When They See Us* (2019), a four-episode dramatisation of the infamous story of the 'Central Park Five', and on Liz Tigelaar's

Little Fires Everywhere (2020), a television adaptation of Celeste Ng's novel of the same name from 2017. This work is all connected by an interest in structural racism in America's past and present, but Locke's profile as both a crime writer and a prestige television writer means her work is of particular interest in debates and discussions about the changing hierarchies of value in contemporary culture, and the sometimes fallow divisions between 'literary' and 'genre' writing. Locke's crime fiction also frequently combines elements of another popular genre, the 'legal thriller', and certainly the Darren Mathews books benefit from Locke's knowledge of the law and include some well-wrought courtroom set-piece scenes.

In *Bluebird, Bluebird*, we learn early on that Mathews was raised by his Uncle Clayton, a 'onetime defense lawyer and professor of constitutional law', and that he had studied law in Chicago before precipitously deciding on returning to the family home in Texas and becoming a Ranger (16). Mathews had been pulled between the influence of his Uncle Clayton and his Uncle William, Clayton's 'identical twin and ideological foil', who was a Texas Ranger (16). Mathews's uncles were 'giants to him . . . men of stature and purpose, who each believed he'd found in his respective profession a way to make the country fundamentally hospitable to black life' (17). Ultimately, this split between the law and law enforcement, and the two uncles, is a red herring as what really is at stake in both novels, and particularly in *Heaven, My Home*, is the possibility of either of these institutions working for Black Americans; or the very possibility of effecting change from within either of them. That Mathews is a Texas Ranger gives this question a particular inflection. The Texas Rangers is an institution described by the omniscient narrator in *Bluebird, Bluebird* as the 'most revered law enforcement agency in the state', and one that is particular to Texas and thus a source of local pride and prestige (23). This means that the reverence held for the Texas Rangers by other law enforcement officers and citizens is often tested by their racist responses to Mathews's Blackness.

The central case in *Heaven, My Home* is that of a missing nine-year-old boy who is the son of an incarcerated Aryan Brotherhood of Texas (ABT) 'Captain'. The ABT developed in the Texas state prison system in the 1980s and has no formal connection to the Aryan Brotherhood, which originated in California in the 1960s. The Anti-Defamation League describes the ABT as 'one of the largest and most violent white supremacist prison gangs in the United States, responsible for committing dozens of murders and many other violent crimes' (n.p.). Mathews is sent to investigate the disappearance of the boy in the hopes it might help bring down a whole network of ABT terrorists, including '[t]welve captains and twenty other Brotherhood rank and file' (40).

There is also a larger 'case' or story involving an ABT associate, that bridges the two novels. At the beginning of *Bluebird, Bluebird*, Mathews is in court, testifying about his involvement in the murder of Ronnie Malvo, a petty criminal with 'ties to the Aryan Brotherhood of Texas' (18). The suspect is a long-time Mathews family friend, Rutherford 'Mack' McMillan (18). Mathews had intervened in a stand-off between Malvo and Mack which ended without harm. Doing his job diligently, he writes up a report, detailing the personal call from Mack to Mathews (instead of a call to the police), only for Malvo to be found dead two days after the stand-off, and for Mack's gun to disappear – leaving questions around the initial encounter he reported. This results in Mathews being suspended as the case is investigated, which compounds his marital trouble and drinking problem. With this convergence of pressures, he leaves town and gets involved in a case in Lark, Texas, which is the central mystery of the novel. However, though the Lark case is solved, the narrative ends with the revelation that Mathews's malicious mother, Bell, has the missing gun and therefore holds his fate in her hands. *Heaven, My Home* begins with the suspension lifted and the marriage in recovery, while Mathews works mostly as a 'desk jockey' supporting a 'task force' investigating ABT activity; but also, with Bell revelling in her bribing of Mathews (14).

As connective tissue for the two novels, the 'Mack' story is instructive, as it deals with contemporary and historical manifestations of violent white supremacist terrorism. In *Bluebird, Bluebird* we learn that Mack is a 'seventy-year-old black man who remembered the Klan, remembered huddling behind his daddy and a shotgun, fears of nighttime raids and tales of Klansmen riding up from towns like Goodrich and Shepherd' (19). Not only does the Mack story connect white supremacist terrorism of the past to that of the present – a core tenet of the main story of *Heaven, My Home* – but it also speaks to a key underpinning question asked by these books: is there any possibility of 'justice' within the system, for Black Americans?

As in *Bluebird, Bluebird*, the present-day case of *Heaven, My Home* is linked to a particular regional history of racial injustice. The missing child of ABT Captain Bill King, Levi, leads Mathews to pursue King's genteel grandmother, Rosemary, a society denizen of Jefferson, Texas in Marion County, and owner of the upmarket hotel where he stays during the investigation. The child goes missing from a small hamlet nearby, called Hopetown, which sits on the banks of Lake Caddo. Hopetown, we learn, was originally established by slaves who swam to freedom from a sinking steamboat. They first sought refuge on an island, where they established a community with local indigenous people, sharing and exchanging ideas, 'creating a love and trust' (242) over a period of generations. After the Civil War, some of the Black inhabitants decided to establish a freedmen community on the banks of the lake – Hopetown – and eventually they were joined by some of the indigenous community. When Mathews first encounters Hopetown, it is still occupied by the descendants of the original settlers more than a century later. However, imposing themselves on this community are a group of white supremacist squatters, who have colonised a section of town with trailers, and Mathews puzzles over the oddity of 'a freedmen's community sharing real estate with Nazis' (71). We eventually learn that a 'legal and cultural loophole' had allowed the 'white nationalists in the trailer park' to 'usurp a whole swath of Hopetown, terrorizing' the Black and indigenous community (242). These include Levi's mother, Marnie, and step-father, Gil, a 'wannabe' ABT, and a whole trailer park of 'mean and underfed' white supremacists (60, 66). Ultimately, Mathews discovers that this loophole is linked to a nefarious property deal orchestrated by Rosemary King and an opportunistic developer called Sandler Gaines that will allow them to build a casino. The Hopetown story is explicitly presented as a 'part of a larger historical story of what black freedom looks like', and the attention *Heaven, My Home* pays to the way the law has been used as a tool of white supremacism is supplemented by its ongoing interest in the way other histories have been erased (239). In an intriguing exchange with a local historian, Mathews discusses the ways tourism has displaced memories of Ku Klux Klan (KKK) terrorism with celebratory narratives of the genteel South – of Southern gothic without the real horror. The historian asks Mathews rhetorically, 'On any of the ghost tours in town, they got a stop for the slaves that were killed on plantations in town, the men who were lynched? . . . It's all white ladies in distress' (239). What makes these exchanges so affecting is the way they echo Mathews's experiences of MAGA-era escalations being tracked by the ABT task force, including 'every church and mosque defacing, every black doll hung from a tree as a joke, and every real black body found the same way' (110). But this history also underpins a set of connections the novel establishes between the poor, trailer-dwelling ABT sympathisers, and the wealthy and imperious Rosemary King, who all help sustain the broader web of American white supremacism. These class-divided white supremacists are connected by what Mathews describes as a kind of 'blind fury' (67). And it is under the thrall of this rage that, Mathews muses, 'white voters had just lit a match to the very country they claimed to love – simply because they were being asked to share it' (67).

As noted, *Heaven, My Home* is at pains to identify the ABT as a terrorist organisation. This emphasis has two effects. One is to signal just how infrequently neo-Nazi organisations that clearly meet consensus definitions of terrorism are referred to as terrorist organisations, and the second is to note the emotional power of the term – used so stridently by conservative American institutions since 9/11 as a catch-all term for all that is evil; or as Herman has it, 'violence you don't like by people you don't like' (5). When Mathews's lieutenant offers him the case, as part of a multi-agency operation, he states, 'six years. Six years, Ranger, we've been trying to take down this terrorist organisation' (40). Mathews is taken aback by the language here: 'Terrorist organisation. He'd never heard his lieutenant describe the ABT this way' (40). Though Mathews notes that this language may be 'for his benefit', the lieutenant also refers to the changing landscape – and alludes to the possibility of material changes in the law in the Trump era, citing the need for an indictment before 'a Trump Justice Department mistakes the Aryan Brotherhood for some sort of honor guard' (40).

The use of this term by the omniscient narrator, in specific application to the ABT, as a 'form of homegrown terrorism', is also conspicuous and it often functions comparatively (83). As mentioned, Mathews evokes the clichés of radicalisation in describing the home environment of Levi King as 'some ISIS shit': 'Mix an unhappy home life with few legal economic opportunities, shake and stir, then let ferment' (111). Here the language and rhetoric of 'terrorism' – as framed in the post-9/11 landscape – is used in application to people it normally is not, but in ways that are entirely appropriate. There are yet other ways in which the novel's identification of the ABT as a 'terrorist organisation' engages more searchingly with the post-9/11 discourses of terrorism. At points it poses serious questions about the extent to which one might compare forms of Islamism to the form of ethnonationalist terrorism exemplified by the ABT. For instance, in one scene Bill King's 'humanity' is questioned, and this invites comparison to the way other kinds of terrorists have been figured as 'inhuman'. The prevalence of stereotypical images of craven Islamist fundamentalists after 9/11 is well known, and this led to imperatives for literary and cultural narratives to 'humanise' terrorists in order to better understand them. But this discourse has also been rightly questioned by Nouri Gana, who points to 'the bankruptcy of the deeper rationale' that begins from a point of 'differential allocations of humanity' (22). As Herman notes, though, the meaningful depiction of the internal world of a white supremacist terrorist is a very different prospect, and the laudable imperative to move beyond stereotypes and caricatures only really works 'when the author or film-maker has some degree of sympathy or agreement with the terrorists' perspective' (203). In *Heaven, My Home*, Mathews does not seek to 'humanise' the terrorist but rather emphasises a loss of humanity. Referring to the ABT Captain Bill King, he states, 'He'd murdered a man who hadn't done anything to him, a man whose name he didn't even know, just to prove to other white folks that he was loyal to a toxic ideology' (225). Ultimately, we learn that Mathews 'relished the chance to sit across from Bill King and have his humanity reaffirmed. Bill King had ceased to be a man to him' (225). I note this here as another example of the novel's engagement with the post-9/11 discourse of terrorism and insistence that the ABT be considered as a terrorist organisation.

As an aside, this particular scene in some ways affirms Arun Kundnani's assertions about the problems inherent in any kind of expansion of the term 'terrorism'. In a *Jacobin* article written with Jeanne Theoharis, entitled 'Don't Expand the War on Terror in the Name of Antiracism', Kundnani directly addresses the policing of white supremacist terrorism and asks, rhetorically:

> What could be wrong with wanting to remove the racial biases in the application of counterterrorism? Why wouldn't we want the full force of federal law to be applied to racist mass murderers? But to think that would be a mistake. It would actually end up worsening the problem of white supremacy and further expanding the reach of law enforcement. (n.p.)

In *Heaven, My Home* the insistence on the term 'terrorism' is more about addressing a racist discrepancy or a lack of willingness to include certain forms of terrorism within consensus definitions or categories, even when they clearly meet the terms. This said, Kundnani's argument has resonance here as the novel questions the very viability of the institutions of policing in America.

Another part of the twenty-first century discourse of terrorism the novel addresses, that is critical to my broader argument, is the question of the 'event'. As noted, Mathews's explanation for giving up on a legal career and joining the Texas Rangers is the horrific murder of James Byrd Junior, who was dragged to death in Jasper, Texas, in 1998. Mathews states evocatively in *Bluebird, Bluebird*, 'that was my September eleventh' (243). But even if that sets up a before and after in the protagonist's life, or points to a new resolve, what the two novels are really interested in is the entrenched forms of systemic violence that function at the level of government, the law, and certainly in policing.

Ultimately, in *Heaven, My Home*, Mathews finds the missing child, restores the land to the indigenous and Black families to whom it belongs, and certain wrongdoers are punished or arrested. However, there is a pervasive sense of futility in the novel. The genteel operator Rosemary King is not punished, the child Levi seems destined to become a violent white supremacist, and Mathews's victories feel small in relation to the unabated systemic malaise. Even before the novel's conclusion, we learn that Mathews is more doubtful than ever about the possibilities of intervening in the activities of the ABT, and that this is because of just how entangled their extremism is in mainstream structural forms of white supremacism:

> In truth, he was the least optimistic he'd ever been that the Brotherhood and what it stood for would ever truly be eradicated. There were too many of them; in tattoos or neckties, they were out there. Everywhere. The country seemed to grow them in secret, like a nasty fungal disease that spread in the dark places you don't ever dare to look. (83)

There are many things that connect the violent terrorism of the ABT to forms of white supremacism that are more socially accepted, in *Heaven, My Home*. Most obvious are the familial ties of Rosemary, Bill and Levi King: the mother is (ostensibly) an exemplar of Southern gentility, and the son is a terrorist. Such connections are also made visible by MAGA iconography that appears everywhere from the sheriff's office to the trailers of the white supremacists in Hopetown. Indeed, after seeing the iconic red MAGA hats on the heads of the white supremacists in the trailer park, it is notable that Mathews sees the same hat on the edge of the Sheriff's desk: 'red like a siren, a warning signal' (150). These connections emphasise the fact that ultimately, in America, the violent actions of groups like the ABT must be considered as forms of 'conservative' or 'pro-state terrorism': defined by Goodwin as terrorism that works in 'defense of the status quo' rather than towards revolutionary causes, with the KKK as an exemplar of this form (259). This reality complicates the comparative gestures the novel makes but it mostly informs the sombre tone of the conclusion.

The entanglements, in *Heaven, My Home*, between a violent terrorist organisation, law enforcement and the pillars of the genteel South mean that Mathews's inner conflict about his job are more acute than ever by the novel's end. This is especially the case given that the MAGA-era surges of violence are connected to deeper histories and entrenched systemic malaise. The omniscient narrator frames his inner conflict in an intriguing way, given these brutal realities: 'Say what you would about Darren's struggles with what the badge meant to him, he was at least living out the question every day. He was in the struggle right now' (242). This valorisation of the ongoing process of questioning 'the badge' is as positive as one could be about Mathews's sense of identity as a law enforcement officer, and the novel's conclusion actually suggests that Mathews may leave his career behind. But this is a useful way of thinking about the project of *Heaven, My Home* and *Bluebird, Bluebird* – as unresolved explorations of the struggle against a form of pro-state terrorism that is both part of the existing structures of white supremacism in American, and deeply resonant with America's history of domestic terrorism.

A Deadly Divide

Ausma Zehanat Khan's *A Deadly Divide* – the fifth of the Rachel Getty and Esa Khattak novels (there is also an ebook-only novella) – is the most formally conventional work under discussion in this chapter. However, if the Getty and Khattak novels adhere to archetypal genre formulas, their Muslim lead detective and the breadth of specialist subject knowledge they draw on make them unique. Khan has a PhD in international law and specialism in war crimes, and in *The Unquiet Dead* (2015) the series begins by tracing the legacies of the genocide in Bosnia. The novels are unashamedly didactic and have elements of what Karl Ågerup has described, in relation to Yasmina Khadra's 'fundamentalism trilogy', as 'didactic aesthetics' (183). But where Ågerup critiques Khadra's 'didafiction' for what he sees as a 'polarizing rhetoric . . . integrated in a didactic aesthetics', the Getty and Khattak mysteries are focused on challenging binary logic (183). Khan's novels certainly have a 'didactic aesthetic', though: each book has a 'further reading', 'afterword' and/or an 'author's note', outlining real-world inspirations and non-fiction sources relating to their core themes. They also include diegetic moments that explicitly offer correctives to elided histories. For instance, in the second novel, *The Language of Secrets* (2016), when one of the antagonists quotes from Adonis's 1971 poem, 'A Grave for New York', the omniscient narrator provides layers of context and critique, in relation to what I have described as 'clash logics':

> It was the reworking of a line from a poem that had galvanized the Arab world. A cataclysmic poem that well predated Huntington's thesis on the clash of civilizations, the thesis that read Islam as a monolithic force hostile to the West, due to an ingrained inferiority and a permanent sense of inadequacy. The thesis paid scant attention to historical encounters with deeply damaging, long-term consequences, reinforced by new incursions into the Islamic world. (111)

Such didactic contextual asides are common in the series, and perhaps most prevalent in the third novel, *Among the Ruins* (2017), in which Khattak works a case in Iran under the guise of tourism. The reader follows his journey, learning from and with him as he visits sites of historical and cultural significance, uncovering hidden histories.

The genre conventions of these works also propel their didactic functions. As Marcia Lynx-Qualey notes, Khan's novels work towards 'decriminalizing Muslim identity' and they do this 'safely within the boundaries of detective series tropes and expectations' (191, 203). Lynx-Qualey notes that detective fiction might be 'an unlikely genre for North American Muslim authors, when Canadian and US Muslims alike, have been put under increased rates of surveillance because of their religious affiliation' (203). However, it is also the case that the narrative conventions and expectations of genre are effective at absorbing change and difference. As Phyllis M. Betz (also cited by Lynx-Qualey) notes, 'the reliance on formula and repetition gives popular fiction the ability to contain the potentially dangerous. By relying on the reader's familiarity with form while simultaneously allowing for adaptation, popular fiction facilitates a balancing of old and new' (8).

In this section I build on Lynx-Qualey's analysis of Khan's use of genre to 'decriminalize Muslim identity', through analysis of a related function of the series, which is to intervene in definitional debates about what terrorism is, and comment on the effects of the post-9/11 rhetoric of terrorism. Indeed, the genre coding, seriality and preoccupation with different forms of political violence combine forcefully in these novels, and I focus on the fifth in the series, *A*

Deadly Divide (2019), where this critique is most potent. Though Khan has indicated there will be further additions, she has moved away from the series for now, and her latest novel, *Blackwater Falls* (2022), begins a new series with another Muslim lead detective, Inaya Rahman. However, while *A Deadly Divide* ends with some conspicuously unresolved plot strands, it is summative. It is substantially longer than the previous four novels, and the different forms of violence that are explored in those texts contextualise the central act of terrorism in this one, a mosque shooting in St. Isadore, Quebec. Crucially, the wide narrative scope, and substantial cast of characters that seriality allows, makes the novel's story of the way 'all levels of law enforcement have been infiltrated by the far right' or 'neo-Nazis' particularly persuasive (228).

Another element of *A Deadly Divide*, which draws on a kind of affective accumulation, is the way the mercurial but measured Esa Khattak is personally impacted by the case. If endemic police brutality and police shootings of Black citizens mean that Locke's Darren Mathews carries a particular burden, then the weight carried by Khattak is similar. He is a devout Muslim and faces discrimination from within and outside the structures of law enforcement. Perennially facing Islamophobic stereotypes, he remains open-minded in his approach to policing, and this is presented as part of his nature but also as a practised strategy: as mentioned earlier, in *Among the Ruins* we learn that '[c]areful and measured consideration was the only way he knew to answer the assumption of Muslim rage' (290). In *The Unquiet Dead*, when pressed to take a position on the 'Ground Zero Mosque' furore, he describes it as a 'volatile situation'; and when reminded of the various injustices Muslims have faced, he notes that there is 'fear and injustice everywhere. It's not exclusively practiced against Muslims. Look at Rwanda. Or Nazi Germany. Or the barriers Hispanic immigrants face' (138). Indeed, we learn early on that Getty and Khattak do not 'deal in ultimate truths' but instead seek to interrogate the 'underground cities of doubt and discrepancy where human frailty revealed itself in layer upon layer of incongruity' (2017, 265). Yet despite Khan's and her protagonist's aversion to binary logic, Khattak grapples with the experience, as a Canadian Muslim, of a 'duality he had never chosen to articulate' – and he often wrestles with this in the face of binary thinking: 'He knew what he was, what his community was. So different from what he saw on the news nightly – the lone wolves, the well-armed gunmen, the rabid mobs, the blistering flags, the overturned tanks, the rocket launchers, the blood-doomed faces' (2016, 141).

Khattak is averse to clash logics, but also a proponent of Muslim solidarity through the broadly defined notion of '*Ummah*'. This is particularly moving in the fourth novel, *No Place of Refuge*, in which Getty and Khattak work with a group of Syrian refugee children in Lesvos to try to find a missing person. When one of the boys feels dehumanised by the rhetoric of the 'migrant crisis', Khattak's response calls back to his actions in Iran in *Among The Ruins* and foreshadows his compulsion to 'take a side' in *A Deadly Divide* (192):

> Khattak looked at the boy with great compassion. These were thoughts he hadn't wanted to own to; this wasn't the first time he'd had them. The question of *ummah* was always with him; it was a question of community, of rootedness in a common history, and the sharing of a present moment of crisis and decline. It was why he'd chosen to go to Iran, why he followed the news in the time he had free from work. It was instinctive to him as a man of faith to be deeply concerned about the *ummah*. (164)

Though Lynx-Qualey argues that Esa's conception of ummah 'is not exclusively the province of Muslims, and includes an abundance of secular, usually white characters', the novels build towards a situation where Khattak, so insistent on resisting clash logics, begins to feel obliged to, in some senses, 'take a side'. In fact, he is directly called upon to do so at the outset of *A Deadly Divide*. Though he is deeply affected by the mosque shooting, Khattak begins the investigation cautiously, aware of extreme institutional bias. Even when Diana Shehadeh, an activist and spokesperson for the Muslim Civil Liberties Union, reproaches him, asking, 'Just whose side are you on?', he remains circumspect and suspicious of her logic: 'These were the kinds of comments he loathed, where people were either with or against you, with no common ground in between' (91). Nevertheless, Khattak grows increasingly fatigued and embattled as the case develops. He also grows his beard as a 'signifier of faith; he hadn't wanted the Muslim community to harbor any doubt' (324).

As noted, the depiction of terrorism in *A Deadly Divide* is contextualised by the forms of violence the series has previously covered, and this makes the novel's commentary on definitional debates powerful. These forms of violence are connected by the work of the Community Policing Section (CPS), the unit led by Khattak with Getty as his partner. The status and reputation of the unit evolves over the course of the series, but it begins in *The Unquiet Dead* as a new initiative with a 'deliberately vague' remit, partly because it was conceived of as a 'fig leaf for the most problematic community relations issue of all – Islam' (10). At the level of genre and form, the CPS is an intriguing device, as it represents a layer of remove from the police proper, allowing for scrutiny of the police within the narrative logic of the detective novel. This is an idea Khan returns to in *Blackwater Falls*, where detective Inaya Rahman works in the Community Response Unit (CRU) in Colorado. In that novel the CRU is designed after the 2020 protests for social justice, to operate 'outside the existing police structure' and to intervene in cases where 'police accountability' is required, or to provide 'complete transparency to overpoliced communities' (2). In the Getty and Khattak series, the focus on institutional white supremacism grows steadily before becoming central in *A Deadly Divide*, and the CPS is explicitly mandated to police the police while simultaneously dealing with the mosque shooting. Additionally, as the CPS is introduced in the first novel of the series, as a 'fig leaf' for the over-policed Islamic community, perennially presented as a dangerous security threat, the series also models key aspects of Lindsay Thomas's history of the fictions of 'preparedness' after 9/11. Thomas shows how this discourse of preparedness and security insists that some disasters are normal while refusing to engage with others. As Thomas reveals, the discourse of preparedness 'is designed to uphold the ethnonationalism of the national security state – to protect whiteness, and to protect the homeland as an implicitly white space – by teaching people to ignore or deny the existence of the many disasters of white supremacy' (5). This is precisely the phenomenon that Khan's series dramatises, over five novels, to connect the Islamophobic practices of policing during the war on terror to the continued rise of white nationalist terrorism.

Before attending directly to *A Deadly Divide*, it is worth considering the different forms of political violence readers encounter before this fifth novel. The series begins with *The Unquiet Dead*, when a Serbian war criminal who had been living under an assumed identity is found dead in Toronto. The genocide of Bosnian Muslims in 1995 and the traumatic memories of torture and rape carried by survivors are vividly interspersed throughout the novel. Additionally, the discourse and rhetoric of terrorism emerges at key points in the case. When a group of Bosnian Muslims are questioned for the murder, and for 'terrorizing' the war criminal with threatening letters, this language is sternly rebuked:

> 'Terrorized?' he spit at her. 'You don't know what terror is. Talk to me when you've spent three years strangled and starved by Serb guns,

when every member of your family has been taken to an execution site, bulldozed into a grave, and then excavated to a secondary grave, their bones scattered over our homeland to disguise the monstrosities committed against them . . . A few letters sent to a man like Krstić do not terrorize.' (307)

This is a pivotal moment in the novel, but given that the discourse of terror and perceived threat of terrorism is so central to the work of the CPS, it also invites reflection on semantic debates about what constitutes 'terror'. It is also significant that it emerges through the logic of reversal – where the perpetrator of crimes is figured as a victim – a phenomenon the series repeatedly returns to, particularly in *A Deadly Divide*, when the mosque shooting is thought by some to have been committed by a Muslim.

In the second novel, *The Language of Secrets*, which revolves around a potential jihadi terror plot in Toronto, semantic questions are again central. Getty and Khattak are repeatedly asked to consider grievances about the persecution of Muslims around the world, as part of their investigation – something made more urgent given Khattak's sister's entanglement with one of the antagonists. Crucially, these arguments are made in ways that challenge prevalent uses of the term 'terrorism':

"we find ourselves called terrorists . . . isn't the murder of Rohingya in Burma terrorism? The Indian army's atrocities in Kashmir – isn't that terrorism? The destruction of Chechnya, the obliteration of Baghdad, the bombardment of Gaza, the murder of children at play on a beach – are these things not terrorism?" (99)

These moments are augmented by Getty's reflections on the different incarnations of Islam she has encountered in her role. Getty polices her own assumptions, reminding herself that entangled questions of faith, geopolitics and cultural difference require her to cut through the prevalent discourses of terrorism. She even evokes images of 'state terrorism', insisting on

an understanding of history, of the power vacuum that erupted in the aftermath of invasions of the longue durée outcomes of occupations and looted capitals, of bombs that levelled the infrastructures of cities, of drones that did their killing without accuracy or due process, of those who rose to fill the vacuum of the deposed and despised, of the dialogue between civilizations, of decades-long struggles for right and democracy. (272)

In the fourth novel, *No Place of Refuge*, the ongoing discussion of another misused term, 'migrant', furthers the continued scrutiny the series gives to the discourse and rhetoric of 'terrorism'. In particular, the media's role in attaching the rhetoric of terror to stories about migration is considered in depth. Early in the narrative, the omniscient narrator notes the prevalent use by politicians of 'migrant' rather than 'refugee', and that 'whenever an opening presented itself, they raised the specter of a terrorist slipping through the net to wreak havoc on Canadian soil' (24). The European press gets serious scrutiny, too, with a focus on language: 'They'd been described as hordes, as swarms, as a flood, as an invasion, as groups of gangs, as "rapefugees," with the British press leading the charge' (140). Finally, in *A Deadly Divide*, when an act of violence that should unambiguously – according to consensus definitions – be considered an act of terror, Getty and Khattak must fight for the case to be understood as such.

This emphasises the war on terror's disproportionate focus on Islam, and institutional racism in the Canadian police, and the work done in the first four novels means that Getty's and Khattak's arguments are potent. *A Deadly Divide* also attends to another dimension of the definitional debate over terrorism: its legal and criminal definitions. At a dramatic highpoint in the novel, one chapter closes and another one begins with expressions of the importance of understanding and categorising the incident as an 'act of terror'. In the mosque, an acquaintance and ally of Khattak's, Alizah, addresses the local Muslim community, insisting that the attack was 'an act of terror' and that the 'terrorist is still at large', before solemnly reciting the names of the dead (326). On the next page, Khattak listens as Diana Shehadeh implores the detectives to ensure the case is 'prosecuted as an act of terrorism, with hate crimes added to the indictment' (327). This emphasis is partly related to the ongoing discrepancies in the way the term 'terrorism' is applied within legal and criminal frameworks, and weaponised to vilify migrants and Muslim citizens. It is also about ensuring that the danger of rising white supremacism is properly recognised under the law. This latter point is reinforced in the 'author's note' which discusses the real case of Alexandre Bissonnette, who killed six people and injured nineteen others in a terror attack at a mosque in Quebec in 2017, noting his obsessions with mainstream white supremacists like Laura Ingraham, Tucker Carlson, Alex Jones and Donald Trump, and noting the reluctance – of various commentators – to describe the incident as an act of terror.

A final dimension of the way the series envisions terrorism is via a set of intertextual moves that again recall Don DeLillo's notion of a 'curious knot that binds novelists and terrorists', who are seen to be simultaneously engaged in a 'zero-sum game' competition for the 'shape mass consciousness' and oddly similar (41, 157). Repeated imbrications of literary writing and terrorist plotting in the Getty and Khattak mysteries certainly suggest that writers and terrorists are both antithetical and strangely linked. *The Language of Secrets* focuses on poetry and the use of figurative language as code. It revolves around the plotting of a potential 'Nakba' attack in which an old friend of Khattak's, Mohsin, is implicated. In the novel's first chapter Mohsin is recalling lines of poetry as he bleeds out in the Algonquin. His final act is to carve lines of verse in a tree for Khattak to read. We eventually learn that poetry is the titular 'language of secrets' that 'Mohsin expected Khattak to decipher' in order to intervene in the Nakba plot (298). The plot also involves a 'hip hop fusion' artist whose 'spoken word poetry' tapes contain coded messages central to the plot, and it is revealed that poetry is a great passion of Khattak's and of the novel's terrorist antagonist, Hassan Ashkouri (196). These ideas recur in the next novel in the series, *Among the Ruins*, in which a play within a play contains coded meanings; again the literary (or dramatic) art aids other kinds of plotting. DeLillo's interest in the changing 'role of the writer' in the new age of terror is also echoed in the series. The case in *Among the Ruins* revolves around an artist regarded as subversive and dangerous by the Iranian government, who is abducted; and music, poetry and writing are again ubiquitous points of interest and discussion. In one memorable scene the writer, Nathan Claire, Khattak's best friend and romantic interest of Getty's, muses on the role of the writer: 'a man could be a fool at least once in his life, he believed: a fool about money, love, friendship, family. Any or all of those. And a writer needed to be, if his books were to traverse the shared experiences of his audience' (255). Indeed, Khattak's best friend is a writer, and Getty's brother is an artist – and their roles are both prominent even if, for Getty, such people were in some ways (like common notions of the 'terrorist other') 'unknowable': they 'belonged to their own world. An undiscovered country' (2018, 203).

A Deadly Divide draws on existing knowledge of, and some of the stereotypes of, white supremacist terrorism in North America and addresses questions about the levels of connection between ostensibly 'lone wolf' terrorists and the wider networks of white supremacy in which they circulate and participate. The novel explores, and in some instances interrogates, what the CSIS has identified as three commonalities in contemporary instances of white nationalist terrorism: 'a decentralized model', where the threat 'comes from individuals, not groups', even if the individuals are linked to group identities; a practice of organising online, 'challenging law enforcement efforts to identify potential attackers'; and finally, a tendency to adopt 'foreign terrorist organization tactics' (n.p.). The most immediately visible of these features is the second (which relates to the first), as one of the novel's few formal innovations is to intersperse transcripts from the forums, platforms and broadcasts in which – we eventually learn – the attackers have circulated. These include transcripts from the 'Wolf Allegiance Chat Room', an online forum where users like 'broadswordben' and 'nineinchnailer' discuss the events in unambiguously racist and conspiratorial language; posts from a local conservative Christian blogger, Elise Douet, who wants 'a responsible immigration policy' that protects 'our culture, our language, our values'; along with transcripts from a locally based alt-right 'shock jock', Pascal Richards, whose excessively toxic masculinity and dog-whistle racism – and apparently mostly financial motivation for extremist views – approximates hateful broadcasters like Alex Jones (31). These transcripts appear throughout the text alongside ones from more moderate radio broadcasts, and crucially, the terrorists are revealed to have been participants in each, emphasising their imbrication in fringe and mainstream forms of white supremacism. By setting up the terrorist(s) (part of the case is the question of whether there were multiple assailants) as 'lone wolves', while meticulously mapping out their networks, the novel directly addresses Mondon and Winter's observation that the 'increasing emphasis on the individual' in the contemporary discourses of terrorism elides structural white supremacism (20).

A Deadly Divide is also interested in highlighting the emergence of new kinds of organised terror groups though its depiction of the 'Wolf Allegiance' points conspicuously to the past. When Khattak first encounters the group's iconography – a set of graphics taped to the walls of a vandalised Muslim Student Association office at the local university in St. Isadore – the link is conspicuous. Khattak gravitates towards one particular graphic:

> It pictured a bearded man in a turban being chased down a street by a long row of marchers wearing hoods that resembled bishops' miters. But something about the way the hoods were drawn could also have

represented the Ku Klux Klan. Except that the faces were unmasked. The same hoods appeared on the graphic next to it, this time worn by a group of men kicking a woman in a burqa who was curled up in a ball on the ground. (59)

Getty and Khattak focus on the Christian dimension of the group's identity and explore other antecedents in doing so. In some instances, Khattak uses this to try to convey the seriousness of their activities. Speaking to the local priest, Père Étienne, he points out that '[g]roups like the Allegiance often identify with their Christian heritage. The Nazis did as well' (266). Ultimately, the Wolf Allegiance is shown to be organised and violent, and to include several members of law enforcement, but it is also just one tentacle of the novel's vision of structural white supremacism.

A Deadly Divide uses several strategies that illustrate the connections between a white supremacist terrorist and entrenched, systemic white supremacism. The setting is one example: the novel's fictionalised St. Isadore, Quebec, is established as a hotbed of '*pure laine*' Quebec nationalism, and an early adopter of a legal 'Code of Conduct' designed to 'protect the values that Quebecois hold dear' (52). The Code of Conduct and other such 'veil laws' mandate 'the uncovering of one's face when providing or receiving state services' and prohibit 'public sector employees from wearing conspicuous religious symbols' (52). When Khattak unexpectedly reunites with an acquaintance from a previous case, Alizah, she informs him that these features make St. Isadore an important location: 'this town is an emblem of what that code might become' (56). St. Isadore's white supremacist web includes the Wolf Allegiance terror group, a group of 'alt-right' student activists, and it is the home of the Alex Jones-esque shock jock Pascal Richard. In the novel's final reveal, we learn that the mosque attack was carried out jointly by one of Richard's security guards – a Wolf Allegiance member – and Isabelle Clément, the press liaison for the Quebec Provincial Premier. Thus, while the mosque attack is committed partly by a member of a known terror group, it is also connected to the right-wing media and political mainstream. This means that the 'lone wolf' identification is challenged twice over: first, as the attack is the work of two unlikely but ideologically linked collaborators, and second, as the attackers are linked to institutional white supremacism. Given the procedural part of the novel works to show how 'all levels of law enforcement have been infiltrated by the far right', to also insist on the complicity of the media and mainstream politicians is a powerful indictment (228).

While this might seem schematic, there are some resonant moments of human drama here, too.

The already-mentioned scene of white nationalist, *'pure laine'* protesters 'carrying bamboo torches' and 'dressed alike in white polo shirts and dark slacks, the torchlight flickering across their clean-cut faces' is an undoubted reference to the deadly 'Unite the Right' event in Charlottesville, NC (207). The most affecting, perhaps, is Getty's reflection on the already-mentioned scene of white nationalist protesters. Getty asks a colleague, 'You know what they're protesting, right? It's not the prayer in the park. It's the people themselves' (201).

The Trees

Percival Everett's twenty-second novel, *The Trees* (2021), explores the legacies of lynching – America's most gruesome and pervasive form of domestic terrorism. Through a crime genre narrative framework, it connects this form of historical violence to contemporary police shootings and to an imagined form of revolutionary counter-violence. Because these three forms of violence are depicted here as shocking spectacles and have clear ideological dimensions, they are each figured as terrorism. Consequently, while *The Trees* offers new and persuasive forms of critique of white supremacist violence of the past and present by understanding it as terrorism, it also questions the limits and value of this term. Though Everett's oeuvre is famously eclectic, *The Trees* is usefully read in relation to his other recent depictions of neo-Nazi violence in *Wounded* (2005), *Assumption* (2011) and *Telephone* (2020), as well as earlier novels such as *Watershed* (1996), in which members of the American Indian Revolution carry out actions in response to a government conspiracy to contaminate indigenous lands. The genre modes of these novels remind us of how infrequently white supremacist violence appears in westerns, procedurals, campus novels and other kinds of American stories with prominent ideological components. Like the novels by Locke and Khan, *The Trees* radically upends the procedural genre's 'continuing thematization of whiteness as the core American value'; a phenomenon that has persisted despite the potent critiques offered by Black-authored hard-boiled fictions from Chester Himes to Walter Mosely (Reddy 2010, 139). Indeed, Everett uses the procedural framework to connect historical and contemporary forms of violence, considering the ways terrorism functions in the context of ongoing structural violence, and registering the charged and emotive nature of this term.

A third of the way through the novel, there is a rich exchange between two Special Detectives of the Mississippi Bureau of Investigation (MBI) and a 105-year-old 'root doctor' or self-described 'witch', called Mama Z. Their discussion addresses questions about policing and terrorism (and policing *as* terrorism) in the American past and present that are central concerns of this chapter. *The Trees* is set in 2018, and the two Special Detectives, Jim Davis and Ed Morgan, both officers of colour who are uncomfortable with the structures of law enforcement in which they work, are investigating two unsettling double murders in Money, Mississippi. Two of the murdered men are Wheat Bryant and Junior Junior Milam, fictionalised sons of Roy Bryant and J.W. Milam, the men who lynched Emmett Till in 1955, a brutal event now widely understood as a key flashpoint that helped ignite the American Civil Rights movement. But at each crime scene there is also an unidentified, dead Black man whose mutilated body resembles Till's.[2] Adding to the macabre spectacle of the murder scenes, the dead Black men are clutching the torn-off testicles of the white men. Yet somehow the corpses disappear or are lost by the bumbling local police. Unable to make sense of these events, the Special Detectives seek out Mama Z for her deep historical knowledge of the town and community, and it is soon clear she represents the heart of the novel.

There are two especially resonant moments in their conversation. First, Mama Z makes a comment that suggests a re-reading of the novel's title, which initially seems to be an unambiguous reference to the trees that at least 4,743 lynching victims were hung from before 1968. When it is put to her that these recent murders are crimes of revenge that seem to have a supernatural element, she states:

> If the spirits are out for revenge, there's going to be a lot more killing around here. Those spirits are going to have a field day around here. Every White person in this county, if they didn't lynch somebody themselves, then somebody in their family tree did. (102)

Mama Z's evocation of the white supremacist 'family tree' offers another vector of meaning to the title, as a pointed reminder that many Americans are intimately connected to this form of terrorism and that white supremacy is historically entrenched. Mama Z's comment also aligns with the formal features of the novel, as it begins to structurally 'branch out' at this moment. I will return to its narrative shape shortly, but thematically, this notion of a 'family tree' of white supremacist violence recalls the final lines of Claude McKay's 1917 poem, 'The Lynching', which emphasises the intergenerational and participatory nature of these heinous acts: 'And little lads, lynchers that were to be, / Danced round the dreadful thing in fiendish glee'. Numerous studies have traced the entrenchment of white supremacy in America, and the structural connections between the KKK and US government, but the public discourse of lynching usually stops short of understanding it as a kind of state-sponsored terrorism that implicates a significant portion of the public.

The second point that Mama Z makes to the two Special Detectives presents precisely this argument, and crucially she asserts to them that there is a contemporary manifestation of lynching in America: 'You should know I consider police shootings to be lynchings. No offense' (103). The idea that police brutality is a form of terrorism – and specifically a form of lynching – is not, strictly, an original idea. Derrick Johnson, President of the National Association for the Advancement of Colored People (NAACP), characterised the murder of George Floyd in these terms, describing 'the same public spectacle: someone in broad daylight with onlookers around, being killed at the hands of a law enforcement officer who has just complete disregard for human life and felt he was above the law' (n.p.). But Mama Z is uniquely able to make this connection between a deeper history of lynching and contemporary state violence – conceived of here as state terrorism. We learn that her real name is Adelaide Lynch, that she was born in 1913 shortly after her father was lynched, and that she has built an archive in her house of 'almost everything ever written about every lynching in these United States of America since 1913' (103). The archive fills a room, and a later chapter of the novel simply lists each name – including victims of police shootings – which also appear in the background of the book's US cover, barely visible in small print, in a blue on a dark blue backdrop.

The first of these two points – about the 'family tree' of domestic terrorism in America – is reinforced in the very next chapter, where Klan activity is explicitly described as terrorism. After a cross burning viewed by the local sheriff, Red Jetty, the omniscient narrator observes that 'not a single masked member of the terrorist exercise was unknown to anyone in the town. It was a long-running joke in Money, Mississippi, that the way to discover who belonged to the Klan was to wait at Russell's Dry Cleaning and Laundry' (107). This is one of several instances in the novel where the shocking nature of Klan violence is juxtaposed with the banal, and foreshadows later discussions of how, despite the spectacle of lynching, the victims have often been erased from history. *The Trees* begins to explore questions about the links between terrorism and policing through such observations, and diegetically through Mama Z, but also at the level of form.

The Trees has some obvious genre codes, moving from redneck satire, to buddy cop drama, to Southern gothic, and it sustains elements of the crime or mystery genres throughout: the fast pace, short chapters, emphasis on detection and the unravelling of a mystery, and grim humour, for example. These generic modes and modulations give the novel a sense of propulsion and cohesion, which is particularly important given the scope of the narrative, which grows precipitously until the two MBI agents are only barely focalising protagonists. Eventually, it includes 65 characters appearing in 108 chapters that sometimes are only one or two paragraphs long. To extend the titular tree metaphor, the novel discursively traces the branches and offshoots – as well as the roots – of the initial murders and ultimately the growth of an uprising. In one sense, it narrows down to the generic concerns of discovery, cause and effect, and in another it expands outwards in ways that suggest connection and implication. In his *New Yorker* review, Julian Lucas understands this oppositional movement as creating a 'chasm' that 'opens up between form and content' between the 'open-and-shut-conventions of the crime novel and the immensity of Everett's subject' (n.p.). There is certainly much at stake here, but the crime novel framework of *The Trees* also enables it to explore the kinds of connections between policing and terrorism that make its historical gestures so powerful. In this sense the novel both stretches the conventions of genre while fundamentally relying on them for its social and historical critiques.

While terrorism is by nature – and, for some, by definition – spectacular, there are many reasons why the literature of terrorism has moved away from a central focus on singular, traumatic events. In Critical Terrorism Studies, the questioning of event-based logic is fundamental and has been connected to the prioritisation of 'particular subjects ... while others, such as state-terrorism or right-wing extremist violence, are by this same logic left un- or under-examined' (Schuurman 464). Indeed, the core project of this book has been to consider recent narratives of terrorism in relation to a broader turn towards systemic phenomena and 'slow violence', and away from certain formations of trauma, as exemplified by Lauren Berlant, Rob Nixon and others. In the fiction of terrorism, this movement away from notions of trauma and rupture is paradoxical, in that terrorism usually takes the form of a spectacle or visceral event. This is one of the few points of consensus on the term. Even those who disagree about whether terrorism is the territory of non-state actors only, there is some basic agreement that it is (a) ideologically motivated and (b) designed to cause fear or panic via shock. Yet, despite this, something approaching the logic of slow violence – usually understood as the opposite of shock – comes into view in *The Trees*, in relation to lynching. A young friend of Mama Z, Gertrude, who initially claims to be her great-granddaughter, but who has actually been a kind of accomplice to her in the initial crimes against the descendants of Emmett Till's murderers, tells the Special Detectives late in the novel that 'when the killing is slow and spread over a hundred years, no one notices. Where there are no mass graves, no one notices. American outrage is always for show' (291). This is a powerful notion: that a kind of terrorism like lynching that is so visible – fundamentally designed as a kind of shocking, gruesome display – is understood as being unnoticed or invisible. This contradiction also relates to the extraordinary discrepancy between the brutality of lynching and the kinds of 'offences' for which people such as Emmett Till were lynched. Marita Sturken addresses this in 'The Memory of Racial Terror', the final chapter of her study *Terrorism in American Memory* (2022). Sturken discusses the National Memorial for Peace and Justice in Montgomery, AL, which opened in 2018, and notes how it attends to 'the banality of lynching's horror' in the listings of the 'reasons' for lynching, including 'addressing a white police officer without the title "mister"' and 'reprimanding white children who threw rocks at her' (221). The contradictory elements of brutal violence and the everyday are also visible in the famous protest song 'Strange Fruit', written by Abel Meeropol (and made famous by Billie Holiday), which is performed in a memorable scene in *The Trees*. 'Strange Fruit' also uses paradoxical language: 'Strange fruit hanging from the poplar trees / Pastoral scene of the gallant South / The bulging eyes and the twisted mouth / Scent of magnolia sweet and fresh / Then the sudden smell of burning flesh'. But Gertrude's comments point towards the specific contradictions of violent spectacles that are also part of historically and systemically entrenched patterns of brutality.

This aporia is explored via a character who provides a historiographic metafictional component and is at the centre of one of the novel's most resonant formal moves. Professor Damon Thruff is a friend of Gertrude's whom she brings to Money to help make sense of Mama Z's archive and of the events that are unfolding. We learn, in a rich instance of academic satire that recalls some of Everett's previous novels including *Erasure* (2001), *I Am Not Sidney Poitier* (2009),

American Desert (2006), and *Telephone* (2020), that Thruff has a 'PhD in molecular biology from Harvard, a PhD in psychobiology from Yale, and a PhD in Eastern Philosophy from Columbia', has published three books with Cambridge University Press and two books with Harvard University Press, and is struggling after a failed tenure bid at the University of Chicago where he is getting a second chance, labelled an 'affirmative reconsideration' (111). Gertrude enlists Thruff as an expert who might write about the archive and the crimes of revenge she, Mama Z and a small group of conspirators have committed. Thruff is overwhelmed by the power of the archive but describes it in the same paradoxical terms that Gertrude does:

> the crime, the practice, the religion of it, was becoming more pernicious as he realized that the similarity of their deaths had caused these men and women to be at once erased and coalesced like one piece, like one body. They were all number and no number at all, many and one, like one body. (171)

This is a rich reflection, that could describe instances of suicide terrorism or, more pointedly, police shootings. Thruff is overcome by the shocking nature of these atrocities, but also how the individual people have been erased by the sheer volume of the occurrences, despite their spectacular or 'unspeakable' nature. In a metafictional move that circles back to Mama Z's insistence that 'police shootings are lynchings, too', *The Trees* then provides a chapter which simply lists names of victims of lynchings (and police shootings), immediately evoking Claudia Rankine's famous passage in *Citizen: An American Lyric* (2014), where the names of victims of police shootings are listed on a page where the typeface slowly fades to white, as if the sheer number of names means the individuals fade from view – the act of repetition functioning as erasure. In *The Trees*, this list comprises ten pages replicating a list made, in the diegesis, by Thruff in pencil on a yellow legal pad. He tells Mama Z:

> When I write the names they become real, not just statistics ... it's almost like they get a few more seconds here. Do you know what I mean? I would never be able to make up this many names. The names have to be real. Don' they? (190)

But if *The Trees* echoes *Citizen* in emphasising the irony of extreme and brutal violence being erased through repetition, then it adds another dimension as Thruff plans to do his own erasing, too, only as an act of liberation. Thruff tells Mama Z, finally, 'When I'm done, I'm going to erase every name, set them free' (190). This is an evocative sentiment and relates to both the disappearances of the bodies that resemble Till's at the early crime scenes, and perhaps the wave of revolutionary counter-violence that begins to rapidly expand at this point in the novel – as if Thruff has released vengeful ghosts on the white supremacist nation.

In Everett's *The Trees*, this sense of conflict and discomfort experienced by the Black MBI agents, as well as a Black FBI agent, Herberta Hind, who joins the investigation, is particularly acute and a near constant point of discussion, as well as a primary source of the novel's comedy. When the Special Detectives meet Gertrude, passing as a waitress under the name 'Dixie' at a local diner, they are intuitively drawn to her and have a genial and humorous dynamic:

> 'I hate to tell you, but we're cops,' Jim said.
> 'Why do you hate to tell me?'
> Jim sipped some coffee and put down his mug. 'Because people either love cops or hate them. It's been my experience that most interesting people hate them. Hell, I'm a cop and I hate them.'
> 'Me too,' Ed said. 'I especially hate him. Hate myself too, on occasion.' (40)

These reflections become much more serious, though, as they begin understanding the historical weight of the crimes they are investigating, and as the case branches out. Moreover, when Agent Hind posits a version of the argument used by Darren Mathews in Locke's books and Esa Khattak in Kahn's – that surely there needs to be a Black presence in law enforcement and government – she is rebuffed by Mama Z, who says that this represents 'bad company' and states flatly, 'I don't keep bad company' (176).

The question of what it means to be an officer of colour in America is turned over repeatedly in *The Trees*, and its importance amplified by the novel's depiction of the white, local police officers, all attached in some way to the KKK. In this context, Everett's novel depicts a mystery that connects domestic terrorism of the past to the present, and exemplifies the historiographic crime fiction mode that has been a prominent and popular sub-genre in recent years. Eric Sandberg's opening comment in a special issue of *Crime Fiction Studies*, on 'Crime Fiction and the Past', is obviously resonant here:

> The body never stays buried. If a field of cultural production as diverse and multifaceted as crime fiction could be said to have a single, over-arching principle, this might well be it. In the narratives

of mystery, detection, transgression, and punishment of all sorts that constitute the broad literary field of the genre, the past is frequently a tangible presence. (153)

However, while Sandberg's assertions nicely describe *The Trees*' interest in giving visibility to crimes of the past – and the ghostly presence of Emmett Till – Theodore Martin's theorisation of the 'drag and drift' of genre in *Contemporary Drift: Genre, Historicism, and the Problem of the Present* is an even more useful way of thinking about how genre helps us understand the past in relation to the present, which is clearly a core element of Everett's novel. Martin argues that:

> Genre, as I understand it ... describes how aesthetic forms move cumulatively through history. The accretive history of genre is a measure of both change and continuity, diachrony and synchrony, pastness and presentness ... Genres lead distinctly double lives, with one foot in the past and the other in the present; they contain the entire abridged history of an aesthetic form while also staking a claim to the form's contemporary relevance. (6)

This is precisely what *The Trees* is doing in using – and, in some ways, abandoning – its crime fiction framework. It connects the lack of visibility of lynching – diegetically discussed by Gertrude, Mama Z and Damon Thruff – to the lack of visibility or representation this form of domestic terrorism has had in crime fiction and in fiction more broadly.

With this in mind, I want to consider a final element of the novel: its depiction of a Black uprising, which is launched via a set of violent crimes that have their own symbolic dimensions, and in some ways mirror or respond to the white supremacist terrorism of the past. This extends and problematises the novel's engagement with definitional debates about terrorism. It ultimately transpires that the first three murders of individuals directly linked to the lynching of Emmett Till were orchestrated by Mama Z and Gertrude along with a group of seventeen young people who have been training in a secret dojo outside of Money, located behind a soul-food restaurant. The disappearing corpses are explained when it transpires that one member of the group stole a truck of cadavers in Chicago, the implication being that the Black corpses were theatrically placed at the crime scenes. However, the initial murders inspire a nationwide crimewave that extends far beyond the original murders. In the final few chapters this develops rapidly, and eventually mobs of roving marauders are seen on the streets. These scenes are described in the language of a different genre – the zombie narrative. In trying to make sense of the way the group's crimes have precipitously expanded, Thruff suggests to Gertrude that it is 'some kind of mass hysteria' (238). Half joking, he continues, 'Maybe its even viral. You're infected, that's what it is' (238). Ultimately, though, the mob is described as an 'undulating mass', a 'throng' and a 'horde' in the final chapters of the novel and there is clearly a supernatural dimension – possibly linked to Thruff's will to 'set free' the thousands of victims he encountered in the archive (253, 306). This additional genre modulation obviously bears further consideration, but I want to focus on how it relates to the novel's larger, crime fiction framework. It is here, after all, where the term 'terrorism' becomes particularly stretched and where the question of whether counter-violence, which responds to such profound histories of violence and injustice, should be understood in the same terms.

To address this question, we might begin by noting that this vision of Black uprising – supernatural or not – also mirrors another under-recognised aspect of the history of lynching: that it was carried out in mobs. As Elizabeth Hinton points out in *America on Fire: The Untold History of Police Violence and Black Rebellion Since the 1960s* (2021):

> The Jim Crow era was defined by riot. In August, 1908, a lynch mob as large as five thousand people, many of them from out of town, descended on the Black community of Springfield, Illinois ... White supremacist violence only escalated as Black migrants fled the terror of the segregationist south. (5)

In the final movement of *The Trees*, violent mobs responding to this history of white supremacist violence proliferate. However, for the original plotters of the revenge crimes, it was clearly an imperative to include a symbolic – even theatrical – component to the crimes and this is made clear when Gertrude is confessing her role to Thruff. She implores him, as someone who she had hoped would write about and understand the events, 'there has to be some way to have these deaths be symbolic' (237). That these crimes were intended to shock and convey a message takes them clearly into the terrain of terrorism, which is affirmed by the MBI Special Detectives, when they learn of the stolen cadavers and warn that this means the crimes will likely 'be construed' as acts of 'terrorism' (289). The implication here is that while these crimes clearly meet some broad definitions of terrorism, they should not be considered as such.

At this point, *The Trees* has positioned historical acts of lynching, police shootings and Black rebellion all as potential acts of terrorism, clearly applying pressure on this term. Here, a set of connections between *The Trees* and Spike Lee's 2017 film *BlacKkKlansman* are useful. In both cases, Black police officers, who are made uncomfortable in their professions and constantly struggle against systemic racism, are investigating crimes linked to the KKK, and both texts depict or raise the possibility of Black counter-violence. In Lee's film, the KKK are depicted in sustained contrast to the Black Panthers and their affiliates, and both groups are named by the FBI as 'terrorist organisations' in the film. It is notable that Lee's depiction of Black revolutionaries is in absolute contrast to KKK terrorists, and this is very similar in *The Trees*. Additionally, both narratives connect the past to the present, and like *BlacKkKlansman*, which concludes a narrative set primarily in the 1970s, with documentary footage of the violent 'Unite the Right' rally at Charlottesville, NC, and of Donald Trump's absurd commentary on this event, in which he identified 'very fine people on both sides', *The Trees* also features a chapter narrated by an only slightly caricatured Donald Trump.

In both *The Trees* and *BlacKkKlansman*, there is a will and desire to understand white supremacism as terrorism that coincides with an entirely sensible discomfort with the notion that this be equated in any way to revolutionary counter-violence. Consequently, notions of perspective, or the adage that 'one person's terrorist is another person's freedom fighter', are rejected. In *The Trees*, the discourse of terrorism is a useful way of connecting the history of lynching with contemporary policing and police shootings; and these connections are established via the crime fiction frame of the novel, and the formal innovations that I have discussed already. These connections help us better understand the pervasiveness yet lack of visibility of these atrocities, and of how their accumulation erases individuality. Moreover, the emphasis on terrorism that is more than just sporadic but linked to systemic phenomena problematises conventional definitions and theoretical formations. *The Trees* further complicates definitions and theories of terrorism by noting that Black rebellion can also be defined in this way, and this pushes definitional debates into new and different terrain, stretching the limits of an already endlessly contested term. While *The Trees* finds productive uses for the discourse of terrorism, it at the very least urges us to insist on a better understanding of relationality, history and context when using it.

Notes

1. In the essay 'Literary Fiction and the Genres of Genre Fiction', Jeremy Rosen points out that there is a long-standing but usually unrecognised distinction between meanings when referring to 'genre' and 'genre fiction'. For Rosen the distinction is between 'genre' as 'an existing literary framework or recipe that writers may adapt and vary according to their needs, and "genre fiction" as a subfield of literary production that is largely synonymous with "popular fiction," an arena composed of particular institutions of publishing, distribution, and reception, in which genre functions as a fundamental organizing principle, and which is often distinguished from the subfield of "serious" or "literary fiction"' (n.p.).
2. Emmett Till's mother, Mamie, famously made the photos of her fourteen-year-old son's body available for publication in *Jet*, and the shocking images were eventually seen by millions.

Works Cited

Ågerup, Karl, 'Knowing an Arab: Yasmina Khadra and the Aesthetics of Didactic Fiction', *Critique: Studies in Contemporary Fiction*, 59.2 (2018), 180–90.

Anti-Defamation League, 'Aryan Brotherhood of Texas', 4 April 2013 <https://www.adl.org/resources/profile/aryan-brotherhood-texas> [accessed 31 August 2023].

Berlant, Lauren, *Cruel Optimism* (Durham, NC: Duke University Press, 2011).

Betz, Phyllis M., *Lesbian Detective Fiction* (Jefferson, NC: McFarland, 2006).

Boxall, Peter C., *Twenty-First-Century Fiction: A Critical Introduction* (Cambridge: Cambridge University Press, 2013).

CSIS (Center for Strategic and International Studies), 'The Escalating Terrorism Problem in the United States', 17 June 2020 <https://www.csis.org/analysis/escalating-terrorism-problem-united-states> [accessed 21 July 2020].

DeLillo, Don, *Mao II* (London: Vintage, 1991).

Everett, Percival, *Assumption* (Minneapolis: Graywolf, 2009).

Everett, Percival, *Telephone* (Minneapolis: Graywolf, 2020).

Everett, Percival, *The Trees* (Minneapolis: Graywolf, 2021).

Everett, Percival, *Watershed* (Minneapolis: Graywolf, 1996).

Everett, Percival, *Wounded* (Minneapolis: Graywolf, 2005).

Gana, Nouri, 'Reel Violence: *Paradise Now* and the Collapse of the Spectacle', *Comparative Studies of South Asia, Africa and the Middle East*, 28.1 (2008), 20–37.

Goodwin, Jeff, 'The Causes of Terrorism', in *The Oxford Handbook of Terrorism*, ed. by Erica Chenoweth, Richard English, Andreas Gofas and Stathis N. Kalyvas (Oxford: Oxford University Press, 2019), pp. 253–67.

Herman, Peter C., *Unspeakable: Literature and Terrorism from the Gunpowder Plot to 9/11* (Abingdon: Routledge, 2020).

Hinton, Elizabeth, *America on Fire: The Untold History of Police Violence and Black Rebellion Since the 1960s* (London: Collins, 2021).

Houen, Alex, *Terrorism and Modern Literature* (Oxford: Oxford University Press, 2002).

Jackson, Richard, 'Afterword', in *The Figure of the Terrorist in Literature and Visual Culture*, ed. by Maria Flood and Michael Frank (Edinburgh: Edinburgh University Press, 2023).

Johnson, Derrick, 'The History of Lynching in America', NAACP (2020) <https://naacp.org/find-resources/history-explained/history-lynching-america> [accessed 31 August 2023].

Khan, Ausma Zehanat, *Among the Ruins* (Harpenden: No Exit Press, 2018).

Khan, Ausma Zehanat, *Blackwater Falls* (New York: Minotaur Books, 2022).

Khan, Ausma Zehanat, *A Deadly Divide* (Harpenden: No Exit Press, 2019a).

Khan, Ausma Zehanat, *The Language of Secrets* (New York: Minotaur, 2016).

Khan, Ausma Zehanat, *No Place of Refuge* (Harpenden: No Exit Press, 2019b).

Khan, Ausma Zehanat, *The Unquiet Dead* (Harpenden: No Exit Press, 2017).

Kundnani, Arun, and Jeanne Theoharis, 'Don't Expand the War on Terror in the Name of Antiracism', *The Jacobin*, 11 January 2019 <https://jacobin.com/2019/11/war-on-terror-domestic-terrorism-act-racism-muslims> [accessed 31 August 2023].

Locke, Attica, *Bluebird, Bluebird* (London: Serpent's Tail, 2017).

Locke, Attica, *Heaven, My Home* (London: Serpent's Tail, 2019).

Lucas, Julian, 'Percival Everett's Deadly Serious Comedy', *The New Yorker*, 20 September 2021 <https://www.newyorker.com/magazine/2021/09/27/percival-everetts-deadly-serious-comedy> [accessed 31 August 2023].

Lynx-Qualey, Marcia, 'An Attempt to De-criminalize Muslims: The Detective Novels of Ausma Zehanat Khan', *The Muslim World*, 111.2 (2021), 191–203.

Martin, Theodore, *Contemporary Drift: Genre, Historicism, and the Problem of the Present* (New York: Columbia University Press, 2017).

Mondon, Aurelien, and Aaron Winter, *Reactionary Democracy: How Racism and the Populist Far Right Became Mainstream* (London: Verso, 2020).

Nixon, Rob, *Slow Violence and the Environmentalism of the Poor* (Cambridge, MA: Harvard University Press, 2011).

Rankine, Claudia, *Citizen: An American Lyric* (London: Penguin, 2014).

Reddy, Maureen T., 'Race and American Crime Fiction', in *The Cambridge Companion to American Crime Fiction*, ed. by Catherine Ross Nickerson (Cambridge: Cambridge University Press, 2010), pp. 135–47.

Reddy, Maureen T., *Traces, Codes and Clues: Reading Race in American Crime Fiction* (London: Rutgers University Press, 2003).

Rosen, Jeremy, 'Literary Fiction and the Genres of Genre Fiction', *Post45 Peer Reviewed*, 8 July 2018 <https://post45.org/2018/08/literary-fiction-and-the-genres-of-genre-fiction/> [accessed 31 August 2023].

Sandberg, Eric, 'Introduction: Crime Fiction and the Past', *Crime Fiction Studies*, 1.2 (2020), 153–6.

Schuurman, Bart, 'Topics in Terrorism Research: Reviewing Trends and Gaps 2006–2017', *Critical Studies on Terrorism*, 12.3 (2019), 463–80.

Soufan Center, *White Supremacy Extremism: The Transnational Rise of the Violent White Supremacist Movement* (September 2019) <https://thesoufancenter.org/wp-content/uploads/2019/09/Report-by-The-Soufan-Center-White-Supremacy-Extremism-The-Transnational-Rise-of-The-Violent-White-Supremacist-Movement.pdf> [accessed 31 August 2023].

Sturken, Marita, *Terrorism in American Memory: Memorials, Museums, and Architecture in the Post-9/11 Era* (New York: New York University Press, 2022).

Taneja, Preti, *Aftermath* (Oakland: Transit Books, 2021).

TE-SAT (European Union Terrorism Situation and Trend) report 2020, 23 June 2020 <file:///C:/Users/user/Downloads/european_union_terrorism_situation_and_trend_report_te-sat_2020_0%20(1).pdf> [accessed 21 July 2020].

Thomas, Lindsay, *Training for Catastrophe: Fictions of National Security After 9/11* (Minneapolis: University of Minnesota Press, 2021).

Conclusion: New Event-Based Narratives of Terrorism

Aftermath

When details about the Fishmongers' Hall terror attack emerged on 29 November 2019, I am ashamed to say that my thoughts moved precipitously to the ways this tragedy might be politicised. The proper response would have been to focus on the victims, including the individuals who were brutally murdered: Jack Merritt and Saskia Jones. Merritt was a course coordinator and Jones a volunteer in the Learning Together programme, an acclaimed prison education initiative sponsored by Cambridge University. Learning Together was celebrating five years of achievements at a special event when a course participant, Usman Khan, attacked. This was just days before the UK general election, and I wondered: how might a Conservative party known for entrenched Islamophobia and emboldened by a rising tide of nationalism, instrumentalise this moment for political capital and to advance its 'tough on crime' agenda? But it quickly became clear that there would be limits to what the Tories could do on this front. Merritt's father made a strong statement condemning political opportunism and the use of his son's name to promote the punitive justice policies Jack had opposed (Merritt's belief in rehabilitation was well known: his master's thesis was on the over-representation of Black, Asian and other ethnic minority men in the United Kingdom's criminal justice system).

Ultimately, the Conservatives did not need to harness the emotive power of a terror attack to bolster their campaign, as they swept away a Labour platform built around the progressive politics of a Green New Deal. Brexit played a role, for sure, but there is no avoiding the fact that the Conservatives won with ugly rhetoric, including the promise to create a 'hostile environment' for migrants. In any case, because of election fallout, ongoing Brexit discourse and, in a few short months, the COVID-19 pandemic, the Fishmongers' Hall attack quickly became old news.

Preti Taneja's *Aftermath*, referenced at various points in this book, brings this event vividly back into view. But despite the title, this is not a conventionally 'event-centred' narrative of terror and trauma, and it is about much more than the aftermath of a single event. In fact, Taneja's book questions the extent to which narrative *can* adequately represent such events. Taneja tells the story from her unique vantage point, as someone for whom Jack Merritt was a colleague and friend, and as someone who had taught creative writing to Usman Khan in the Learning Together programme. *Aftermath* is a book of extraordinary heart and intellectual force that probes the power of trauma and interrogates the ideologically inflected meanings of terrorism. Its achievement lies in its generosity and intimacy, and, crucially, in how it shows the way traumatic rupture can occur amid the less visible but equally pernicious forces of systemic violence. Taneja immerses the reader in what she calls the 'atro-city', probing its painful edges. In *Aftermath* the 'atro-city' is at once a single event that is all-encompassing and, conversely, a world of structural violence crystallised in a single event. It is 'the outside world turned inwards', a place where endemic poverty, lack of opportunity, entrenched prejudice, and punitive justice violently collide (2).

Aftermath is highly referential, and while Taneja is a novelist, the book cites theory and poetry more than it does fiction. Yet it is usefully understood in relation to the novel of terrorism, which as I have argued in this book, has had a particular trajectory in relation to 'events' in the early twenty-first century. As we have seen, since the anglophone 9/11 novels published in the 2000s, and discussed in my first chapter, which reinforced the exceptionalisation of '9/11', the novel of terrorism has moved steadily away from event-centred narratives. This has been a welcome development, and this book has examined the ways novels have resisted and challenged formations that have underpinned this exceptionalisation such as the alleged clash of civilisations. It has considered the way novels have articulated new and more persuasive visions of what terrorism is, responding to the narrow definitions shaped by, as Arun Kundnani shows, 'ideological projection and fantasy' that persists still today; as 'the assumption remains that the term "terrorist" is reserved for acts of political violence carried out by Muslims' (17, 23). It has examined contemporary fictions of earlier twentieth-century instances of terror, which include powerful resonances with our present, and it has examined novels depicting the kinds of terrorism that are largely absent from post-9/11 security paradigms, but which actually represent the most significant terror threat in the world today: right-wing extremism. In these analyses it has explored the ways these works have not so much focused on 'events' as they have depicted the impact of various forms of slow and systemic violence.

Of course, acts of terrorism rely on shock and spectacle, so to move away from event-based narrative means to focus on the contexts in which terror, extremism and radicalisation occur or might occur. *Aftermath* recentres the event while insisting on locating it in the context of systemic racism, incarceration and the legacies of colonialism. Taneja writes from a position of grief, vulnerability and trauma, but also from experience and knowledge, and with an urgent desire for accountability and understanding, braiding these emotions, imperatives and subject positions together over 230 pages. It is a work of precision, unfolding over three parts and twenty-five chapters, but even in its moments of sharp and robust analysis, it also feels like an urgent uncoiling. Part memoir, part essay, part polemic, it resists easy categorisation and might most usefully be thought of as a trauma narrative, though each of these terms is inadequate. That said, it makes two interventions in the literature of terrorism that resonate strongly with my analysis in this book. First, in the way it situates trauma within the context of particular forms of slow violence, and second, as a radical refiguring of Don DeLillo's famous notion of a 'curious knot that binds novelists and terrorists', an idea that has echoed across many of the novels I have discussed. In DeLillo's 1991 novel *Mao II*, a novelist, Bill Gray, argues that writers are no longer able to 'alter the inner life of the culture', that they are losing ground to the explosive narratives of terrorists, who 'make raids on human consciousness' (41). For Gray, 'novelists and terrorists are playing a zero-sum game' and the power of the novel is losing out to spectacle and crisis. *Mao II* circles around this notion, suggesting, also, that there are similarities between writers and terrorists, who both rely on plot, symbolism, myth and rhetoric; in one place, an explosion is described as 'logical', 'legitimate' and 'well argued' (182).

Margaret Scanlan's analysis in *Plotting Terror: Novelists and Terrorists in Contemporary Fiction* (2001) – published just two months prior to September 11 – focused precisely on the connections

DeLillo explores. Scanlan argued that in a set of novels published in the 1980s and 1990s, novelists and terrorists are consistently 'doubled', and that these novels are metafictionally obsessed with 'exploring the influence of fiction on history and politics, the relation between language and violence, the nature of power, and the impetus to resist' (14). But while such binaries can be productive and illuminative, they can also fold inwards and, as we have seen in my first chapter, '9/11 metafiction' obsessed over the proper way to represent 9/11 without exploring the questions Scanlan and others have raised. In some instances, these binaries have even tacitly reinforced the 'us against them' mantra of the Bush administration's 'war on terror'.

Aftermath is also – like so many of the novels I have considered in this book – interested in the relationship between writing and terror, and Taneja discusses Usman Khan's interest in writing in depth. Khan was imprisoned in 2012 for plotting a terrorist attack, and Taneja notes that his interest in writing after release was taken by some as an indication of 'deradicalisation' (49). However, Taneja concludes that he simply 'valued the form, a conduit for control and self-expression: the art of convincing others' (49). Khan used these rhetorical skills in plotting his deadly attack; as Taneja notes, 'his greatest skill was *passing*: he was a product of the state' (50). He deceived and manipulated many but was ultimately a product of poverty, discrimination, limited horizons of opportunity, and incarceration. And this is the terrain on which the 'curious knot' is recalibrated in *Aftermath* – not to build connections between Khan's writing and his violent extremism, or to posit a zero-sum competition between writers and terrorists, or to in any way excuse his awful actions, but to stake a claim for the power of shared or solitary acts of creativity against the overwhelming force of institutional violence, in spite of this single, undermining act of violence. Taneja makes a persuasive case for the impact of a programme in which inmates were allowed to feel human, where people could get together and 'practice a few hours of creativity against the highest set of odds an advanced late-capitalist society can make, within its own borders' (157–8). This recalibration of the curious knot, and interest in reading and writing as refuge can be seen throughout this book: from middle sister's refuge in books in *Milkman* to the archival writings of Damon Thruff in *The Trees*, this particular kind of metafiction is an integral part of the contemporary novel of terrorism.

The theme of writing and creativity set against institutional violence recurs in numerous contexts in *Aftermath*. In one affecting episode, the author describes a conversation with a South Asian cab driver in New York City in October 2018; it happens that he, too, is a writer, and he recounts the experience of being detained after 9/11 and having his notebooks – full of children's stories – seized by the authorities. His life's work was never returned and he 'hadn't been able to bring himself to write again', but he promises Taneja that, when she starts her next book, 'he would start as well' (101). This small gesture is one of many acts of creative solidarity positioned against the forces of state violence. These acts offer respite or distraction, or maybe the opportunity 'to build incremental moments of self esteem against the state's efficient machinery' (196). And this really is the core project of *Aftermath*, which marshals numerous citations of all kinds of writing – poetry, theory, fiction – towards its call for 'a government of heart, mind and tongue, that does not treat lives as contingent' (100).

In addition to the way *Aftermath* rethinks DeLillo's 'curious knot', it also reflects on and responds to the experience of trauma, a phenomenon often associated with terrorism, and with 9/11 and 9/11 novels such as DeLillo's *Falling Man* (2007). But as Lucy Bond has noted, '9/11 trauma fiction' is different from other kinds of trauma writing and has mostly been characterised by 'uncritical recycling of paradigms inherited from orthodox trauma theory', usually in service of insular narratives of American victimhood (409). *Aftermath* refuses such impulses, continually defining and redefining trauma as the narrative unfolds. It wilfully interrogates the circularity or repetitions of trauma – 'an event happens and happens and happens: this is a definition of trauma' – and the paradoxical compulsion to narrate the 'unspeakable' (13): 'Writing makes me hypervisible: so much remains unspeakable. This is trauma as definition' (42). These sentiments are echoed and repeated throughout the book, and it is notable that Taneja is careful to offer *a* definition, not *the* definition: 'this is a definition of trauma. Not the thing itself, but the repetition of the event' (90). Though there is much meta-reflection on trauma here, several formal devices draw out the traumatic realism in *Aftermath*. There is an unpredictable movement from first to third person, alongside commentary on the empathetic qualities of the second-person address. There are gaps in the text and missing punctuation, suggesting a loss of words or incomplete thought, and there are discursive leaps in some chapters, particularly the earliest ones. Additionally, the precipitous modulations of the narrative are reminiscent of what Roger Luckhurst, in his 2008 book *The Trauma Question*, describes as one particular response to trauma: 'the manic production of retrospective narratives that seek to explicate' (80).

While *Aftermath* refigures DeLillo's 'curious knot' and probes the extent to which traumatic events can be adequately narrated, it also simply wants to better understand what happened at Fishmongers' Hall. It asks and addresses the question, 'how far must we go back to find a beginning?' (21). And it reframes this question as an interrogation of systems/institutions: 'why do we know so little about why and how the algorithm of radicalization works so compellingly in our current systems . . .?' (178). *Aftermath* insists on context, no matter how unsettling or uncomfortable it might be, and it examines the phenomenon head on, with love, sorrow, intimacy and honesty.

A Burning

Though *Aftermath* is not a novel, it is aligned with and exemplifies a new way in which fiction is beginning to address 'events'. Karan Mahajan's *The Association of Small Bombs* (2016), discussed in my third chapter, is an early example of this. As we have seen, Mahajan's novel traces the aftermath of the 1996 Lajpat Nagar Market bombing, only to *associate* it with systemic and historical violences. Megha Majumdar's *A Burning* (2020), another novel set in India – in this case Kolkata – is even more conspicuous in the way it uses an event-based narrative framework to look outwards and to explore systemic and institutional failures. Like *The Association*, Majumdar's novel concerns the aftermath of a terror attack, family tragedy, Hindu nationalism and political corruption. However, where Mahajan traces a particular historical narrative, concentrating on a period between 1996 and 2003, *A Burning* is very much a novel of the neoliberal present in Narendra Modi's India; even if the train attack – the event that begins the novel – is a clear reference to the 2002 train burning in Ghodra, which was the catalyst for the 2002 Gujarat pogrom, in which over 1,000 mostly Muslim citizens were killed, sometimes with the aid of the police. After the fictional Kolabagan train attack, instead of depicting the traumatic aftermath of victims, survivors and their families, or even the attackers themselves, the novel turns focus to the wrongly accused and the complicit.

Majumdar also focuses on the climate of neoliberalism in which the attack occurs – not unlike the way Ayad Akhtar focuses on neoliberalisation in America in *Homeland Elegies* (2020) – and particularly on aspiration. *A Burning* centres on three characters whose lives intersect in unexpected ways; it is structured by short, alternating chapters oriented by each character, along with brief interlude chapters or vignettes that add thematic texture and often emphasise systemic Hindu supremacism. Jivan, a young Muslim woman living with her family in a Kolkata slum, witnesses a deadly terror attack at Kolabagan train station. Her own life is upended after she makes a flippant comment about the attack, and subsequent police inaction, on Facebook: 'if the police watched them die, doesn't that mean that the government is also a terrorist?' (7). Jivan is soon arrested, incarcerated and pilloried by the media, and much of her backstory is then narrated by her from prison. Lovely is a hijra woman who had been learning English from Jivan while trying to launch an acting career. She faces daily discrimination but is defiantly hopeful despite the heartache she suffers after splitting with her partner. Lovely's joyful monologues, delivered in the continuing present tense, are the soul of the novel. PT Sir is a jaded PE teacher who once taught and took pity on Jivan, a 'charity student'. He becomes enthralled by the nationalist rhetoric of the corrupt Jana Kalyan Party (JKP) in which he begins to make waves. Both Lovely and PT Sir are in a position to intervene in Jivan's case, and the novel's suspense steadily builds in relation to whether their personal ambitions will deter them from doing so.

All three characters share a defining trait – aspiration – and this conceit allows Majumdar to address a set of questions: when does the desire for upwards mobility cloud judgement? What is the nature of its intoxicating power? What are its moral dimensions? Can it be a positive social force? What does it reveal about inequality? Jivan, whose parents experienced violence while working in precarious jobs, simply wants stability, good food and modest material pleasures, and she is rightly proud of the advances that her job as a shop assistant at Pantaloons affords: 'I was moving up . . . from an eater of cabbage, I was becoming an eater of chicken. I had a smartphone with a big screen' (38). She feels affinity with Lovely's aspirations, too, and is proud of their shared endeavours: 'Lovely believed she would have a better life someday, and so did I . . . English is the language of the modern world. Can you move up in life without it? We kept going' (38). Jivan and Lovely strive against entrenched prejudice, and Lovely's desire for fame is frequently expressed as a simultaneous desire for acceptance. Eventually, though, both characters question themselves. Jivan reproaches herself for wanting to be 'not even rich, just middle class', and Lovely faces the awful conundrum of whether to risk ruining her chance of fame by supporting Jivan. *A Burning* does not condemn their dreams, but it shows how, in a rigged and unequal system, they can be destructive. PT Sir's ambitions are of a different kind. Two chance experiences at JKP rallies fill him with patriotic zeal and he seeks to do something 'meaningful, bigger than the disciplining of cavalier schoolgirls' (49). He criticises his students' desires to study abroad as unpatriotic 'brain drain' (170). His own acts of patriotism soon lead to personal gain and he becomes increasingly embroiled in the corruption of the JKP.

A common observation about *A Burning* has been that its depiction of Kolkata, where Majumdar grew up, holds up a mirror to the US, where she now lives. Certainly, the novel's portrayal of nationalism, corruption, prejudice and violence supports this more generalised reading, and Majumdar has spoken of parallels. It is important to consider the setting's specificities, as these parallels with contemporary US politics complicate the novel's discussion of aspiration. After all, it is easy in the West to associate aspiration with the discontents of neoliberal individualism – and David Cameron's rhetoric of an 'aspiration nation' is interrogated in depth in Kamila Shamsie's *Home Fire*, discussed in Chapter 3. Majumdar dramatises the aspiration for survival, dignity, pleasure and fame – all in sympathetic ways – while at the same time showing how it can lead to negative, even destructive outcomes in the context of structural inequality.

Aftermath and *A Burning* do not purport to suggest that the complexities of failing systems or the nuances of historical currents are crystallised in the 'events' they depict. Instead, they suggest that the events must be understood in relation to these systems and currents. This book has traced the ways a diverse set of novels have moved towards these ideas and moved away from the notions of a defining moment that were so prevalent after '9/11'.

Works Cited

Bond, Lucy, '9/11', in *The Routledge Companion to Literature and Trauma*, ed. by Colin Davis and Hanna Meretoja (New York: Routledge, 2020), pp. 407–17.
DeLillo, Don, *Mao II* (London: Vintage, 1991).
Kundnani, Arun, *The Muslims Are Coming: Islamophobia, Extremism, and the Domestic War on Terror* (London: Verso, 2015).
Luckhurst, Roger, *The Trauma Question* (London: Routledge, 2008).
Mahajan, Karan, *The Association of Small Bombs* (London: Vintage, 2016).
Majumdar, Megha, *A Burning* (New York: Knopf, 2020).
Scanlan, Margaret, *Plotting Terror: Novelists and Terrorists in Contemporary Fiction* (Charlottesville: University of Virginia Press, 2001).
Taneja, Preti, *Aftermath* (Oakland, CA: Transit Books, 2021).

Index

1990s, the, 9, 20, 22, 24, 32, 34, 52, 65, 104, 128, 137, 163, 174, 180, 200–1, 206, 236, 246, 294
9/11 or September 11, 2001, terror attacks, 2–11, 17, 18–19, 20–2, 25, 27, 28–32, 34–9, 40, 111–15, 118, 122–3, 125–30, 132–6, 138, 144, 149, 152–6, 162, 164–7, 168–9, 179–82, 184, 185, 189, 191, 192, 199, 2001, 202–3, 206, 207, 208, 213–14, 260, 265–6, 269, 272, 289, 292–5, 298
  9/11 exceptionalism, 2, 4, 32, 63, 93, 162
  9/11 fiction and the '9/11 novel', 6, 8–9, 21, 28–30, 40–110, 114–16, 121, 127–8, 135–6, 166, 182, 208, 257, 292, 295

A Burning (Majumdar, Megha), 11, 22, 31, 37, 296–8
A Deadly Divide (Khan, Ausma Zehanat), 257–60, 268–78
A Disorder Peculiar to the Country (Kalfus, Ken), 28, 44, 53–6, 65, 102
  Aftermath (Taneja, Preti), 11, 15, 19–20, 27, 31, 38, 163, 167, 253, 290, 292–8
  Akhtar, Ayad, 10, 30, 34, 170, 200–7
  Homeland Elegies, 10, 30, 34, 170, 200–7
Alexander, Michelle, 26
American exceptionalism, 2, 4, 63, 90–1, 111, 162, 166
Among the Ruins (Khan, Ausma Zehanat), 259, 260, 269, 270, 271, 275, 289

Aryan Brotherhood of Texas (ABT), 258, 260, 262–8, 288
Aslam, Nadeem, 29, 34, 115, 152–63, 168
  The Blind Man's Garden, 29, 34, 115, 152–63, 168
  The Wasted Vigil 152, 159

Baader Meinhof Group, 231, 239
Begum, Shamima, 30, 191, 197, 205, 208
Beigbeder, Frédéric, 34, 40, 46, 48, 105, 115
  Windows on the World, 3–40, 46–8, 115
Berlant, Lauren, 2, 12, 13, 23, 24, 34, 281, 288
bin Laden, Osama, 63, 145, 203–4
Blackkklansman, 287
Blackwater Falls (Khan, Ausma Zehanat), 270, 272, 289
Bleeding Edge (Pynchon, Thomas), 27, 28, 32, 37, 41, 47, 54, 89, 95, 104, 105, 89–110, 231
Bluebird, Bluebird (Locke, Attica), 253, 257, 258, 260–8, 278, 284, 289
Bouziane, Anissa M., 40
  Dune Song, 40
Boxall, Peter, 27, 35, 115, 118–20, 164, 257, 288
Brexit, 192, 247, 248, 259, 291, 292
Brown Album (Khakpour, Porochista), 5
Burns, Anna, 10, 30, 37, 169, 175, 210, 251, 252 255
  Milkman, 10, 30, 37, 210–15, 233–48
  No Bones, 234, 236, 243, 250

Burnt Shadows (Shamsie, Kamila), 191
Bush, George W., 69, 105, 185

Caruth, Cathy, 24, 34, 35
Chambers, Claire, 195
'clash of civilisations' thesis, 27, 29, 81, 85, 97, 111–67, 168, 255, 269, 292
Cole, Teju, 2, 5–7
  Open City, 2–5, 7
colonialism, 19, 27, 78, 102, 181, 293
counterterrorism, 18, 33, 94, 266
Critical Race Studies (CRS), 26
Critical Terrorism Studies (CTS), 13, 15, 16, 18, 19, 33, 36, 165, 196, 256, 281

Deckard, Sharae, 27, 35, 103, 105, 106, 135–7, 190
DeLillo, Don, 8, 10, 11 21, 27–8, 35, 42–4, 46, 53–7, 61, 63, 65, 67, 80, 95, 105–7, 115, 127, 139–40, 151, 162, 164, 185–6, 200, 206–7, 211–12, 232, 235, 246–51, 275, 288, 293–6, 298
  Falling Man, 10–11, 28, 35, 44, 46–7, 49, 53–67, 76, 83, 90, 95, 103, 105, 106, 107, 115, 139, 140, 206, 207, 232, 295
  'In the Ruins of the Future', 56, 106, 162, 164, 185, 207
  Mao II, 10, 21, 35, 65, 106, 107, 151, 165, 200, 207, 232, 246, 250, 288, 293, 298
  Underworld, 8
  drone programme, 17, 22, 115, 142, 163, 191, 195, 273
Dune Song (Bouziane, Anissa M.), 40

event-centred / event-based narratives, 1–13, 18, 19, 22–3, 31, 40–2, 45, 52, 65, 135, 180, 185, 191, 213–14, 233, 235, 239, 255, 256, 281, 291–8
Everett, Percival, 9, 23, 31, 35, 138, 253, 255, 278–88, 289
  American Desert, 283
  Assumption, 258, 278, 288
  Telephone, 258, 278, 283, 288
  The Trees, 9, 9, 31, 138, 253, 257, 278–88
  Watershed, 258, 278, 288
  Wounded, 258, 278, 288
Extremely Loud and Incredibly Close (Safran Foer, Jonathan), 9, 28, 38, 46, 48–53, 109, 127

Falling Man (DeLillo, Don), 10–11, 28, 35, 44, 46–7, 49, 53–67, 76, 83, 90, 95, 103, 105, 106, 107, 115, 139, 140, 206, 207, 232, 295
Friel, Brian, 211
Fanon, Frantz, 142, 163, 164
  The Wretched of the Earth, 142, 163, 164
Fishmongers' Hall terror attack, 19, 253, 292–6
Frankenstein in Baghdad (Saadawi, Ahmed), 11, 29, 38, 169, 170–80, 205, 206, 207, 208

genre, 8, 9, 28–31, 40–2, 45, 47, 67–8, 79–82, 89–93, 95–7, 105, 114, 119, 127, 135–46, 152–5, 179, 182, 200, 252, 253–90
  genre and 'literary' divide, 8, 136, 139, 152, 154, 255–7
  genre turn, 8
Gilroy, Paul, 193, 194, 207
Greene, Graham, 102, 106, 122
  The Quiet American, 102, 106, 122
Greenwald Smith, Rachel, 9, 32, 36, 41, 46, 51, 52, 65, 67, 100, 101, 104–7, 163, 165, 199, 206, 207, 211, 217, 248, 250

Hamid, Mohsin, 29, 36, 44, 54, 83, 114, 117, 121, 123, 126, 127, 129
  Moth Smoke, 116
  The Reluctant Fundamentalist, 29, 36, 44, 54, 83, 114, 116–26, 127, 129
Hartnell, Anna, 12, 105, 122
Heaney, Seamus, 20
Heaven My Home (Locke, Attica), 31, 138, 253, 257, 258, 260–8, 284, 289

Herman, Peter C., 13, 20, 36, 37, 60, 106, 165, 172, 184, 212, 251, 256
Hindu supremacism, 181, 186–8, 297
Hirsch, Marianne, 4, 5, 7, 36, 51, 106
Holloway, David, 7, 36, 42, 48, 106, 111, 112, 113, 165
Home Fire (Shamsie, Kamila), 9, 17, 22, 30, 35, 38, 138, 169, 191
Houen, Alex, 13, 20–3, 36, 42, 107, 162, 165, 256, 289
Huntington, Samuel P., 27, 111, 155, 165, 269

I Dream of Jeannie, 131–2
'In the Ruins of the Future' (DeLillo, Don), 56, 106, 162, 164, 185, 207
Islamic Revolution in Iran 1979, 5, 44, 117, 126, 128
Islamism, 14, 17, 115, 118, 136–7, 141, 175, 232, 253–5, 259, 265
Islamophobia, 1, 6, 20, 26, 27, 32, 36, 37, 40, 47, 71, 78, 79, 81, 84, 107, 111–13, 115, 116, 120, 126, 129, 137, 138, 159, 160, 163, 164, 165, 166, 169, 272, 183, 191, 193, 200, 205, 206, 207, 208, 250, 270, 291, 298
ISIS (Islamic State of Iraq and Syria), 191, 192, 260, 265
IRA, 233–5

Jameson, Frederic, 120–1, 125, 165
Jackson, Richard, 6, 16, 36, 111, 165, 257
Javid, Sajid, 30, 169, 191, 197, 205, 209

Kalfus, Ken, 28, 44, 53–6, 65, 102
  A Disorder Peculiar to the Country, 28, 44, 53–6, 65, 102
Kapadia, Ronak, 3, 17, 36, 113, 156, 165, 182, 207
Khadra, Yasmina, 10, 29, 114, 135–52, 163, 164, 168, 268, 288
  The Attack, 10, 29, 135–44
  The Sirens of Baghdad, 135–40, 144–52

Khakpour, Porochista, 5, 44, 114, 116–17, 126–35
  Brown Album, 5
  Sick, 5–7
  Sons and Other Flammable Objects, 5, 114, 116–17, 126–35
  The Last Illusion, 5, 127
Khan, Ausma Zehanat, 31, 138, 253, 257–60, 268–78
  A Deadly Divide, 257–60, 268–78
  Among the Ruins, 259, 260, 269, 270, 271, 275, 289
  Blackwater Falls, 270, 272, 289
  No Place of Refuge, 259, 271, 274, 289
  The Language of Secrets, 259, 269, 273, 275, 289
  The Unquiet Dead, 259, 268, 270, 271, 272, 289
Khair, Tabish, 192
Ku Klux Klan (KKK), 15, 257, 264, 267, 277, 280, 284, 287
Kumar, Deepa, 15, 26, 37, 79, 112, 115, 129, 159, 165
Kundnani, Arun, 18, 26, 37, 115, 165, 168, 207, 240, 250, 266, 289, 292, 298
Kushner, Rachel, 30, 101, 210, 221, 248, 252
  Telex From Cuba, 227, 249, 251
  The Flamethrowers, 30, 37, 101, 210–34, 246–52
  The Hard Crowd, 227, 250–51

Leaving the Atocha Station (Lerner, Ben), 7, 37
Lee, Spike, 36, 287
  Blackkklansman, 287
Lerner, Ben, 7, 37
  Leaving the Atocha Station, 7, 37
Livingstone, Ken, 193, 208
Locke, Attica, 31, 138, 253, 257, 258, 260–8, 278, 284, 289
  Bluebird, Bluebird, 253, 257, 258, 260–8, 278, 284, 289
  Heaven My Home, 31, 138, 253, 257, 258, 260–8, 284, 289
  The Cutting Season, 261
Lorentzen, Christian, 81, 107, 231, 251

McInerney, Jay, 28, 42, 44, 46, 54, 55, 56, 65–6, 103, 107, 127
   The Good Life, 28, 44, 46, 55, 56, 65–6, 103, 108
Make America Great Again (MAGA) movement, 261, 264, 267, 268
Mahajan, Karan, 30, 37, 169, 180–90, 207
   The Association of Small Bombs, 30, 37, 169, 180–90, 207
Malone, Patricia, 23, 37, 212, 215, 233–5, 237, 241, 243, 249
Majumdar, Meghan, 11, 22, 31, 37, 296–8
   A Burning, 11, 22, 31, 37, 296–8
Mao II (DeLillo, Don), 10, 21, 35, 65, 106, 107, 151, 165, 200, 207, 232, 246, 250, 288, 293, 298
Messud, Claire, 28, 44, 46, 53–4, 56, 65–6, 80, 95, 127
   The Emperor's Children, 28, 44, 46, 53–4, 56, 65–6, 95, 127
#MeToo, 236, 247
metafiction, 10, 22, 28, 40, 45–8, 51–4, 56, 62–5, 67–8, 72, 80, 86, 106, 110, 126, 171, 174, 176, 179, 180, 195, 201, 202, 205, 207, 230, 235, 282, 283, 294
Milkman (Burns, Anna), 10, 30, 37, 210–15, 233–48
Modi, Narendra, 31, 181, 182, 184, 189, 190, 296
Morey, Peter, 27, 37, 83, 85, 108, 112–13, 116–19, 122, 146, 163, 166
Moth Smoke (Hamid, Mohsin), 116
multiculturalism, 2, 4, 30, 47, 72, 98, 169, 170, 193–7, 207

neoliberalism, 2, 5, 9, 10, 27, 28, 30, 31, 32, 35, 36, 48, 52, 89–93, 95–103, 104, 105, 106, 107, 108, 109, 118, 163, 165, 168, 169, 182, 191–9, 206, 207, 208, 212, 217, 231, 248, 251, 296
neoliberal multiculturalism, 98, 169, 193
neo-Nazism, 253, 254, 265, 270, 278

Netherland (O'Neill, Joseph), 8, 28, 31, 44, 47, 54, 55, 67–78, 106, 110, 115
Nixon, Rob, 12, 13, 23, 24, 37, 104, 281, 290
No Bones (Burns, Anna), 234, 236, 243, 250
No Place of Refuge (Khan, Ausma, Zehanat), 259, 271, 274, 289

Obama, Barrack, 115, 116, 156, 261
O'Neill, Joseph, 8, 28, 31, 44, 47, 54, 55, 67–78, 106, 110, 115
   Netherland, 8, 28, 31, 44, 47, 54, 55, 67–78, 106, 110, 115
Omar, Ilan, 6, 32
Open City (Cole, Teju), 2–5, 7

Park51 Community Center, 71, 79, 116
periodisation, 7–9, 42, 101, 104, 163
policing, 30, 186, 253, 258, 260, 266–7, 270–2
   policing as terrorism, 279, 281
'Portraits of Grief', 43, 109
postmodernism, 8, 21, 28, 48, 67, 200, 235
Pynchon, Thomas, 27, 28, 32, 37, 41, 47, 54, 89, 95, 104, 105, 89–110, 231
   Bleeding Edge, 27, 28, 32, 37, 41, 47, 54, 89, 95, 104, 105, 89–110, 231
Prevent Programme (UK), 138, 163

racism, 6, 11, 12, 26–8, 29, 40, 47, 71, 86, 111–67, 200, 204, 205, 253–98
   institutional racism, 12, 26–8, 11–167, 205, 253–98
Rankine, Claudia, 283
Red Army Faction, 47, 56, 61, 231, 232
Red Brigades, 30, 211, 213, 214, 216, 220, 222–30, 247, 249, 250, 251
Rothberg, Michael, 11, 24, 37, 41, 44, 53, 75, 87, 97, 99, 104, 109, 182, 208
Roy-Bhattacharya, Joydeep, 191, 209
   The Watch, 191, 209

Saadawi, Ahmed, 11, 29, 38, 169, 170–80, 205, 206, 207, 208
  Frankenstein in Baghdad, 11, 29, 38, 169, 170–80, 205, 206, 207, 208
Said, Edward, 112, 141, 204
Safran Foer, Jonathan, 9, 28, 38, 46, 48–53, 109, 127
  Extremely Loud and Incredibly Close, 9, 28, 38, 46, 48–53, 109, 127
Scanlan, Margaret, 21–2, 38, 154, 155, 166, 180, 208, 246, 251, 293, 294, 298
Schwartz, Lynne Sharon, 28, 44, 46, 53–67, 106, 109, 110
  The Writing on the Wall, 28, 44, 46, 53–67, 106, 109, 110
September 11, 1973 attack, 48, 89, 101, 213
September 11, 2001 attack ('9/11'), 2–11, 17, 18–19, 20–2, 25, 27, 28–32, 34–9, 40, 111–115, 118, 122–3, 125–30, 132–6, 138, 144, 149, 152–6, 162, 164–7, 168–9, 179–82, 184, 185, 189, 191, 192, 199, 2001, 202–3, 206, 207, 208, 213–14, 260, 265–6, 269, 272, 289, 292–5, 298
  9/11 exceptionalism, 2, 4, 32, 63, 93, 162, 192
  fiction of 9/11 or '9/11 novel', 6, 8–9, 21, 28–30, 40–110, 114–116, 121, 127–8, 135–6, 166, 182, 208, 257, 292, 295
Shamsie, Kamila, 9, 17, 22, 30, 35, 38, 80, 109, 138, 169, 191–200, 206–9
  Burnt Shadows, 191
  Home Fire, 9, 17, 22, 30, 35, 38, 138, 169, 191
  Review of *The Watch* (Bhattacharya, Joydeep), 191, 209
  Review of *The Submission* (Waldman, Amy), 80, 109
Shapiro, Stephen, 27, 33, 103, 105, 107, 165, 199, 208
Sick (Khakpour, Porochista), 5–7
slow violence, 4, 12

Smith, Zadie, 'Two Paths for the Novel' 2, 4, 8, 31, 38, 68, 103, 109
social media, 22
Sons and Other Flammable Objects (Khakpour, Porochista), 5, 114, 116–17, 126–35
state violence 11, 15, 17, 19, 29–31, 45, 113–15, 138, 142, 144–7, 163, 169
Sykes, Rachel, 32, 57
systemic violence 1, 2, 4, 12, 19, 23, 24, 27, 37, 105, 256, 281, 282, 290, 293

Taneja, Preti, 11, 15, 19–20, 27, 31, 38, 163, 167, 253, 290, 292–8
  Aftermath, 11, 15, 19–20, 27, 31, 38, 163, 167, 253, 290, 292–8
Telephone (Everett, Percival), 258, 278, 283, 288
Telex From Cuba (Kushner, Rachel), 227, 249, 251
terrorism
  definitional debates, 14–23
  ecoterrorism, 14
  Islamist terrorism, 14, 17, 115, 118, 136–7, 141, 175, 232, 253–5, 259, 265
  lone wolf terrorism, 235, 275, 277
  lynching, 9, 15, 17, 23, 31, 254, 257–8, 278–88
  neoliberal terrorism, 90, 200
  right wing terrorism, 13–14, 16, 253–88
  state terrorism, 1, 6, 13, 16–18, 31, 33, 113, 115–16, 137, 163, 168, 181, 191, 255–7, 267, 268, 273, 280, 281
  white nationalist terrorism, 14, 31, 33, 253, 255, 257–60, 264, 272, 276, 278
'terror sex', 57, 107, 134, 165
The Addams Family, 131–2
The Association of Small Bombs (Mahajan, Karan), 30, 37, 169, 180–90, 207
The Attack (Khadra, Yasmina), 10, 29, 135–44

The Cutting Season (Locke, Attica), 261
The Good Life (McInerney, Jay), 28, 44, 46, 55, 56, 65–6, 103, 108
The Emperor's Children (Messud, Claire), 28, 44, 46, 53–4, 56, 65–6, 95, 127
The Flamethrowers (Kushner, Rachel), 30, 37, 101, 210–34, 246–52
The Hard Crowd (Kushner, Rachel), 227, 250–1
The Language of Secrets (Khan, Ausma Zehanat), 259, 269, 273, 275, 289
The Last Illusion (Khakpour, Porochista), 5, 127
The Quiet American (Greene, Graham), 102, 106, 122
The Reluctant Fundamentalist (Hamid, Mohsin), 29, 36, 44, 54, 83, 114, 116–26, 127, 129
The Sirens of Baghdad (Khadra, Yasmina), 135–40, 144–52
The Submission (Waldman, Amy), 28, 29, 44, 47, 67–71, 78–89
The Trees (Everett, Percival), 9, 9, 31, 138, 253, 257, 278–88
The Unquiet Dead (Khan, Ausma Zehanat), 259, 268, 270, 271, 272, 289
The Wretched of the Earth (Fanon, Frantz), 142, 163, 164
The Writing on the Wall, Schwartz, Lynne Sharon, 28, 44, 46, 53–67, 106, 109, 110
The Zero (Walter, Jess), 44, 90, 92–4
torture, 17, 18, 77, 116, 153, 158–9, 162, 163, 181, 183, 184, 188, 191, 204, 272
trauma, 1–5, 11–12, 14, 19–22, 23, 24–5, 28–30, 40–89, 93, 104, 111, 114, 122–3, 128, 130, 140, 160, 183, 186, 203, 212–15, 233–4, 237, 240–2, 256, 272, 282, 292–6, 298

cultural trauma, 24–5
collective trauma 24–5
The Troubles (NI), 20, 30, 233–48, 251
Trump, Donald J., 6, 30, 32, 169, 200, 201, 202, 204, 258, 259, 261, 265, 274, 287

Underworld, DeLillo, Don, 8
Up Against the Wall Motherfucker (UAW/MF), 214–15, 220, 225
'United the Right' march and terror attack in Charlottesville, NC, 259, 278, 287

Waldman, Amy, 28, 29, 44, 47, 67–71, 78–89
  The Submission, 28, 29, 44, 47, 67–71, 78–89
Wallerstein, Immanuel, 25, 27, 38
Walter, Jess 44, 90, 92–4
  The Zero, 44, 90, 92–4
war on terror, 1–10, 16–20, 29, 42, 50, 57, 64, 69–71, 75, 78, 91, 112–13, 116–19, 122, 136, 138, 145–7, 154, 159, 162, 168–203, 255, 266, 272, 273, 274, 294, 298
Warwick Research Collective (WReC), 25–6, 32, 39, 248, 252
Waugh, Patricia, 45, 64, 65, 67, 110
Watershed (Everett, Percival), 258, 278, 288
Wounded (Everett, Percival), 258, 278, 288
Whitehead, Anne, 24, 41
white nationalism, 14, 31, 33, 253, 255, 257–60, 264, 272, 276, 278
Windows on the World (Beigbeder, Frédéric), 3, 40, 46–8, 115
Wood, James, 8, 228, 248
world-systems, 3, 6, 13, 25, 27, 30, 32, 38, 194, 198, 199, 222, 224–5, 229, 230, 232, 233, 248

Yaqin, Amina, 27, 37, 83, 85, 108, 112–13

EU representative:
Easy Access System Europe
Mustamäe tee 50, 10621 Tallinn, Estonia
Gpsr.requests@easproject.com

www.ingramcontent.com/pod-product-compliance
Lightning Source LLC
Chambersburg PA
CBHW050207240426
43671CB00013B/2242